COVERED BRIDGES TODAY

by BRENDA KREKELER

DARING PUBLISHING GROUP, INC.

DARING BOOKS • LIFE ENRICHMENT PUBLISHERS
CANTON • OHIO

About The Author

Brenda Krekeler grew up in the small, rural community of Williamsburg, Ohio located about 35 miles east of Cincinnati in Clermont County. Throughout her childhood and all through her teens, Ms. Krekeler's mother was always taking the family to outdoor recreational activities. Her father would take the family up to the Cincinnati Zoo, museums, and expose them to ''city life'' in downtown Cincinnati, always encouraging the educational aspects through books, music and experience.

The existence of covered bridges quite naturally falls into Historical Geography. Researching the history of the bridges (a skill she developed in graduate school), physically locating the bridge with the use of maps, and finally witnessing and photographing the skill of the bridge building craftsmen, all tantalize the geographer in Ms. Krekeler.

Ms. Krekeler has received her Master's degree in Geography from the University of Cincinnati and she has taught many different social science classes. She now resides with her husband, Michael, and son, Mark, in Cincinnati, Ohio.

Published by Daring Books
P.O..Box 20050, Canton, Ohio 44701

Library of Congress Cataloging-in-Publication Data

Krekeler, Brenda C., 1951-
    Covered bridges today.

    1. Covered bridges--United States. I. Title.
TG23.K74 1988   624'.38   88-6997
ISBN 0-938936-72-7

Printed in the United States of America.

THIS BOOK IS DEDICATED TO MICHAEL

Table of Contents

FOREWORD 6

ACKNOWLEDGMENTS 7

INTRODUCTION 9
   Why Covered Bridges?
   The Condition of Covered Bridges Today

ABOUT THE BRIDGE 13
   Identifying the Parts of a Covered Bridge

TRUSSES IN THE UNITED STATES TODAY 15

EXPLANATION OF THE TEXT 27

HOW TO FIND COVERED BRIDGES AND OBTAIN COUNTY MAPS 29

SPECIAL BRIDGES, EVENTS AND ORGANIZATIONS 32
   Counties That Are Especially Interesting to Bridge
   Covered Bridge Festivals
   Covered Bridge Associations
   Some of My Favorite Bridges

TERMS 37

CONNECTICUT 39

INDIANA 41

PHOTO GALLERY 1 65

KENTUCKY 99

MAINE 107

MARYLAND 111

MASSACHUSETTS 115

MICHIGAN 119

NEW HAMPSHIRE 123

NEW YORK 147

OHIO 157

PHOTO GALLERY 2 193

PENNSYLVANIA 251

PHOTO GALLERY 3 289

VERMONT 313

VIRGINIA 339

WEST VIRGINIA 345

COVERED BRIDGE SIGNS 353

BIBLIOGRAPHY 359

Foreword

This book is an historical, pictorial documentation of the condition of our covered bridges today. The text will provide you with historical information on 412 covered bridges found in fourteen states, and expose you to the the individual characteristics of each bridge.

Photographs of the exterior display the beautiful landscapes where the covered bridges are found throughout the United States. Interior photographs will link you with the craftsmen of 100 to 175 years ago who built these magnificent structures. The different types of trusses used and the men who designed them are also noted within the text.

You will learn about aspects of our architectural heritage through the presentation of historical data and actual photographs to assist you in discovering the talents of the bridge designers, the stone masons, and the builders. *Covered Bridges Today* is a book that is educational, but presented in a visually enjoyable manner.

The education and enjoyment is a feature of this book I hope you will come to treasure, but there is another aspect of this book which you can pursue to provide an even more rewarding experience. *Covered Bridges Today* is designed for the reader to become a participant in an activity known as "Bridging." This book will, hopefully, teach you how and where to find covered bridges!

Acknowledgments

My husband, Michael, gave me his understanding, assistance and direction. I could not have completed this book without him. My son, Mark, who traveled with me to untold bridges, was always there for me with support and positive reinforcement.

Without the time and assistance of many people, my task would have been more difficult. I want to expressly thank the following people for their time, help and support: Charlene Speeg, Joe Speeg, Dolores Krekeler, Terry Sawyers, Carole Wells, Shannon Fassler, and the Geography Department at the University of Cincinnati, especially Lynn Winterman and Bev Mueller.

Introduction

At one time the United States had as many as 12,000 covered bridges. Today an estimated 840 remain. Some covered bridges still exist due to the efforts of preservationists in historical societies, covered bridge organizations and township, county and state officials. If it were not for the determination of the preservationists and craftsmanship of the builders, we would not have these historic structures to admire. Our remaining covered bridges would have met the same fate as over 11,000 other covered bridges.

There is something that is incredibly fascinating about finding covered bridges. First of all, when searching for covered bridges, you will drive on roads that are seldom traveled except by local residents. On these roads, you will see landscapes not found on interstates or in national parks. The roads to covered bridges often have many examples of historic sites seldom seen, such as: old mills, wooden dams, round barns, stone houses, octagonal, stone, one-room schoolhouses and old train depots. The roads traveled to find the covered bridges are full of interesting features. The actual search for the bridge is exciting. With map in hand, an eye for the tree-lined stream, and the approach of a valley, signaling an approaching bridge; bridging is a lot of fun. When you drive down a hill, around a bend, following a creek, you know you are close. All of a sudden, there it is, looming over the stream with its massive structure! The experience of finding each bridge is an accomplishment and it is rewarding. It is rewarding because you are aware of the historical implications, and you can inspect the precise stonework in the abutments, admire the craftsmanship of the build and touch the hand-hewn beams that support the bridge. When photographing the bridge, each season offers a different background. The configuration of the bridges is a natural topic for photography. Each bridge is individually unique. Although you will find bridges that have the same truss design, each bridge is constructed to meet the demands of its location. The length, height, width and covering are all unique for each bridge. One major characteristic changing at each bridge site is the landscape. Some bridges span meandering brooks, while others cross roaring streams

filled with waterfalls. Hills, valleys and mountains also present spectacular backdrops for the bridge to be photographed.

The search for the bridge, the inspection and recording of it in photographs are all exciting aspects of bridging.

The text for each bridge offers a map. This map is to be used in conjunction with a county map that you can obtain from each state. For additional information on locating covered bridges and how to acquire the county maps, refer to the chapter entitled, "How to Find Covered Bridges and Obtain County Maps."

The condition of these covered bridges needs to be brought to the attention of the public in the hope that their preservation will be promoted. Preservation starts with us as individuals being aware of the few existing bridges. With the continuing preservation of our covered bridges, we, and following generations, will be able to contribute to our heritage.

Bridging, the search and location of covered bridges, will take you to some of the most remote locations in America. You will see beautiful scenery, wildlife, and interesting buildings and places. I hope you have the opportunity to use this book in its fullest capacity, to find covered bridges!

WHY COVERED BRIDGES?

Wooden bridges were covered with a roof and siding to protect them from the weather. Bridges left unprotected, deteriorated. The superstructure would last only a few years if exposed to the ravages of nature.

The importance of the covering of the truss was recognized in 1805. The contract for the first covered bridge in the United States, built by Timothy Palmer over the Schuylkill River in Philadelphia, required that it be covered to protect the wooden beams. Covered bridges have been discovered as far back as the 16th Century in Europe.

The covering, if reasonably maintained, protects the interior wooden members and extends the bridge's life from ten years to 100 or more years. Many of our historic structures are used today by modern traffic, and are 100 to 175 years old. Their longevity is attributed to the protection the truss has received. In some bridges, the age of the wood used is easily noticeable. First, observe the truss members. Many of the massive beams used in the trusses were hand-hewn, and the imprint of the broadaxe or adze (tools used to shape the beams) enhances the character of the bridge as well as indicates its history.

You will also want to pay attention to the floor. Many of the bridges have new floors, especially the ones that are exposed to heavy traffic. There are, however, many bridges open to traffic that have their original floor. You can tell by the amount of separation between the planks. When the planks are separated, it is indicative of an old floor. When the floor is originally laid, the planks are placed close together. Over the years, the moisture from the planks evaporates and dries out the wood, which makes them shrink, causing gaps between the planks. When this occurs, the planks develop a flaky appearance. They look like boards full of splinters. When the planks dry out to such a degree, the wood is dryrotting and the planks will soon need to be replaced because they become brittle and can easily crack under stress.

The wooden members in a truss usually do not suffer from dry rot, but when they do, they also need to be replaced.

The longevity of the wooden truss bridge is attributed to a combination of things. Primarily, the covering protects the wood from weather damage.

Secondly, the bridge's life span is determined by the builder of the bridge. The builder must check each beam to see that it is free from defects, cut preferably through the heart of the tree, and is straight. All ensure the bridge's longevity.

Finally, the builder, although he uses a patented truss, must design the bridge to fit exactly onto the abutments. All truss designs have their benefits, some more than others, but the basic equation necessitated to achieve a long life for a covered bridge, is the craftsmanship of the bridge builder.

Historically, our covered bridges are 100 to 175 years old. These structures were built by craftsmen whose skill has virtually disappeared. The knowledge that these old bridges will never be duplicated, should appeal to our sense of heritage. Each of the remaining covered bridges is individually unique; no two are the same. Because they represent one aspect of our nation's heritage, we intuitively want them preserved for us and future generations to appreciate and enjoy.

The covered bridges were originally built for the public to allow them dependable transportation to obtain supplies from town, take their grains to the mill, and give safe passage for school children. The intention of the covered bridges, paid for with public funds, was to serve the public. Today, whether the bridge is still used, bypassed, or preserved in a park, it is still serving the public. Its mere existence allows us to inspect and enjoy the craftsmanship of our ancestors.

Beyond the historical attributes of the covered bridges, their physical settings are aesthetically appealing, and pleasant for anyone to visit. Always located in a valley, the bridge can span a little brook or a roaring stream. The action of the water, whether in a meandering creek or a rocky mountain river with numerous waterfalls, creates an exciting location.

The charm of our covered bridges, whether for their historical implications, the skill of their builders, or their beautiful valleys and streams, is something for everyone to enjoy.

THE CONDITION OF COVERED BRIDGES TODAY

Today, with only an estimated 840 covered bridges left in the U.S., we wonder what became of the other 11,000 bridges.

First of all, 11,000 covered bridges is probably a conservative estimate. In the early 1800s, hundreds of bridges were built that had no records. These bridges were destroyed by floods. Their record of existence is gone forever. Covered bridges were replaced sometimes five and six times, due to flood destruction. Through the history of covered bridges, floods have been their greatest enemy. In March of 1987, Maine lost one more of its few remaining covered bridges in a flood which resulted from three inches of rain and melting snows.

Arson, another major factor in the destruction of bridges, occurred even during the 1800s. The Civil War, however, was responsible for the burning of many hundreds of covered bridges in the south. Today, only a few covered bridges are left in the south that were built prior to the Civil War. Unfortunately, we are still losing some of our bridges that were one of a kind to arson. The Roberts Bridge (35-68-05) in Preble County, Ohio was burned by arson in August of 1986. Roberts Bridge was Ohio's oldest (1829) and only double-barrelled bridge. With the destruction of this double-barrelled bridge, there are only five left in the United States.

The Hillsboro Railroad Bridge (29-06-01) in Hillsborough County, New Hampshire was burned by arson in 1985. With only a few railroad covered bridges left, the loss of the Hillsboro Bridge was sad.

In 1981, the Sulphite Railroad Bridge (29-07-09) in Merrimack County, New Hampshire was also burned by arson. The Sulphite Bridge was extraordinary because it was the only example left that carried the train on top of the bridge rather than through it. Photographs of the charred remains of this bridge are included in the text.

Arson has taken its toll on our bridges over the years. Signs appear on many bridges warning that prosecution will result for damage to the bridge. This has been followed through on several cases, and, hopefully, it will act as a deterrent in the future.

Collapse is another way we have lost many of these bridges. The bridge loses some of its roof and siding, exposing the truss to water. The joints become weakened, and the bridge, under the stress of its own weight, just collapses.

Occasionally, loads too heavy for the bridge will try to pass through it and fall through the floor. Usually, this can be repaired.

Most of our covered bridges have been lost through demolition and replacement by a concrete/steel bridge.

Another cause of covered bridges disappearing is that many new dams have been constructed since 1950 which flood the river valleys, forming a recreation flood control lake. The creation of these new lakes has eliminated many covered bridges.

Floods, arson, collapse and replacement have resulted in the disappearance of thousands of covered bridges. More often than not, the fate of the covered bridge has been destruction and replacement.

PUBLIC ROAD

I was amazed at just how many of our covered bridges are in use. Over two-thirds of them are open to traffic. Most of them are on township and county roads that are not heavily traveled. It seems as though the bridges used are in much better condition than those that are bypassed. Once bypassed, the bridge seems to be forgotten and it begins to deteriorate, much like a vacant house. When a covered bridge is used by traffic, it is maintained. Many of the open

covered bridges have been restored. At the time of restoration, they had concrete piers and abutments added, and steel beams placed under the bridge. Although this changes the original character of the bridge, it does preserve the structure, allowing daily use and keeping it in the mainstream of public transportation.

Keeping a covered bridge open to traffic is an expense and requires upkeep. The expense of maintaining a covered bridge can be nominal when viewed in the light of a new replacement bridge costing as much as $500,000. The small inconvenience of occasional maintenence such as replacing missing siding and shingles, is far outweighed by the aesthetic value produced by the bridge's continued existence.

The covered bridge that is open to traffic continues to be well maintained and allows the public to have a greater participation factor with the bridge than if it were bypassed and forgotten. Vermont and New Hampshire try to keep all of their covered bridges open to traffic. Their townships and counties, as well as the states, take great pride in their covered bridges and insist on their maintenance and preservation.

BYPASSED

Often, you will find covered bridges that are bypassed. Bypassed is a more acceptable condition than having the covered bridge demolished and replaced. Usually when a covered bridge is bypassed, an area around the bridge is maintained by the township or county. Sometimes the park-like area has picnic tables and grills. The public has easy access to these bridges which have been preserved. The majority of the bypassed bridges are reasonably maintained. Some are simply bypassed and forgotten, and have fallen into a state of disrepair.

Unfortunately, some of the bypassed covered bridges have fallen into private ownership. Shortsightedness on the part of the county or township, allowed the public bridge to become privately owned. This is no problem when the owners are willing to share their bridge with the public. But when the private bridge is wired shut and posted, "NO TRESSPASSING", the once public bridge is no longer accessible for all to enjoy. Because a covered bridge demands occasional maintenance, the private bridge very often falls into disrepair.

If bypassed, I feel that the covered bridge should remain on public land so the public can enjoy its heritage without having to intrude on someone's private property.

PRIVATE PARKS

Some of the covered bridges are located in privately owned parks. These parks house and preserve historic buildings and offer a variety of activities for the family. Each park is fun to visit. They generally require an admission fee during the season. Off season, you may be able to obtain access to the bridge without paying admission.

Greenfield Village in Wayne County, Michigan (22-82-01) is open most of the year and always requires admission. Shelburn Museum in Chittenden County, Vermont (45-04-06) is only open in season. The covered bridge is only accessible in season with admission. Billie Creek Village in Parke County, Indiana (14-61-19) and Meadowcroft Village in Washington County, Pennsylvania (38-63-35) have admission during season, but access to the covered bridges is possible off season. Carillon Park in Montgomery County, Ohio (35-57-03) is open to the public all year.

All of these historic villages maintain their covered bridges and old buildings beautifully. The structures are fun to see for the whole family.

CLOSED

More than a few of the covered bridges are found closed. This means one of three things. First, it is scheduled to be replaced. Secondly, it is in such poor condition that it is no longer safe and there are no funds to fix it or replace it. Finally, it is going to be renovated. Because there are fewer and fewer covered bridges left, townships and county officials are becoming aware of their potential resource, and more of the bridges are being repaired and strengthened to accept everyday traffic.

Just because you see "bridge closed" signs, it does not always mean the ultimate destruction of the covered bridge.

ABANDONED

Abandoned covered bridges are sorrowful sites. Usually isolated on roads long since forgotten, pieces of siding and roof are missing, and the floor and truss members are rotting. The floor sags severely and much of the planking is missing.

Overgrown with trees and thick vegetation, the poor old bridge is struggling with its imminent extinction.

PRIVATELY OWNED

Occasionally, covered bridges are often left in their original locations, but have fallen into private ownership. Sometimes the road that the bridge once served has been abandoned, and owners of the surrounding land assume the bridge. Other times, the covered bridge is bypassed and government officials allow the covered bridge to be assumed by the nearby neighbor. This practice of taking a public bridge and placing it into private ownership is a shortsighted act of the township or county. The bridge was originally paid for by public funds. What has probably happened in the past was that the township or county did not want the upkeep involved, so they just relinquished the bridge to the original land owner. Unfortunately, many of the private owners are not able or do not want to maintain the bridges, and they deteriorate. The bridge is barricaded with fencing and subsequently allows no access to the public. Some of the privately owned covered bridges are used as barns for cows, a shed to store wood, or protection for machinery and carriages.

In the future, hopefully, the local officials will recognize the resource of the existing covered bridges and do everything possible to keep them open. If it is impossible to keep the covered bridge open, a public park should be established around the bridge. When bypassed, the new bridge should be a comfortable distance away from the covered bridge. There are many instances where a covered bridge was bypassed and the new bridge was built right next to the covered bridge, preventing visual access of the covered bridge.

If a covered bridge is privately owned, always ask permission before inspecting it.

About The Bridge

IDENTIFYING THE PARTS OF A COVERED BRIDGE

The main structure of a covered bridge is the truss. The truss is the part of the bridge which absorbs the stress when a vehicle passes over the bridge, and transfers the weight to the abutments.

There are two trusses in each bridge, one on either side. If the bridge has more than one span, the bridge can have another set of trusses, depending on the design. A truss is composed of wooden beams designed in such a manner as the vertical members (posts) and diagonal members meet to form one or many triangles. Triangles are strong and easily distribute the weight of a passing load, so the stress does not fall on one member. The diagonal beams of the triangles are called compression members because they squeeze together as a load passes over the bridge. The vertical posts are called tension members because they are pulled down as a vehicle crosses the bridge. The truss members are attached to an upper and lower chord. The upper and lower chords are horizontal beams that hold the truss together. The chords can consist of one massive beam, or many beams, depending on the truss and the length of the bridge. There are eighteen different trusses exhibited in covered bridges throughout the United States today. Each of these trusses is discussed in the chapter on trusses.

The floor joists are wooden beams usually 4″ x 12″, but can be quite massive, set on or connected into the lower chord of the truss. These joists, which run perpendicular to the truss, support the planking of which the floor is made. Often, a second layer of joists is used, laid opposite the first, to help distribute the load evenly upon the trusses. A second layer of planking is sometimes used for the floor covering, which runs opposite the first layer, and, occasionally, lengthwise planking is laid down where the wheels run, forming two runners. At times, a solid runner will be found laid lengthwise, occupying the center two-thirds of the floor space.

The truss and floor are protected by the roof and siding. The roof can be covered with tin or shake, which are both very common. Rarely, tar paper and asphalt shingles are used.

Siding is mostly composed of wooden planks (vertical) and occasionally lap (horizontal) planks. There are a few bridges that are sided with tin. Especially in Pennsylvania, and Parke County, Indiana, the plank siding has batten; one inch strips of wood that cover the seams between planks. The wooden siding can be found naturally weathered, painted bright red, dark red, brown or white. Often the portals are trimmed in white or red. The portals are the ends of the bridge; the entrances.

Another aspect of the covered bridge that demonstrates the craftsmanship of the early bridge builders is the abutments. The abutments are the stone or concrete bases built on the stream's banks that support the bridge. It is the abutments which absorb the weight of the vehicle as it passes over the bridge. The truss distributes the weight along to the abutments.

Especially in New England you will find many of the stone abutments laid with no mortar. This technique is called dry stone. The appearance of a dry stone abutment is impressive because the only thing that holds the stone together is the method in which the stones were originally laid, and the weight of stone and bridge. Many of these dry stone abutments are in excellent condition even after being constructed over 100 years ago.

Prevalent in eastern Pennsylvania in Bucks and Lancaster Counties, the stone abutments have been extended at either portal to form wingwalls. The stone and mortar walls at each entrance are excellent examples of the stonemason's work.

The stones used in abutments are as varied as the bridges. Cut stone, bedrock or creek stone were all used. The cut stone is usually sandstone. These quarried stones range in size from 8″ x 12,″ to pieces 3′ by 6′ and larger. The symmetry of the cut stone abutments is beautiful. Bedrock abutments are also attractive. You can even find some bedrock laid dry. It is amazing how the abutments maintain their condition over so many years. When creek stone is used in abutments, usually, (not always) it is laid up with mortar because the creek stones are often round.

A pier is used to support a covered bridge when the bridge is too long to span the stream without additional support. When one pier is used, and placed in the center of the stream, the bridge has two spans.

When two piers are used, the bridge has three spans. The pier is usually constructed of the same materials as the abutments. If the pier was added after the original construction, during a renovation of the bridge, the pier will usually be made out of concrete.

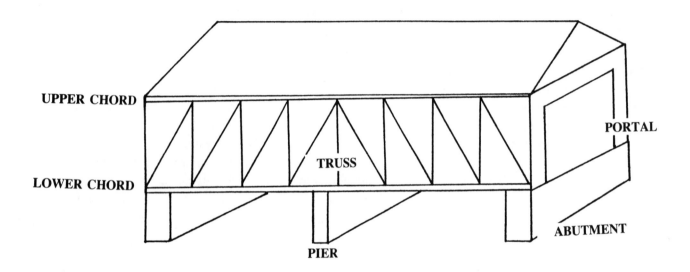

Trusses in the United States Today

The kingpost truss was the first known truss. The queenpost and multiple kingpost trusses followed the kingpost truss because they could span wider streams. It was only the kingpost, queenpost and multiple kingpost trusses that were used prolifically from the 16th Century through the 19th Century. It was in the early 1800s that wooden bridge building was revolutionized in North America by innovative bridge building engineers.

The early 1800s found a growing demand for bridges to span wider streams to assure dependable transportation. With the abundance of timber available, impressive wooden bridges were designed and constructed.

The first covered bridge in America was constructed by Timothy Palmer in 1805. This bridge was in Philadelphia over the Schuylkill River on Market Street. The bridge was a three span, 550-foot structure built with impressive cambers.

The next famous bridge builder of the early 1800s was Lewis Wernwag, who in 1812 built the Colossus, a 340-foot bridge over the Schuylkill River. Wernwag built over 300 such structures between 1810 and 1838.

Another famous bridge builder of this time was Theodore Burr. In 1804, Burr was the first to patent his bridge truss in the United States, the Burr arch. This was the first of a series of patents for covered bridge trusses.

There are eighteen existing covered bridge truss designs left in the U.S. today. Some of these trusses, which once had hundreds of examples, now only have a few remaining examples, such as the Wernwag, Warren, Haupt, Brown, Post, and Bowstring. Other trusses have over one hundred examples, such as the Howe, Town and multiple kingpost.

Each truss, although the same design, is distinctly different from any other. Each truss is unique because it must be constructed to fit the exact length between abutments. Each bridge has its own height and width which is a product of its intended use.

The truss's design, length, height, width, and materials used all combine to make each bridge one of a kind.

(Allen, 1957; American Society of Civil Engineers, 1934; Donovan 1980).

THE EXISTING COVERED BRIDGE TRUSSES IN THE UNITED STATES

TRUSSES/DESIGNERS/BUILDERS	PATENT DATE
1. Kingpost	
2. Multiple kingpost	
3. Queenpost	
4. Theodore Burr	1804
5. Ithiel Town	1820, 1835
6. Lewis Wernwag	1829
7. Stephen H. Long	1830, 1836, 1839
8. James Warren	1838
9. Herman Haupt	1839
10. William Howe	1840
11. Thomas Willis Pratt	1844
12. Enoch Child	1846
13. Josiah Brown, Jr.	1857
14. Simeon S. Post	1863
15. Robert S. Smith	1867, 1869
16. Reuben Partridge	1872
17. Peter Paddleford	no patent
18. Bowstring Suspension	no patent known

KINGPOST TRUSS

Illustration 1

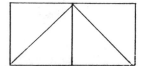

Ackley Bridge

The oldest bridge truss design is the kingpost. The kingpost design was initially used under the roadway. This truss, with its two diagonals and kingpost, made two right triangles and used a basic engineering principle: a triangle will hold its shape when carrying a load until its side members or joints are broken. A frame that has four sides or more will shift and lose its shape and its capacity to carry a load. Soon it was discovered that the kingpost truss would be just as efficient if it were built above the floor, and it would permit high water to pass without the bridge acting as a dam.

The diagonal beams of the kingpost truss are called compression members because they squeeze together as a load passes over the bridge. The vertical member of the kingpost panel is called the tension member because it is pulled down as a load crosses the bridge. The kingpost design is not capable of spanning more than 25 to 30 feet normally. Illustration 1 shows the members of the kingpost truss.

The Ackley Bridge (22-82-01) in Wayne County, Michigan, is a classic example of a kingpost truss. This bridge was constructed in 1832 with hand-hewn beams.

(Allen, 1957; American Society of Civil Engineers, 1934; Donovan, 1980)

MULTIPLE KINGPOST

Illustration 2

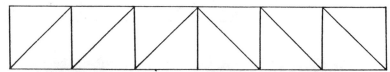

Oldtown Bridge

The multiple kingpost was designed to cross larger spans than the simple kingpost, up to 100 feet. A multiple kingpost truss has one kingpost in the center and many right angle panels to either side of the kingpost, pointing toward the center as in Illustration 2.

Oldtown Bridge (17-45-02) in Greenup County, Kentucky, illustrates a multiple kingpost truss. This example, which differs from Illustration 2, has each member doubled. This characteristic is common in the few covered bridges left in Kentucky and is found periodically throughout the United States.

MULTIPLE KINGPOST WITH DOUBLE CENTER PANELS

Illustration 3

QUEENPOST

Illustration 4

Bucher's Mill Bridge

Cox Bridge

Bucher's Mill Bridge (38-36-12) is found in Lancaster County, Pennsylvania. The center of the double kingpost is sometimes referred to as an empty center panel with an "X" bracing. There are examples of the multiple kingpost truss with an empty center panel and right angle panels pointing toward the center, in this book. This particular bridge is also supported by a half-size Burr arch. These are easily confused with a queenpost center panel that has multiple right angle panels. To distinguish the difference, a horizontal beam under the upper chord must be present for it to be a queenpost. Trusses that do not have the horizontal upper beam over the center panel are multiple kingpost trusses with an empty center panel.

(Allen, 1957; American Society of Civil Engineers, 1934: Donovan, 1980)

The queenpost truss followed the kingpost truss. The top of the kingpost truss was replaced by a horizontal member, which simply stretched the kingpost design and enabled the bridge to span a stream wider than 25 to 30 feet, and gave greater structural strength. The queenpost has a large square or rectangular box in the center of the truss, and vertical and diagonal beams forming right angles, pointing toward the center of the bridge. The center panel of the queenpost has a horizontal beam under the upper chord. It is this horizontal beam that is attached to the vertical member of the right angle panel on either end of the open center panel.

Illustration 4 depicts the traditional queenpost truss.

Cox Bridge (35-82-10) in Vinton County, Ohio, photographed above, displays a pure queenpost truss. The queenpost truss is often used in conjunction with a multiple kingpost truss and a burr arch. A good example of such a combination can be found in the Landisburg Bridge (38-50-10) in Perry County, Pennsylvania. The Mount Pleasant Bridge (38-50-12) also in Perry County, Pennsylvania combines the queenpost and multiple kingpost truss.

(Allen, 1957; American Society of Civil Engineers, 1934; Donovan, 1980)

BURR TRUSS

Illustration 5

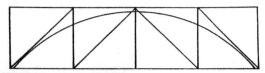

Medora Bridge

Theodore Burr was born in Torringford, Connecticut in August, 1771. He died in Middletown, Pennsylvania on November 21, 1822 and lived in Massachusetts during his bridge building career, which lasted from 1800 through 1820. Burr built many bridges in his career, some of which are especially noteworthy. In 1804, Burr built his first bridge in New York between Lansingburgh and Waterford, spanning the Hudson River. In 1806, he built a bridge at Trenton, New Jersey over the Delaware River that had two roadways and two walkways. Its structure had five arches. At Schenectady, New York in 1808, Burr built a bridge over the Mohawk River. His fourth major bridge was built in 1816 over the Susquehanna River in Harrisburg, Pennsylvania. This bridge's design was different from his previous trusses. It had twelve spans.

Burr patented his design in 1804, but he only claimed the wooden arch in combination with any truss. It was the Waterford Bridge which served as a model for all of the wooden bridges incorporating the Burr arch. The general rule was if the bridge exceeded fifty feet, it required a Burr arch. The Burr truss was the first innovative bridge design in the U.S. in the early 1800s. Typically, the Burr arch consists of a wooden arch attached to a multiple kingpost truss. The Burr arch can be seen as a single arch or a double arch, where it encases the multiple Kingpost truss. The Burr arch was the forerunner of the new wooden trusses that would be engineered over the next seventy years. The oldest Burr truss in existence in the U.S. today was built in 1812. There are three Burr truss bridges that are thought to be built as early as 1812 and they are all in Pennsylvania. The longest Burr truss bridge in the U.S. today can be found in Jackson County, Indiana. Built in 1875, the Medora Bridge (14-36-04) has been bypassed and is 434 feet long with three spans. The second longest Burr truss covered bridge is also located in Indiana in Rush County. The Moscow Bridge (14-70-07) is 334 feet long with two spans and was built in 1886. It has two sets of Burr arches and the interior is geometrically interesting. The bridge is still open to traffic but it displays, "UNSAFE BRIDGE" signs. This bridge is beautiful and demands to be bypassed for preservation. The Burr truss has been used in building covered bridges since the early

1800s, and thousands were constructed. Today, there are an estimated 299 Burr arch truss covered bridges in existence in the United States. Illustration 5 depicts a typical Burr arch. There is a close-up of a multilayered, laminated arch that was added in the early 1980s. The huge arch is found in the Benetka Road Bridge (35-04-12) in Ashtabula County, Ohio, in the Ohio section of this book.

BURR ARCH WITH AN "X" PANEL TRUSS

Illustration 6

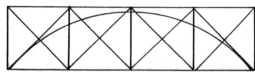

Philippi Bridge

The "X" panel truss was used in conjunction with a Burr arch in the early 1800s. Theodore Burr built some of his bridges using the "X" panel encased with the double arches. Today the "X" panel truss is extremely rare. This photo shows the truss found in the "double-barrelled" Philippi Bridge (48-01-01) in Barbour County, West Virginia. Notice the notches visible in the center truss where the legs of the "X" panel are attached.

(Allen, 1957; American Society of Civil Engineers, 1934; Donovan, 1980)

TOWN TRUSS

Illustration 7

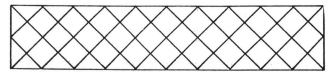

State Road Bridge

Ithiel Town (1784-1844) was born in Thompson, Connecticut. Ithiel Town claimed his first patent in 1820 on a lattice truss. It was one of the first popular new covered bridge designs. In 1835, he patented a similar design but with double webbs and secondary chords. Town was not a bridge builder. He traveled the country promoting his lattice design and sold the rights to build the Town lattice truss to local communities across the country.

The Town lattice was very popular for the following reasons: 1) it used small, reasonably sized lumber for the planking, 2) required a limited amount of framing, 3) additional materials consisted of only bolts and some metal rods, making construction in remote regions possible, 4) local unskilled labor could build the bridge because it was such a simple design, 5) it could span up to 200 feet and serve for 50 to 100 years, and, 6) this design showed stress long before collapse would occur.

The longest Town truss covered bridge existing today is in Blount County, Alabama. It was built in 1932 and is 385 feet long and has four spans. The longest single span Town lattice is in Georgia in Oglethorp County. Date of construction is not known. It is 168 feet long.

There are two Town truss covered bridges on record that were built in 1830, making them the oldest Town truss bridges in existence in the United States. One is in Bucks County, Pennsylvania and is 110 feet long, the Uhlerstown Bridge (38-09-08). The second is in Cheshire County, New Hampshire and is 118 feet long, the Coombs Bridge (29-03-03).

Because the Town truss was such a popular and durable covered bridge truss, thousands were built, and, fortunately, there are an estimated 137 in existence today in the United States. Most of the Town truss covered bridges are preserved in the northeastern United States.

Illustration 7 pictures the lattice pattern. Ashtabula County, Ohio boasts of ten of the historic Town lattice truss bridges. This photo pictures the new State Road Bridge in Ashtabula (35-04-58). State Road Bridge was constructed with galvanized bolts. All of the historic Town lattice trusses are constructed with treenails (wooden nails) instead of bolts. Examples of the treenails are pictured throughout the book.

(Allen, 1957: American Society of Civil Engineers, 1934; Donovan, 1980)

WERNWAG TRUSS

Illustration 8

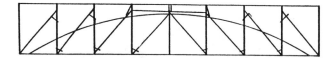

Governor Bebb Park Bridge

Lewis Wernwag was born in Riedlingen, Germany on December 4, 1769. Lewis Wernwag built bridges for twenty-seven years in Pennsylvania, Maryland, Virginia, Kentucky, Ohio and Delaware. He was a bridge building genius. His most spectacular feat was called the "Colossus." Built in 1812, it had a clear span of 340 feet over the Schuylkill River at Fairmount, Pennsylvania. Wernwag took out a patent in 1829 that included iron rods in every panel. A technique used by Wernwag to prevent dry-rot, was sawing the timbers through the heart to detect defects. Also, he kept timbers separated from one another by iron links and screw-bolts. The timbers were never mortized or tenoned. This unique type of construction allowed each piece of timber to be replaced without injuring the superstructure. Lewis Wernwag died in Harpers Ferry, Virginia on August 12, 1843.

This photo is the only example of a Wernwag truss design. It is the Governor Bebb Park Bridge (35-09-02) in Butler County, Ohio. Illustration 8 is the truss design used in the Governor Bebb Park Bridge. Although Wernwag did not build this bridge, the bracing and vertical beams exhibited by this truss characterize it as a Wernwag design. There is some dispute that this truss is just a multiple kingpost truss with a double Burr arch.

(American Society of Civil Engineers, 1934; Donovan, 1980; Southern Ohio Covered Bridge Association, Inc. Ohio Covered Bridge Guide. Columbus: Southern Ohio Covered Bridge Association.)

LONG TRUSS

Illustration 9

Bement Bridge

WARREN TRUSS

Illustration 10

Salt Creek Bridge

Stephen H. Long (1784-1864) was born in Hopkinton, New Hampshire. Long first patented his truss in 1830, and subsequently in 1836, and 1839, with improvements. Long was more of a promoter than a builder. Like Town, he went around the country selling the rights to communities to build his bridge design. Long's truss design consisted of boxed panels with an "X" designed inside the box. One leg of the "X" has a single beam encased by the other leg which has two beams. The oldest Long truss in existence in the U.S today is in Merrimack County in New Hampshire, and was built in 1854. This photo shows the Bement Bridge, which has one span and is 63 feet long. The longest Long truss stands in Miami County, Ohio with 234 feet and has two spans. Called the Eldean Bridge (35-55-01), it was built in 1880 and has been bypassed. A variation of the Long truss is found in the Odaville Bridge (48-18-01) in Jackson County, West Virginia. The Odaville Bridge has two vertical members instead of one. Another characteristic of a typical Long is that the double leg of the "X" panel is opposite on either side of the center panel. The center panel of Bement Bridge has a single, and the double legs point away from the center of the truss. The panel of Odaville Bridge has just two vertical beams and the double legs point toward the center of the truss.

One of the most interesting Long truss bridges today is the Blenheim Bridge (32-48-01) in Schoharie County, New York. This is a double-barrelled bridge and the truss is composed of massive beams. The truss of the bridge is excessively tall. One of the most amazing characteristics about this bridge is that it is 228 feet long and is a single span.

There are an estimated 29 Long truss covered bridges left in the U.S today. Between 1830 and 1840, the Long truss was used extensively. Unfortunately, only a few remain.

(Allen, 1957; American Society of Civil Engineers, 1934; Donovan, 1980)

The Warren truss was patented by James Warren and T. W. Morzani in 1838. The truss is a simple construction of panels of diagonal wooden beams meeting in the form of an inverted "V" depicted in Illustration 10. There are only three Warren trusses in existence today in the United States. All of the remaining Warren truss bridges were built in the 1870s and are found in Ohio. Montgomery County has two Warren truss bridges, the Carillon Park Bridge (35-57-03) and the Mud-Lick Creek Bridge. Muskingum County has the Salt Creek Bridge (35-60-31). This photo is the only pure Warren truss left. The other two have added arches.

One bridge in Greenup County, Kentucky, Bennett's Mill Bridge (17-45-01), is labeled a Warren in the *World Guide to Covered Bridges*. However, the truss appears to be some variation of an "X" panel, rather than a Warren because only one leg of the "X" panel is solid. The other leg is composed of two beams attached to the solid leg, off center.

(American Society of Civil Engineers, 1976; Donovan, 1980)

HAUPT TRUSS

Illustration 11

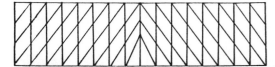

Sayres Bridge

Born March 26, 1817, Herman Haupt graduated from West Point in 1835. After constructing the Gettysburg Railroad across South Mountain in Pennsylvania, Haupt was principal assistant for York and Wrightville Railroad in 1840. It was in this position that he became interested in bridge construction. In 1847, Haupt worked in the capacity of principal assistant engineer for the Pennsylvania Railroad. In 1852, he published *The General Theory of Bridge Construction* which became the text of bridge building for engineers. In 1853, Chief Engineer Haupt constructed the Allegheny tunnel and mountain division of the Pennsylvania Railroad.

During the Civil War, Haupt was in charge of military railroads. In 1862, *Haupt on Military Bridges* was published. Subsequently, Haupt worked for and managed numerous railroad companies. Haupt was an engineering genius. The Haupt truss was patented in 1839. There are two examples of this truss today. One is in Catawba County, North Carolina. Called the Bunker Hill Bridge (33-18-01), it is 85 feet long and was built in 1894. The second example is located in Orange County, Vermont. The Sayres Bridge (45-09-06) has a variation Haupt truss. Built in 1839, it is 134 feet long with a single span. This photo shows a section of the Sayres Bridge truss.

(Donovan, 1980; The National Cyclopaedia of American Biography, Wilson, 1888)

HOWE TRUSS

Illustration 12

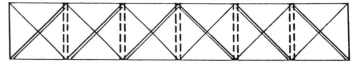

McCafferty Road Bridge

William Howe (1803-1852) was born in Spencer, Massachusetts. Howe obtained a patent for his truss design in 1840. His design resembles that of the Long truss, but the vertical wooden post of the long truss was replaced with iron tie-rods (Illustration 12) that could be adjusted with turnbuckles. In 1840, the Howe truss was patented because of its superior design, and gave the Long truss such intense competition that many more bridges were built using the Howe design instead of the Long truss. For years, Long claimed that Howe had infringed upon his patent rights, but to no avail.

The Howe design was a superior truss in that it made each bridge stronger than any all-wood bridge. It was the Howe truss design that was the forerunner of iron bridges, which caused the eventual end of the era of wooden bridges. The Howe truss was used extensively for railroad bridges because it was easy to ship by rail. Pre-cut timbers and iron parts were loaded on several flat bed rail cars in New England, shipped to the bridge site and erected in one or two days, with the covering to be added after the bridge was in use.

The McCafferty Road Bridge (35-08-04) is a typical example of a Howe truss.

The Howe's superior design is characterized by the fact that there are an estimated 124 Howe truss covered bridges in existence in the United States today, compared to only an estimated 29 Long truss covered bridges. The Howe design is structurally more durable. Consequently, more Howe covered bridges have withstood time than the Long covered bridges.

It was 1837 when the oldest Howe truss covered bridge was built that is still in existence in the United States today. The bridge can be found in Middlesex County, Connecticut. Named the Comstock Bridge (07-04-01), it is closed and is 80 feet long, but due to time constraints, I could not visit this bridge.

PRATT TRUSS

Illustration 13

Caine Road Bridge

Thomas Pratt (1812-1875), the son of an architect, worked with his father and later pursued a career as an engineer. Thomas Pratt's career was spent in the employ of various railroad companies as chief engineer of construction. In 1844, Pratt patented the famous Pratt truss. Originally, it was built of all wood, but with the advent of readily available iron and steel, the Pratt truss received its greatest exposure because its design was conducive to the use of metal. It was the iron Pratt design which won the Pratt truss fame, but it was so long in the development that Pratt did not benefit financially for this invention. Illustration 13 of the Pratt truss, has solid and dashed lines. The solid lines represent wooden members and the dashed lines represent iron rods.

There are only five covered bridges in the U. S. that have the Pratt truss. Two are in California, one is in Butte County and the other is in Santa Cruz County.

The photo illustrates a new Pratt truss covered bridge which is located in Asbtabula County, Ohio. The Caine Road Bridge (35-04-59) was built in 1986 and is 175 feet long.

The other two Pratt trusses are found in the northeast. The County Bridge (29-06-02) in Hillsborough County, New Hampshire was built in 1937 and is 84 feet long. Lower Sheffield Bridge (21-02-02) in Berkshire County, Massachusetts is an excellent example of a Pratt truss. Built in 1952, this Pratt truss uses wooden beams in place of the standard diagonal iron rods.

(American Society of Civil Engineers, 1934; Donovan, 1980; Malone, 1935)

CHILD'S TRUSS

Illustration 14

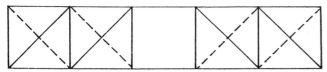

Barronvale Bridge

Illustration 15

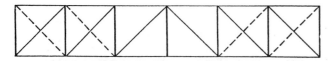

Brubaker Bridge

The Child's truss was designed by the three brothers, Enoch, Warren and Horace. Horace was the carpenter, Warren was the stone mason, and brother Enoch was a graduate from Yale University and was the architectural engineer. The Child brothers built many railroad and highway bridges throughout northeastern United States.

The Child's truss consists of steel tie-rods and opposing diagonal wooden members which cross to form an "X". The center panel can be open or have a kingpost. Illustrations 14 and 15 depict the Child's truss. The dashed lines represent the steel tie-rods and the solid lines represent wooden beams. Illustration 15 has the kingpost center panel and Illustration 14 has the open center panel.

There are an estimated nine covered bridges with a Child's truss left in the United States today. One is in Delaware County in Ohio. The Chambers Bridge (35-21-04) was built in 1874 and is 74 feet long. Six are in Preble County, Ohio and were built between 1887 and 1895 and range from 52 to 109 feet long.

There are two Child's truss bridges in Somerset County, Pennsylvania, Trostletown Bridge (38-56-10) and Barronvale Bridge (38-56-03). Barronvale Bridge shows the only two span Child's truss known. Each span has a kingpost center panel which is graphically shown in Illustration 15.

The Child's truss is very interesting because they used the diagonal steel tie-rods in conjunction with a wooden truss. The Brubaker Bridge (35-68-06) in Preble County, Ohio is an excellent example of the Child's truss. Two-thirds of the sides of the bridge have been removed to expose oncoming traffic. Consequently, the truss is also exposed. Brubaker Bridge has the open center panel which is graphically depicted in Illustration 14. Although hundreds of the Child's trusses were used in covered bridge construction for railroads and highways, only nine still are known to exist in the U.S. today.

(Allen, 1957; American Society of Civil Engineers, 1934; Donovan, 1980)

BROWN TRUSS

Illustration 16

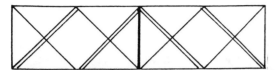

White's Bridge

Josiah Brown, Jr. patented the Brown truss in 1857. The Brown truss is a series of "X" panels, however, the "X" panels are not divided by wooden post or steel tie-rods like the Long and Howe trusses.

Brown truss resembles the Smith truss in that there are no vertical members between the "X" panels. The difference being that the Smith's double diagonal of the "X" panel changes direction in each panel, while the Brown's double diagonal always points toward the center of the truss (Illustration 16). Fallasburg Bridge (22-41-02) has an unusual character in that each member of the truss is placed at an angle rather than having each "X" panel square to one another.

There are only two examples of the Brown truss in existence in the United States today. The oldest and longest is located in Ionia County, Michigan. White's Bridge (22-34-01), is 116 feet long with one span and was built in 1869. The second remaining Brown truss is in Kent County, Michigan. The Fallasburg Bridge (22-41-02) is 100 feet long and was built in 1871 with one span.

(American Society of Civil Engineers, 1976; Donovan, 1980)

POST TRUSS

Illustration 17

Bell's Ford Bridge

The Post Truss was patented in 1863 by Simeon S. Post. The Post truss is very unusual. As can be seen in Illustration 17, the truss has wooden posts that are set on an angle pointing toward the center. Steel rods encase the wooden beams in a crisscross manner. There is only one example of this truss in the United States and that is in Jackson County, Indiana.

Bell's Ford Bridge (14-36-03) is 330 feet long and was built in 1869 with two spans. The bridge hovers over the East Fork White River, adjacent to a new concrete bridge which is now serving the local traffic. Bell's Ford Bridge has foot traffic access only by a narrow, wooden, elevated walkway. The bridge's interior is very exciting because of its unique truss design. The exterior is rotting and in need of repair.

Because the bridge is the only one in the United States with the Post truss, it makes it an especially interesting adventure to see.

(American Society of Civil Engineers, 1976; Donovan, 1980)

SMITH TRUSS

Illustration 18

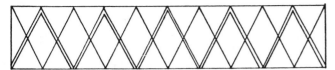

Everitt Road Bridge

Robert W. Smith was born in 1833 in West Charleston, Miami County, Ohio. The son of a cabinet maker, Robert Smith was educated at home by his mother. He attended school for six weeks when he was fifteen and studied geometry, which became a valued tool in his bridge construction career. At age 34, Smith had one patent, a truss for a covered bridge, and had successfully formed the Smith Bridge Company at Tippecanoe City, Ohio (now known as Tipp City). In 1867, Smith moved to Toledo to obtain supplies and expedite shipments for his company. In 1867, he built five covered bridges. In 1868, he built twenty-two and in 1869, he built seventy-five. In 1869, he obtained another patent for an improved combination truss.

The Smith Bridge Company had a unique distribution system. Smith would build an ordered bridge in Toledo, disassemble it, ship it to the location and rebuild it. If shipping costs were prohibitive, arrangements for local lumber and construction were made. Whether Smith's Company did the actual erection or local builders used his patented truss, the design was guaranteed. The Smith Bridge Company's business extended as far as Oregon. Robert Smith died at the age of 65 in 1898.

There are an estimated twenty-one Smith truss covered bridges in existence in the United States as of 1986. Thirteen are in Ohio, seven are in Indiana and one is in Pennsylvania.

The oldest Smith truss in existence is located in Mercer County, Pennsylvania. Called the Kidd's Mill Bridge, it is 124 feet long, a single span, and was built in 1869. The longest Smith truss is 170 feet long, built in 1875, and can be found in Gibson County, Indiana.

Everitt Road Bridge (35-77-01) in Summit County, Ohio has a Smith truss with all "X" panels consisting of single diagonals. Eagle Creek Bridge (35-08-18) in Brown County, Ohio, illustrates the Smith truss with the "X" panel, consisting of one double diagonal and one single diagonal changing direction at every "X" panel. Illustration 18 graphically shows how this occurs.

(Donovan, 1980; Gould, 1977; "Highlights of the Life of Robert W. Smith"; Wilson, 1967)

PARTRIDGE TRUSS

Illustration 19

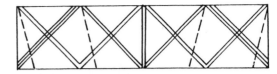

Little Darby Creek Bridge

Born in 1823 in Essex County, New York, Reuben Partridge and his widowed mother moved to Marysville, Union County, Ohio, in 1836, to be close to relatives. Partridge learned the wagon and carriage trade at an early age.

In 1855, at age 32, Partridge built his first self-supporting bridge in Union County. In 1872, he patented the "high bridge truss improvement." Reuben Partridge built over 200 bridges in Union County. His patent was used throughout contiguous counties and a few were built in other states. At age 77, Partridge fell while working on one of his bridges, causing fatal injuries in 1900 at Blues Creek in Union County.

There are only six known Partridge truss bridges left today. One is in Franklin County, Ohio and five are in Partridge's home county, Union County, Ohio. All of these bridges are kept in excellent repair and are serving the local traffic except for one in Union County.

Illustration 19 shows the Partridge truss. The solid lines represent wooden members and the dashed lines represent steel rods. The photograph is an excellent example of the Partridge truss, which can be found in the Little Darby Creek Bridge (35-80-04). Other Partridge trusses incorporate diagonal steel rods in conjunction with the diagonal wooden members.

(Donovan, 1980; "Our Heritage: R.L. Partridge"; Reuben L. Partridge)

PADDLEFORD TRUSS

Illustration 20

Durgin Bridge

BOWSTRING SUSPENSION TRUSS

Illustration 21

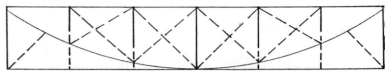

Germantown Bridge

The Paddleford truss was designed by Peter Paddleford from Littleton, New Hampshire. Paddleford had built several Long truss bridges when, in 1846, he modified the Long truss into what is referred to as the Paddleford truss. He took one diagonal of the "X" panel, extended its length and placed it at such an angle so that it extended into each of the panels beyond the original "X" panel (see Illustration 20). Paddleford never patented this truss design but it was used extensively throughout New England.

There are twenty-one Paddleford truss bridges left in the U.S. today. They are all located in the New England States of Maine (five bridges), New Hampshire (thirteen bridges), and Vermont (three bridges).

The oldest and longest Paddleford truss is found in Bath Bridge (29-05-03) in Grafton County, New Hampshire. Built in 1832, the four span structure is 400 feet long. With multiple Burr arches, the Paddleford truss is impressive.

Whittier Bridge (29-02-08) in Carroll County, New Hampshire has an added multi-layered laminated arch. This Paddleford truss was constructed in 1870. This photograph is a close up of a panel of the Paddleford truss used in the Durgin Bridge (29-02-07) also found in Carroll County, New Hampshire.

With an estimated 21 Paddleford trusses left in the U.S. today, they are a rare find. Their geographic isolation in Vermont, New Hampshire, and Maine make them seem exotic to the midwesterner. The Paddleford's geometric pattern adds to the truss' provocative nature.

(American Society of Civil Engineers, 1976; Donovan, 1980)

The only bowstring suspension bridges in the world are exemplified in Ohio by two bridges. One is located in Montgomery County (35-57-01). The Germantown is 105 feet long and was built in 1870. Germantown Bridge is especially exciting. It is the only pure bowstring suspension bridge left in the world. The bridge does not have any sides, therefore allowing the bowstring suspension to be exposed, which is geometrically enticing. Illustration 21 shows the wooden members as solid lines and the steel suspension as dashed lines. The steel bowstring is the solid curved line.

The second bowstring suspension bridge is the John Bright Bridge (35-23-10) in Fairfield, County, Ohio. With an added arch, the John Bright Bridge was built in 1881 and is 72 feet long. The photographs of the John Bright Bridge in the text depict a decrepit, vandalized bridge. The siding is virtually gone and the roof has shotgun holes.

The uniqueness of this bridge has aroused local concern and stimulated plans to move and preserve the John Bright Bridge to Ohio University Lancaster Campus in Lancaster.

(Donovan, 1980)

Explanation of the Text

The text includes 412 covered bridges in fourteen states. Those states include Michigan, Indiana, Ohio, Kentucky, Pennsylvania, West Virginia, Virginia, Maryland, New York, Vermont, New Hampshire, Maine, Connecticut and Massachusetts. The 412 bridges examined in this book include excellent examples from each of the fourteen states. Pennsylvania has more covered bridges than any other state, with an estimated 228. Pennsylvania's bridge trusses are dominated with 129 Burrs, 40 queenposts and 19 Towns. The remaining 40 represent mostly multiple kingpost combinations. Pennsylvania does not offer a great variety of trusses but each of their bridges has its own allure because of the tremendous landscapes. You will find 76 examples of Pennsylvania bridges in the text, which represent the Keystone State's covered bridges as they exist today. As the state with the largest number of covered bridges, Pennsylvania is striving to preserve them.

Ohio has 142 remaining covered bridges and is second to Pennsylvania in the number of them left. I researched Ohio first because it is my home state. Initially, I wanted to see the condition of our covered bridges. Ohio proved to be the basis for my covered bridge education. With only 18 truss designs in existence today in the United States, Ohio has 14 of them. Where Pennsylvania holds the record for the greatest quantity of covered bridges, Ohio holds the record for the greatest variety of trusses. This book contains all 142 covered bridges in Ohio.

For the state with the third largest number of covered bridges, there is a tie between Vermont and Indiana. Because we continue to loose covered bridges periodically, it's difficult to assess an exact figure. I estimate that Vermont has 100 and Indiana has 98. Because the figures are so close and the count is so variable, I consider them a tie. Each state has excellent examples of their existing bridges in the text. Indiana has 65 and Vermont has 43 examples.

Of the fourteen states, Indiana, Ohio, Pennsylvania and Vermont originally had the most covered bridges because of their populations and topographies. The most important factor in the number of surviving covered bridges is the preservation efforts of these states, and their local communities.

In this text, you will find such varied examples from exquisite restorations, to abandoned, soon-to-collapse bridges. The condition of our covered bridges by township, county and state will be evidenced throughout the book.

The text is presented in alphabetical order; first, according to state and secondly, according to county. Each bridge will be identified with its county, state and number. The number is assigned to each bridge by the National Society for the Preservation of Covered Bridges (NSPCB). The number is presented in three segments such as 45-01-05. The first two digits represent the state according to alphabetical order. The second two digits represent the county and the third two digits represent the designated bridge. If you would like to obtain a list of all known covered bridges in the world, request a copy of *World Guide to Covered Bridges* from the National Society for the Preservation of Covered Bridges, whose address appears with the covered bridge associations.

The text presents each bridge with the designated number assigned by the NSPCB, along with the county and state. Each bridge has a name and, in many cases, more than one. The names will appear in the heading for each bridge. The text addresses the bridge by the first name that appears in the heading. The names of the bridges are very interesting and come from a variety of sources. Many covered bridge sites had a mill site close by. Usually the mill existed prior to the construction of the covered bridge. Wagons would cross the stream to take their grains to the mill. The place where they forded the stream became known as a crossing and usually adopted the Mill owner's name, such as Sawyer's Crossing (29-03-05). When the covered bridge was built, the crossing was replaced with the term, bridge, and names such as Wagoner's Mill Bridge (38-50-15) developed.

Bridge names are also assumed from the people who owned the surrounding land, or nearby neighbors. Sometimes the bridge has the name of its builder. Other times the bridge assumes the name of the nearby town or village. Often the bridge is named after the road it serves or the stream that it spans.

The text includes all of the historical data that was available for the bridges. Usually, dates of construction are known, but, occasionally, not even that information was available. Some counties have bridge building records, but most do not, especially prior to 1870. Dates of construction prior to 1850 are questionable as far as accuracy is concerned because of the complete absence of records. If the builder of the bridge is known, it is included in the text. Dates of renovation and restoration are also included if known.

The information presented in this book is a compilation of many historical references. Due to the inherent nature of historical data, which dates as far back as 1812, there are incongruities that exist. Often I would find three or four references that would contradict one another. Information that I present in this book is based on my experience and judgments. I have determined these facts to be the most accurate, based on accessible historical data. If you find information that you feel is in error and have a reference you wish to share with me, I would sincerely appreciate your assistance so that the historical documentation in this book can be maintained with as much accuracy as possible.*

*Brenda Krekeler, c/o Daring Books, P.O. Box 20050, Canton, Ohio 44701.

How to Find Covered Bridges and Obtain County Maps

Finding the covered bridges is half the fun of bridging. Their locations will take you places that, ordinarily, you would never see. Covered bridges are usually found on backroads. The covered bridges on main roads were the first to be replaced by concrete and steel structures. The covered bridges remaining in America are generally the ones not used by heavy traffic. Consequently, they are normally located on township or county roads which are not well traveled. It is on these rural roads you will discover unique parts of American life, past and present. If you are an interstate driver, like myself, you will be impressed just by the interesting scenery normally missed on interstates. Instead of heavy traffic and interchanges, you will witness tremendous farms, intricate rock walls (early 1800s), and quaint towns and villages. The beautiful barns in Indiana, the bubbling mountain streams in New Hampshire and Vermont, and the hills and mountains of Pennsylvania are viewed from roads few people, other than the local residents, travel. Each state with covered bridges has a fascinating landscape for the bridger to discover.

To start bridging, there are some tools you will need. Using these tools, you will soon become skilled in locating bridges by interpreting the landscape. Let us first start with the basics. Maps and a compass are mandatory tools. It is my suggestion to obtain county maps available from each state, for the counties you intend to bridge. Addresses for all the states covered in this book are provided at the end of this chapter. I also suggest obtaining a local county map from the Chamber of Commerce located in each county seat. They are usually available, and sometimes even have the bridges identified. Also, some of the maps provided locally are easier to use. Another avenue you might want to pursue in your quest for maps is to find an atlas and gazetteer of the state. The atlas will have all of the county maps for the state. This can prove to be the most economical approach, especially when bridging states such as Vermont, New Hampshire, Pennsylvania, Ohio and Indiana. These states have many bridges in many counties.

The maps and directions provided for you in the text can be used in the following manner. Take my direc-tions and map and locate the bridge's position on your county map, obtained from the state. First, identify the township if the information is provided and if townships are demarcated on your county map. Next, identify the stream that your bridge spans. Finally, find the point of origin, usually a town or village, and coordinate the information. This process will enable you to: 1) locate the bridge, 2) develop a sense of the landscape, and 3) get the big picture—just where the bridge is in relation to the entire county. This will allow you to plan your expedition more efficiently.

Please do not be fooled by this methodical approach. There are some pitfalls to be aware of before attempting your first bridging exploration. If you are an experienced bridger, then you are acquainted with the traps maps can cause. The problem is that a map can have roads which are nonexistent. Other times, the map will not have roads that do exist. This can be a formidable trap, especially when the directions show you "left on the second road," when there are actually several roads at that point. This brings us to the problem of identifying the roads. Most all roads have numbers. Township roads, county roads, state roads, United States roads and interstates are identified as CR, SR, US, and I-roads, respectively, in the directions provided in this book and on many maps. Many roads also have names, especially the township and county roads. This can present a problem when your map provides numbers and the roads are identified with names, or vice versa. This is where it comes in handy to have a local county map obtained from the Chamber of Commerce. In the directions provided in the text, if it states, "from a 'town', three miles on SR 221," the mileage is calculated from the town's outer limits.

Signs that will help locate your bridge include "ROAD CLOSED," "LOW CLEARANCE," "BRIDGE WEIGHT LIMIT 3 TONS," and on rare occasions, "COVERED BRIDGE AHEAD." These signs occur periodically and can help lead you to your bridge. Other signs, consistent and dependable, are provided for you by the landscape. From your map you can interpret which way the stream is flowing. When a tributary meets another stream, a larger stream, that point of entry is called their confluence. The direction in which the tributary is pointing at the confluence is the direction the stream is flowing. When you drive over streams in the area of your bridge, you will soon learn how to interpret your location in respect to your bridge, assuming you are familiar with the stream's identification. Rivers, creeks and small streams will help locate your bridge. The streams' banks are always vegetated. Soon you will notice a pattern of vegetation along a stream's banks. One of the best clues in locating covered bridges is they are always found in a valley, never on a hill. As obvious as it might seem, I have found myself on more than one occasion looking for a bridge on a hill.

As long as your covered bridge is in its original location, these skills can be incorporated. Even if your bridge is bypassed, the same rules apply. However, when you are searching for a bypassed bridge, be sure to look carefully in either direction from the new bridge because, occasionally, they are well concealed.

Finding relocated covered bridges is another matter entirely. Many bridges have been placed and restored in parks, and sometimes finding the parks inside city limits prove frustrating. Because they are dryland, or over a pond, you do not have the natural indications provided by the landscape, such as tree lines along the streams, and the direction of water flows in the creeks and hills and valleys. City parks are usually located amid a myriad of streets. County maps do not usually provide street names or any type of identification of the park's existence. I found most of the city parks by asking local residents, who all were very helpful. Covered bridges in parks are difficult to find but even though they are not in their natural locations they are usually never a disappointment. They have been restored at the time of relocation and the parks take excellent care of them.

Covered bridges that are privately owned are also difficult to find at times. If they are still in their original location, the bridges can be found easier. If, however, they are dryland, on private grounds, it can sometimes be impossible to locate. When you do locate a covered bridge that is identified as being privately owned, always ask permission to see their bridge.

Each state has similarities associated with discovering their covered bridge locations. Even more apparent are the similarities associated with finding covered bridges within a county. For example, some counties, although rare, label roads that have a covered bridge. Some counties have covered bridge festivals and provide color-coded tours of their bridges. For more information concerning the covered bridge festivals, please see the chapter on "Special Bridges, Events and Organizations." Other counties consistently use "LOW CLEARANCE 6′ " signs or "BRIDGE LIMIT 3 TONS" signs. You will soon become familiar with how each county identifies their covered bridges.

The last resource I want to mention is a most valuable one. Once you know you are in the immediate vicinity of your bridge, and are having some difficulty finding it, simply ask someone directions. People who live close to our historic structures are proud of them and are always very helpful. Do not be shy about asking for directions because you can save yourself miles of driving and a considerable time investment.

At this point I want to reiterate that finding some of our old historic bridges can be a challenge. The directions I have provided are to the best of my knowledge correct. However, I remember on one specific occasion in Noble County, Ohio, my husband and I drove for three hours on countless graveled trails, over hundreds of hills and through numerous valleys hunting one bridge. We finally found the bridge but we were not sure where we were! I tried to write down specific directions to guide you but when some roads have no names or numbers and other roads have names contrary to that found on a map, you and I can find ourselves LOST!

The best advice I can provide for you to prepare for your bridging adventures is to be familiar with your maps, do not forget your compass, and have a full tank of gas! Many covered bridge locations are remote, so do not be caught stranded. Because the covered bridges are located in remote areas, the local towns do not have any fast food establishments. It is best to pack your lunch. Insect repellent is another supply that can definitely come in handy, especially around the creek and river banks. It is always wise to travel with a first aid kit.

Now you have the basics of bridging. When you are becoming a little frustrated, trying to figure out just where your bridge is hiding, remember where you packed your sense of humor. Have FUN!!

ADDRESSES TO OBTAIN COUNTY MAPS

CONNECTICUT
Connecticut Department of Transportation
P.O. Drawer A
Wethersfield, Connecticut 06109

INDIANA
Print Graphics Inc.
2502 East 52nd
P.O. Box 55161
Indianapolis, Indiana 46205

KENTUCKY
Kentucky Department of Highways
Map Sales
Frankfort, Kentucky 40622

MAINE
State of Maine Department of Transportation
State House
Station #16
Child Street
Augusta, Maine 04333

MARYLAND
State Highway Administration
Map Sales
2323 West Joppa Road
Brocklandville, Maryland 21022

MASSACHUSETTS
Massachusetts Department of Public Works
10 Park Plaza
Room 4150
Boston, Massachusetts 02116

MICHIGAN
Department of Transportation Contracts Division
P.O. Box 30050
Lansing, Michigan 48909

NEW HAMPSHIRE
State of New Hampshire, Department of
Transportation
John O. Morton Building
Concord, New Hampshire 03301

NEW YORK
Map Information Unit
New York State Department of Transportation
State Office Campus Building 4
Room 105
Albany, New York 12232

NORTH CAROLINA
North Carolina Department of Transportation Location
& Survey Unit
P.O. Box 25201
Raleigh, North Carolina 27611

OHIO
Ohio Department of Transportation
25 South Front Street, Room B100
P.O. Box 899
Columbus, Ohio 43216-0899

PENNSYLVANIA
Department of Transportation
Penn DOT Sales Store
P.O. Box 2028
Harrisburg, Pennsylvania 17105

TENNESSEE
Tennessee Department of Transportation
Map Sales Suite 1000, James K. Polk Building
505 Deaderick
Nashville, Tennessee 37219

VERMONT
Vermont Agency of Transportation Project Planning
Division
133 State Street
Montpelier, Vermont 05602

VIRGINIA
Department of Transportation
1401 E. Broad Street
Richmond, Virginia 23219

WEST VIRGINIA
West Virginia Department of Highways
Planning Division
1900 Washington Street
Charleston, West Virginia 25305

If you require additional addresses from other states, call information in the capitol of the state in question, and ask for the phone number of the Department of Transportation, Highway Department, and, sometimes, map sales has a listed number under one of the previously mentioned headings.

Special Bridges, Events and Organizations

COUNTIES THAT ARE ESPECIALLY INTERESTING TO BRIDGE

JACKSON COUNTY, INDIANA has three remaining covered bridges. All three are over 300 feet long and span the East Fork White River.

Shieldstown Bridge (14-36-02) is 331 feet and was built in 1876. With two spans, Shieldstown Bridge has two sets of double Burr arches.

Bell's Ford Bridge (14-36-03) is 330 feet long and was constructed in 1869. Bell's Ford Bridge is the only covered bridge left in the United States that has a Post truss. The Post truss is fascinating because its wooden posts are set diagonally, and steel rods encase the posts in a crisscross fashion.

Medora Bridge (14-36-04) is the second longest covered bridge left in America. At 434 feet, it is the only covered bridge with three sets of double Burr arches known to this author. The three sets of arches are quite spectacular.

Although Jackson County has only three bridges left, each has exciting characteristics.

PARKE COUNTY, INDIANA has 34 covered bridges, more covered bridges than any other county in the United States. Parke County celebrates their covered bridges each year with a ten-day, covered bridge festival, in which an estimated 800,000 people visit their bridges.

The quantity of covered bridges that Parke County has to offer is overwhelming. Jeffries Ford Bridge (14-61-03) and West Union Bridge (14-61-27) have two spans and each span has a significant camber. These are the best examples of double humpback bridges. Many of Parke County's single span covered bridges exhibit cambers. It is this feature which makes Parke County bridges so interesting to photograph.

Mansfield Bridge (14-61-20) and Bridgeton Bridge (14-61-04) still have mill sites. The old mill buildings have been preserved and their mill races create spectacular falls. Both bridges and mills are extremely in-teresting because there are very few bridge and mill combinations left in the midwest.

The open fields and farmlands of Indiana help to make Parke County's many bridges a pleasant bridging experience.

CARROLL COUNTY, NEW HAMPSHIRE is an interesting area to bridge because it has seven covered bridges, all with the Paddleford truss. With only an estimated 21 of these trusses left, finding seven of them clustered is pleasing. And, as with much of New England, the locations are often quite beautiful.

MERRIMACK COUNTY, NEW HAMPSHIRE is an exciting county to visit, with eight historic covered bridges, two of them are old railroad bridges. Unfortunately, the Sulphite Railroad Bridge (29-07-09) was burned by arson. Only the shell remains. What is so fascinating about the Sulphite Railroad Bridge is that the train tracks ran on top of the bridge, not through it. Although this type of construction was common in the late 1800s, this was the only example left in our country.

Merrimack County's other six covered bridges are interesting in their own right as they are well maintained and have attractive locations.

SULLIVAN COUNTY, NEW HAMPSHIRE has two railroad covered bridges. Pier Railroad Bridge (29-10-03) and Wright Railroad Bridge (29-10-04) span Sugar River within a mile of each other. Both of these railroad bridges are imposing, but both are abandoned. With so few examples of railroad covered bridges left, these two need to be preserved.

Sullivan County, New Hampshire shares the Cornish/Windsor Bridge (29-10-09) with Windsor County, Vermont. Spanning the Connecticut River, the Cornish/Windsor Bridge is the longest covered bridge in the United States, with 460 feet and only two spans. The Cornish/Windsor Bridge is Sullivan County's crowning jewel. The fast streams and beautiful scenery combine to create beautiful landscapes for the bridges.

ASHTABULA COUNTY, OHIO is one of Ohio's

most fascinating counties to bridge. With fourteen covered bridges, Ashtabula has ten Town lattice trusses, three Howe trusses and one Pratt truss. The fourteen covered bridges include two new bridges, State Road Bridge (35-04-58) and Caine Road Bridge (35-04-59). Ashtabula's historic structures have been restored and are used daily. Ashtabula County represents a county that is dedicated to the preservation of their bridges. Each fall Ashtabula has a covered bridge festival to celebrate its covered bridges.

BROWN COUNTY, OHIO has eight covered bridges, five of which are constructed with a Smith truss. There are only an estimated 21 Smith truss bridges left in the U.S. and finding five of them together is exciting. Brown County has an interesting landscape with hills and deeply entrenched valleys. This landscape provides a lovely setting for these covered bridges, all of which are well maintained.

PREBLE COUNTY, OHIO has seven historic covered bridges, all of which have the Child truss. Some exhibit an open center panel and others have a kingpost center panel. Over and above having seven of the nine existing Child truss bridges in America in one county, Preble County's bridges are all very picturesque. The landscape has gently rolling hills and offers a wonderful setting for the bridges, all of which are well maintained.

COLUMBIA COUNTY, PENNSYLVANIA has 22 covered bridges. Each fall, Columbia County and their neighbor, Montour County, have a covered bridge festival.

Columbia County's bridges span swift flowing, rocky mountain streams, which create exciting landscapes for the bridges. The most fascinating site is at East Paden Bridge (39-19-11) and West Paden Bridge (38-19-12), the only twin covered bridges left in the United States. Although not identical twins, they are fun to see. West Paden is 103 feet long with a Burr truss, and East Paden is only 79 feet long with a queenpost truss. They are superbly maintained and located in a public park in their original location. Fortunately, Columbia County had the foresight to save the "twins."

All of Columbia County's covered bridges are breathtaking as a result of their mountainous location and because they are well maintained.

LANCASTER COUNTY, PENNSYLVANIA has 28 covered bridges, which makes it the second largest number of covered bridges in one county. Lancaster County's covered bridges are especially interesting because almost all of them were located near a mill site. At many of the locations, remnants of the mill race and mill buildings can still be found.

Lancaster does not presently offer a covered bridge festival. With the quantity of bridges and their beautiful locations, a covered bridge festival seems like a natural occurrence.

What makes bridging in Lancaster County even more exciting is that many of the bridges are in the heart of Amish country. The sight of black carriages drawn by a horse, the sound of the horse's clop clop across the covered bridges, and the perfect fields, plowed by horse-drawn equipment, creates an environment that will take you over 100 years back in time. The unique lifestyle of the Amish creates a landscape that presents the covered bridges as they appeared over a century ago. Lancaster County is a fascinating experience.

PERRY COUNTY, PENNSYLVANIA has thirteen covered bridges. Most of the bridge locations were near old mills which still have remnants of the mill race and mill buildings. There are seven covered bridges that span Shermans Creek within 14 miles of each other. Shermans Creek flows in a wide valley between the Tuscarora Mountains and the Blue Mountains. Some of the most impressive scenery in Pennsylvania is found in this valley. All of the covered bridges over Shermans Creek are well maintained and each one has its own alluring charm.

Wagoner's Mill Bridge (38-50-15) which spans Bixler Run, north of Shermans Creek, is possibly one of the oldest covered bridges left in the United States. It is thought to have been built in 1812. The site is also fascinating because there is a three story stone mill and mill race still present in excellent condition. The mill operated into the 1940s.

Perry County has excellent examples of our historic covered bridges and as a bonus, magnificent scenery.

ADDISON COUNTY, VERMONT has five covered bridges. Station Bridge (45-01-01) is fascinating because it is located on Swamp Road, appropriately named because the bridge spans Otter Creek, which is surrounded by miles of swamp. Pulpmill Bridge (45-01-04), built in 1830, is a double-barrelled bridge, one of only five left in America.

Rutland Railroad (45-01-05) is an excellent example

of a preserved railroad bridge. With a massive Howe truss, and 108 feet long, the Rutland Railroad Bridge has a most inspiring environment with the Green Mountains in the background.

Although all of Vermont's covered bridges are spectacular, Addison County offers some exciting representatives.

COVERED BRIDGE FESTIVALS

For more information about the covered bridge festivals please write:

WASHINGTON COUNTY, PENNSYLVANIA
Washington County Tourism
P.O. Box 877
Washington, Pennsylvania 15301

ASHTABULA COUNTY, OHIO
Ashtabula Covered Bridge Festival
25 West Jefferson Street
Jefferson, Ohio 44047

PARKE COUNTY, INDIANA, DATES:
Parke County Covered Bridge Festival
October 14-23, 1988
Tourist Information Center
Parke County, Inc.
October 13-22, 1988
P.O. Box 165
October 12-21, 1990
Rockville, Indiana 47872-0165

COLUMBIA-MONTOUR COUNTY, PENNSYLVANIA
Columbia-Montour County Covered Bridge Festival
RD 2 Box 109
Bloomsburg, Pennsylvania 17815

For information about a covered bridge tour each year please write:
The National Society for the Preservation of Covered Bridges, Inc.
M. Marion Bonnet - President
17 Beaumont Street
Dorchester, Maine 02124

COVERED BRIDGE ASSOCIATIONS

NORTHEASTERN STATES:

Connecticut River Valley Covered Bridge Society
10 Congress Street
Greenfield, Massachusetts 01301

(Alternate Address)
Connecticut River Valley Covered Bridge Society
Richard E. Roy - Treasurer
73 Ash Street
Manchester, New Hampshire 03104

INDIANA:

Indiana Covered Bridge Society Inc.
965 Broadway Drive (North)
Plainfield, Indiana 46168

(Alternate Address)
Indiana Covered Bridge Society Inc.
John Sechrist - Treasurer
725 Sanders Street
Indianapolis, Indiana 46203

KENTUCKY:

Kentucky Covered Bridge Society, Inc.
62 Miami Parkway
Fort Thomas, Kentucky 41075
(Not Active)

NEW YORK:

New York State Covered Bridge Society
Henry Messing - Treasurer
958 Grove Street
Elmira, New York 14901

OHIO:

Ashtabula County Covered Bridge Publication
Ashtabula County Historical Society
P.O. Box 206
Jefferson, Ohio 44047-0206

Fairfield Covered Bridge Association
c/o Jim Walter
5905 Lancaster / Kirk Road
Baltimore, Ohio 43105

Northern Ohio Covered Bridge Society
Mrs. Pat Eierman
6622 Balsam Drive
Bedford Heights, Ohio 44146

The Southern Ohio Covered Bridge Association
3155 Whitehead Road
Columbus, Ohio 43204

OREGON:

Oregon Covered Bridge Society
Fred Kildow - Corresponding Secretary
9070 South West Rambler Lane
Portland, Oregon 97223

PENNSYLVANIA:

Theodore Burr Covered Bridge Society
of Pennsylvania, Inc.
1121 Colonial Drive
Lancaster, Pennsylvania 17603

NATIONAL:

The National Society for the Preservation
of Covered Bridges, Inc.
M. Marion Bonnet - President
17 Beaumont Street
Dorchester, Maine 02124

The National Society for the Preservation of Covered
Bridges, Inc.
Richard Donovan
Bucknell View Court #4
RD 1 Box 213
Milton, Pennsylvania 17847

The National Society for the
Preservation of Covered Bridges, Inc.
Roger D. Griffin - Treasurer
31 Federal Street
Beverly, Maine 01915

SOME OF MY FAVORITE BRIDGES

White Water Canal Aqueduct, Franklin County, Indiana (14-24-11). This is the only covered bridge that is designed to carry water for a canal that is still in existence.

Bell's Ford Bridge, Jackson County, Indiana (14-36-03). This is the only Post truss bridge.

Medora Bridge, Jackson County, Indiana (14-36-04). The only covered bridge that has three sets of double Burr arches. Medora Bridge is the second longest covered bridge left in the United States.

Upper Village Bridge, Cheshire County, New Hampshire (29-03-02). The best example of a village style bridge, it has two external walkways. The bridge is 170 feet long and both of the Town trusses are exposed.

Cornish/Windsor Bridge, Sullivan, New Hampshire (29-10-09). The longest covered bridge in the United States, Cornish/Windsor is 460 feet.

Blenheim Bridge, Schoharie County, New York (32-48-01). The longest single span bridge in America, with 228 feet, the Blenheim Bridge is a double-barrelled structure.

Benetka Road Bridge, Ashtabula County, Ohio (35-04-12). Benetka Road Bridge has a beautiful 38-layer laminated arch.

Germantown Bridge, Montgomery County, Ohio (35-57-01). Germantown Bridge is the only pure bowstring truss left today.

Little Darby Bridge, Union County, Ohio (35-80-04). An excellent example of the rare Partridge truss, Little Darby Bridge is painted white and beautifully maintained.

Humpback or Geer's Mill Bridge, Vinton County, Ohio (35-82-06). Humpback Bridge is one of only two examples of humpback bridges left in the United States. This bridge is 180 feet long, with three spans, and rises over eight feet above the road level.

East Paden and West Paden Bridges, Columbia County. The only example of twin bridges today, is in Pennsylvania. East (38-19-11) and West (38-19-12) Paden are well preserved in a county park.

Wagoner's Mill, Perry County, Pennsylvania (38-50-15). Wagoner's Mill Bridge is possible one of the oldest covered bridges left in the U.S. today, built as early as 1812. The bridge site has a three story mill and mill race which have been preserved and present a spectacular site.

Rutland Railroad Bridge, Addison County, Vermont (45-01-05). Rutland Railroad Bridge has been preserved and has a splendid background, the Green Mountains.

Swanton Railroad Bridge, Franklin County, Vermont (45-06-10). The longest existing railroad bridge, Swanton Bridge is preserved and one of the most striking structures because of its immense size. Beautiful Swanton Railroad Bridge shown in the color photograph on page 326, has since been burned by arson. This was a tragic loss.

Old Humpback Bridge, Allegheny County, Virginia (46-03-01). Old Humpback is the shorter of the two remaining humpbacks left in the United States. This bridge also has an eight foot rise in the center of the bridge, above the road level.

Terms

ABANDONED - A covered bridge that is no longer in use and is not maintained.

ABUTMENT - The bridge foundation upon either bank, usually built of cut stone, bedrock or concrete.

ADZE - A small axe used to smooth a beam.

ARCH - A curved timber or timbers used in conjunction with all truss designs for additional structural support. The arch is most commonly used with a multiple king post truss.

AUGER - An instrument used to drill holes for the wooden pegs.

BACKBONE - See HUMPBACK.

BARN SIDING - Planking that runs vertically.

BATTEN - One inch strips of wood covering the seams of the plank siding.

BEETLE - An instrument used to drive treenails into their openings.

BRACE - Diagonal timbers that slant toward the center of the bridge for structural support.

BRIDGER - A covered bridge enthusiast.

BROADAXE - A large axe with a beveled sharp blade on one side. A broad axe was used to hew a round log into a square beam.

BYPASSED - A term used to describe a covered bridge that has been left in its original location with a new bridge built nearby.

CAMBER - A hump built into the chords that allows the bridge to level after the weight of the bridge settles.

CHORD - The upper and lower chords are horizontal timbers encasing the top and bottom members of the truss.

COMPRESSION MEMBERS - These timbers are diagonal beams that are subjected to squeeze when a load passes over the bridge.

CONFLUENCE - The physical location where two streams merge.

COUNTER-BRACE - This brace is a diagonal timber in a truss that points away from the center of the bridge.

DOUBLE-BARRELLED BRIDGE - This covered bridge has two lanes that are divided by a truss which is structural support for the bridge.

DRY ROT - Very old wood that has dried and shrunken. The board appears as if it is full of splinters and becomes very brittle. It must be replaced because it will soon crack under pressure.

DRY STONE - A cut stone or bedrock abutment or pier that is laid up without mortar.

EVES - This part of the covered bridge is the portion of the roof hanging over the sides of the covered bridge.

FLOOR JOIST - Wooden beams 4″ x 12″ or larger, set into or on the lower chord. These joists, which run perpendicular to the truss, support the floor planking. Often a second layer of joists are used, laid opposite the first.

HUMPBACK - A humpback bridge is one that has a distinct arch built into the bridge, and the center of the bridge is noticeably elevated above road level. The arch is called a camber.

INFERIOR BRACE - This brace acts as a support which runs from the face of the abutment to the lower chord.

LAMINATED ARCH - Multiple planks bolted together to form an arch, used in place of a solid beam.

LATERAL BRACING - This bracing is made of timbers that are between the two upper chords and between the two lower chords to keep the truss evenly separated and in place.

LAP SIDING - Horizontal wooden siding that laps over one another.

MAUL - An all wood hammer used to pound in wooden pegs. The hammer head resembles a club.

MORTISE - A timber with a notched opening that will accept another timber for an exact fit. The timber that fits into the mortise is a tenon.

NUMBER DESIGNATION - A number with three segments such as 45-01-85 designates a specific bridge. The first two digits represent the state (alphabetically), the second two digits represent the county, and the last two digits identify the bridge.

PANEL - Individual sections of a truss separated by a vertical post.

PATENTED TRUSS - A truss design that has been granted a patent by the United States Patent Office.

PIER - A foundation made of stone, concrete or steel that supports the center of the bridge.

PITSAW - Used to cut a beam in half. One man was in a pit and one man was on top of the pit, to use the saw.

PLANE - An instrument used to add smoothness to the timbers.

PORTAL - The entrance and exit of a covered bridge and the surrounding wood used to protect the end of the bridge.

POST - A vertical timber in a bridge truss.

RAFTER - Small wooden beams that form the roof's truss.

RUNNER - Lengthwise planking laid down on the floor where the wheels run.

RENOVATED - Major structural additions have been made on the bridge.

RESTORED - Replaced old members but did not change the bridge design.

ROD - Vertical iron rods were used to replace the vertical wooden members in some trusses. These rods connected the upper and lower chords and were capable of being adjusted.

SHAKE - Wooden shingles. Roofs are commonly covered with shake or tin. Rarely, asphalt shingles or tar paper is used.

SHELTER PANEL - The first panel at each end of the bridge that is boarded to protect the truss from the weather.

SIDING - Planking that covers the exterior of the bridge. Vertical siding is called planking and horizontal siding is called lap.

SPAN - The length of the bridge from one abutment to the other. When a bridge has a pier in the center, the bridge has two spans.

SUSPENSION ROD - An iron rod used to attach an added arch to the floor beams in an old bridge.

TRIBUTARY - A stream that drains into a larger stream.

TENON - The timber that fits into the notched opening of a mortise joint.

TENSION MEMBER - Vertical posts that are pulled down when a vehicle passes over the bridge.

TREENAILS - Wooden pegs which were turned in a lathe and soaked in linseed oil. These treenails can be seen in Town lattice truss covered bridges. The treenails were pounded into holes slightly smaller than the diameter of the treenails.

TWIN BRIDGES - Two covered bridges aligned end to end, separated by land or an artificial abutment.

TRUSS - Timbers arranged in such a manner to form a series of triangles, which are the side structures of a covered bridge. The truss will support the bridge's own weight and the weight that crosses over the bridge.

Connecticut

ACKNOWLEDGMENTS

I would like to thank the following people of Connecticut for their time, information and suggestions:
Alesandra M. Schmidt, Reference Librarian, The Connecticut Historical Society
Michael R. Gannett, President, Cornwall Historical Society, Inc.
Mrs. Barbara J. Todd, Assistant Director, The Litchfield Historical Society

CONNECTICUT

At one time, Connecticut had 50-60 railroad and highway covered bridges (Allen, 1957, p.73). Today there are only three still in existence. One is no longer in use and is located in East Hampton in Middlesex County (04-04-01), the Comstock Bridge.

The two bridges that are still functioning are located in Litchfield County, Bull's Bridge (07-03-01) in Kent and West Cornwall Bridge (07-03-02) in West Cornwall. Both of these bridges are conveniently located just off US 7.

Connecticut's place in covered bridge fame comes not from the three covered bridges, but more from its two famous bridge designers that called Connecticut home, Theodore Burr and Ithiel Town. Connecticut is also the birthplace of many other famous bridge builders such as Jonathon Walcott, Colonel Ezra Brainerd, Zenas Whiting and Samuel Mack.

The two preserved, functioning covered bridges in Connecticut have the unusual combination of a Town and queenpost truss and are in interesting geographic locations.

(Allen, 1957; Donovan, 1980)

BRIDGE NAME	COUNTY	NUMBER
Bull's	Litchfield	07-03-01
West Cornwall	Litchfield	07-03-02

Bull's Bridge

Bull's Bridge crosses the Housatonic River on the western edge of Litchfield County.

Bull's Bridge was built in 1858 by Jacob Bull of Dover Plains, New York for $3,000 (Allen, 1950, p. 19). The 109-foot bridge has naturally weathered plank siding, a shake roof and four small square windows on each side. The single span rests on creek rock abutments encased in concrete. The interior is most interesting with a combination Town lattice truss and a queenpost truss. The queenpost has steel rods in place of the traditional wooden vertical members and there is an inverted "V" bracing at the center of the queenpost panel, as well as additional diagonal bracing. The floor has a lengthwise solid runner centered on three-fourths of the floor space. The bridge is still open and carries a tremendous amount of traffic.

Just north of the bridge site is an elaborate dam which diverts water to supply a race that flows the same direction as the river and whose channel is located just east of the bridge site. The water eventually drops to a hydroelectric plant several miles downstream. The dam creates a spectacular waterfall into a gorge filled with huge boulders, producing an exciting view at the bridge. In the photograph of the exterior, you will note how smooth the water appears. Actually, the water was rather choppy and flowing very swiftly. It was late one evening and almost dark at the time, and required a time lapse shot.

The bridge site has a well defined trail on one side that allows easy access to the creek. This location offers a good opportunity for photographers.

DIRECTIONS: Just west of US 7 in Kent (Allen, 1950; Donovan, 1980)

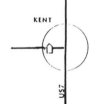

West Cornwall Bridge

West Cornwall Bridge spans the Housatonic River at West Cornwall in central Litchfield County.

A flood took out the first covered bridge at this location in 1837. It is thought that sometime between 1837 and 1856, the present bridge was erected (Allen, 1950; "Covered Bridge Links Town's Past, Present").

The 242-foot West Cornwall Bridge is open to traffic and has enough room in the interior to accept two lanes. The truss, similar to Bull's Bridge (07-03-01), the only other open covered bridge in Connecticut, is a Town truss with a double queenpost encasing the Town. There is a separate queenpost over each span. The queenpost has two steel rods in place of the traditional vertical beams and there is diagonal bracing through the truss. The floor has diagonal planking. The interior has electricity and is well lighted.

West Cornwall Bridge's exterior has a shake roof, red plank siding with batten and seven small square windows with glass panes. The bridge has two spans and is supported by stone abutments encased in concrete and one concrete pier.

Plans were presented by the Department of Transportation to replace the West Cornwall Bridge in 1968, but there was such resistance from the local community that, instead, West Cornwall Bridge was strengthened with steel and raised two feet to prevent flood damage. In 1961, a serious ice jam was threatening the pier of the bridge. The jam was dynamited and the bridge was left unharmed.

The river banks of the Housatonic are relatively clear and easily accessible. The rapids at the bridge site give the bridge an enticing quality.

DIRECTIONS: Just east of US 7 in West Cornwall. (Allen, 1950; "Covered Bridge Links Town's Past, Present"; Donovan, 1980)

Indiana

At one time, 70 of Indiana's 92 counties had covered bridges. Between 1834 and 1923, there were over 600 covered bridges built in Indiana. Indiana now has 98 remaining covered bridges in 30 counties. In 1987, 62 of the remaining 98 bridges were open to traffic: 16 bypassed, 9 in parks, 8 closed, 2 used as private barns and one is an aqueduct (Indiana Covered Bridge Society).

This study of the historic covered bridges of Indiana includes 64 of the 98 bridges in sixteen different counties. Although this is not a comprehensive list, it is thought to be representative of Indiana's covered bridges today.

Indiana ranks fourth in total number of covered bridges by state, in the United States.

The majority of Indiana's covered bridges exist in the southern half of the state. Indiana experienced the wrath of continental glaciation during the ice age, which left northern Indiana relatively flat. Southern Indiana has a much more diverse terrain with steep hills and river valleys. Deeply entrenched, meandering rivers prone to flooding, created the demand for a means to cross the streams safely. Southern Indiana has such major drainage systems as: West Fork White River, East Fork White River, Sand River, Laughery River, Muscatatuck, Sugar Creek, Big Raccoon Creek, Flat Rock, Big Blue and Driftwood. All of these rivers presented formidable barriers to transportation.

INDIANA'S TRUSSES

Indiana has a rich representation of trusses. There are eight different designs. Fifty-eight of the 98 bridges are constructed with a Burr arch truss. The most popular use of the truss in Indiana is the double Burr arch encasing a multiple kingpost truss. The second most prolific truss design in existence today, is the Howe truss, with 24 examples.

The Smith truss is used in seven of Indiana's covered bridges. Three are in Gibson County, two are found in Wabash, one is located in Howard and one in Owen County.

Two queenpost trusses exist. One each in Franklin and Parke Counties. Both, however, are private barns and their trusses cannot be viewed by the general public. There is one multiple queenpost truss in Vigo County in Fowler Park.

Two multiple kingpost trusses are represented. One is in Parke County, the Phillips Bridge (14-61-12), and the other is in Rush County, the Homer Bridge (14-70-18). The more unusual Long truss has two examples. One is in Marion County, the Brownsville Bridge (14-49-02), and the other is in Bartholomew County, the Clifty Bridge (14-03-01).

In Brown County, the Bean Blossom Bridge (14-07-01), has the extremely rare Howe Single truss. Jackson County, Bell's Ford Bridge (14-36-03), has the only Post truss still existing in the United States today.

INDIANA'S RARE AND UNUSUAL BRIDGES

The only known covered bridge in the United States that is used as an aqueduct, exists and is functioning in Franklin County, Indiana. At historic Metamora, the Whitewater Canal Aqueduct (14-24-11) is carrying the waters of the restored Whitewater Canal.

Multiple span covered bridges were, at one time, very common throughout Indiana. There are still some excellent examples of the long, 300 foot-plus structures. In Jackson County, Shieldstown Bridge (14-36-02), can be found at 331 feet displaying two sets of double Burr arches. Bell's Ford (14-36-03), in Jackson County, is also a double span, with 330 feet. The second largest bridge in America, is found in Jackson County (14-36-04); the three span Medora Bridge, which is 434 feet long and has three sets of impressive, double Burr arches. Lawrence County's Williams Bridge (14-47-02), is 376 feet long with only two spans and is constructed with a Howe truss. The Moscow Bridge (14-70-07), in Rush County, has 334 feet, two spans and two sets of double Burr arches.

There are more covered bridges in Parke County than any other county in the United States. Parke County has a total of 33 covered bridges. Over

800,000 people visit Parke County during their annual 10-day fall Covered Bridge Festival. There is no admission charged at the Covered Bridge Festival. The Festival is growing each year and is expected to top over one million visitors soon!

Indiana's parks take pride in their restored covered bridges. An excellent example is the Longwood Bridge (14-21-01), in Roberts Park; located in Connersville, in Fayette County.

Jackson County claims the only covered bridge with a Post truss left in the United States. The 330-foot Bell's Ford Bridge (14-36-03) is bypassed and offers a unique experience.

The Darlington Bridge (14-54-01), in Montgomery County, has one of the most spectacular floors that exists in covered bridges today. Three inch by six inch blocks of wood are laid in such a manner as to expose the tree's growth lines. Care was taken so that almost every block displays the center of the tree. This floor is the work of skilled craftsmen.

Brown County has two unique covered bridges. Bean Blossom (14-07-01), has a rare Howe Single truss, the only one in the state. Ramp Creek Bridge (14-07-02) is the oldest covered bridge in Indiana, built in 1838. Ramp Creek is also the only double-barrelled covered bridge in Indiana, and one of only five left in America.

INDIANA'S BRIDGE BUILDERS

The Kennedy Family

Archibald McMichael Kennedy and sons, Emmett and Charles, built the first Kennedy bridge in 1870 over the East Fork White Water River, close to Dunlapsville in Union County. From 1870 through 1918, the Kennedy family built 58 or more bridges. From 1881 through 1884, they built 23 bridges. The Kennedy Bridge was finished in 1918, and spanned Noland's Fork near Fountain City, in Wayne County. (Gould, 1977)

The Kennedy family had a timber yard in Rushville, where the bridges were prefabricated. They preferred the multiple kingpost truss encased by a double Burr arch, but also built several Howe truss bridges. Most of their bridges were single spans. They did, however, build six 2-span, three 3-span and one 4-span, and one village-type bridge that had two external walkways. Located in Shelbyville, the Vine Street

Bridge, now destroyed, had enclosed arched ceilings in the two walkways and interior of the bridge. The Vine Street Bridge was an example of their finest work. (Gould, 1977)

Joseph J. Daniels

Joseph J. Daniels was the son of one of Stephen Long's bridge builders. J.J. Daniels' father built Long truss bridges throughout southern Ohio. J.J. Daniels worked with his father for years, then, at age 24, Daniels built his first covered bridge in Indiana on the Rising Sun Versailles Pike. Daniels preferred the Burr arch truss, but sometimes built the Howe truss.

In 1853, Daniels started building bridges for Evansville and Crawfordsville Railroad. His most spectacular railroad bridge was a 600-foot, four span structure over the White Water, near Hazelton, in Gibson County. In 1861, Daniels moved to Rockville in Parke County, and began a new company. The first bridge built by his new company, was a 207-foot single span that is still serving local traffic. Daniels built his bridges in Parke, Putman, Vermillion, Montgomery, Owen and Vigo Counties.

A spectacular example of his work is the Medora Bridge (14-36-04), in Jackson County. Bypassed, the Medora Bridge is 434 feet long and has three spans.

Daniels built a total of 50-60 bridges. His method of construction was characterized by the use of iron tie rods. Daniels' last bridge was the Neet Bridge (14-61-18), in Parke County, built in 1904.

Daniels died in 1916 in Rockville, Parke County. (Gould, 1977)

Joseph Albert Britton and Sons

The son of a carpenter, J. A. Britton was born in 1839. He built his first bridge in 1882, the Narrow's Bridge in Parke County (14-61-36). Over the next 40 years, J. A. Britton and sons built as many as 40 bridges (Allen, 1970). There are 17 of these short, single spans still standing, with 15 still being used by traffic.

Britton used iron tie rods in all his bridges. The differences between Daniels' and Britton's structures are hard to identify, since both used the Burr arch truss and iron rods. After 1882, Daniels and Britton were in competition. (Gould, 1977)

OTHER INDIANA BUILDERS

Robert Smith and his company, built 45 covered bridges in Indiana. From 1870 to 1885, Thomas Hardman built 8 covered bridges. One is still in existence in Versailles State Park, Busching Bridge (14-69-04). Aaron Wolf built six covered bridges in Parke and Putman counties. Portland Mills (14-61-21) and Crooks Bridges (14-61-17) are still serving traffic.

There are a number of other builders whose bridges are still standing. Barnhart & Ahrens built the Wallace Bridge (14-23-01) in 1871 with a Howe truss in Fountain County. Clark McDaniels built the Catlin Bridge (14-61-15) in 1907 with a multiple kingpost truss and a Burr arch in Parke County. Daniel Barron built the James Bridge (14-40-02) in 1887 with a Howe truss in Jennings County. Robert Patterson built Bell's Ford Bridge (14-36-03) in 1869 with the unique Post truss which is found in Jackson County. D. M. Brown built the Tow Path Bridge (14-61-29) in 1907 with a multiple kingpost truss and a Burr arch in Parke County. J. Van Fossen built Conley's Ford Bridge (14-61-02) in 1907 with a Burr arch attached to a multiple kingpost truss, also found in Parke County. Frankfort Construction Company built Beeson Bridge (14-61-24) in 1906 with a multiple kingpost truss with a Burr arch in Parke County. William Hendricks built the Rush Creek Bridge (14-61-31) in 1904 and the Wilkins Mill Bridge (14-61-35) in 1906. Both of Hendricks' bridges were constructed with a multiple kingpost truss with a Burr arch and both are found in Parke County.

COUNTY BACKGROUND

BARTHOLOMEW COUNTY - originally had seven covered bridges. There is only one covered bridge, Clifty Bridge (14-03-01), left; and it was moved into Mill Race Park in Columbus in 1966.

BROWN COUNTY - has two covered bridges. Bean Blossom Creek Bridge (14-07-01) is the only original Brown County covered bridge left. It has an unusual Howe Single truss. Ramp Creek Bridge (14-07-02), was moved into Brown County from Putnam County and is the only double-barrelled covered bridge that Indiana has.

DEARBORN COUNTY - at one time had more than 12 covered bridges. Some of them were railroad covered bridges. Only one, Guilford Bridge (14-15-01), remains preserved in a park. Guilford Bridge has a unique block floor.

FAYETTE COUNTY - had three covered bridges, only one is left. Longwood Bridge (14-21-01), is now preserved in Roberts Park in Connersville.

FOUNTAIN COUNTY - has three Howe truss bridges left out of five original covered bridges.

FRANKLIN COUNTY - at one time had 21 more covered bridges. Today only five remain. One is a private barn and another one is the only covered bridge in America that is a functioning aqueduct, at Metomora, the White Water Canal Aqueduct (14-24-11).

JACKSON COUNTY - has three extremely long covered bridges. Shieldstown (14-36-02), is 331 feet long, Bell's Ford (14-36-03), is 330 feet long and Medora (14-36-04), is the second longest bridge in the United States, at 434 feet long. All three are unusual examples, with multiple sets of double Burr arches creating a most interesting symmetrical pattern.

JENNINGS COUNTY - has two remaining bridges.

LAWRENCE COUNTY - has one covered bridge left. The Williams Bridge (14-47-02), is a 376-foot Howe truss construction.

MONTGOMERY COUNTY - has two of its original eight covered bridges left. The Darlington Bridge (14-54-01), has a remarkable block floor.

PARKE COUNTY - has 33 covered bridges left out of a possible 57. Parke County has an annual Covered Bridge Festival each fall for 10 days, which draws over 800,000 visitors each year.

PUTMAN COUNTY - has lost 23 of its original 32 covered bridges.

RIPLEY COUNTY - has two of its original eleven covered bridges left. Ripley County lost some of its covered bridges during the Civil War.

RUSH COUNTY - has seven existing covered bridges out of its original 19. All 19 were built by the Kennedy family.

VERMILLION COUNTY - had twelve or more bridges at one time. Four are still in existence, one on dry land. (Gould, 1977)

HOW TO LOCATE COVERED BRIDGES
IN INDIANA

The directions and maps provided with the text on each bridge, are to be used in conjunction with the county maps provided by the state of Indiana (please see addresses on how to obtain county maps). Although the directions are as precise as possible, and the map looks like it will lead you directly to the bridge, do not be fooled! Location information is provided to assist you in locating covered bridges; a skill you will develop! The numbers enclosed with the directions such as 500E or 425S, coordinate with a map grid on the county maps available from the state. The numbers used in the directions are an estimate of what the road number is, because many of Indiana's roads are *NOT* identified. Another problem with the maps, which is also true for all maps, is sometimes the map will show a road that is not there. The reverse is also true. There might be a road in existence, but it does not show up on the map. Anyhow, finding Indiana's covered bridges is not all that terrifying, it is just my desire to caution you as to the kind of adventures you will be encountering.

The county map is your main tool. You should also carry a compass, because, on cloudy days you can easily get turned around the wrong way! The rest of the equipment you will need is time, patience, and alertness!

Some of the key landscape features to watch for are tree lines, indicating the existence of a creek or river, and a valley (covered bridges are always located down in a valley—never upon a hill). Another feature that will indicate the existence of your bridge is a "road closed", "bridge out", "weight reduced", "height limit" or "one lane bridge" signs. And, although rare, there is the "covered bridge" sign.

Sometimes you will find only abutments or possibly some crumbled beams, remnants of what was once a covered bridge. When a bridge is closed, you may have to walk a short distance. Usually, they block the bridge at its entrance. Private and park bridges can also present a challenge because the natural terrain is not available to help clue you into where the bridge might be located.

Bridging in Indiana can be a lot of fun. When you go, do not forget your maps, compass, a full tank of gas, and a sense of adventure!

ACKNOWLEDGMENTS FOR INDIANA

I would like to thank the following people of Indiana for their effort and generosity. They supplied me with additional sources, materials and personal data. Thank you:

John Sechrist, Treasurer of Indiana Covered Bridge Society

Mrs. Patricia Selig, Madison-Jefferson County Public Library, Madison, Indiana

Kathy Risk, Crawfordsville-Montgomery County Chamber of Commerce, Crawfordsville, Indiana

Mildred I. Heller, Brownstown, Indiana

David E. Penturf, Putnam County Surveyor, Greencastle, Indiana

Mrs. Birney A. Bailey, Nashville, Indiana

Helen Horstman, Genealogy & Local History, Jennings County Public Library, North Vernon, Indiana

Bloomfield-Eastern Green County Public Library, Bloomfield, Indiana

Jerry L. Gobin, Surveyor Fayette County, Connersville, Indiana

Eleanor Arnold, Indiana Extension Homemakers Association, Rushville, Indiana

Sally Stegner, Ripley County Library, Versailles, Indiana

Greensburg Public Library, Greensburg, Indiana

Vivian Watterson, Lawrence County Historical-Genealogical Society, Bedford, Indiana

Paulette Hayes, Fayette County Public Library, Connersville, Indiana

Margret Tucker, Owen County Auditor, Spencer, Indiana

Dee Smith, Parke County Tourism Information Center

Pricilla Ohaver, Parke County Tourism Information Center

BRIDGE NAME	COUNTY	NUMBER
Clifty	Bartholomew	14-03-01
Bean Blossom	Brown	14-07-01
Ramp Creek	"	14-07-02
Guilford	Dearborn	14-15-01
Westport	Decatur	14-16-01
Longwood	Fayette	14-21-01
Wallace	Fountain	14-23-01
Cade's Mill	"	14-23-02
Stockheughter	Franklin	14-24-05
Snow Hill	"	14-24-09
Whitewater Canal Aqueduct	"	14-24-11
Shieldstown	Jackson	14-36-02
Bell's Ford	"	14-36-03
Medora	"	14-36-04
Scipio	Jennings	14-40-01
James	"	14-40-02
Williams	Lawrence	14-47-02
Darlington	Montgomery	14-54-01
Deer's Mill	"	14-54-03
Big Rocky Fork	Parke	14-61-01
Conley's Ford	"	14-61-02
Jeffries Ford	"	14-61-03
Bridgeton	"	14-61-04
Nevins	"	14-61-05
Jessup/Adams	"	14-61-06
Thorpe Ford	"	14-61-07
Roseville/Coxville	"	14-61-09
Harry Evans	"	14-61-10
Zacke Cox	"	14-61-11
Phillips	"	14-61-12
Mecca	"	14-61-13
Sim Smith	"	14-61-14
McAllister	"	14-61-16
Crooks	"	14-61-17
Neet	"	14-61-18
Billie Creek	"	14-61-19
Mansfield	"	14-61-20
Portland Mills/Dooley Station	"	14-61-21
Beeson	"	14-61-24
Melcher/Klondyke	"	14-61-26
West Union	"	14-61-27
Jackson	"	14-61-28
Tow Path/Mill Creek	"	14-61-29
Coal Creek/Lodi	"	14-61-30
Rush Creek	"	14-61-31
Marshall	"	14-61-32
Bowsher Ford	"	14-61-33

BRIDGE NAME	COUNTY	NUMBER
Cox Ford	Parke	14-61-34
Wilkins Mill	"	14-61-35
Narrows	"	14-61-36
State Sanatorium	"	14-61-38
Hills/Baker's Camp	Putnam	14-67-02
Pine Bluff	"	14-67-03
Rollingstone	"	14-67-04
Edna Collins	"	14-67-06
Holton	Ripley	14-69-02
Busching	"	14-69-04
Ewbank/Smith	Rush	14-70-01
Offutt's Ford	"	14-70-02
Forsythe Mill	"	14-70-04
Ferree	"	14-70-06
Moscow	"	14-70-07
Norris Ford	"	14-70-08
Newport	Vermillion	14-83-04
Eugene	"	14-83-05

Bartholomew County
14-03-01

Clifty Bridge

Clifty Bridge was moved into Mill Race Park in Columbus in 1966. The Clifty Bridge was 145 feet long at its original location. When it was moved, its length had to be cut down to 100 feet. The bridge spans Mill Run Creek which had been drained at the time of the photograph. Date of construction is unknown.

Clifty Bridge has natural plank siding with batten and a shake roof. The truss is listed in the *World Guide to Covered Bridges* and the *Indiana Covered Bridge Guide* as a Howe truss. Because of the wooden vertical beams, it meets the criterion of a Long truss. The Howe truss is characterized by the vertical members being steel rods.

Clifty Bridge is well maintained and Mill Race Park allows easy access to the stream. Mill Race Park is an interesting, well maintained city park.

DIRECTIONS: Columbus Township. On left of SR. 46 at west edge of town in Mill Race Park. (Donovan, 1980; Indiana Covered Bridge Society, Inc.; Indiana Department of Highways, 1982; Puetz)

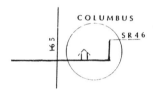

Brown County
14-07-01

Bean Blossom Bridge

Bean Blossom Bridge spans Bean Blossom Creek with 60 feet. The single span structure was built in 1880 by P. Hutti of Kentucky for $1,175.00. His name appears carved in the northern foundation. The exterior of the bridge has dark brown plank siding with batten, and a rusting, corrugated tin roof. Bean Blossom is supported by one stone abutment with concrete poured at the base and one solid concrete abutment/pier. The concrete abutment/pier supports the end of the bridge that has a wooden, 30-foot approach ramp. Access to the creek is easy.

The interior has diagonal floor planking interfaced with two runners. The most unique characteristic about Bean Blossom is its truss. The truss is technically defined as a Howe Single. It does not have the traditional "X" wooden panel separated by two or more steel rods. The Howe Single is identical in appearance to a multiple kingpost truss, but all of the vertical wooden beams are replaced with steel rods. Brown County struggled to save their last county road covered bridge and its singularly unique truss. In March of 1982, the bridge that had served for 105 years was closed for repairs. In June of 1982, Bean Blossom Bridge was reopened. A crumbling stone abutment has been replaced by concrete and a new approach ramp was added.

DIRECTIONS: Jackson Township. From Bean Blossom, south on SR. 135, one-fourth mile, first right, one-half mile. (Bailey, 1987; "Bean Blossom Bridge Closes"; "Council Votes to Fix the Bean Blossom Bridge"; Donovan, 1980; Gould, 1977; Indiana Covered Bridge Society, Inc.; Indiana Department of Highways, 1982; "Once Again Open for Automotive Traffic"; Puetz)

Ramp Creek Bridge

Ramp Creek Bridge is one of only five double-barrelled covered bridges left in the United States. Ramp Creek Bridge was moved to its current location in Brown County State Park in 1932. Built by Aaron Wolf, Ramp Creek Bridge was originally located on the New Albany-Fafayette State Road near Fincastle in Putman County. The two-lane bridge now spans Salt Creek at the north entrance to the Brown County Park.

Built in 1838, this is the oldest covered bridge in Indiana. Although the bridge has been well maintained and parts of the bridge have been replaced; the truss members are the original timbers.

The exterior of Ramp Creek Bridge has a brown shingled roof, red lap siding and white portals. The single span is supported by cut stone abutments. The interior has three Burr arch trusses, one in the middle of the bridge dividing the two lanes.

Although Ramp Creek Bridge is the shortest double-barrelled bridge left in the United States, at 96 feet, it is the most natural in appearance because it has been authentically maintained.

Access to the creek is easy and the bridge is open, serving patrons of Brown County State Park.

DIRECTIONS: Washington Township. From Nashville, east on SR 46, one and one-half miles, turn right into the Brown County State Park entrance. (Donovan, 1980; Gould, 1977; Indiana Covered Bridge Society, Inc.; Indiana Department of Highways, 1982, Puetz)

NASHVILLE

SR 46

Guilford Bridge

The Guilford Bridge spans a small tributary of the West Fork Creek. Their confluence is in the park where the Guilford Bridge is located. The 104-foot bridge was built in 1879 by the Kennedy Family. At one time, Dearborn County had twelve known covered bridges. Some of these were railroad covered bridges. Guilford is the last of Dearborn's covered bridges and has been preserved in the park.

The exterior has white plank siding, shake roof and three small roofed windows on both sides. The single span structure is supported by concrete abutments. The interior has a double Burr arch with additional supports in the multiple kingpost truss. Blocks of wood about the size of bricks are laid down to form the surface of the floor.

The bridge's location in the park makes it visibly accessible.

DIRECTIONS: Miller Township, at Guilford. (Donovan, 1980; Gould, 1977; Indiana Covered Bridge Society, Inc.; Indiana Department of Highways, 1982; Puetz)

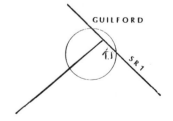

GUILFORD

SR 1

Decatur County
14-16-01

Westport Bridge

The Westport Bridge spans Sand Creek in southern Decatur County.

Built in 1880 by A.M. Kennedy and Sons, the single span bridge is 115 feet long. The exterior has a rusted, flat tin roof, white lap siding and a three-foot tall window with a shingled roof, that extends the full length of the bridge on both sides. Supported by cut stone abutments, the bridge is in good repair. The interior has experienced graffiti attacks. The truss is a multiple kingpost encased by a double Burr arch. The floor has crosswise planking with two runners.

Bypassed in 1975, the new bridge is a distance away and in no way interferes with the Westport Bridge's appearance. The creek has reasonable access. This is an excellent example of a bypassed covered bridge that has not been bypassed and abandoned. The bridge has been well maintained.

DIRECTIONS: Sand Creek Township. From Westport. South on SR 3, left on Main Street, through town, one and one-half miles beyond the town limits, left. (Donovan, 1980; Gould, 1977; Indiana Covered Bridge Society, Inc.; Indian Department of Highways, 1982; Puetz)

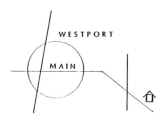

Fayette County
14-21-01

Longwood Bridge

Longwood Bridge was moved to its current location in Roberts Park, Connersville, in 1984 for preservation. The bridge's original location was over Williams Creek, four miles west of Connersville at CR 75N and CR 525W.

Longwood Bridge was built in 1884 by the Kennedy Brothers. The 94 foot bridge has fresh paint, white lap siding, a rusted, flat tin roof and rests on cut stone and mortar abutments. The interior has a double Burr arch encasing a multiple kingpost truss that is missing the traditional kingpost center panel.

Longwood Bridge spans a dry depression in Roberts Park. Care was taken with the placement of the old covered bridge, evidenced by its landscape and its reconstruction. The bridge has dirt approaches, but is only used by foot traffic.

DIRECTIONS: In Connersville at Central (SR 1) and 30th Street (north of the city core). (Donovan, 1980; Gobin, 1987; Indiana Covered Bridge Society, Inc.; Indiana Department of Highways, 1982; Puetz)

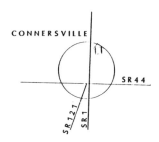

Wallace Bridge

The Wallace Bridge crosses Sugar Mill Creek, which drains the far southeastern corner of Fountain County. Sugar Mill Creek has a 40 foot bed width at the bridge site.

The Wallace Bridge was built in 1871 by Barnhart and Ahrens and is 81 feet long. The exterior has a rusted-gray tin roof, dark red plank siding and white portals. The single span bridge is supported by cut stone abutments that have been partially encased by concrete. The interior is constructed with a Howe truss. The floor has lengthwise planking but it has been blacktopped.

The Wallace Bridge has been bypassed, with the new bridge a comfortable distance from the covered span. The ground surrounding Wallace Bridge offers a park-like area which makes the creek accessible.

DIRECTIONS: Jackson Township. East of Wallace, one mile at 1000S. (Donovan, 1980; Gould; Indiana Covered Bridge Society, Inc.; Indiana Department of Highways, 1982; Puetz)

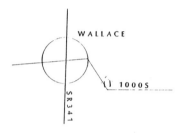

Cade's Mill Bridge

Cade's Mill Bridge spans Coal Creek, which drains the southwestern quarter of Fountain County.

Built in 1854, the 150 foot bridge is a single span and rests on cut stone abutments with concrete facing the two steel piers. The exterior has a rusty tin roof, red plank siding and white portals. The interior has a Howe truss and crosswise floor planking with two lengthwise runners.

The bridge was bypassed in 1975 and offers a very small park area.

DIRECTIONS: Wabash Township. Two miles west of Mackie at about 425S. (Donovan, 1980; Gould, 1977; Indiana Covered Bridge Society, Inc.; Indiana Department of Highways, 1982; Puetz)

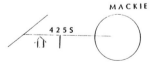

Stockheughter Bridge

Stockheughter Bridge spans Salt Creek in southwestern Franklin County.

Built in 1887, the 92-foot single span rests on concrete abutments and is also supported by a concrete pier. The exterior has red plank siding and roof. The interior was constructed with a Howe truss and lengthwise plank flooring.

Access to the creek is convenient. The bridge is open and serves local traffic.

DIRECTIONS: Ray Township. One-half mile east of Enochsburg. (Donovan, 1980; Indiana Covered Bridge Society, Inc.; Indiana Department of Highways, 1982; Puetz)

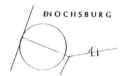

Franklin County
14-24-09

Snow Hill Bridge

Snow Hill Bridge spans Johnson's Fork in the southeastern corner of Franklin County.

Snow Hill Bridge was built in 1894. The 75-foot bridge rests on stone abutments. The exterior is in poor condition. Many pieces are missing from the naturally weathered, gray siding. The shake roof is also in serious need of repair. The interior has a Howe truss and the remains of two lengthwise runners.

The bridge is closed, with boulders blocking the entrances. Snow Hill is in critical condition. The entire structure is sagging in the center.

Access to the creek is extremely difficult and visual access of the bridge is prevented by the surrounding foliage.

DIRECTIONS: Whitewater Township. From Rockdale, north by northwest, one mile. (Donovan, 1980; Indiana Covered Bridge Society, Inc.; Indiana Department of Highways, 1982)

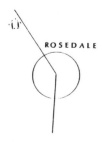

Whitewater Canal Aqueduct

A distinctively unique covered bridge, the Whitewater Canal Aqueduct was not designed to carry traditional traffic, but to carry water for a canal that carried traffic. The 81-foot aqueduct was necessitated because the canal had to cross over an existing stream, Duck Creek. The canal system was abandoned with the advent of trains, but this section of the Whitewater Canal has been preserved in historical Metamora, Indiana. The Whitewater Canal and aqueduct were acquired in 1946 by Whitewater Canal Association and the Indiana Department of Conservation. The area was restored in three years (Allen, 1970). The water for the canal system is channeled from the Whitewater River, a favorite for canoeing enthusiasts.

Built in 1846, the interior of the bridge has a walkway on one side and is constructed with a multiple kingpost truss encased by a double-Burr arch. The lower chords are protected against the canal water by a lining of tin.

The exterior of the bridge is also very intriguing. The bridge has a rusty-red tin roof and natural wood stained plank siding. One side of the bridge that has easy access to Duck Creek, exhibits an exterior wooden walkway. The lower chord, joist and floor beams are also exposed on this side. The bridge has several openings where some of the water pours out into Duck Creek. These openings are there to release excess water from the canal system.

The bridge rests on cut stone abutments and is a clear span bridge. The Whitewater Canal Aqueduct is striking due to its individual character. Its location in Metamora, Indiana also adds a greater historical perspective to the bridge.

Metamora is of historical interest because of the preserved canal and aqueduct, but it also has an operating flour mill powered by a wooden wheel in the canal. Metamora also operates an old train and a flat boat pulled by horses on the canal. Metamora has many gift shops and celebrates our national holidays in grand style with thousands of visitors.

DIRECTIONS: Metamora Township. At Metamora. (Allen, 1970; Donovan, 1980; Indiana Covered Bridge Society, Inc.; Indiana Department of Highways, 1982; Puetz)

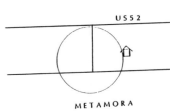

US 52

METAMORA

Shieldstown Bridge

Shieldstown Bridge spans the East Fork White River, the largest river in Jackson County. The river dissects the county diagonally from the northeastern corner to the southwestern corner.

Shieldstown Bridge was built in 1876 by Joseph J. Daniels. The exterior of the bridge is most impressive because of its 331-foot length. Shieldstown Bridge has a rusty red tin roof and faded red plank siding. The siding is in need of repair. The bridge is supported by cut stone abutments and one cut stone pier. The bridge has two immense spans, each over 150 feet. Each span has a multiple kingpost truss encased with an extremely long, double Burr arch. The floor has diagonal planks with two lengthwise runners.

Access to the creek is difficult. The bridge that bypassed Shieldstown Bridge is so close to the covered bridge that the view of the covered bridge is seriously hampered.

DIRECTIONS: Brownstown/Hamilton Township. At Shields approximately at 200E and 275N. (Donovan, 1980; Gould, 1977; Indiana Covered Bridge Society, Inc.; Indiana Department of Highways, 1982; Roeger)

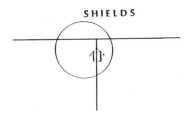

Bell's Ford Bridge

Built in 1869, Bell's Ford Bridge spans the East Fork White River. The East Fork White River has an average bed width in this area of 200 to 250 feet. The river dissects Jackson County from its northeastern corner to its southwestern corner and is the major drainage channel for this region.

Built by Robert Patterson for the Seymour Bridge Company, Bell's Ford Bridge is a 330-foot, two span structure. It rests on cut stone abutments and one cut stone pier. The exterior has a gray shingled roof and the siding is mostly rusty-red, with some of the wood planks freshly painted red. Some of the siding is missing.

The covered bridge is bypassed by a new adjacent bridge. There is a narrow wooden walkway that leads to the east portal. This covered bridge is unusual because it is the only one left in the United States that has been constructed with a Post truss. The Post truss has wooden beams that connect the upper and lower chords diagonally, slanting toward the center of the bridge. Steel rods encase the wooden beams in a criss-cross manner.

Although access to the river bed itself is very difficult, the bridge can be viewed easily from the surrounding park area. Bell's Ford Covered Bridge is inviting because of its long span across the East Fork White River and because it has the exclusive Post truss. The park area that surrounds the bridge and the bridge itself is now under the care of the Jackson County Park Board.

DIRECTIONS: Hamilton/Jackson Township. From Seymour, SR 258 west, two miles. (Donovan, 1980; Gould, 1977; Indiana Covered Bridge Society, Inc.; Indiana Department of Highways, 1982; Roeger)

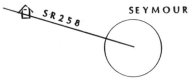

Medora Bridge

The longest covered bridge in Indiana is the Medora Bridge with 434 feet. The Medora Bridge also has the distinction of being the second longest covered bridge in the United States. The longest covered bridge is located between Vermont and New Hampshire over the Connecticut River. The Cornish/Windsor Bridge (29-10-01) is 460 feet long.

The Medora Bridge crosses the East Fork White River with three spans. The East Fork White River is the region's major river and has an average bed width of 350 feet at the bridge site.

The Medora Bridge was built in 1875 by J.J. Daniels with a multiple kingpost truss encased with a double Burr arch. There is a separate truss over each span of the bridge. The interior, therefore, exhibits a total of six multiple kingpost trusses with a double Burr arch. The exterior of the Medora Bridge has a gray shingled roof and faded red plank siding. The portals are a weathered white. The bridge is supported by stone abutments and two stone piers.

The Medora Bridge is unequaled in the United States because of its 434 foot length combined with the interior's display of three sets of double Burr arches. The bridge has been bypassed and there is a park area surrounding the bridge site.

DIRECTIONS: Driftwood Township. From Medora, east on SR 235, one mile (Donovan, 1980; Gould, 1977; Indiana Covered Bridge Society, Ind.; Indiana Department of Highways, 1982; Roeger)

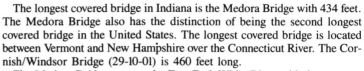

MEDORA

SR235

Scipio Bridge

Scipio Bridge spans Sand Creek on the northwest corner of the village of Scipio. Sand Creek drains a northern portion of Jennings County and has a normal bed width of 125 feet at the bridge site.

Built in 1886 by the Smith Bridge Company of Toledo with a Howe truss, the 146-foot single span structure rests on cut stone with mortar abutments. The exterior has a corrugated tin roof and red, four-inch wide plank siding. The floor is treated 2″ x 4″ timbers laid on edge.

The bridge's location offers convenient access to the creek. Scipio Bridge is open to local traffic.

DIRECTIONS: Geneva Township. West of Scipio. ("Covered Bridge"; Donovan, 1980; Indiana Covered Bridge Society, Inc.; Indiana Department of Highways, 1982; Puetz)

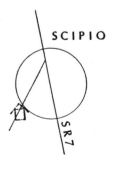

SCIPIO

SR 7

James Bridge

The James Bridge spans Big Graham Creek. Big Graham Creek drains the southeastern portion of Jennings County and has a 90-foot normal bed width at the bridge site.

Built in 1887 by Daniel Barron, the 124-foot structure has faded red plank siding with batten, a rusted, corrugated tin roof and rests on cut stone abutments. The interior has a Howe truss and diagonal floor planking with two runners.

Accessibility of the creek is very difficult and the area is thick with vegetation.

DIRECTIONS: Lovett Township. From Vernon, south on SR 3, six and one-half miles, left at 650S, one-half mile. (Donovan, 1980; Gould, 1977; Indiana Covered Bridge Society, Inc.; Indiana Department of Highways, 1982; Puetz)

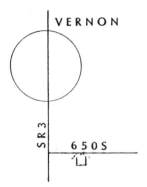

VERNON

SR 3

650S

Williams Bridge

The Williams Bridge spans the East Fork White River at the western edge of central Lawrence County. East Fork White River dissects the county from east to west and is the county's largest river.

Williams Bridge was built in 1884 by the Massillon Bridge Company of Ohio for a cost of $18,700. The stones for the abutment were brought to the bridge site by river from a nearby quarry. The wood and steel were also shipped in by river from Bedford.

The immense Williams Bridge is 376 feet long and has two spans supported by thirty-foot sandstone abutments and one massive stone pier. Located in a flat river valley, the bridge level was elevated by a long ramp to avoid flood waters.

The exterior has a green corrugated tin roof and dark red plank siding with batten. The interior has a Howe truss and lengthwise floor planking. The sides are fenced into the first six feet inside the bridge to discourage vandals and prevent accidents.

The 376 foot structure can be viewed for some distance through the river valley. Trails lead down to the river banks. Williams Bridge was restored and reopened in 1984 after major repairs. Williams Bridge is listed in the National Register of Historic Places.

DIRECTIONS: Spice Valley Township. From Williams, south, one-half mile. (Donovan, 1980; Indiana Covered Bridge Society, Inc.; Indiana Department of Highways, Merrell, 1987; Puetz)

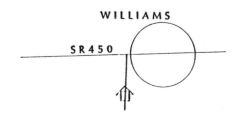

WILLIAMS

SR 450

Darlington Bridge

The Darlington Bridge is located just west of the village of Darlington. Spanning Sugar Creek, the bridge is 166 feet long. Sugar Creek has a 150-foot bed width at the bridge site and is the principle drainage system in Montgomery County.

Built in 1867 by Joseph Kress, Darlington Bridge has a brown shingled roof, weathered white plank siding and cut stone abutments. The pier is also cut stone, but it is encased with concrete and has a concrete ice breaker. The interior of the bridge has a Howe truss. A fascinating characteristic of this bridge is its unique floor. The floor is made of 3″ X 6″ pieces of wood laid in such a manner as to show the growth lines of the tree. Formerly blacktopped, the floor now has large areas of exposed blocks, making this bridge extremely attractive to bridgers. The entire floor is sunken about 12″ below the road surface.

Access to the creek is convenient. The external view is not as rewarding as the interior because pieces of the siding are missing. The bridge is closed to traffic.

DIRECTIONS: Franklin Township. At Darlington. About 500N and 575E. (Crawfordsville-Montgomery County Chamber of Commerce (b); Donovan, 1980; Indiana Covered Bridge Society, Inc.; Indiana Department of Highways 1982; Puetz)

DARLINGTON

Deer's Mill Bridge

Deer's Mill Bridge crosses Sugar Creek, a major drainage channel that diagonally dissects Montgomery County from the northeastern corner to the southwestern corner. Sugar Creek has a normal bed width of 225 feet at the bridge site.

The 275-foot bridge structure was built in 1878 by Joseph J. Daniels. The configuration of the bridge is uncommon because of the slope towards the center. Deer's Mill Bridge exhibits a camber in each of its two spans. The exterior has dark red plank siding with batten, a brown shingled roof and rests on huge cut stone abutments and cut stone pier that has been faced with concrete. The interior shows slight evidence of the cambers on the lengthwise floor, that at one time had some blacktop. There are two sets of double Burr arches encasing the multiple kingpost truss over each span. The interior is provocative due to the existence of the cambers and the geometrical appeal of Burr trusses.

Deer's Mill Bridge has been bypassed. In 1971, the bridge was repaired by the Indiana Department of Natural Resources. The bridge is now part of a private park which maintains the grounds along the river bank. During the summer season, there is a charge to enter the park.

DIRECTIONS: Ripley/Brown Township. East of Shades State Park. (Crawfordsville-Montgomery County Chamber of Commerce (a); Crawfordsville-Montgomery County Chamber of Commerce (b); Donovan, 1980; Indiana Covered Bridge Society, Inc; Indiana Department of Highways, 1982 Puetz)

SHADES

SR234

Big Rocky Fork Bridge

Big Rocky Fork Bridge spans Big Rocky Fork Creek with 72 feet. The creek has a normal bed width of 60 feet and is a tributary of Big Raccoon Creek, the major drainage channel for southern Parke County.

Built in 1900 by J.J. Daniels, the exterior has a rusted, flat tin roof, red plank and batten siding and rests on cut sandstone abutments with a single span. The portals are painted white and the first six feet of siding on either end is also painted white. The exterior is in need of repair and paint. The bridge exhibits a slight camber in both the roof and floor. The interior is in fair condition, with a double Burr arch encasing the multiple kingpost truss which does not have a kingpost center panel. The height of the arch extends only halfway up the truss, but is secured into the abutments four feet below the lower chord. The floor has crosswise planks with two lengthwise runners.

The bridge is still open and serving local traffic. Access to the creek is easy.

DIRECTIONS: Jackson Township. From Mansfield, SR 59 south one mile left at 710S, one and three-quarters mile. (Donovan, 1980; Indiana Covered Bridge Society, Inc.; Indiana Department of Commerce, 1986; Indiana Department of Highways, 1982)

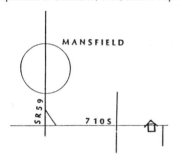

Conley's Ford Bridge

Conley's Ford Bridge crosses Big Raccoon Creek which has an average width of 160 feet at the bridge site and is the major drainage channel for southern Parke County.

Conley's Ford Bridge is a 192-foot, single span structure. This bridge is the second longest single span still in service in Parke County. Constructed in 1906 and 1907, the bridge was built by J. Van Fossen with white pine.

The exterior has faded red plank siding with batten, white portals and one small roofed window centered on either side. The bridge is supported by concrete abutments.

The interior is well preserved. A double Burr arch composed of two separate large beams, encases the multiple kingpost truss. The floor has two lengthwise runners laid on crosswise planking.

Access to the creek is difficult to obtain.

DIRECTIONS: Raccoon Township. From Bridgeton, east on 800S, one mile left at 425E, one and one-half miles, right at 550E, one-fourth mile. (Donovan, 1980; Indiana Covered Bridge Society, Inc.; Indiana Department of Commerce, 1986; Indiana Department of Highways, 1982)

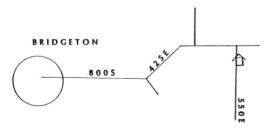

Jeffries Ford Bridge

Jeffries Ford Bridge, at 204 feet long, spans Big Raccoon Creek, the largest river in southern Parke County, which has a normal bed width of 180 feet at the bridge site.

Built in 1915, the bridge was constructed by J. A. Britton. Jeffries Ford Bridge is a double span bridge and is supported by concrete abutments and one concrete pier. One of two similar bridges in Parke County (Parke 27), Jeffries Ford has a distinctive camber in each span. The exterior's rusted tin roof exhibits two evident humps.

The interior floor also shows the two cambers, illustrated by the interior photograph. The low point in the floor is the center of the bridge, where the bridge rests on its pier.

The exterior has been well maintained. The siding is plank with batten and is a faded brown. The portals are painted white. The interior, interesting because of the two cambers, has crosswise planks with two lengthwise runners. Each span has a multiple kingpost truss encased by a double Burr arch. The bridge, therefore, has four multiple kingpost trusses and two sets of double Burr arches.

Access to the stream is difficult and visual access of the bridge from the stream is seriously hidden by brush. The bridge would appear quite majestic if some brush were removed from the creek banks.

DIRECTIONS: Raccoon Township. From Bridgeton, south on 300 E, two miles, left on 1000, one mile, first right on 150E, one-half mile. (Donovan, 1980; Indiana Covered Bridge Society, Ind.; Indiana Department of Commerce, 1986; Indiana Department of Highways, 1982)

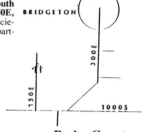

Bridgeton Bridge

The Bridgeton Bridge is located in the town of Bridgeton. The two span structure crosses Raccoon Creek, the major drainage channel in southern Parke County. The bridge is 245 feet long and the creek has a similar bed width.

The bridge, built in 1868 by J.J. Daniels, has a gray tin roof, red plank siding with batten and white portals. Six roofed windows are unevenly distributed throughout the bridge. The abutments and pier are made with cut stone and mortar, and the pier has a concrete ice breaker. The interior is extremely narrow. Each span has a multiple kingpost truss and a set of double Burr arches. The floor has lengthwise planking.

The bridge has a spectacular location, sitting virtually on top of a mill race that extends the full length of the 245-foot bridge. The Weise Mill was built the same year as the bridge and is still producing corn meal, wheat, rye and buckwheat flours during the Parke County Covered Bridge Festival.

DIRECTIONS: Raccoon Township. At Bridgeton. (Donovan, 1980; Hardesty; Indiana Covered Bridge Society, Inc.; Indiana Department of Commerce, 1986; Indiana Department of Highways, 1982)

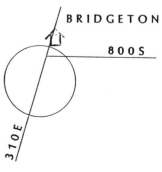

Nevins Bridge

Nevins Bridge spans Little Raccoon Creek, which is a tributary of Big Raccoon Creek, the major drainage channel in southern Parke County.

Nevins Bridge is 155 feet long, with a single span which has a camber noticeable in the roof and floor. Nevins Bridge was the last bridge built by J. A. Britton and son in 1920.

The exterior of the bridge has faded red plank siding with batten, a charcoal-gray shake roof and white portals. The single span structure is supported by concrete abutments. The interior is in good condition.

A multiple kingpost truss is encased by a double Burr arch. The floor has crosswise planks with two lengthwise runners.

The bridge site has an excellent location. The area around the bridge has been cleared which allows easy visual access.

DIRECTIONS: Raccoon Township. From Catlin, east on 500S, one and one-forth miles, right on 200E, three-quarter mile. (Donovan, 1980; Indiana Covered Bridge Society, Inc.; Indiana Department of Commerce, 1986; Indiana Department of Highways, 1982)

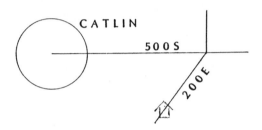

Jessup/Adams Bridge

The 155-foot Jessup/Adams Bridge carries two names because the original Adams bridge, built in 1907 by the Frankfort Construction Company, was destroyed by a flood in 1969, and was subsequently replaced by the Jessup Bridge which had been bypassed at its original location in 1966. The Jessup Bridge was built by J.L. Van Fossen in 1910, and when it was placed onto the abutments from the lost Adams Bridge, it fit perfectly.

Jessup/Adams Bridge spans the Little Raccoon Creek, which is a tributary of the largest river in southern Parke County, Big Raccoon Creek.

The exterior of Jessup Bridge has severely weathered red plank siding with small roofed windows on either side. The portals are painted white. The roof is red tin. The bridge rests on concrete abutments and has additional concrete poured over the original.

The interior has a multiple kingpost truss encased by a double Burr arch. All of the floor beams are new and steel supports for the arches have been added at the abutments. The floor has dried and shrunken crosswise planks with two lengthwise runners.

There are trails around the bridge that allow easy access to the creek.

DIRECTIONS: Washington/Adams Township. From Nyesville, east on 100N, one and one-half miles. (Donovan, 1980; Indiana Covered Bridge Society, Inc.; Indiana Department of Commerce, 1986; Indiana Department of Highways, 1982)

Photograph by Michael Krekeler

NYESVILLE

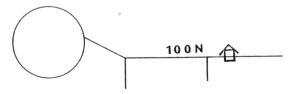

Parke County
14-61-07

Thorpe Ford Bridge

Thorpe Ford Bridge spans Big Raccoon Creek, the major drainage channel in southern Parke County. Big Raccoon Creek is 150 feet wide at the bridge site.

Built in 1912 by J. A. Britton, the 163-foot structure has a single span and is supported by concrete abutments. The exterior exhibits a camber in the roof and entire structure. The roof is a charcoal-gray shake, the siding is dark red planks with batten and the portals are painted white. The interior is representative of Parke County's covered bridges, with a multiple kingpost truss encased with a double Burr arch. Each arch has two separate beams. The floor has lengthwise planks.

Thorpe Ford Bridge has been bypassed. The bridge that bypassed Thorpe Ford sits so close to it that visual access is impossible without full view of the new adjacent bridge. Thorpe Ford would be much more picturesque if the new bridge had been placed several more yards away.

Access to the creek is easy but not necessary to appreciate the bridge in its entirety. A park-like area surrounds the bridge.

DIRECTIONS: Florida Township. From Rosedale, north on 175W, one-half mile. (Donovan, 1980; Indiana Covered Bridge Society, Inc.; Indiana Department of Commerce, 1986; Indiana Department of Highways, 1982)

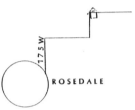

Parke County
14-61-09

Roseville/Coxville Bridge

The Roseville Bridge is located in Coxville and is sometimes referred to as the Coxville Bridge. This bridge spans the Big Raccoon Creek, which is the largest river in southern Parke County.

Roseville Bridge has two spans and is 263 feet long. The pier and northern abutments are cut sandstone. The southern abutment has cut stone encased in concrete. The stone abutments and probably the pier were the originals used by the first covered bridge at this site built by J. J. Daniels, which was destroyed in 1910 by arson. The story about the fire was that two men were refused liquor at a nearby saloon patronized by the local coal miners. They became angry and took their frustration out on the bridge.

J. L. Van Fossen built the Roseville Bridge in 1910. The exterior has red plank siding, a natural shake roof and two small roofed windows on either side. The interior has a multiple kingpost truss encased with a double Burr arch over each span. The floor has crosswise planking and two lengthwise runners.

Access to the creek is easy but not necessary. The surrounding area has the brush removed and the bridge is visibly accessible.

DIRECTIONS: Florida Township. At Coxville. (Donovan, 1980; Hardesty; Indiana Covered Bridge Society, Inc.; Indiana Department of Commerce, 1986; Indiana Department of Highways, 1982)

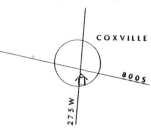

Harry Evans Bridge

The Harry Evans Bridge spans Rock Run, which is a tributary of the largest drainage channel in southern Parke County, Big Raccoon Creek. Harry Evans Bridge spans Rock Run with 65 feet and the normal bed width of the stream is 30 feet.

This bridge was built in 1908 by J. A. Britton. The exterior has a natural shake roof, dark red plank siding and white portals. The bridge displays a slight camber in its configuration and sits on concrete abutments with one span. The interior has lengthwise floor planking and a multiple kingpost truss encased by a double Burr arch. The arch is segmented and attached at each panel on the vertical beam.

The Harry Evans Bridge is located in an isolated valley, is well preserved and is still serving local traffic. Access to the creek is easy because the surrounding area is maintained.

DIRECTIONS: Florida Township. From Coxville, northwest one-half mile (do not make a right turn). (Donovan, 1980; Hardesty; Indiana Covered Bridge Society, Inc.; Indiana Department of Commerce, 1986; Indiana Department of Highways, 1982)

COXVILLE

Zacke Cox Bridge

The Zacke Cox Bridge spans Rock Run, a tributary of Big Raccoon Creek. Rock Run has a normal bed width of 25 feet at the bridge site.

Zacke Cox Bridge was constructed in 1908 by J.A. Britton. The exterior presents a very slight camber across its 54-foot length. The roof is shake, the siding is dark red plank and the portals are white. The bridge rests on stone abutments that have been faced with concrete. The concrete facing is cracking and falling off the stone. The interior has a crosswise floor planking with two lengthwise runners. The multiple kingpost truss is encased by a double Burr arch. The height of the arch extends three-quarters up the center kingpost panel.

Zacke Cox Bridge is located in a pleasant, isolated valley and is still open. The creek has easy access and offers photographers excellent opportunity.

DIRECTIONS: Florida Township. From Coxville, northwest (do not take an immediate right) three and one-fourth miles, turn right at 500S, one-half mile. (Donovan, 1960; Indiana Covered Bridge Society, Inc.; Indiana Department of Commerce, 1986; Indiana Department of Highways, 1982)

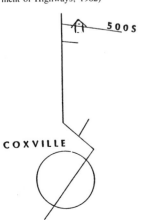

500S

COXVILLE

Phillips Bridge

Phillips Bridge spans Big Pond Creek, which is located on the western edge of central Parke County. Big Pond Creek is a tributary of Big Raccoon Creek.

The 42-foot structure was built by J. A. Britton in 1909. The exterior has dark red plank siding, a natural shake roof and white portals. This bridge has no suggestion of a camber and sits on concrete abutments. The interior has crosswise floor planking with two lengthwise runners. The truss is a multiple kingpost and is the only covered bridge in Parke County that does not have the characteristic Parke County Burr arch.

Phillips Bridge is the shortest bridge in Parke County and is still serving local traffic. Unfortunately, access to the creek is impossible because fencing is secured at all four corners.

DIRECTIONS: Wabash Township. From Rockville, west on US 36, four miles, forth left at 400W, one-quarter mile, turn left. (Donovan, 1980; Indiana Covered Bridge Society, Inc.; Indiana Department of Commerce, 1986; Indiana Department of Highways, 1982)

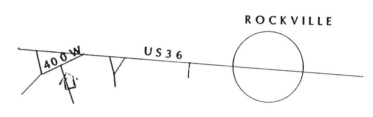

Mecca Bridge

Mecca Bridge spans Big Raccoon Creek, which is the largest river in southern Parke County.

Mecca Bridge was constructed in 1873 by J. J. Daniels for a cost of $7,000. The 150-foot single span structure has a shake roof, faded red plank siding and white portals. The bridge is supported by large cut stone abutments with mortar. The interior has lengthwise floor planking, a double Burr arch encasing the multiple kingpost truss and a utility pipe boxed on the floor on the right side of the photograph.

The Mecca Bridge was bypassed in the 1960s for preservation. Access to the creek is easy because the area is maintained.

The local history of Mecca is interesting. At the bridge site there is an iron jail cage which was used during the late 1800s and early 1900s. Mecca was a thriving town during that time due to an abundance of coal and clay locally deposited. Mecca not only had six coal mines and was considered the clay capital of the world in 1905, but it also had flour and textile mills. Huge clay tiles can still be seen at the site of the old clay factory that once fired 34 kilns. The factory closed in the 1960s after exhausting the clay deposit.

DIRECTIONS: Wabash Township, At Mecca. (Donovan, 1980; Hardesty; Indiana Covered Bridge Society, Inc.; Indiana Department of Commerce, 1986; Indiana Department of Highways, 1982)

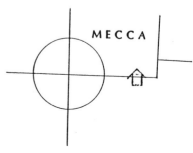

Sim Smith Bridge

The Sim Smith Bridge spans Leathewood Creek, a tributary of Big Raccoon Creek, with 84 feet.

The single span bridge was constructed in 1883 by J. A. Britton. The exterior of the bridge is representative of Parke County's covered bridges with a shake roof, dark red plank with batten siding, and white portals. The interior has crosswise flooring with a solid lengthwise runner covering the center two-thirds of the floor. The bridge displays a slight camber and is supported by cut stone and mortar abutments.

Sim Smith Bridge is characterized because each portal has a different shape and because the bridge has a local reputation of being haunted, no doubt due to the portal controversy. Sim Smith is still serving traffic.

DIRECTIONS: Wabash Township. From Rockville, US 36 west, four miles, forth left at 400W, three-quarters miles (Donovan, 1980; Indiana Covered Bridge Society, Inc.; Indiana Department of Commerce, 1986; Indiana Department of Highways, 1982)

McAllister Bridge

McAllister Bridge spans Little Raccoon Creek, a tributary of Big Raccoon Creek.

Built in 1914 by J. A. Britton, the single span structure exhibits a camber throughout its 126-foot length.

The exterior has a rusty-red tin roof, red plank with batten siding and white portals. The interior has the Parke County customary multiple kingpost truss with a double Burr arch. The floor has crosswise planking with a new solid runner centered on two-thirds of the floor.

Some steel has been added to the underside for support. McAllister Bridge is supported by concrete abutments. Access to the creek is easy, as the immediate area is well maintained. The bridge is still serving local traffic.

DIRECTIONS: Adams Township. From Catlin, north on 20E, one mile, first right at 400S, one and one-fourth miles, turn left, one-fourth mile, turn right at 400S, one mile. (Donovan, 1980; Indiana Covered Bridge Society, Inc.; Indiana Department of Commerce, 1986; Indiana Department of Highways, 1982)

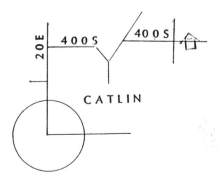

Crooks Bridge

Crooks Bridge spans Little Raccoon Creek, a tributary of Big Raccoon Creek, with 132 feet.

Crooks Bridge boasts of being the oldest covered bridge in Parke County. Built in 1856 by Henry Wolf, the bridge was damaged and rebuilt in 1867 by General Arthur Patterson.

The bridge has a red tin roof, red plank siding with batten and white portals. The bridge has three roofed windows on one side and one on the other side. The interior has a multiple kingpost truss encased by a double Burr arch. Each arch consists of two separate beams. The crosswise floor planking is interfaced with two lengthwise runners. The bridge has unique characteristics not only because it is the oldest covered bridge in Parke County, but because of its configuration. The floor of the bridge is wider than the roof and gives its portals the appearance of falling in toward the center. The bridge rests on cut stone abutments and is still open.

DIRECTIONS: Adams Township. From Rockville, east on US 36, two miles, right at 300E, one and one-fourth mile, right on 200S, one-half mile, left at 250E, one and one-fourth miles, left. (Donovan, 1980; Indiana Covered Bridge Society, Inc.; Indiana Department of Commerce. 1986; Indiana Department of Highways, 1982)

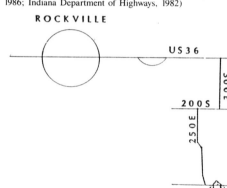

Neet Bridge

The Neet Bridge spans Little Raccoon Creek, a tributary of Big Raccoon Creek.

Neet Bridge is 126 feet long and its entire length displays a camber. Built in 1904 by Joseph J. Daniels, the bridge has a tin rusting roof, faded dark red plank siding with batten and white portals.

The interior has a solid lengthwise runner centered on two thirds of crosswise floor planking. The truss is unique in Parke County in that it has two kingposts side by side to form the center panel (demonstrated in the interior photograph).

Visual access of the bridge is easy in the winter and spring. Neet Bridge is open and still serving local traffic.

DIRECTIONS: Adams Township. From Catlin, north one mile at 25E, first right on 400S, two miles, right on 225E, one-half mile. (Donovan, 1980; Indiana Covered Bridge Society, Inc.; Indiana Department of Commerce. 1986; Indiana Department of Highways, 1982)

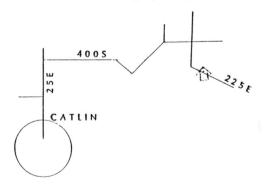

Bissel Bridge   21-06-04   Massachusetts

North Pole Bridge   35-08-23   Ohio

McAllister Bridge   14-61-16   Indiana

Christman Bridge   35-68-12   Ohio

Brubaker Bridge   35-68-05   Ohio

Bowman Mill Bridge   35-64-06   Ohio

Cain Road Bridge   35-04-59   Ohio

Buskirk Bridge 32-58-04 New York

Scottown Bridge   35-44-05   Ohio

Fletcher Bridge   48-17-03   West Virginia

Whittier Bridge   29-02-08   New Hampshire

70

Scofield Bridge   35-08-21   Ohio

Engle Mill Bridge   35-29-03   Ohio

Shade Bridge   35-23-20   Ohio

John Bright Bridge   35-23-10   Ohio

71

Corbin Bridge   29-10-05   New Hampshire

Ackley Bridge   22-82-01   Michigan

Black Bridge   35-09-03   Ohio

Shieldstown Bridge   14-36-02   Indiana

Treacle Creek   35-80-03   Ohio

Langley Bridge   22-75-01   Michigan

Medora Bridge   14-36-04   Indiana

Keniston Bridge   29-07-02   New Hampshire

Upper Village/Ashuelot Bridge 29-03-02 New Hampshire

Jediah Hill Bridge 35-31-01 Ohio

Creamery Bridge 45-13-01 Vermont

75

Root Bridge   35-84-08   Ohio

Williams Bridge   14-47   Indiana

Center Point Bridge   48-09-07   West Virginia

McDaniels Bridge   38-05-20   Pennsylvania

Rupert Bridge   38-19-33   Pennsylvania

Jericho Bridge   20-12-01   Maryland

Waterloo Station Bridge   29-07-04   New Hampshire

Biedler Bridge   46-83-01   Virginia

Swiftriver Bridge   29-02-05   New Hampshire

East and West Paden Twin Bridge   38-19-11   New York

Billie Creek Bridge

The 62 foot Billie Creek Bridge spans Williams Creek, a tributary of Big Raccoon Creek. Billie Creek Bridge was built in 1895 by J. J. Daniels.

The bridge is supported by cut stone abutments and displays a camber evident in the roof and floor. The exterior has a shake roof, red plank siding with batten and white portals. The interior has a multiple kingpost truss encased by a double Burr arch that is only one-third the height of the kingpost center panel. The arch is exposed six feet below the floor and is secured into the abutments.

Billie Creek Bridge is located in Billie Creek Village. The bridge is open to the public, but during Village hours, a fee is charged to enter the park. Billie Creek Village is a park which displays restored historic structures.

DIRECTIONS: Adams Township. From Rockville, east on US 36, one mile on right at Billie Creek Village. (Donovan, 1980; Indiana Covered Bridge Society, Inc.; Indiana Department of Commerce, 1966; Indiana Department of Highways, 1982)

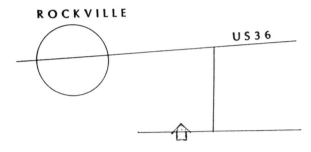

ROCKVILLE

US 36

Mansfield Bridge

Mansfield Bridge spans Big Raccoon Creek in southeastern Parke County.

The 247-foot, two span structure was built in 1867 by Joseph J. Daniels. Huge cut stone abutments and one pier support the bridge. The exterior has a tin roof and faded red plank siding with batten and white portals. The interior has lengthwise floor planks and a multiple kingpost truss encased by a double Burr arch over each span. The bridge is serving local traffic.

Mansfield Mill is located close to the bridge and it has a concrete mill race that was built in 1913, which replaced a previous mill race constructed of wood.

The combination of the covered bridge, mill and mill race offer a picturesque location.

DIRECTIONS: Jackson Township. At Mansfield. (Donovan, 1980; Indiana Covered Bridge Society, Inc.; Indiana Department of Commerce, 1986; Indiana Department of Highways, 1986)

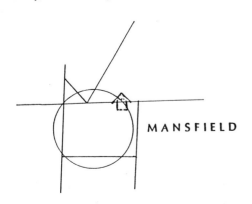

MANSFIELD

Portland Mills/ Dooley Station Bridge

Portland Mills Bridge was moved from its original location and replaced the Dooley Station Bridge in 1960, when Dooley Station Bridge was destroyed by arson. Four men spent 104 days in jail and paid $8,000 in fines.

Portland Mills crosses the Little Raccoon Creek with 130 feet and a single span.

Built in 1856 by Henry Wolf, the bridge's exterior is in poor condition. The white lap siding is missing many pieces, especially in the center where it seems to be a favorite place for vandals to kick. The interior has crosswise planking and two lengthwise runners. A multiple kingpost truss is encased by a double Burr arch which is constructed with two separate beams for each arch.

The bridge is closed and blocked by huge boulders. Resting on concrete abutments, the floor sags 12 inches below the road level.

DIRECTIONS: Greene Township. From Guion, north on SR 236/59, one mile, second left, one mile. (Donovan, 1980; Gould, 1977; Indiana Covered Bridge Society, Inc. Indiana Department of Commerce, 1986; Indiana Department of Highways, 1982)

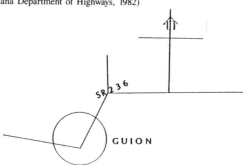

Beeson Bridge

Beeson Bridge is located in Billie Creek Village, where historical buildings are restored and maintained. Beeson Bridge spans Williams Creek with 55 feet. The Beeson Bridge was built in 1906 by the Frankfort Construction Company. The bridge is in good condition with a shake roof, dark red plank siding with batten and white portals. Resting on concrete abutments, the bridge has a camber. The interior has a multiple kingpost truss with a double Burr arch that is visible only four feet high against the center kingpost panel. The arch extends six feet below the floor and is attached to the abutments.

The bridge is used to store picnic tables and equipment for Billie Creek Village in the off-season. The east end of the bridge appears to have been burned at some time.

DIRECTIONS: Adams Township. From Rockville, US 36, one mile, on the right at Billie Creek Village. (Donovan, 1980; Gould, 1977; Indiana Covered Bridge Society, Inc.; Indiana Department of Commerce, 1986; Indiana Department of Highways, 1982)

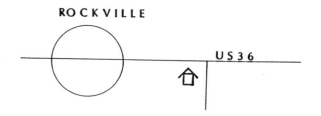

Melcher/Klondyke Bridge

The Melcher Bridge is also referred to as Klondyke Bridge after the nearby community. Melcher Bridge spans Leatherwood Creek, a tributary of Big Raccoon Creek.

The 83-foot bridge was built in 1896 by Joseph J. Daniels. The bridge exhibits a slight camber and rests on cut stone abutments with some concrete assistance. The exterior has red plank siding, a shake roof and white portals. The interior is a clone of many Parke County covered bridges with a multiple kingpost truss encased with a double Burr arch.

Open and serving local traffic, the bridge site has easy access to the creek. Visually the bridge is best appreciated when the leaves are off the trees, in late fall or winter.

DIRECTIONS: Wabash Township. At Klondyke. (Donovan, 1980; Indiana Covered Bridge Society, Inc.; Indiana Department of Commerce, 1986; Indiana Department of Highways, 1982)

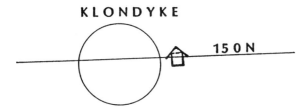

West Union Bridge

West Union Bridge crosses Sugar Creek, which is a major drainage system in northern Parke County. West Union Bridge was built in 1876 by J. J. Daniels. The 315-foot bridge has two spans and is the longest double span bridge in Parke county. West Union Bridge has a unique configuration, as each span displays a significant camber. The abutments and pier are made of cut stone and mortar. The exterior has a tin roof and red plank siding with batten and white portals. The interior has a multiple kingpost truss encased by a double Burr arch. The floor has lengthwise planking. The bridge has been bypassed for preservation. A park-like area surrounds the bridge and offers excellent visual access.

DIRECTIONS: Reserve Township. From West Union, north on 500W, one mile. (Donovan, 1980; Indiana Covered Bridge Society, Inc.; Indiana Department of Commerce, 1986; Indiana Department of Highways, 1982)

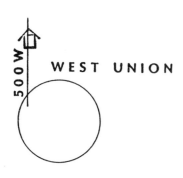

Jackson Bridge

Jackson Bridge spans Sugar Creek with 207 feet, making it the longest single span still in service in Parke County.

Built in 1861 by J. J. Daniels, the bridge has lap siding that was painted white over red. The red paint is now bleeding through white. There is siding missing, and the tin roof is rusted. Generally, the exterior of Jackson Bridge is ugly. The interior has been preserved. The floor has two lengthwise runners and the double Burr arch encases a double multiple kingpost truss, which is evident in the interior photograph.

The bridge rests on stone abutments. The bridge site does not allow access to the creek.

DIRECTIONS: Penn Township. From Turkey Run State Park, west on SR 47, south on US 41, one and one-half miles, right at 625N, three-fourths mile, right at 125W, one and one-half miles, left, three quarters mile. (Donovan, 1980; Indiana Covered Bridge Society, Inc.; Indiana Department of Commerce, 1986; Indiana Department of Highways, 1982)

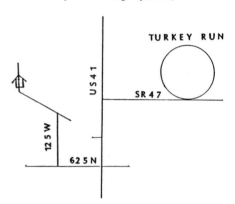

Tow Path/Mill Creek Bridge

Tow Path Bridge spans the Mill Creek, which is a tributary of the Wabash River, the major drainage channel for western Indiana. The Wabash forms the western boundary of Parke County.

Built by D. M. Brown in 1907, the 92-foot bridge has faded red plank siding with batten, a galvanized tin roof and the traditional Parke County white portals. The single span is supported by concrete abutments. The interior has a solid lengthwise runner occupying the center two-thirds of the floor space. The multiple kingpost truss is encased by a double Burr arch. The bridge is open to local traffic and accessibility to the creek bed is convenient.

DIRECTIONS: Liberty Township. From Howard, east on 1025N, one mile. (Donovan, 1980; Indiana Covered Bridge Society, Inc.; Indiana Department of Commerce, 1986; Indiana Department of Highways, 1982)

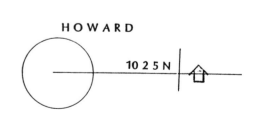

Coal Creek/Lodi Bridge

The 170 foot Coal Creek Bridge spans the creek of the same name in the community of Lodi, in the most northwestern corner of Parke County. Coal Creek empties into the Wabash River one mile west of the bridge site.

Originally built in 1869 by J. J. Daniels, a flood caused serious damage in 1898 and Daniels rebuilt the bridge.

The exterior has a shake roof, red plank siding and traditional white portals. The interior has two lengthwise runners and a multiple kingpost truss encased by a double Burr arch. Resting on cut stone abutments, the bridge is still open. Due to fencing, access to the creek is very difficult. The location is not conducive for photographs.

DIRECTIONS: Liberty Township. At Lodi. (Donovan, 1980; Indiana Covered Bridge Society, Inc.; Indiana Department of Commerce, 1986; Indiana Department of Highways, 1982)

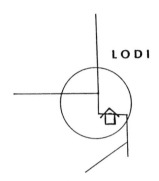

Rush Creek Bridge

Rush Creek Bridge spans Rush Creek, which is a tributary of Sugar Creek. Built in 1904 by William Hendricks, the bridge has the familiar Parke County covered bridge exterior. The bridge is 80 feet long. The shake roof, red batten siding and white portals, combined with an interior of a multiple kingpost truss encased with a double Burr arch, are representative of Parke County's covered bridges.

The creek is easily accessible but thick vegetation prevents a good view.

DIRECTIONS: Liberty Township. From Tangier, south at 420W, one and one half-mile, left at 900N, one fourth mile. (Donovan, 1980; Indiana Covered Bridge Society, Inc.; Indiana Department of Commerce, 1986; Indiana Department of Highways, 1982)

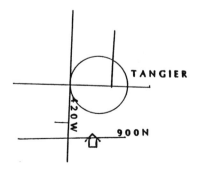

Parke County
14-61-32

Marshall Bridge

The Marshall Bridge spans Rush Creek, a tributary of Sugar Creek, a major drainage channel of northern Parke County.

Built in 1917 by J. A. Britton, the bridge shows a camber in its roof and there is slight evidence of the camber in the floor.

The 56-foot structure has a rusted tin roof and red plank siding. The interior has the customary multiple kingpost truss encased by a double Burr arch, with crosswise floor planking interfaced with two lengthwise runners.

The bridge is nestled in a valley and is open to traffic. The bridge site also allows easy access to the creek, but the bridge offers its best appearance when the leaves are gone.

DIRECTIONS: Liberty Township. From Tangier, South on 420W, two and one-half miles, left on 810N. (Donovan, 1980; Indiana Covered Bridge Society, Inc.; Indiana Department of Commerce, 1986; Indiana Department of Highways, 1982)

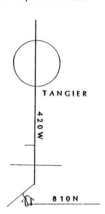

Parke County
14-61-33

Bowsher Ford Bridge

The 72-foot Bowsher Ford Bridge spans Mill Creek in northwestern Parke County. Mill Creek is a tributary of the Wabash River. Their confluence is two miles southwest of the bridge site.

Bowsher Ford Bridge was built in 1915 by J. A. Britton's son, Eugene Britton. The exterior has the customary shake roof, red batten siding and white portals. The interior displays a multiple kingpost truss encased by a double Burr arch that extends only half of the height of the center kingpost panel. The floor has a solid lengthwise runner that occupies the center two-thirds of the floor space.

Bowsher Ford Bridge is open to vehicles and sits on stone abutments with poured concrete headers.

The bridge has an attractive location but, unfortunately, it is impossible for one to view the bridge from the creek because the surrounding land is secured by fencing.

DIRECTIONS: Liberty Township. From Howard, north, one mile on 700W, right on 1125N, one mile. (Donovan, 1980; Indiana Covered Bridge Society, Inc.; Indiana Department of Commerce, 1986; Indiana Department of Highways, 1982)

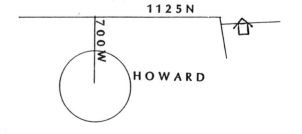

Cox Ford Bridge

Cox Ford Bridge spans Sugar Creek, which is the major drainage channel for northern Parke County.

Built in 1913, Cox Ford Bridge was constructed by J. A. Britton. The exterior has faded dark red plank siding with batten, a charcoal shake roof and white portals. The single span bridge is 176 feet long and sits on cut stone abutments. The interior's floor is different than most of Parke County's covered bridges in that the planking is laid diagonally and interfaced with two lengthwise runners. The standard multiple kingpost truss is encased by a double Burr arch.

Cox Ford Covered Bridge replaced an iron bridge that was destroyed in a flood in 1912. In 1913, a covered bridge near Armiesburg was destroyed by a flood and its arches, built by Henry Wolf, were used by Britton in the construction of Cox Ford Bridge. The arches in Cox Ford Bridge are 60 years older than the timbers used in the truss.

Access to the creek is easy and the river banks offer an excellent view of the bridge. The bridge is still open.

DIRECTIONS: Penn Township. From Turkey Run State Park west on SR 47, one mile, first right at 120 E. three-fourths mile. (Donovan, 1980; Hardesty; Indiana Covered Bridge Society, Inc.; Indiana Department of Commerce, 1986; Indiana Department of Highways, 1982)

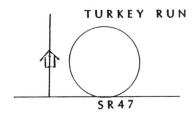

Wilkins Mill Bridge

Named after a nearby mill, Wilkins Mill Bridge spans Sugar Mill Creek, a tributary of Sugar Creek which is the principle drainage channel for northern Parke County.

Built in 1906 by William Hendricks, Wilkins Mill Bridge is 102 feet long. The exterior has the conventional shake roof, faded red batten siding and white portals. The interior has the traditional Parke County truss and floor.

Resting on concrete abutments, the bridge is still open for traffic and access to the creek is easy.

DIRECTIONS: Sugar Creek Township. From Turkey Run State Park, west on SR 47, two miles, right on US 41, one and one-half miles right at 910N. (Donovan, 1980; Indiana Covered Bridge Society, Inc.; Indiana Department of Commerce, 1986; Indiana Department of Highways, 1982)

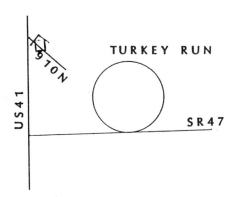

Parke County
14-61-36

Narrows Bridge

Narrows Bridge spans Sugar Creek in Turkey Run State Park. Built in 1882 by J. A. Britton, the Narrows Bridge is 121 feet long and its single span is supported by stone abutments. The exterior has plank siding that was painted red, but has since weathered and faded pink. The roof is shake. The interior displays a narrow passageway with a dilapidated solid lengthwise runner centered on two-thirds of the floor, and a multiple kingpost truss encased by the prolific double Burr arch.

Due to its prominent location in Turkey Run State Park, the Narrows Bridge has a continuous line of visitors. The Narrows was bypassed in 1960. The bridge spans a sandstone, rocky gorge that offers a spectacular location for photographers. Afternoon is the time to visit this bridge; with the sun at your back, the photography opportunity is great.

DIRECTIONS: Sugar Creek Township. In Turkey Run State Park. From SR 47, north at 300E, three-quarter mile. (Donovan, 1980; Indiana Covered Bridge Society, Inc.; Indiana Department of Commerce, 1986; Indiana Department of Highways, 1982)

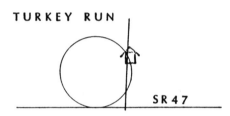

TURKEY RUN

SR 47

Parke County
14-61-38

State Sanatorium Bridge

The State Sanatorium Bridge spans Little Raccoon Creek.

Built in 1913 by Joseph A. Britton, the 154-foot bridge has beautifully weathered, gray plank siding with batten, a gray tin roof and rests on concrete abutments. The interior has the familiar multiple kingpost truss with a double Burr arch and crosswise floor planking. It is difficult to identify on the exterior photograph of the bridge, but it is said to be the only known covered bridge with lightening rods.

Access to the creek is easy, but vegetation has overgrown the surrounding area, making it difficult to see the entire bridge.

DIRECTIONS: Adams Township. From Rockville, east on US 36, two miles, left at 420 E, one-half mile, right, one-tenth mile. (Donovan, 1980; Indiana Covered Bridge Society, Inc.; Indiana Department of Commerce, 1986; Indiana Department of Highways, 1982)

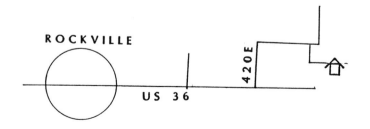

ROCKVILLE

420 E

US 36

Hills/Baker's Camp Bridge

The Hills Bridge spans Big Walnut Creek which runs diagonally across Putnam County. Big Walnut Creek crosses from the northeastern corner through the southeastern corner.

Built in 1901, Hills Bridge is a single span and rests on cut stone and mortar abutments. The 128-foot bridge has a dark red tin roof and dark red plank siding. The interior has a Burr truss with crosswise floor planking interfaced with two lengthwise runners.

The creek is easily accessible.

DIRECTIONS: Flood Township. From Bainbridge, east on US 36, one and one-half miles, right at 475E, one-half mile, right at 650N, one-half mile. (Donovan, 1980; Indiana Covered Bridge Society, Inc.; Indiana Department of Highways, 1982; Puetz)

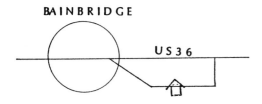

Pine Bluff Bridge

Pine Bluff Bridge spans Big Walnut Creek with 211 feet. The date of construction is unknown. The two span structure is supported by cut stone abutments and one cut stone pier. The bridge has a rusted tin roof and dark red plank siding with batten. The interior was constructed with a Howe truss and lengthwise floor planking.

Pine Bluff Bridge is closed and appears to be abandoned. Floor planking has been removed from the area at the portals, preventing interior inspection. The bridge is located in a picturesque valley and the 211-foot span over the Big Walnut Creek makes an intriguing image. The bridge could still be saved in its current condition, but left to the elements it will soon fall into a state beyond repair.

DIRECTIONS: Jackson Township, From Carpentersville, south on 250E one-half mile, left at 950N, one and one-half miles. (Donovan, 1980; Indiana Covered Bridge Society, Inc.; Indiana Department of Highways, 1982; Puetz)

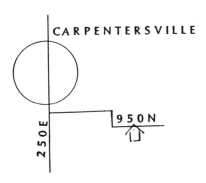

Rollingstone Bridge

Rollingstone Bridge crosses Big Walnut Creek.

The 1915 bridge is a 103-foot single span. The structure has a camber noticeable in both the floor and roof. Resting on concrete abutments, the exterior has a galvanized tin roof and dark red plank siding with batten. The interior has a Burr arch truss and a solid runner centered on two thirds of the floor space, laid on diagonal planking.

The bridge is open to traffic. Access to the creek is limited to the east side.

DIRECTIONS: Floyd Township. Northeast of Bainbridge, at 78ON and 375E. (Donovan, 1980; Indiana Covered Bridge Society, Inc.; Indiana Department of Highways, 1982; Puetz)

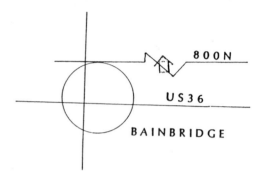

Edna Collins Bridge

The Edna Collins Bridge spans Little Walnut Creek. The 80-foot bridge was built in 1922 with a Burr truss. The floor is lengthwise planking. The exterior has a rusting tin roof and weathered, dark red plank siding with batten. There is no access to the creek due to fencing secured at all four corners.

DIRECTIONS: Clinton Township. From Clinton Falls, northwest, one-half mile, turn left at 450N. (Donovan, 1980; Indiana Covered Bridge Society, Inc.; Indiana Department of Highways, 1982; Puetz)

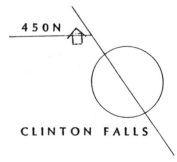

Holton Bridge

Holton Bridge spans Otter Creek on the western edge of central Ripley County. Thomas Hardman built Holton Bridge in 1884. The stone work was done by the John Greerand Company from Seymore, Indiana.

Holton Bridge is a 112-foot single span that rests on one concrete abutment and one cut stone with mortar abutment. The exterior has a rusted, corrugated tin roof and corrugated tin siding. There are four small windows on each side. The interior has a Howe truss and lengthwise floor planking.

The creek has easy access and the bridge is open for traffic.

DIRECTIONS: Otter Creek Township. West of Holton, one mile at about 75N and 810W. (Business and Professional Women, 1968; Donovan, 1980; Indiana Covered Bridge Society, Inc.; Indiana Department of Highways, 1982; Puetz)

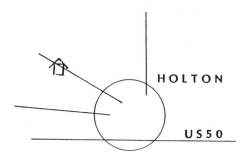

Busching Bridge

Busching Bridge spans Laughery Creek in Versailles State Park.

The bridge was built in 1885 by Thomas A. Hardman from Brookville. The 176-foot bridge is a single span and rest on cut stone abutments. The exterior has a gray tin roof and red plank siding. The interior has a Howe truss and lengthwise floor planking.

The bridge is open and sits in its original location. This road was the old Cincinnati to St. Louis Pike. The road was rerouted and is now U.S. 50. Access to the creek is easy but the vegetation blocks the view of the bridge.

DIRECTIONS: Johnson Township. At Versailles State Park (Business and Professional Women, 1968; "Covered Bridge is on the Original Route of the Cincinnati to St. Louis Pike"; Donovan, 1980 Indiana Covered Bridge Society, Inc.; Indiana Department of Highways, 1982; Puetz)

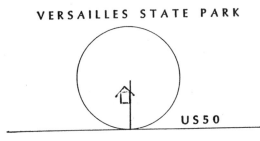

Ewbank/Smith Bridge

The Ewbank/Smith Bridge spans Big Flat Rock River, which drains diagonally across Rush County from the far northeastern corner to the southwestern corner. Big Flat Rock River has a normal bed width of 120 feet at the bridge site.

Built by the Kennedy Family, natives of Rush County, in 1877, the Ewbank Bridge is a 124-foot single span resting on cut stone and mortar abutments. The exterior is in poor condition. The white lap siding has all but disappeared, exposing the multiple kingpost truss encased by a double Burr arch. The interior displays graffiti on the truss members and the lengthwise floor planking.

Access to the creek is convenient but disappointing since the exterior has been so vandalized. The bridge is closed and, unfortunately, scheduled for possible demolition. The Ewbank Bridge is listed on the National Register of Historic Places.

DIRECTIONS: Rushville Township. From Rushville, east on SR 44, one and one-fourth miles, left at 200E, one and one-half miles, left at 150N, one-half mile. (Arnold, 1987; Donovan, 1980; Indiana Covered Bridge Society, Inc.; Indiana Department of Highways, 1982)

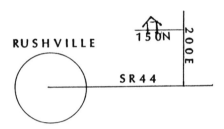

Offutt's Ford Bridge

Offutt's Ford Bridge spans Little Blue River, which drains the northwestern corner of Rush County. The average bed width of Little Blue River is 50 feet at the bridge site.

Built in 1884 by the Kennedy Family, Offutt's Ford Bridge is seriously deteriorated. The exterior has a rusted flat tin roof and unpainted lap siding that has suffered severe vandalism. The 100-foot structure sits on cut stone abutments. The interior has a Burr truss. The floor has lengthwise planking laid over crosswise planks.

Offutt's Ford Bridge is closed and, sadly, is also slated to be destroyed. This bridge is listed on the National Register of Historic Places.

DIRECTIONS: Posey Township. From Rushville, US 52, west, four miles, right at 425W, one and three-fourths miles, left on 300N, one-fourth mile, right at about 475W, one-half mile. (Arnold, 1987; Donovan, 1980; Indiana Covered Bridge Society, Inc.; Indiana Department of Highways, 1982)

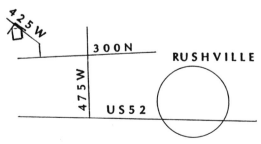

Forsythe Mill Bridge

Forsythe Mill Bridge spans Flat Rock River in the southwestern corner of Rush County.

Built by the Kennedy Family in 1888, the Forsythe Mill Bridge is a single span supported by cut stone abutments. The 196-foot bridge is the longest single span in Rush County.

This bridge and the Moscow Bridge (14-70-07) are the only two bridges that will definitely be preserved in Rush County. Consequently, the bridge has been well maintained. The exterior is all intact with white lap siding and a tin roof. The interior, although it has experienced some graffiti, is also in good repair. The Burr truss and lengthwise floor is characteristic of the Kennedy's construction.

The Forsythe Mill Covered Bridge is open to local traffic. The creek is easily accessible in the winter months. Forsythe Mill Bridge is listed in the National Register of Historic Places.

DIRECTIONS: Orange Township. From Gowdy, east on 800S, one and one-half miles, turn right. (Arnold, 1987; Donovan, 1980; Indiana Covered Bridge Society, Inc.; Indiana Department of Highways, 1982).

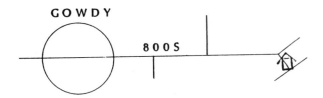

GOWDY

800S

Ferree Bridge

Ferree Bridge spans the Little Flat Rock River which drains the southeastern corner of Rush County. Little Flat Rock River has a 50-foot bed width at the bridge site.

Built by the Kennedy Family in 1873, Ferree Bridge is the oldest covered bridge left in Rush County, which once had nineteen covered bridges. The 100-foot bridge has not been maintained and, consequently, has fallen into disrepair. Only half of the faded, white lap siding remains. The tin roof is all intact and the single span rests on cut stone abutments. The interior Burr truss members are aged due to exposure.

Although in sad repair, the bridge remains open, serving local traffic. This bridge could easily be repaired and strengthened to serve for many years. Unfortunately, Ferree Bridge is scheduled to be replaced.

Ferree Bridge is listed on the National Register of Historic Places.

DIRECTIONS: Anderson Township. From Rushville, south on SR 3, five miles, left at 600S, one mile, right at 00, one-half mile. (Arnold, 1987; Donovan, 1980; Gould, 1977; Indiana Covered Bridge Society, Inc.; Indiana Department of Highways, 1982)

RUSHVILLE

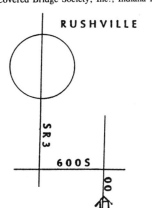

SR 3

600S

00

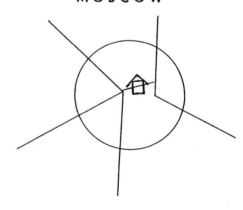

Moscow Bridge

Moscow Bridge is located in the southwestern corner of Rush County at the edge of the small village of Moscow. The Moscow Covered Bridge crosses the Big Flat Rock River which is a major drainage channel for Rush County. The normal river bed width is 150 feet but there is ample river bed to accept a width of over 300 feet.

The bridge has two spans. One span crosses the normal river bed and the other span crosses the elevated river bed that is dry most of the year. Spanning 334 feet, the Moscow Bridge is the longest bridge in Rush County. The bridge rests on cut stone abutments and one stone pier. The bridge hovers thirty feet over the river.

The exterior of the bridge has a rusty-red tin roof and fresh white lap siding. Each span has two sets of double windows with canopies. The bridge was built in 1886 by the Kennedy family, with a multiple kingpost truss and two sets of double Burr arches, one over each span. The interior of the bridge is beautiful with the two sets of Burr arches, the massive timbers of the multiple kingpost truss and the 334-foot passage.

The bridge is open for traffic but each road that leads to the bridge, and the bridge itself displays an "UNSAFE BRIDGE" sign. While I was standing at the middle of the bridge, a small postal jeep drove across the bridge, which shook terribly.

The Moscow Bridge is a classic example of a double Burr truss, and the bridge's exterior has been well maintained. However, if the bridge continues to serve the local traffic without being repaired soon, it will fail under the weight of modern traffic.

The Moscow and Forsythe Bridges are the only two bridges definitely scheduled to be preserved at this time in Rush County.

Access to the river bed is very easy and the bridge is quite awesome as it looms over the river bed. The Moscow Bridge is listed in the National Register of Historic Places.

DIRECTIONS: Orange Township. At Moscow. (Arnold, 1987; Donovan, 1980; Indiana Covered Bridge Society, Inc.; Indiana Department of Highways, 1982)

MOSCOW

Norris Ford Bridge

The Norris Ford Bridge spans Big Flat Rock River in the northeast section of Rush County. Big Flat Rock River has a 90 foot normal bed width at the bridge site.

The 169-foot bridge was constructed by the Kennedy Family builders in 1916. The single span structure has white lap siding and a red tin roof. The photograph shows much of the siding missing.

Since the picture was taken, efforts have been made to restore the bridge. The interior has the Burr arch which was the Kennedys' favorite truss construction. The floor has crosswise planking.

The creek banks are convenient but the climax vegetation blocks the view of the bridge. Norris Ford Bridge is open to traffic and is listed in the National Register of Historic Places.

DIRECTIONS: Jackson Township. From Rushville, north on SR 3, three miles, right at 300N, two miles. (Arnold, 1987; Donovan, 1980; Indiana Covered Bridge Society, Inc.; Indiana Department of Commerce, 1986; Indiana Department of Highways, 1982)

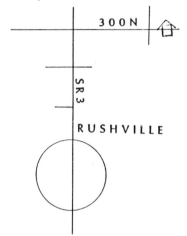

Newport Bridge

Newport Bridge crosses the Little Vermillion River, which is a tributary of the Wabash River. Their confluence is four river miles east of the bridge site.

Newport Bridge was built in 1885 with a single span. The entire bridge exhibits a camber. The 190-foot structure has a gray, rusting tin roof, and dark red plank siding with batten and white portals. Newport Bridge is supported by cut stone abutments with some concrete assistance. The interior has a double Burr arch encasing a multiple kingpost truss. Each arch is constructed with two separate beams. The floor is in excellent condition with lengthwise planking.

Newport Bridge is open and still serves local traffic. Access to the creek is easy.

DIRECTIONS: Vermillion Township. West of Newport, west of SR 63 at about 50N. (Donovan, 1987; Indiana Covered Bridge Society, Inc.; Indiana Department of Highways, 1982; Puetz)

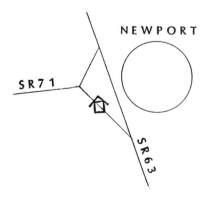

Eugene Bridge

Eugene Bridge spans the Vermillion River, which is a principle drainage channel for northern Vermillion County. Vermillion River empties into the Wabash River two miles east of the bridge site. The Wabash River forms the eastern boundary for Vermillion County.

The Eugene Bridge was built in 1885. The single span is 192 feet long and rests on cut stone with mortar abutments. Concrete has been poured around the base of each abutment. The bridge has a galvanized tin roof and red plank siding with batten. The interior has a massive double Burr arch truss and lengthwise floor planking with some planks missing.

Eugene Bridge has been bypassed and the new bridge was built far enough away from the covered span so as not to detract from it. The exterior photograph was taken from the new bridge.

DIRECTIONS: Eugene Township. From Eugene, north at 20N, one and one-half miles.
(Donovan, 1980; Indiana Covered Bridge Society, Inc.; Indiana Department of Highways, 1982; Puetz)

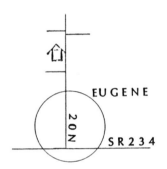

Dearborn County
14-15-01

Guilford Bridge

An unusual block floor in the Guilford Bridge (14-15-01) in Dearborn County, Indiana.

Franklin County
14-24-04

Lower Blue Creek Bridge

The remains of Lower Blue Creek Bridge (14-24-04) in Franklin County, Indiana. Sometimes only the abutments remain after a collapse.

Montgomery County
14-54-01

Darlington Bridge

A unique block floor used in the Darlington Bridge (14-54-01) in Montgomery County, Indiana.

Parke County
14-61-19

Billie Creek Bridge

Billie Creek Bridge (14-61-19) exhibits hundreds of rusty nails which are remnants of old advertisements in Parke County, Indiana.

Kentucky

ACKNOWLEDGMENTS

I would like to thank the following people of Kentucky for their assistance in providing me with suggestions, resources and information:

Betty B. Dillow, Lewis County Historical Society

Dianne Wells, Manager, Kentucky Historical Society

Lyla Lee Humphries, Librarian, Fleming County Library

Ms. Dorthy K. Griffith, County Librarian, Greenup County Public Library District

Susan C. Eades, Paris-Bourbon County Library

Shirley A. Hinton, Clerk, Lewis County Engineer's Office

Frances H. Gaitskill

Mr. L. K. Patton

Fleming County Library

INTRODUCTION

Today, Kentucky has fifteen covered bridges. Five of the historic structures are open to traffic. Of the remaining ten, eight have been bypassed and are now closed. Kentucky's existing covered bridges are all found in the northeastern quarter of the state. Mooresville Bridge (17-115-01) has the farthest southwestern location, in Washington County, 60 miles southwest of Lexington. The remaining bridges are found northeast of Lexington.

Eastern Kentucky is known for its hilly terrain, which has many streams that need to be forded. This necessitated the demand for many covered bridges. Subsequently, the region of Kentucky still possessing the covered bridges is that which had the most abundant supply originally. Another reason for their existence is the hilly, northeastern section of Kentucky did not see much Civil War activity, which destroyed most of the South's old bridges.

OLDEST & LONGEST

Kentucky's oldest covered bridge can be found in Bracken County, the Walcott Bridge (17-12-01), built in 1824. This bridge has been preserved by the Kentucky Historical Society. Walcott Bridge is beautifully maintained and in excellent condition (Kentucky Historical Society).

Until 1981, Bath and Fleming Counties shared Kentucky's longest covered bridge, the Sherburne Bridge, with 265 feet. In that year, the bridge was burned by arson and destroyed. Today, Kentucky's longest covered bridge is found in Washington County, Mooresville Bridge (17-115-01). With 226 feet and two spans, the bridge was bypassed in 1982. Mooresville Bridge, unfortunately, appears to have been forgotten; graffiti and vandalized siding scar the bridge's appearance.

KENTUCKY'S TRUSSES

Kentucky has several unusual truss designs and combinations. The most distinguishing characteristic about the fifteen bridge trusses, is that five of them exhibit multiple kingpost trusses built with double members. These bridges include the Colville (17-09-03), Ringo's Mill (17-35-04), Grange City (17-35-05), Oldtown (17-45-02) and Mackey (17-68-03) Bridges.

Kentucky has two bridges displaying one of a kind trusses. The first rare truss is found in Bennett's Mill Bridge (17-45-01) in Greenup County. This truss has a peculiar "X" panel truss with one solid leg, and the other leg is in two pieces, but attached off-center to form an off-balance "X" panel. This is the only truss of its kind in the eastern United States known to this author. The second rare truss is located in Robertson County. The Johnson Creek Bridge (17-101-01) has a variation of a Howe truss. The steel tie rods are vertical and placed into the "X" panel, rather than where the rods traditionally divide the panels.

Walcott Bridge (17-12-01) in Bracken County, displays an interesting combination of a kingpost and queenpost truss. Dover Bridge (17-81-01) in Mason County, has a most interesting double queenpost truss combination.

Goddard/White Bridge (17-35-06) in Fleming County, has Kentucky's only Town lattice truss. Switzer Bridge (17-37-01) in Franklin County has a Howe truss. The three covered bridges built in the 1900s have the following trusses: Yatesville (17-64-02)—Howe (1907), Trinity (17-64-01)—kingpost (1924), and Bouldin (17-81-02)—kingpost (1925).

FINDING KENTUCKY'S COVERED BRIDGES

Kentucky's covered bridges are easy to find, but they are widely distributed in ten eastern Kentucky counties. Fleming County has the most covered bridges with three examples. Ringo's Mill (17-35-04), Grange City (17-35-05), and Goddard/White Bridges (17-35-06) are all well preserved and are guaranteed not to be a disappointment. Each have beautiful locations and their sites are maintained and allow easy visual access.

Directions and maps accompanying the text are to be used in conjunction with county maps available from the state (Please see the chapter on How to Find Covered Bridges and Obtain County Maps).

If you wish to see all of Kentucky's covered bridges, plan on at least two or three days because they are so dispersed.

The landscape Kentucky offers is beautiful. The flat bluegrass horse ranches around Lexington and the hills and mountains in eastern Kentucky offer picturesque landscapes while bridging.

BRIDGE NAME	COUNTY	NUMBER
Colville	Bourbon	17-09-03
Walcott/Bracken/White	Bracken	17-12-01
Ringo's Mill	Fleming	17-35-04
Grange City/Hillsboro	"	17-35-05
Goddard/White	"	17-35-06
Switzer	Franklin	17-37-01
Bennett's Mill	Greenup	17-45-01
Oldtown	"	17-45-02
Mackey/Huges/Jones Farm	Lewis	17-68-03
Dover	Mason	17-81-01
Johnson Creek	Robertson	17-101-01
Mooresville	Washington	17-115-01

Bourbon County
17-09-03

Colville Bridge

Colville Bridge spans Hinkston Creek with 120 feet in the northern corner of Bourbon County. Hinkston Creek forms the county boundary of the northeastern section.

Built in 1877, Colville Bridge presently rests on new concrete abutments. Protected by a shake roof and natural plank siding, the bridge's truss is a multiple kingpost. The truss is unusual because each vertical and diagonal member of the traditional multiple kingpost is doubled. The floor has crosswise planking and two lengthwise runners. Sadly, the truss members have been the object of many graffiti attacks.

Colville Bridge has easy access to the creek, but the area is heavily vegetated, preventing easy visual access.

DIRECTIONS: From Millersburg, west on SR. 1896, three miles, right on Colville Road, one and one-half miles (keep left). (Donovan, 1980; Kentucky Transportation Cabinet)

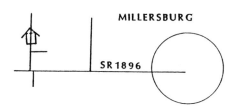

Bracken County
17-12-01

Walcott/Bracken/White Bridge

Three miles south of the Ohio River, Walcott Bridge spans Locust Creek. Locust Creek is a small stream with a 60-foot bed width at the bridge site and drains into the Ohio River.

Built in 1824, Walcott Bridge is the oldest covered bridge in Kentucky. Built to replace another covered bridge, Walcott was constructed on property owned by the Murray family. The 75-foot structure served the local community of Walcott until 1954, when it was bypassed. Today, Walcott Bridge is surrounded by a small park and picnic area. Protected by a silver tin roof and freshly painted white plank siding, Walcott Bridge has a unique truss. Hand-hewn timbers form a combination queenpost and kingpost truss. The roof has been repaired with new boards and the floor is made of crosswise planking.

Preserved by the Bracken County Historical Society, Walcott is the last covered bridge in the county. The bridge and surrounding area are well maintained and easily accessible. The hills surrounding the bridge present an attractive background. Walcott Bridge is listed on the National Register of Historic Places.

DIRECTIONS: At Walcott. (Donovan, 1980; Kentucky Historical Society; Kentucky Transportation Cabinet; ''Kentucky's Covered Bridges'')

Ringo's Mill Bridge

Ringo's Mill Bridge spans Fox Creek with 86 feet. Fox Creek drains into the Licking River, five miles west of the bridge site. Licking River forms Fleming County's southwestern boundary.

Built in 1867, Ringo's Mill Bridge is protected by a silver tin roof and beautifully weathered, natural gray plank siding. The single span is supported by red stone abutments covered with concrete. The truss is a multiple kingpost. What is rare about the truss's construction is that all of the members are double. The floor has crosswise planking.

Bypassed, Ringo's Mill Bridge has a park area and is well maintained. The bridge, its surrounding hills and valley are very picturesque. Ringo's Mill is listed in the Nation Register of Historic Places.

DIRECTIONS: At Ringo's Mill. (Donovan, 1980; Kentucky Historical Society; Kentucky Transportation Cabinet; "Kentucky's Covered Bridge")

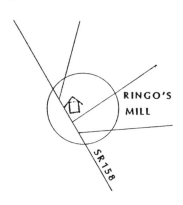

Grange City/Hillsboro Bridge

Grange City Bridge is three miles west of Ringo's Mill Bridge (17-35-04). Spanning Fox creek, Grange City Bridge is 86 feet long. Fox Creek drains into the Licking River two miles west of the bridge site.

Built between 1865 and 1870, the truss is covered with a silver tin roof and natural plank siding. The siding is only several years old. The west side has turned gray from receiving all the weather. The east side, shown in the photograph, still retains the wood's original color. The single span is supported by cut stone abutments covered with a concrete facing. The truss is identical to the multiple kingpost truss used in Ringo's Mill Bridge (17-35-04), each of the truss members are double. The floor has crosswise planking and two lengthwise runners.

Bypassed, Grange City Bridge has a park area and an attractive location. Grange City Bridge is listed in the National Register of Historic Places.

DIRECTIONS: From Grange City, north on SR 111, one and one-half miles. (Donovan, 1980; Kentucky Historical Society; Kentucky Transportation Cabinet; "Kentucky's Covered Bridges")

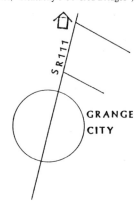

Fleming County
17-35-06

Goddard/White Bridge

The Goddard/White Bridge spans Sandlick Creek with 63 feet.

The date of construction is unknown. Covered with a tin roof and naturally weathered gray plank siding, the single span rests on one dry creek stone abutment and one concrete abutment. The end with the concrete abutment has an uncovered wooden approach that is 50 feet long, with two spans. The center pier and other abutment are made of bedrock. Steel bracing has been installed under the bridge to add structural support. Goddard/White Bridge's interior is constructed with a Town lattice truss which is Kentucky's only example of this. The floor has crosswise planks and two lengthwise runners.

In 1968, Louis Bower, Jr. of Flemingsburg, Kentucky, restored the bridge. Open for traffic, the bridge offers an attractive location with hills and a church as a background. Goddard/White Bridge is listed in the National Register of Historic Places.

DIRECTIONS: In Goddard just off of SR 32 on Maddox Road (CR 1101). (Donovan, 1980; Kentucky Historical Society; Kentucky Transportation Cabinet; ''Kentucky's Covered Bridges'')

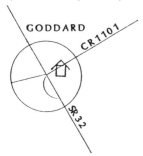

Franklin County
17-37-01

Switzer Bridge

Switzer Bridge crosses North Elkhorn Creek on the far eastern edge of Franklin County. One of only fifteen covered bridges left in Kentucky, Switzer Bridge is the only one left in Franklin County, which is home to Frankfort, Kentucky's State Capitol. Switzer Bridge is located four miles northeast of Frankfort.

Built in 1855, by George Hockensmith, the single span structure is supported by one cut stone abutment with a concrete facing and one that is dry cut stone without mortar. The bridge is 120 feet long and protected with a tin roof and naturally weathered, gray plank siding that is missing many pieces. The truss is a Howe and the floor has crosswise planking.

Switzer Bridge was bypassed in 1954. The bridge is in need of siding and renovation if it is to be preserved. North Elkhorn Creek provides an attractive location at the bridge site. Switzer Bridge was listed on the National Register of Historic Places in 1974.

DIRECTIONS: From Frankfort, US 460 east, two miles, left on SR 1689, four miles, right on SR 1262, one-tenth mile, on left. (Donovan, 1980; Kentucky Transportation Cabinet; (''Kentucky's Covered Bridges'')

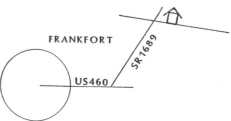

Bennett's Mill Bridge

Bennett's Mill Bridge spans Tygart's Creek with 145 feet.

Built in 1875, the bridge is covered with a corrugated tin roof and natural plank siding. The single span is supported by cut stone abutments. Steel has been added to the underside. The interior is particularly interesting. The truss consists of "X" panels, and at the center of the bridge is two vertical beams. All of the truss members are double. One leg of each "X" panel is solid and its upper portion points away from the center of the bridge. The other leg of the "X" is two separate pieces, attached, not mortized to the solid beam. I have not been able to identify what type of truss is used in the Bennett's Mill Bridge. I have referred to it as a version of an "X" panel in the chapter on trusses. The floor is also interesting. Planking is laid diagonally, but changes direction every 20 feet. Two lengthwise runners interface with the planking.

Open to traffic, the floor beams appear to be broken down. The bridge needs major repairs and should be closed. It would be unfortunate to lose a bridge with such a rare truss.

DIRECTIONS: From Lynn on SR 7, north on SR 7, four miles, on right. (Donovan, 1980; Kentucky Transportation Cabinet)

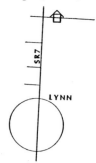

Oldtown Bridge

Oldtown Bridge crosses Little Sandy River with 194 feet. Built in 1880, the bridge cost $4,000.

Protected by a shake roof and natural plank siding, the two span structure is supported by one pier and abutments made of huge cut sandstone. The short span (50 feet) has a single member multiple kingpost truss. The long span has a double multiple kingpost truss. The floor has diagonal planking with two lengthwise runners.

The Green Thumb Program restored Oldtown Bridge in 1972-1973. February of 1987 found the bridge closed and in poor condition. Oldtown Bridge is listed on the National Register of Historic Places.

DIRECTIONS: At Oldtown. (Donovan, 1980; Kentucky Historical Society; Kentucky Transportation Cabinet)

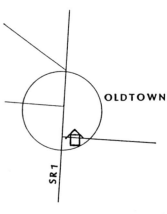

Lewis County
17-68-03

Mackey/Huges/Jones Farm Bridge

The Mackey Bridge spans Cabin Creek with 114 feet. The single span structure rests on concrete abutments. A steel and concrete lateral brace has been recently added on the south side of the bridge. The brace consists of a concrete pillar and a steel A-frame with turnbuckles to pull the trusses perpendicular again.

Built in 1867, the Mackey Bridge is covered with a tin roof and naturally weathered black plank siding. The interior is extremely interesting. First of all, it has a double multiple kingpost truss. Secondly, each diagonal wooden member is opposed by a steel tie rod forming an ''X'' panel with one leg that is steel and the other wood. What is so fascinating about the truss' configuration is that this technique is used in the Child's truss. It was formally thought that the only example of the Child's truss existed in Ohio. This bridge's truss definitely exhibits the Child's design. The floor has crosswise planking with two lengthwise runners.

Bypassed in 1983, Mackey Bridge is well preserved and has an attractive bridge site.

DIRECTIONS: From Herron Hill on SR 10, west on Poplar Flat Road, three miles, right on Cabin Creek Road, five miles. (Donovan, 1980; Kentucky Transportation Cabinet)

Photograph by Michael Krekeler

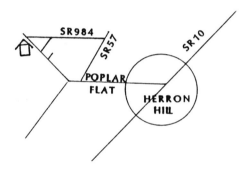

Mason County
17-81-01

Dover Bridge

Dover Bridge spans Lee Creek with 63 feet. Lee Creek has a 50-foot bed width at the bridge site and drains into the Ohio River one mile north. Dover Bridge was built in 1835.

Protected by a rusted tin roof and natural gray plank siding, the single span is supported by concrete abutments poured over the old bedrock abutments. Massive steel I-beams have been installed under the bridge to support modern traffic. The interior has a complex double queenpost truss. Each truss is made of four beams. This truss is very unusual. The floor has crosswise planking.

Dover Bridge is open to traffic and access to the creek is easy.

DIRECTIONS: At Dover. (Donovan, 1980; Kentucky Transportation Cabinet)

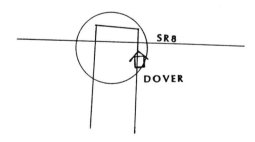

Johnson Creek Bridge

Johnson Creek Bridge spans Johnson Creek with 110 feet and two spans.

Built in 1862, the structure is protected by a tin roof and new plank siding. The abutments are stone with concrete caps, the stone pier has a concrete base to protect it from ice damage. The bridge has received some major restoration recently. Several of the Howe truss panels have been replaced. This truss is a rare example of a variation of the Howe truss. This truss differs from the traditional Howe in two ways. First, the adjustable steel tie rods are placed into the "X" panel rather than between the panels. Secondly, the "X" panel members are very thick at the portals. The members become thinner as the "X" panels approach the center. The truss is reinforced by a 4-ply single Burr arch that is composed of 4″ X 4″ beams. The floor has crosswise planking.

Although the bridge has been repaired, when you walk across it, you can feel the structure bounce. Johnson Creek Bridge is found in a remote area and is closed to traffic. The stream has difficult access and the area is heavily vegetated, preventing easy visual access in the summer months.

DIRECTIONS: From Mount Olivet, east on US 62, one mile, right on SR 616 one and one-half mile, left on Ogden Ridge Road, three miles, right on SR 1029, one-half mile, on left. (Donovan, 1980; Kentucky Transportation Cabinet)

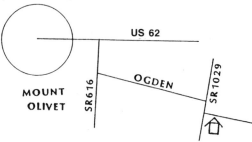

Mooresville Bridge

Mooresville Bridge spans Little Beech Fork, which is a tributary of Beech Fork. Beech Fork delineates a portion of the northwest boundary of Washington County. Their confluence is one and one-half miles northwest of the bridge site.

Built in 1876 by Henry Cornelius Barnes of Mt. Washington, Kentucky, the two span structure is supported by abutments and one pier constructed of cut stone and mortar. Mooresville Bridge is now the longest covered bridge left in Kentucky with 226 feet.

The bridge exhibits a camber that is most apparent over the pier. The roof is covered with brown galvanized tin. The siding is naturally weathered planking, but many pieces are missing. The interior has a multiple kingpost truss and a single Burr arch over each span, so that there are two sets of single arches. The floor has crosswise planking interfaced with lengthwise planking that occupies the center two-thirds of the floor space. The entrances have at one time, been blacktopped, Unfortunately, the interior has experienced much graffiti.

Mooresville Bridge was bypassed in 1982. Today, the structure sits a comfortable distance from the new bridge, but the bridge site is not maintained. The bridge appears as if it has been bypassed and forgotten.

Access to the stream is extremely difficult.

DIRECTIONS: From the Blue Grass Parkway, south on SR 555, two miles, right on SR 1796, four miles, left on SR 458, two miles, on right. (Donovan, 1980; Kentucky Transportation Cabinet; "Kentucky's Covered Bridges")

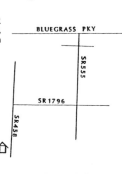

Maine

Being a mid-westerner, the Northeastern states fascinated me. Maine was no exception. Hills, mountains, lakes, rivers, and swamps were all spectacular. The rocky coastline is as beautiful as it is reported to be. Maine is definitely an interesting state to search for its covered bridges. At one time there were over 120 known covered bridges in Maine (Allen, 1957, p. 33). Today, Maine only has eight survivors. One was lost in a spring flood in 1987 (name unknown) and another was burned by arson in 1983. The burned bridge was a 236-foot Howe truss located in Bangor, the Morse Bridge (19-10-01). Of Maine's eight remaining bridges, there are four truss designs represented: queenpost, Howe, Long, and the geographically isolated Paddleford truss.

Finding the covered bridges in Maine can present quite a challenge. For example, after driving a considerable distance through, at times, torrential rains; (March 1987) and roads with water standing up to 10 inches from the melting snows, we finally located the road where the Hemlock Bridge (19-09-02) was located. However, the road was not serviced all winter and there was still 20″ of snow, making it impassable. Thus, we were not able to view this bridge.

The maps and text provided in the text are to be used in conjunction with a local map or one obtained from the State of Maine (see chapter on "How to Find Covered Bridges and Obtain County Maps").

We were fortunate though to be able to see three excellent examples of Maine's Paddleford truss covered bridges and they have been included in the book.

Maine's covered bridges are extremely interesting as well as the diverse landscape offered by the state. This is not a state that will disappoint bridgers. (Ewing, 1987; Burbank; Donovan, 1980)

ACKNOWLEDGMENTS

I would like to express my appreciation to Abigail Ewing, Curator at Bangor Historical Society for her time and information.

BRIDGE NAME	COUNTY	NUMBER
Lovejoy	Oxford	19-09-01
Sunday River	Oxford	19-09-04
Portor/Parsonfield	York	19-16-01
	Oxford	19-09-05

Lovejoy Bridge

Lovejoy Bridge spans Ellis River, which has an average bed width of 80 feet at the bridge site.

Built in 1867, this is the shortest covered bridge in Maine and is 80 feet long. The exterior has weathered plank siding with batten, a shake roof, and portals trimmed in red. The single span sits on cut stone abutments without mortar. Lovejoy Bridge has one of an estimated 21 Paddleford trusses still in existence today. The floor has crosswise planking with two lengthwise runners. The bridge is open and continues to serve traffic. It is easy to get to the creek and the banks are mostly free from vegetation.

DIRECTIONS: Andover Township. From Andover south on SR 5, three miles, left, one-tenth of a mile. (Burbank; Donovan, 1980; State of Maine)

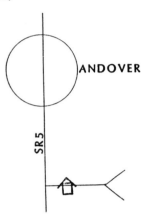

Sunday River Bridge

Sunday River Bridge spans the Sunday River with 100 feet.

The 1870 structure has weathered plank siding only on the lower half, which exposes the top half of the truss. The roof is shake and has eaves that extend two feet beyond the sides. A single span, the bridge rests on cut stone abutments. The interior has lengthwise floor planking and a rare Paddleford truss, found only in the far northeastern United States.

The stream banks have easy access and the bridge has been bypassed.

DIRECTIONS: Newry Township. From North Bethel on US 2, north off US 2, three and one-half miles. (Burbank, Donovan, 1980; State of Maine)

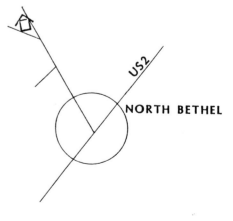

Oxford County
19-09-05

York County
19-16-01

Portor/Parsonfield Bridge

The Portor/Parsonfield Bridge assumed its names from the two towns that built the bridge. This bridge shares its residence with Portor Township in Oxford County and Parsonfield Township in York County. The Porter Bridge spans the Ossipee River with 160 feet, which ties it for Maine's longest covered bridge with the Watson Bridge (19-02-01) in Aroostook County.

Porter Bridge was built in 1858, and is now bypassed. The new bridge is a comfortable distance away and in no way obscures the Porter Bridge setting. The exterior has multicolored plank siding from several repair jobs. There is a three-foot tall ventilation panel that extends the full length of the bridge on both sides. It is open right under the eaves. The two span structure rests on cut stone abutments and a cut stone pier. The interior is particularly fascinating. The Paddleford truss has a 21-ply laminated arch over each of the two spans. The floor is exceptional and the only one of its kind known to this author. It is rectangular 12″ X 24″ slabs of asphalt 2″ thick, cemented into place.

Bypassed, there is a parklike area on one side of the bridge. The bridge is conveniently viewed from the new, adjacent bridge.

DIRECTIONS: Porter Township in Oxford County. From Porter on SR 25, south on SR 160, one-fourth mile. (Burbank; Donovan, 1980; State of Maine)

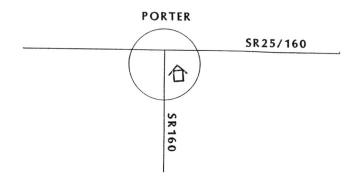

The flooring in this bridge is a unique asphalt tile.

Maryland

ACKNOWLEDGMENTS

To the following people of Maryland, thank you for your information, time and generous materials:
Margaret Shank, Librarian
Harford County Library, Bel Air Branch
William G. Willman, Research Correspondent
The Historical Society of Frederick County, Inc.
Cathy Hurley, Information Services Librarian
Cecil County Public Library
Kathryn J. Flynn, Reference Librarian
Frederick County Public Libraries

INTRODUCTION

Maryland had 52 covered bridges at one time. Today only six of these bridges remain. All are easily accessible except for Foxcatcher Farms Bridge (20-07-02) which is private. Five of the bridges have a multiple kingpost truss. Four of them have a Burr arch. One bridge, Roddy Road (20-10-02) has a kingpost truss.

Maryland's five covered bridges that are publicly owned are well maintained by the state, counties and local historical societies.

Locating Maryland's covered bridges is easy. The directions provided in the text are to be used with the county maps available from the state. (Please see the chapter on "How to Find Covered Bridges and Obtain County Maps")

Although Maryland has only been able to retain 5 bridges, they are not a disappointment. Maryland has incredible scenery, and the stonework found on houses, fences, foundations and bridges is spectacular. The state of Maryland has much to offer bridgers. (Donovan, 1980; Frederick County Parks and Recreation; Maryland Department of Transportation)

BRIDGE NAME	COUNTY	NUMBER
Jericho	Baltimore	20-03-02
	Harford	20-12-01
Gilpin's Falls	Cecil	20-07-01
Utica Mills	Frederick	20-10-01
Roddy Road	Frederick	20-10-02
Loy's Station	Frederick	20-10-03

Baltimore County
20-03-02

Harford County
20-12-01

Jericho Bridge

Jericho Bridge spans Little Gunpowder Falls Creek with 88 feet and connects Baltimore and Harford Counties. Thomas F. Forsyth, a machinist from Baltimore City, built Jericho Bridge in 1865 for $3,125.

Jericho Bridge was closed in 1980 because it was unsafe. In 1981, restoration was begun by the state of Maryland, Baltimore and Harford Counties. The bridge's structure was strengthened, a new floor was installed, the stone-abutments and approaches were repaired and the bridge was painted.

Today, Jericho Bridge is open and serving traffic. The floor of the bridge is 2″ X 4″ boards on edge and is independently supported by a structural steel framework. The shake roof, brown plank siding and multiple kingpost truss encased by a Burr arch are self supporting. The stone abutments laid in mortar are excellent examples of masonry.

Jericho Bridge has an impressive setting and easy access to the creek. One reason the area surrounding Jericho Bridge is so appealing is Little Gunpowder Falls Creek had a number of mills years ago. A flour mill was in Jerusalem. Cotton mills were in both Jericho and Franklinville. Franklinville also had a spade factory and an iron works. The local residents have saved the buildings and are preserving many of their historic relics.

DIRECTIONS: North on Route 1, right on Jerusalem, three miles, right on Jericho. (Donovan, 1980; Maryland Department of Transportation; United States Department of the Interior)

Photograph by Michael Krekeler

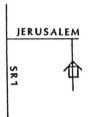

Cecil County
20-07-01

Gilpin's Falls Bridge

Gilpin's Falls Bridge spans Northeast Creek and is 119 feet long.

Built in 1860, Gilpin Bridge was restored in 1959 by the state and the Historical Society of Cecil County. The bridge is located on public land and spans a pool formed by a mill race. The site has been the location of many mills and has the remnants of the mills at the mill race. The earliest mill was a flour mill built by Samuel Gilpins.

Today, the bridge is covered by a shake roof and severely weathered plank siding. The interior has a multiple kingpost truss encased with a double Burr arch. Each arch is composed of two separate beams. The floor has diagonal planking. The bridge has suffered vandalism, with graffiti and much of the siding knocked out.

Gilpin's Bridge is bypassed. The site has a small park around the bridge.

DIRECTIONS: From I-95, north on SR 272, one mile. (Donovan, 1980; Maryland Historical Society; Maryland Department of Transportation)

Utica Mills Bridge

Utica Mills spans Fishing Creek with 100 feet. Originally spanning Monocacy Creek, the Utica Mills Bridge was damaged during the 1889 flood and only half of the bridge survived. It was carried by wagon to its current location at Utica and rebuilt.

Built in 1850, the structure is supported by concrete abutments and one concrete pier. The bridge is covered with red lap siding and a corrugated tin roof. The truss is a multiple kingpost encased with a double Burr arch. The configuration of the multiple kingpost truss is unusual in that the diagonal members are wedged into the vertical members. The floor has crosswise planking.

Open to traffic, the bridge site offers easy access to the creek.

DIRECTIONS: At Utica, three miles northeast of Walkersville, two miles east of US 15 on Utica Road. (Donovan, 1980; Frederick County Parks and Recreation; Maryland Department of Transportation)

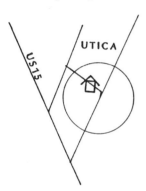

Roddy Road Covered Bridge

Roddy Road Bridge spans Owen Creek with 40 feet, the shortest covered bridge left in Maryland.

Built in 1850, the structure has a steel structure under the bridge. The single span is supported by stone abutments with mortar. The stone abutments are very colorful, using all kinds of stones. The bridge is covered with red lap siding and a gray tin roof. The truss is a kingpost and the floor has crosswise planking.

The site offers excellent access to the creek.

DIRECTIONS: From Thurmont, north on Roddy Road one mile, east of US 15. (Donovan, 1980; Frederick County Parks and Recreation; Maryland Department of Transportation)

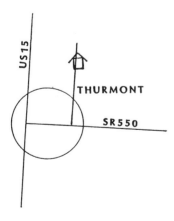

Loy's Station Bridge

Loy's Station Bridge is a double span structure crossing Owen Creek. Named after the nearby train stop, Loy's Station Bridge is 90 feet long.

Built in 1880, the bridge is covered with red lap siding and a gray tin roof. The structure rests on cut stone abutments with mortar and one concrete pier. The multiple kingpost truss has its diagonal members wedged into its vertical members. The floor has crosswise planking.

Open for traffic and preserved in a park, the bridge site offers easy access to the creek.

DIRECTIONS: From Thurmont, east on SR 77, three miles, right on Frederick Road, one-fourth mile. (Donovan, 1980; Maryland Department of Transportation)

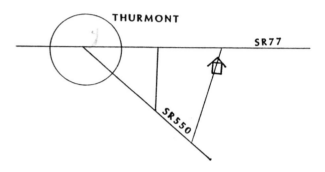

Massachusetts

I would like to thank the following people of Massachusetts for their information, suggestions and materials:

Alice P. Crawford, Curator, Historical Society of Greenfield

Clifton F. Giles, Jr., Library Director, Greenfield Public Library

Ruth T. Dagenhardt, Department Head, Local History and Literature Services, Pittsfield's Public Library

INTRODUCTION

At one time Massachusetts had over 100 covered bridges. Today only five of the historic structures remain. Massachusetts is referred to as "The cradle of covered bridge building in America." (Allen, 1957, p. 64) Massachusetts had its covered bridges built by such famous builders as Timothy Palmer, Ithiel Town, Issac Damon, William Howe, Daniel Harris, Amasa Stone, Jr., Azurich Boody and Richard F. Hawkins. (Allen, 1957, pp. 65-67)

The oldest covered bridge in Massachusetts is the Upper Sheffield Bridge (21-02-01). Built in 1833, it is over 154 years old. Of the five historic structures left, three have Town lattice trusses, one is a Burr arch and one has the most unusual Howe single truss.

Massachusetts also has five modern covered bridges. Two examples have been included in this book, since they were specifically designed for traffic and not for a promotion or decoration. The two are Bissell, (21-06-04) and Lower Sheffield (21-02-02). Each of these bridges replaced a deteriorated covered bridge. These two new bridges were built because of local demand.

Locating covered bridges in Massachusetts is not difficult. Directions and maps provided with the text are to be used in conjunction with the regional maps available from the state of Massachusetts. (See the chapter on "How to Find Covered Bridges and Obtain County Maps".)

Although Massachusetts has not been able to preserve a great number of its covered bridges, the few that have been preserved offer unusual and rare trusses as well as extremely picturesque locations.

BRIDGE NAME	COUNTY	NUMBER
Upper Sheffield	Berkshire	21-02-01
Lower Sheffield	"	21-02-02
Burkville	Franklin	21-06-01
Arthur Smith	"	21-06-03
Bissell	"	21-06-04

Upper Sheffield Bridge

Upper Sheffield Bridge spans the Housatonic River in southern Berkshire County. The Housatonic River is a major drainage channel for western Massachusetts.

At the time of the photograph, March of 1987, the Upper Sheffield Bridge was only several feet away from the swollen waters of the Housatonic. It was difficult to tell what portion of the river the bridge normally spans as the river was flooded and its banks were obscured.

Upper Sheffield is most famous because it is the oldest covered bridge still existing in the state of Massachusetts, built in 1833. The bridge was closed to traffic in 1974. The local residents and Sheffield Historical Commission raised $25,000 in 1981 to match a grant from Massachusetts Historical Commission. These funds were used to restore the bridge and to raise it to avoid ice floes. Upper Sheffield Bridge was rededicated in October of 1981.

In the summer of 1986, the U.S. Army Corps of Engineers started a project to stabilize the banks of the Housatonic River at the bridge site. The project consisted of repairing the abutments and dumping huge boulders into holes in the river bed that the swift waters had displaced. Also, the stabilizing of the banks would prevent the bridge from eventual collapse. The project was still under construction as of the spring of 1987. The town of Sheffield provided $180,000 toward the $430,000 project. Sheffield obtained the funds from a grant through the Department of Public Works of the state of Massachusetts. The balance of the funds was provided by a federal program, The Emergency Streambank Protection Program.

Built in 1833, the 91-foot structure rests on concrete abutments. The exterior has naturally weathered plank siding and a shake roof. The interior has a Town lattice truss and crosswise floor planking.

Every effort is being made to save this bridge. The local residents and Sheffield Historical Commission should be pleased with their accomplishment.

DIRECTIONS: Sheffield Township. At Sheffield. East of US 7 on Covered Bridge Lane. (Commonwealth of Massachusetts: Donovan, 1980; "One Hundred Turn Out In Sheffield for Bridge Rededication"; "Saving Sheffield's Kissing Bridge"; "Town Cost Delays Work on Riverbank"; "Work on Covered Bridge Should Start This Summer")

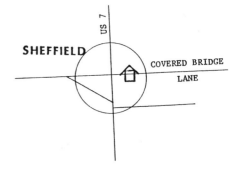

SHEFFIELD

US 7

COVERED BRIDGE
LANE

Berkshire County
21-02-02

Lower Sheffield Bridge

The 135 foot Lower Sheffield Bridge also spans the Housatonic River about one and one-quarter miles south of the Upper Sheffield Bridge (21-02-01).

Lower Sheffield does not have the historical aspect that Upper Sheffield does because it was built in 1952. Lower Sheffield was built to replace a covered bridge that decayed beyond repair. The new bridge cost $250,000. It was designed by the engineers of the Timber Engineering Company of Washington, D.C.

Lower Sheffield was closed in March of 1987 and it is not known whether it will be reopened. The bridge rests on stone abutments and each approach has a wooden ramp. The two features that make Lower Sheffield especially unique are its two-lanes and its all-wood Pratt truss. The bridge is big, not only wide, but tall. The exterior has red plank siding, a shake roof, eight large square windows on each side and a full length ventilation opening. The interior is excessively large; huge beams were used in the Pratt truss, and the floor is 4″ by 8″ planks on edge and blacktopped.

Access to the river is easy but the banks are so thick with foliage that the bridge is obscured. This bridge might be considered a new bridge by today's standards, but if preserved, 100 years from now it would be a real treasure.

DIRECTIONS: Sheffield Township. In Sheffield, east on US 7 on Maple Avenue. (Allen, 1957; Commonwealth of Massachusetts, Donovan, 1980).

Franklin County
21-06-01

Burkville Bridge

Burkville Bridge spans South River with 110 feet. South River has an average bed width of 70 feet at the bridge site.

Built in 1870, Burkville Bridge has naturally weathered plank siding with six windows on one side. The roof is shake and has been recently repaired. The single span structure rests on concrete abutments.

The truss is the most extraordinary feature about Burkville Bridge. It is a most unusual example of a Howe single truss. One other known to this author is the Bean Blossom Bridge (14-07-01) in Brown County, Indiana. The Howe single resembles a multiple kingpost truss, where all of the vertical beams are replaced by iron rods. The floor has crosswise planking and two lengthwise runners.

Access to the creek is difficult and the creek banks are heavily vegetated.

DIRECTIONS: Conway Township. In Conway, south of SR 116 on Main Poland Road. (Commonwealth of Massachusetts; Donovan, 1980)

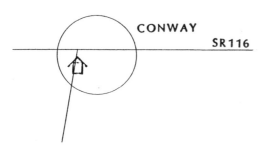

Photograph by Michael Krekeler

Franklin County
21-06-03

Arthur Smith Bridge

Arthur Smith Bridge spans North River in northwestern Massachusetts. Built in 1870, the 100-foot structure has a shake roof and faded red plank siding. Most of the siding is rotten or missing. The single span rests on cut stone abutments. The interior's original truss was a multiple kingpost encased with a double Burr arch. The original arch has since separated in places. An added 11-ply arch was installed. The new arch is attached to the lower chords with iron rods at every vertical beam. The floor has crosswise planking with two lengthwise runners.

The bridge is closed and its future looks dismal. Access to the creek is easy. If the siding were repaired, the bridge would be very attractive because of the beauty of its natural setting.

DIRECTIONS: Colrain Township. South of Colrain in Lyonsville, just west of SR 112. (Commonwealth of Massachusetts; Donovan, 1980)

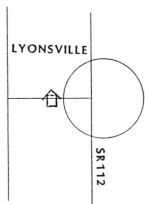
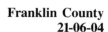

Franklin County
21-06-04

Bissell Bridge

Bissell Bridge spans Mill Brook. The bridge has a beautiful location at an old mill site. The mill itself has disappeared but there is a stone dam that can be seen in the photograph on the right, under the bridge. To the immediate left of the dam, there is a spillway forming an exciting waterfall. From that point, Mill Brook's water rushes down a steep rocky gorge, creating a spectacular series of waterfalls.

The 92 foot Bissell Bridge is a fine example of a modern covered bridge. Built in 1951, the Bissell Bridge will easily accept two lanes of traffic. The bridge is not only excessively wide (24 feet) but it is also extremely tall. The Long truss uses huge treated beams. The truss consists of a double "X" and double vertical beams in each panel. The floor is crosswise planking that has been blacktopped. The single span structure rests on a natural boulder on one end and bedrock and mortar on the other. Bissell Bridge replaced a previous covered bridge that had become decrepit. The new Bissell Bridge uses the same abutment structures as the original covered bridge.

The roof has charcoal gray shingles and is supported by massive roof trusses. The siding is naturally weathered planks. There are five rectangular windows on each side of the bridge. Each window is centered on a vertical beam of the truss. There is also a 12-inch tall ventilation panel that extends the full length of the bridge on both sides.

Access to the creek is difficult but offers a tremendous opportunity for photographers.

DIRECTIONS: Charlemont Township. In Charlemont, north on SR 2 one-fourth mile on Heath Road (SR 8A). (Allen, 1957; Commonwealth of Massachusetts; Donovan, 1980)

Michigan

Michigan has four covered bridges. One is preserved at Greenfield Village in Wayne County and is the oldest covered bridge in Michigan, built in 1832. The other three are still serving traffic at their original locations.

Two are within two miles of each other; the Fallasburg Bridge (22-41-02) and the White's Bridge (22-34-01) in Kent and Ionia Counties, respectively. What is so rare about these two bridges is that they each have a Brown truss and are the only two bridges left in the United States with that distinction. The Brown truss is an unusual design because it has "X" panels similar to that of the Long and Howe truss, but it does not have any vertical beams dividing the panels. The "X" panels in the Fallasburg Bridge (22-41-02) are set at an angle, which makes the design even more unusual.

The remaining bridge, in St. Joseph County, Langley Bridge (22-75-01) is the longest of the four at 282 feet.

Although Michigan has only been able to save four covered bridges, each has very interesting historical attributes.

Traveling through Michigan to see the covered bridges allows one to appreciate what the southern part of the state has to offer. The beautiful scenery consists of lush flat farm lands, hundreds of lakes, and wide, shallow rivers, abundant with fish. The bridger will only find four covered bridges in Michigan, but this state provides a beautiful landscape to bridge!

BRIDGE NAME	COUNTY	NUMBER
White's	Ionia	22-34-01
Fallasburg	Kent	22-41-02
Langley	St. Joseph	22-75-01
Ackley	Wayne	22-82-01

Photograph by Michael Krekeler

White's Bridge

Spanning Flat River with 116 feet, White's Bridge was built in 1867 by Jared N. Bresse, and J. N. Walker for $1,700. The bridge was named after a pioneer family.

Supported with cut stone and mortar abutments, White's Bridge is protected by naturally weathered, dark plank siding and a tin roof. The interior has the rare Brown truss. There are only two known to exist. The other is found two miles northeast, Fallasburg Bridge (22-41-02).

Access to the stream is easy and the bridge is open to traffic. The bridge site has a picturesque location.

DIRECTIONS: Keene Township. From Smyrna, southwest on White's Bridge Road, three miles. (Donovan, 1980; Michigan County Maps; Michigan Department of Transportation)

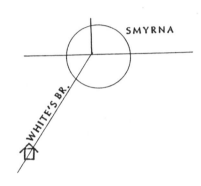

Fallasburg Bridge

Fallasburg Bridge spans Flat River with 100 feet. Flat River is so named because the stream is wide but shallow. Built in 1871 by Jared N. Bresse, the bridge cost $1,500.

Concrete abutments support the single span. Covered with naturally weathered, dark plank siding and a rusted tin roof, the truss is the Brown design. One of only two known Brown trusses in existence, this one is unusual because the "X" bracing is set on an angle. The other Brown is found two miles northeast of this bridge site, in Ionia County, White's Bridge (22-34-01). The floor has crosswise planking.

There is a park area at the bridge site that provides easy visual access of the bridge. Open to traffic, Fallasburg Bridge presents an attractive sight.

DIRECTIONS: Vergennes Township. From Lowell, Lincoln Lake Road north, two miles, right on Covered Bridge Road, one and one-fourth miles. (Donovan, 1980; Michigan County Maps; Michigan Department of Transportation)

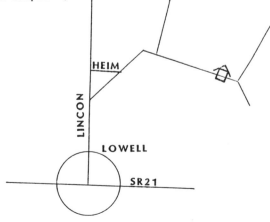

St. Joseph County
22-75-01

Langley Bridge

Langley Bridge, named after a local pioneer family, spans Sturgis Lake, which is part of the St. Joseph River. With 282 feet, Langley Bridge is the longest of the four remaining covered bridges in Michigan.

Langley Bridge was built in 1887 by Pierce Bodner. Sturgis Lake Dam was constructed in 1910. At that time, Langley Bridge had to be raised eight feet to accommodate the lake's level. In 1950-51, the St. Joseph County Road Commission restored the Langley Bridge with major repairs. Today, the three span structure is supported by concrete and steel abutments and piers. Protected by red plank siding and a tin roof, the structure has a Howe truss and lengthwise floor planking that has been blacktopped. There is one 20-foot long, 3-foot tall window at one end of the bridge.

Langley Bridge has a most attractive site as it stands only four feet over the lake. The bridge has a high visibility from many angles around the lake.

DIRECTIONS: Lockport and Nottawa Townships. From Centreville, north three miles on Covered Bridge Road. (Donovan, 1980; Michigan County Maps; Michigan Department of Transportation)

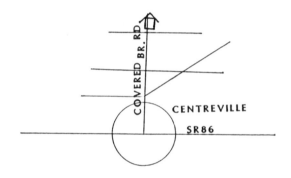

**Wayne County
22-82-01**

Ackley Bridge

Presently spanning a pond, Ackley Bridge was moved into Henry Ford's Greenfield Village in 1937. Greenfield Village has preserved over 100 historic buildings and has them available for the public to inspect.

The 75-foot structure, built in 1832, is one of the oldest covered bridges in the United States. The exterior is covered with naturally weathered, lap siding and has a shake roof. The interior of the Ackley Bridge is its most fascinating characteristic. The truss is constructed with one huge single kingpost. The massive timber members of the truss were hand hewn and display the etching of the builder's adze. The floor has crosswise planking.

The bridge site is extremely attractive. Ackley Bridge spans a pond and rests on cut stone with mortar abutments. Greenfield Village is an exciting place to visit. Among their historic structures, you will find a windmill, an antique merry-go-round, saw mills, Henry Ford's workshop, Edison's workshop, an old machine shop, a printing shop and dozens of other fascinating buildings that house historic aspects of our country's development.

DIRECTIONS: Dearborn Township. At Greenfield Village, just south of US 12. (Donovan, 1980; Michigan County Maps; Michigan Department of Transportation)

New Hampshire

At one time, there were over 200 bridges in New Hampshire (Allen, 1957, p. 40). Today, 50 of these historic structures remain. Saving and preserving twenty-five percent of New Hampshire's covered bridges is quite an accomplishment in light of the fact that most states have retained less than ten percent of their original number.

The 50 covered bridges present a myriad of characteristics unique to New Hampshire.

VARIETY OF TRUSS DESIGNS

Seven of the eighteen known designs that still exist in America are represented in New Hampshire. The Town lattice truss has the most representatives, with 19 examples, two of which have an arch. The rare Paddleford truss is exhibited in 14 bridges, the most in any one state, and more than half of the total Paddlefords in existence. The other Paddleford trusses in existence are three in Vermont and four or five in Maine. Only two of New Hampshire's Paddleford trusses have a pure Paddleford. The other 12 have added arches.

The remaining 17 bridges are represented as follows: Long-5 (three have an added arch), queenpost-4, multiple kingpost-4, Howe-3, and one king and queenpost combination.

CHARACTERISTICS OF NEW HAMPSHIRE'S COVERED BRIDGES

One of the most striking features about New Hampshire's covered bridges is the stone work. Most of the original abutments and piers have been laid with huge cut stones or with bedrock. What characterizes much of the stonework is that it does not have any mortar. Stone abutments without mortar are called dry stone. One of the more impressive features of the dry stone masonry is the abutments and piers constructed out of dry stone are in good repair over 100 years later. The longevity of the dry stone abutments and piers is a

credit to the stone masons. Dry stone masonry also creates an awareness of the days when the bridges were built. In the mid-1800s, most of the time mortar was not available and if it was, it was very expensive. Another reason the eastern states exhibit dry stone more than the mid-west is because the eastern state's covered bridges are generally older and the technology at the time of construction did not incorporate the use of mortar.

A characteristic that makes each bridge in New Hampshire unique is the sense of community pride, evident by the efforts to preserve and maintain each covered bridge. Well-maintained parks surrounding the bypassed bridges, convenient parking, fresh paint and repaired siding are all indicative of the preservation climate. Milton Graton, a well-known covered bridge expert, and his son, Arnold, have repaired and restored many of New Hampshire's bridges. His work has influenced the conservation of New Hampshire's covered bridges presently as well as for the future.

RARE AND UNUSUAL BRIDGES

New Hampshire's covered bridges have a wealth of variety.

The longest covered bridge in the United States is still in service and is shared with the state of Vermont. Cornish/Windsor Bridge (29-10-09) is 460 feet long and spans the Connecticut River connecting Windsor, Vermont and Cornish, New Hampshire.

The longest covered bridge completely in New Hampshire is the Bath Bridge (29-05-03) in Grafton County, with 400 feet spanning the Ammonoosuc River and the B&M Railroad tracks. Bath Bridge is constructed with the rare Paddleford truss and has multiple arches.

The oldest known covered bridge is the 257-foot Bath/Haverhill Bridge (29-05-04). With a Town lattice truss, the bridge was built in 1827, making it over 160 years old. There are quite possibly older covered bridges in New Hampshire but, unfortunately, no date of construction can be confirmed.

New Hampshire has an excellent collection of village-style bridges; those that have external walkways. The best example of a village-style bridge is the Upper Village Bridge (29-03-02) in Cheshire County. This bridge has two walkways, a Town truss, and is painted white with red trim; a spectacular bridge. The Saco River Bridge (29-02-03) in Carroll County is 225 feet long and also has two external walkways but the bridge is closed, in poor condition, and the walkways are dangerously unsafe. Stark Bridge (29-04-05) in Coos County also has two walkways.

West Swanzey Bridge (29-03-04) and Honeymoon Bridge (29-02-01), each have one external walkway. There are many other bridges in New Hampshire that had external walkways but they have since disappeared. Rowell's Bridge (29-07-08) in Merrimack County, is a good example of a bridge that once had two walkways.

Another feature offered by New Hampshire covered bridges is the existence of four remaining railroad covered bridges. All were built between 1889 and 1903. Three have a Town truss and one is a Howe.

Unfortunately, the 91 year old, 180-foot Sulphite Railroad Bridge (29-07-09), built with a Pratt truss, was burned by arson in 1981. Charcoaled beams are all that remain. What is so terribly unfortunate about the loss of this bridge is that it was singularly unique; there is not another bridge even similar to it. The railroad track ran on top of the bridge instead of through it.

The preserved, 219-foot Hillsboro Railroad Bridge was also burned by arson. In 1985, the 1903, Town truss railroad bridge was destroyed. Hillsboro Bridge (29-06-01) was listed on the National Register of Historic Places.

The good news is, of the railroad bridges left in New Hampshire, one is preserved. It is located in Grafton County at Clark's Trading Post, called the Clark's Railroad Bridge (29-05-14).

The remaining three railroad bridges have not been preserved. One, the Contoocook Railroad Bridge (29-07-07) is private, used for storage, and is not easily accessible. Pier Railroad Bridge (29-10-03) and Wright Railroad Bridge (29-10-04) are located in Sullivan County, and are abandoned. The tracks have been pulled out. Much of the shake is missing, allowing water in to destroy the truss. These two bridges are structurally sound and demand to be preserved. Hopefully, some action will be taken before it is too late.

There are only six railroad covered bridges left in the United States today. There are two in Vermont and four left in New Hampshire. Because they are so rare, the few remaining should be saved and preserved.

The railroad covered bridge differs from the traditional covered bridges because they are immense. They can exceed 30 feet in height and 20 feet in width. The timbers in the trusses are massive. The presence of a railroad bridge is awesome and a part of our heritage that should not disappear.

The railroad bridges included in this text for New Hampshire are the remains of the Sulphite (29-07-09), Clark's (29-05-14), Contoocook (29-07-07), Pier (29-10-03) and Wright (29-10-04).

NEW HAMPSHIRE SUMMARY

New Hampshire offers a wide variety of covered bridges, from the southernmost counties of Cheshire with its Town trusses, to northern Coos County with its Paddleford trusses. The bridges are so diverse as to include the longest bridge in America, village style bridges, railroad bridges and fine traditional bridges.

New Hampshire's landscape is as diverse as the covered bridges. Beautiful alpine glaciated mountains, part of the White Mountains, are gorgeous to view. The rocky mountain streams and rivers are fabulous. The winter season offers skiing and snow mobiling. The summer offers fishing, hiking, rafting and lush, beautiful scenery.

Every season has its special attributes. One such example is the experience we had in late March, 1987. While we were bridging, we would often end up on dirt roads. Because it was spring, the snows were melting and the frozen ground was thawing. Consequently, the dirt roads were mud, thick viscous mud that oozed up around the tires, causing the car to slip and slide as if on ice. Although my husband found this experience quite exciting, I did not appreciate it too much, especially since many of the roads followed the edge of a cliff or ravine that dropped into a river!

We were soon to discover that we were visiting Vermont and New Hampshire during "Mud Season." Early spring is when the sap from the maple trees comes in and large trucks carrying huge vats of maple sap travel the mud roads as they collect the sap. As the trucks drive the mud roads, they squeeze the mud and form ditches with their tires. After collecting the sap, it is cooked down to a syrup in ''sugaring houses,'' and this process is called ''sugaring.'' Driving through the countryside we saw dozens of small, barn-like structures with a chimney on the roof, venting steam from the sugaring process. All in all, ''mud season'' was very interesting.

New Hampshire offers a myriad of activities all year long for the bridger to appreciate. Just be wary of the wintertime because the snows can prevent access to many of the covered bridges.

The actual locating of New Hampshire covered bridges can sometimes present a challenge. The maps and directions included with the text are to be used in conjunction with the maps available from the state of New Hampshire (please see the chapter on ''How to Find Covered Bridges and Obtain County Maps''). Even with my directions, maps of the county, and possibly a second backup map, you still might have some difficulty. Most of the bridges are not difficult to find; however, there are always some guaranteed to get you lost. Make sure you have a compass.

Sometimes the roads are not labeled, sometimes there are roads in reality, but not on the map, and other times there are roads on the map that are not in existence. You will soon develop a sense of how to locate covered bridges in New Hampshire, once you become familiar with the landscape, the road system, and the philosophy of just where New Hampshire hides its covered bridges. You will soon discover the covered bridges New Hampshire has to offer are well worth the effort.

ACKNOWLEDGMENTS

To the following people of New Hampshire, I extend my appreciation for the time, efforts and excellent resources that they supplied:

Ann Pierce, Acting Assistant Librarian, Plymouth Public Library

Thomas G. Allen, Hillsborough Historical Society

Alan F. Rumrill, Historical Society of Cheshire County

Debra J. Thompson, Head Librarian, Hillsborough County Law Library

William Copeley, Associate Librarian, New Hampshire Historical Society

Ann M. Cullinan, Henney History Room, Conway Public Library

BRIDGE NAME	COUNTY	NUMBER
Honeymoon	Carroll	29-02-01
Bartlett	"	29-02-02
Saco River	"	29-02-03
Swift River	"	29-02-05
Albany	"	29-02-06
Durgin	"	29-02-07
Whittier	"	29-02-08
Upper Village/Ashuelot	Cheshire	29-03-02
Coombs	"	29-03-03
West Swanzey/Thompson	"	29-03-04
Sawyers Crossing/Whitcomb/Cresson	"	29-03-05
Slate	"	29-03-06
Carlton	"	29-03-07
Swiftwater	Grafton	29-05-02
Bath	"	29-05-03
Bath/Haverhill	"	29-05-04
Bump	"	29-05-08
Blair	"	29-05-09
Smith	"	29-05-10

BRIDGE NAME	COUNTY	NUMBER
Edgell	Grafton	29-05-11
Clark's Railroad	"	29-05-14
Cilleyville/Bog	Merrimack	29-07-01
Keniston	Merrimack	29-07-02
Bement	"	29-07-03
Waterloo Station	"	29-07-04
Dalton	"	29-07-05
Contoocook Railroad	"	29-07-07
Rowell's	"	29-07-08
Sulphite Railroad	"	29-07-09
Blacksmith Shop	Sullivan	29-10-01
Dingleton	"	29-10-02
Pier Railroad/Chandler Sta.	"	29-10-03
Wright Railroad	"	29-10-04
Corbin	"	29-10-05
Meriden/Mill	"	29-10-08
Cornish/Windsor	Sullivan, NH	29-10-09
	Windsor, VT	45-14-14

Honeymoon Bridge

Honeymoon Bridge spans Ellis River with 138 feet. This bridge is sometimes called the Jackson Bridge because it is located in the village of Jackson.

Carroll County is a novelty for the covered bridge enthusiast. With seven covered bridges, Carroll County displays only one type of truss. This phenomena is not unusual throughout the U.S. because each county is usually uniform in the types of trusses used. The Paddleford truss is used in the construction of each of the seven covered bridges in Carroll County and none of them are a disappointment. This is particularly unique because there are only 22 Paddleford trusses left and this truss can only be found in Vermont, New Hampshire and Maine.

Carroll County's Honeymoon Bridge was built in 1876 by an engineer of the Maine Central Railroad. The single span rests on huge cut stone abutments. The courses of the stone have been laid up without any mortar, which displays the skill of yesterday's craftsmen.

Honeymoon Bridge was widened and reinforced in 1939. Route 16, which had passed near the west portal, has now been rerouted about 50 yards west. The old road still passes directly in front of the portal, allowing easy access and parking to enjoy the bridge.

Today the exterior of the Honeymoon Bridge has natural weathered plank siding with a three-foot tall window that extends the full length of the bridge on both sides, exposing the Paddleford truss. The portals are painted red and trimmed in white. The roof is green corrugated tin. The bridge also has a walkway on one side that is under the roof.

The interior of the bridge is spectacular with the Paddleford truss and a 12-ply arch added on each truss. The floor has lengthwise planking.

The bridge's unique design, the rocky stream site and the excellent condition of the bridge make Honeymoon Bridge a choice selection of New Hampshire's covered bridges.

DIRECTIONS: Jackson Township. Off of Route 16 at 16A in Jackson Village. (Donovan, 1980; New Hampshire Department of Public Works and Highways; New Hampshire Department of Resources and Economic Development)

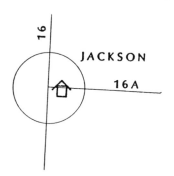

Photograph by Michael Krekeler

This photo shows an external walkway and a dry cut stone abutment.

Bartlett Bridge

Bartlett Bridge spans the Saco River with 183 feet. The single span structure rests on cut stone abutments laid without mortar. The bridge was abandoned in 1939. In 1966, Milton Graton repaired Bartlett Bridge. The bridge is now privately owned and houses a gift shop.

The exterior has plank siding on the bottom third of the sides, exposing the upper two-thirds of the Paddleford truss and the added 12-ply arch.

The bridge is sagging and needs repair. The river has difficult access but the bridge can be viewed from the adjacent concrete bridge.

DIRECTIONS: Bartlett Township. From Bartlett, four miles east on 302. (Donovan, 1980; New Hampshire Department of Public Works and Highways; New Hampshire Department of Resources and Economic Development)

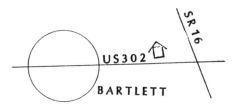

Saco River Bridge

The double-span Saco River Bridge is 225 feet long. Saco River Bridge was built in 1890 by Charles Broughton and his son, Frank for $4,000. This bridge is the third bridge built at this location.

The abutments and one pier are cut stone and mortar. Corrugated tin siding covers the lower third of the sides, exposing the upper two-thirds of the Paddleford truss and two sets of Burr arches, one over each span. The roof is also corrugated tin. All of the tin, siding and roof, is painted orange.

The bridge has two external sidewalks under the roof. The floor is lengthwise planking that had at one time been blacktopped, but has since had most of it worn away. The external walkways are not safe. The entire bridge needs repair if it is to be preserved. Presently, the bridge is owned by the state and is closed.

Access to the river is easy and the bridge, although orange with peeling paint, is impressive as it looms over the Saco River.

DIRECTIONS: Conway Township. At Conway, just west of SR 16. (Donovan, 1980; New Hampshire Department of Public Works and Highways; New Hampshire Department of Resources and Economic Development)

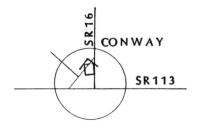

Carroll County
29-02-05

Swift River Bridge

Swift River Bridge was built in 1869 by Jacob Berry and his son, Jacob Jr. The first bridge at this site was built in 1850 by John Douglas, which was destroyed by a flood in 1869.

The 144-foot single span rests on cut stone abutments without mortar. Steel supports have been installed in front of the abutments for additional support. The exterior has red plank siding with a three foot tall window that extends the full length of the bridge on both sides, exposing the Paddleford truss and added 19-ply massive arches. The roof is green corrugated tin. The floor is 2″ X 4″ boards on edge.

From the Swift River Bridge, if you look east you can see the Saco River Bridge (29-02-03). Access to the creek is difficult. Swift River Bridge has been bypassed and is well-maintained by the town of Conway.

DIRECTIONS: Conway Township. At Conway, north of SR 116 on Passaconway Road.
(Donovan, 1980; New Hampshire Department of Public Works and Highways; New Hampshire Department of Resources and Economic Development)

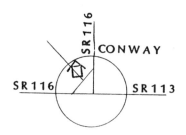

Carroll County
29-02-06

Albany Bridge

Albany Bridge spans Swift River with 129 feet. Amzi Rossell and Leander Morton built the bridge for $1,300. The bridge was blown down before it was completed in 1857 and was not finished until 1858.

The single span is supported by cut stone abutments without mortar. Steel beams were placed under the bridge in 1971-72 by the White Mountain National Forest Service. Plank siding covers the bridge. There are rectangular windows the entire length of the bridge on both sides. The roof is red corrugated tin. The Paddleford truss also has added multi-ply Burr arches. The floor is lengthwise planking. The bridge is open and serves visitors to the Park.

Located in the White Mountain National Forest over the rocky Swift River, the Albany Bridge presents an impressive form against the mountains.

DIRECTIONS: Albany Township. From Conway, six miles west on SR 112, on the right.
(Donovan, 1980; New Hampshire Department of Public Works and Highways New Hampshire Department of Resources and Economic Development)

Photograph by Michael Krekeler

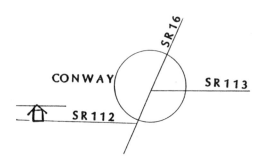

Durgin Bridge

Durgin Bridge spans Cold River with 120 feet. The bridge is named after James Holmes Durgin (1815-1873). Durgin operated a grist mill near the bridge site, drove the stagecoach from Sandwich to Farmington and was a link in the underground slave railroad from Sandwich to Conway.

Built in 1869 by Jacob Berry of North Conway, this is the fourth bridge at this location. The first three were destroyed by floods in 1844, 1865 and 1869.

Milton Graton and his son, Arnold, have worked on Durgin Bridge. Today, Durgin Bridge has black plank siding, a red, flat tin roof and rests on concrete abutments. The interior has the unique Carroll County characteristic Paddleford truss, with arches that were added in 1957. The floor has lengthwise planking with two thick lengthwise runners.

Access to the creek is easy.

DIRECTIONS: Sandwich Township. From North Sandwich, north on 113A, one mile, right on Fellows Hill, one and one-half miles. (Donovan, 1980; New Hampshire Department of Public Works and Highways; New Hampshire Department of Resources and Economic Development)

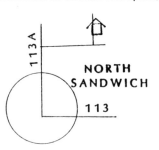

Whittier Bridge

Whittier Bridge spans Bearcamp River. The 144-foot structure was built in 1870 by Jacob Barry.

The exterior has naturally weathered plank siding that covers the lower third of the bridge, exposing the upper two-thirds of the Paddleford truss. The roof is shake. The Paddleford truss has an added, multi-ply Burr arch. The floor has crosswise planking. Steel tie rods were added in 1958 connecting the arch to the lower chord. Milton Graton completed an $85,000 restoration project on Whittier Bridge in 1983. Monies for this project were supplied by Gordon Pops, a summer resident, and the balance was supplied by the state of New Hampshire.

Whittier Bridge is aesthetically appealing. Located in a picturesque river valley, the structure, with its arches and geometric truss, poses a beautiful setting.

DIRECTIONS: Ossipee Township. In West Ossipee, west of SR 16, north of SR 25. (Donovan, 1980; New Hampshire Department of Public Works and Highways; New Hampshire Department of Resources and Economic Development)

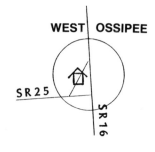

Upper Village/Ashuelot Bridge

The Upper Village Bridge spans the Ashuelot River with 170 feet.

Upper Village Bridge is the best example known to this author of a village style bridge, which is one that has two walkways on the outside of the trusses, under the roof.

The double-span structure was built in 1864 and is described as pure American Gothic Architecture. The abutments are cut stone, faced with concrete ice breakers. The one pier is concrete, possibly encasing cut stone. The roof is orangish-red corrugated tin. The walkways are sided on the lower quarter with the upper three-quarters open. The truss is a Town lattice painted a brilliant white. There is no siding on the bridge but the truss is protected by the extended roof over the walkways. The white Town lattice is attractive not only because it is so well-preserved but because the bridge is not covered with siding and light fills the interior. The portals are also painted white, but the trim is bright red.

Upper Village bridge is in excellent condition and a unique covered bridge because of its double walkways. Access to the creek is easy and the bridge site is appealing, but its portal view is the most impressive. Upper Village bridge is open and serving traffic.

DIRECTIONS: Winchester Township. At Ashuelot, just south of SR 119. (Donovan, 1980; New Hampshire Department of Public Works and Highways; New Hampshire Department of Resources and Economic Development)

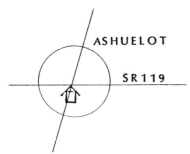

Coombs Bridge

Coombs Bridge is located six miles north of the Upper Village Bridge (29-03-02) over the Ashuelot River. Five of Cheshire County's covered bridges are clustered and span the Ashuelot River. The sixth covered bridge, Carlton (29-03-07), is in the same vicinity but spans the South Branch of Ashuelot River.

Coombs Bridge was built in 1837 and named after its builder. The 118-foot structure has one span and rests on huge cut stone abutments that do not have mortar, which is referred to as dry stone.

Naturally weathered plank siding covers the bridge with an 18-inch full length ventilation panel on both sides of the bridge. One end of the bridge has a 20-foot, 24'' tall window on each side. The roof is tin. The interior has a Town truss and lengthwise flooring. In 1971, the bridge was refurbished at a cost of $13,340. The bridge is maintained by the Winchester Township. Coombs Bridge is open and serving traffic.

DIRECTIONS: Winchester Township. From Westport, south on SR 10, one-half mile, turn right. (Donovan, 1980; New Hampshire Department of Public Works and Highway New Hampshire Department of Resources and Economic Development)

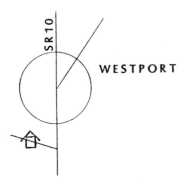

Photograph by Michael Krekeler

West Swanzey/Thompson Bridges

Spanning the Ashuelot River with 159 feet, West Swanzey Bridge was built in 1832 by Zodac Taft for $552.27.

The one hundred and fifty-six year old structure had, at one time, two walkways. Unfortunately, one has disappeared. The bridge has a similar design as the Upper Village Bridge (29-03-02), but has not been as well preserved.

Red plank siding exists on the lower half of the side missing the walkway. The roof is corrugated tin and the portals are bright red trimmed in white.

The double span is supported by cut stone abutments and one pier that was laid with mortar. The remaining exterior walkway is sided on the lower third and has a chain link fence halfway up the side. The interior has a Town lattice truss painted red and a blacktopped floor.

Connecting the two sections of West Swanzey across the Ashuelot River, the bridge has a commercial/residential location which makes photographing the structure difficult. Access to the river is impossible.

DIRECTIONS: Swanzey Township. In West Swanzey, east of SR 10 on Main Street. (Donovan, 1980; New Hampshire Department of Public Works and Highways; New Hampshire Department of Rssources and Economic Development)

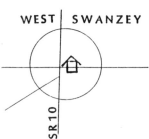

Sawyers Crossing/ Whitcomb/Cresson Bridge

Originally built in 1812, the Sawyers Crossing Bridge was rebuilt in 1859 and spans the Ashuelot River at Sawyers Crossing in Swanzey with 160 feet.

Sawyers Crossing is a two span covered bridge with cut stone abutments laid without mortar and a pier constructed out of cut stone and mortar. Solid, faded red plank siding and a corrugated red tin roof cover the bridge. The interior is built with a Town truss and lengthwise floor planking. The bridge was restored in 1983 at a cost of $45,000; $15,000 of which came from the town of Swanzey and $30,000 came from the state.

Sawyers Crossing Bridge has a distinctively attractive setting. The river banks have easy access and the bridge is still serving traffic.

DIRECTIONS: Swanzey Township. In Swanzey, west of SR 32. (Donovan, 1980; New Hampshire Department of Public Works and Highways; New Hampshire Department of Resources and Economic Development)

Cheshire County
29-03-06

Slate Bridge

Slate Bridge was named after a nearby family. Spanning the Ashuelot River with 145 feet, the Slate Bridge was built in 1862 at a cost of $1,850. This is the second bridge at this site. The first bridge was built in 1800 and collapsed with a team of four oxen upon it, in 1842. I do not know the fate of the oxen.

The single span has naturally weathered plank siding, a shake roof, and red portals trimmed in white. The abutments are dry stone. The interior has a Town truss and an added bowstring suspension with adjustable tie rods for additional structural support. The floor is lengthwise planking.

Access to the river banks is easy. Slate Bridge has an isolated, picturesque location and is still serving traffic.

DIRECTIONS: Swanzey Township. North of Westport Village, south of SR 10. (Donovan, 1980; New Hampshire Department of Public Works and Highways, New Hampshire Department of Resources and Economic Development)

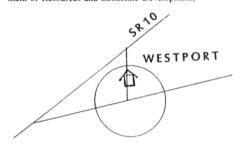

Cheshire County
29-03-07

Carlton Bridge

Spanning the South Branch of Ashuelot River, Carlton Bridge is 69 feet long.

Built in 1869, the single span's exterior is in poor condition. The structure sags in the middle and most of the red plank siding is missing. The rusted corrugated tin roof is all intact. The cut stone abutments, which do not have mortar, are in decrepit condition. The interior was constructed with a queenpost truss. Several of the braces and main members are broken or missing.

The bridge is open to traffic but if not repaired soon, the bridge will be too broken down to restore. Carlton Bridge has an attractive location. It would be a shame to let it collapse.

DIRECTIONS: Swanzey Township. From the Village of Swanzey, south on SR 32, one and one-half miles, left on Carlton Road, one-tenth mile. (Donovan, 1980; New Hampshire Department of Public Works and Highways; New Hampshire Department of Resources and Economic Development)

Photograph by Michael Krekeler

Swiftwater Bridge

Located in Swiftwater Village, the Swiftwater Bridge spans the Wild Am-monoosuc River, which is a tributary of the Ammonoosuc River, and their confluence is two miles north of the bridge site. The Ammonoosuc River is the major drainage channel for Grafton County. The Wild Ammonoosuc River has a normal bed width of 75 feet at the bridge site.

Swiftwater Bridge was built in 1849. Swiftwater Bridge is 158 feet long, a single span and is supported by cut stone abutments set on huge boulders in the river bed. Naturally weathered lap siding with three small square windows on each side, and a gray, corrugated tin roof cover the bridge. There is a three-foot tall ventilation panel right under the eaves which extends the full length of the bridge on both sides. A massive 14-ply, 12″ wide arch has been added to the Paddleford truss. The floor has lengthwise planking.

Swiftwater Bridge has a picturesque location and offers easy access to the creek and is still open to traffic.

DIRECTIONS: Bath Township. In Swiftwater Village, just north of SR 112. (Donovan, 1980; New Hampshire Department of Public Works and Highways; New Hampshire Department of Resources and Economic Development)

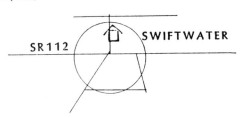

Bath Bridge

Bath Bridge spans the Ammonoosuc River four miles east of the Am-monoosuc River's confluence with the Connecticut River.

Built in 1832, the four span structure is 400 feet long. It is the longest covered bridge that is completely in New Hampshire. The Cornish/Windsor Bridge (29-10-09) is 460 feet, but connects Vermont and New Hampshire.

At the time of the photograph (March 1987), the bridge's siding was being repaired. The covering consists of plank siding and a rusted, corrugated tin roof. The abutments and three piers are cut stone with some sides faced with concrete.

Over and above the excessive length of Bath Bridge the most interesting feature is its truss. With 400 feet, this is the longest and oldest Paddleford truss. Each span has a double Burr arch encasing the Paddleford truss. The bridge was raised to allow the B & M Railroad to pass under the bridge. At this time, three additional 14-ply Burr arches were added, which creates multiple opposing angles resulting from the presence of the many arches. The north side of the bridge has a walkway built up on the interior.

The bridge site has natural waterfalls and a dam, which makes the area interesting. The river has no access but the bridge can be easily viewed from the surrounding roads. Bath Bridge is still in service.

DIRECTIONS: Bath Township. At Bath, just west of US 32. (Donovan, 1980; New Hampshire Department of Public Works and Highways; New Hampshire Department of Resources and Economic Development)

Grafton County
29-05-04

Bath/Haverhill Bridge

Spanning the Ammonoosuc River with 257 feet, the bridge connects Bath and Haverhill Townships near the confluence of the Ammonoosuc River and the Connecticut River. The Connecticut River forms the state boundary for Vermont and New Hampshire.

Built in 1827, Bath/Haverhill Bridge is the oldest covered bridge in New Hampshire. The east side of the bridge has an external walkway that is roofed and enclosed. The west side of the bridge has naturally weathered, gray plank siding. The portals are painted red with white trim. The roof is gray corrugated tin. Dry stone abutments and one pier support the bridge with some concrete assistance. The interior has a Town lattice truss and two sets of multi-layered Burr arches that are tied to the lower chord with iron tie rods. The floor has crosswise planking.

The bridge site has a dam under the bridge, which adds another dimension. Access to the river banks is impossible. Although this bridge has a lot to offer, it is impossible to view without obtaining permission from private land owners who have the area posted, "NO TRESPASSING." It would be so nice if the township could acquire just a small portion of land along the river banks so that interested parties could have access to view the impressive old bridge, especially since there is a small area that could be developed into an excellent little park.

Bath/Haverhill Bridge is still serving traffic.

DIRECTIONS: Bath/Haverhill Township. From Woodsville, north on SR 135. (Donovan, 1980; New Hampshire Department of Public Works and Highways; New Hampshire Department of Resources and Economic Development)

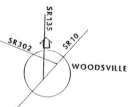

Grafton County
29-05-08

Bump Bridge

Bump Bridge, with 66 feet, spans the Beebe River, which is a tributary of the Pemigewasset River, a major drainage channel.

Built in 1877, the Bump Bridge was named after a nearby family. The lower half of the bridge has lap siding. The upper half is open, exposing the queenpost truss with its wooden bracing and added steel tie rods, which connect the upper and lower chord. The roof is tin and the floor has lengthwise planking. Arnold Graton repaired the bridge in 1972.

Bump Bridge is open for passenger cars only. The bridge site is in an isolated area and offers a picturesque location.

DIRECTIONS: Campton Township. From Campton Hollow, south on Perch Pond Road, one mile on left. (Donovan, 1980; New Hampshire Department of Public Works and Highways; New Hampshire Department of Resources and Economic Development)

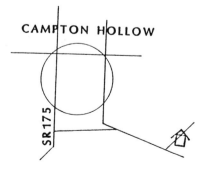

Blair Bridge

Spanning the Pemigewasset River, Blair Bridge is 292 feet long and was built in 1869.

The double span structure is supported by dry stone abutments and one pier. Covered by natural plank siding and a flat tin roof, the bridge has a twenty-foot window over each span. The Long truss has two sets of 9-ply single Burr arches that are tied with iron rods to the lower chord.

Blair Bridge was restored in 1977 by Milton Graton and his son, Arnold, for a cost of $59,000. Blair Bridge offers easy access to the river banks, an attractive location and is still in service.

DIRECTIONS: Campton Township. At Blair, east of US 3. (Donovan, 1980; New Hampshire Department of Public Works and Highways; New Hampshire Department of Resources and Economic Development)

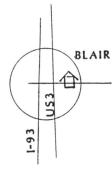

This is a fine example of a pier laid up with dry stone (large cut stone without mortar). Built in 1869, the pier is in excellent condition.

Smith Bridge

Smith Bridge spans Baker River with 149 feet. Baker River has a 140-foot bed width at the bridge site.

Smith Bridge was built in 1880 by Charles Richardson. Naturally weathered plank siding and rusted, green corrugated tin roof cover the structure. The single span rests on dry stone abutments. The Long truss has a 10-ply, 12″ wide Burr arch. The floor has lengthwise planking.

Smith Bridge has had repair in 1940, 1949 and 1958. In 1971, the bridge was restored for $7,876. The bridge has easy access to the river bank and is still open to passenger cars only.

DIRECTIONS: Plymouth Township. From Plymouth, northwest one mile, left on SR 25, one-half mile, right on Smith Bridge Road one-half mile. (Donovan, 1980; New Hampshire Department of Public Works and Highways; New Hampshire Department of Resources and Economic Development)

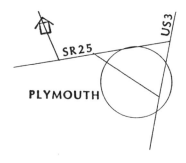

Edgell Bridge

Edgell Bridge, 154 feet long, spans Clay Brook which is a tributary of the Connecticut River which is one-fourth mile from the bridge site.

Edgell Bridge was built in 1885 by Walter Piper for $1,825. Plank siding and a new tin roof cover the bridge. There are windows on one side of the bridge and an 18″ ventilation panel on each side. The interior has a Town truss and lengthwise floor planking.

Edgell Bridge has experienced its share of mishaps. The bridge was raised off its north abutment in 1936 by a flood. It was placed back on the abutment and tied down with cables. In 1971, the state straightened the bridge, installed a new floor and put in concrete abutments for a cost of $23,829. In February 21, 1982, snow collapsed the roof. A new roof was constructed in July of 1982 for $30,000.

Access to the creek is easy.

DIRECTIONS: Lyme Township. From Orford Village in Orford Township, south on SR 10, two miles, right on River Road, one mile. (Donovan, 1980; New Hampshire Department of Public Works and Highways; New Hampshire Department of Resources and Economic Development)

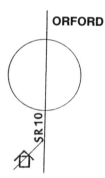

ORFORD

SR 10

Clark's Railroad Bridge

Spanning the Pemigewasset River with 120 feet, the Clark's Railroad Bridge is located at Clark's Trading Post in North Woodstock and is privately owned. In 1965, brothers Ed and Murray Clark dismantled the bridge in East Montpelier, Vermont and reassembled it in its present location. The bridge was originally constructed in 1904.

The single span structure rests on cut stone abutments, has dark, naturally weathered plank siding and a beige, tar papered roof. The peak of the roof has a roofed vent that allows smoke to escape.

This is a rare example of one of the few remaining railroad bridges left in the U.S. today. Because it is a railroad bridge, the structure is much taller than the average covered bridge, to accomodate the large trains. The train parked in the covered bridge in the photograph is a full size train which allows some perspective on just how tall the bridge is.

The bridge is an excellent example of restoration and preservation and is available to the public.

DIRECTIONS: Lincoln Township. In North Woodstock on SR 112. (Donovan, 1980; New Hampshire Department of Pubic Works and Highways; New Hampshire Department of Resources and Economic Development)

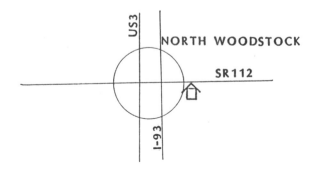

US3

NORTH WOODSTOCK

SR 112

I-93

Cilleyville/Bog Bridge

The Cilleyville Bridge crosses Blackwater River with one span. Built in 1887 by Print Atwood, a local carpenter, the bridge tilts because his assistants, Al Emerson and Charles Wilson became angry and cut some of the timbers short. The original cost of construction was $552.

The 51-foot structure is supported by dry stone abutments. The exterior has plank siding but many of the planks are missing. The roof collapsed on March 9, 1982 and a new steep roof was installed by the town in July of 1982 for $3,400. The interior has a Town truss and lengthwise floor planking laid in four sections.

Cilleyville Bridge was bypassed in 1959 and is listed in the National Register of Historic Places. Access to the river is easy.

In the third picture this portion of the town truss displays the precise engineering of the treenail holes through the two boards.

DIRECTIONS: Andover Township. At Cilleyville, off of SR 11 near SR 4A. (Donovan, 1980; New Hampshire Department of Public Works and Highways; New Hampshire Department of Resources and Economic Development)

CILLEYVILLE

Keniston Bridge

Keniston Bridge spans the Blackwater River with 63 feet. The single span was built by Albert R. Hamilton for $745 in 1882.

Keniston Bridge has its lower third covered with dark plank siding. The upper two-thirds expose the Town lattice truss. The roof is shake and the floor has lengthwise planking with two runners.

In 1972, the bridge had some planking torn off by an ice jam. In 1981, the E. D. Swett Construction Company was employed by the Andover Township to restore Keniston Bridge. Concrete abutments were installed and the bridge was refurbished for $60,000.

Open to traffic, the bridge sits next to the Boston & Maine Railroad. Keniston Bridge is listed on the National Register of Historic Places.

DIRECTIONS: Andover Township. At Andover just south of SR 11. (Donovan, 1980; New Hampshire Department of Public Works and Highways; New Hampshire Department of Resources and Economic Development)

ANDOVER

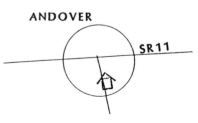

SR 11

Merrimack County
29-07-03

Bement Bridge

Spanning the West Branch of Warner River, the Bement Bridge is 63 feet long. Built in 1854, the bridge was constructed by Stephen H. Long for $500.

The single span Bement Bridge rests on one dry cut stone abutment and the other abutment has concrete facing. The exterior has natural plank siding and a shake roof. The interior exhibits a Long truss and lengthwise floor planking.

Bement Bridge was closed in 1968, repaired for $20,000 and reopened in 1969.

The area is thickly vegetated, making access to the stream difficult. Bement Bridge is open to traffic and is listed on the National Register of Historic Places.

DIRECTIONS: Bradford Township. In Bradford, one-fourth mile south of SR 103 on Bradford Center Road. (Donovan, 1980; New Hampshire Department of Public Works and Highways; New Hampshire Department of Resources and Economic Development)

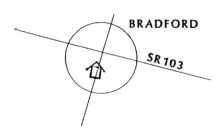

Merrimack County
29-07-04

Waterloo Station Bridge

Waterloo Station Bridge assumes its name from a nearby railroad depot. Waterloo Station crosses Warner River with 72 feet. Originally built in 1840, it was rebuilt in 1857, probably due to flood damage. The bridge was constructed by Dutton Woods from Contoocook, New Hampshire.

Waterloo Station has naturally weathered plank siding with three square windows on each side. The roof is rusted, corrugated tin attached over the old shake roof. The single span rests on creek stone abutments that have a concrete cap. The interior has lengthwise floor planking and a Town truss. Each plank of the Town truss is doubled.

Waterloo Station sits over an old mill pond, which creates a stable pool of water, allowing an almost perfect reflection of the bridge. Waterloo Station Bridge is listed in the National Register of Historic Places.

DIRECTIONS: Warner Township. At Waterloo, just south of SR 103 on New Market Road. (Donovan, 1980; New Hampshire Department of Public Works and Highways; New Hampshire Department of Resouces and Economic Development)

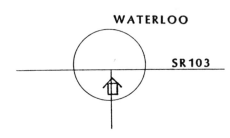

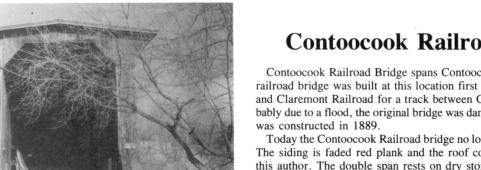

Dalton Bridge

Dalton Bridge spans Warner River three miles east of Waterloo Station (29-07-05) with 75 feet. Dalton Bridge was built in the early 1800s but, unfortunately, a precise year cannot be identified. It could possibly be the oldest covered bridge existing but since a date cannot be determined, Pennsylvania's Roddy's Mill (38-50-15), Rishel (38-49-05) and Sam Wagner (38-47-01) Bridges tie for the oldest covered bridges, all built in 1812. Dalton Bridge was constructed by Joshua Sanborn and the abutments were installed by George Sawyer and Walter S. Davis.

Dalton Bridge's exterior consists of plank siding with four rectangular windows on each side, a rusted, corrugated tin roof, and rests on cut stone abutments with concrete caps. The interior has a combination kingpost truss with bracing and a queenpost truss. The floor has lengthwise planking.

Renovated in 1963 by the Township of Warner and the state, it was restored in 1965 at a cost of $16,933.

Dalton Bridge is open to traffic and offers easy access to the creek. Dalton Bridge is listed in the National Register of Historic Places.

DIRECTIONS: Warner Township. In Warner, just south of SR 103. (Donovan, 1980; New Hampshire Department of Public Works and Highways; New Hampshire Department of Resources and Economic Development)

Contoocook Railroad Bridge

Contoocook Railroad Bridge spans Contoocook River with 157 feet. A railroad bridge was built at this location first in 1849/50 by the Concord and Claremont Railroad for a track between Concord and Bradford. Probably due to a flood, the original bridge was damaged and the present bridge was constructed in 1889.

Today the Contoocook Railroad bridge no longer has the railroad tracks. The siding is faded red plank and the roof construction is not known to this author. The double span rests on dry stone abutments and one pier. The interior has a Town lattice truss and lengthwise floor planking. The bridge is massive, twenty feet wide and thirty feet tall.

It is a magnificent bridge but, unfortunately, the river banks are so thickly vegetated that visual access of the bridge is impossible. The bridge is closed on one end and used for storage and is privately owned. The bridge is an excellent example of the rare old railroad bridges. It would be nice if it were made easily accessible and shared with the public.

DIRECTIONS: Hopkinton Township. In Contoocook, just south of SR 103, (Donovan, 1980; New Hampshire Department of Public Works and Highways; New Hampshire Department of Resources and Economic Development)

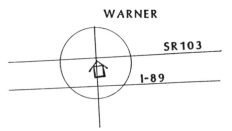

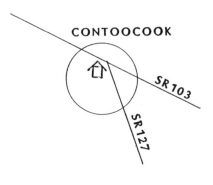

Merrimack County
29-07-08

Rowell's Bridge

Built in 1853, Rowell's Bridge spans the Contoocook River with 167 feet.

Rowell's Bridge is exciting because it was constructed by the Childs brothers, Horace, Enoch and Warren. Horace was the carpenter, Warren was the stone mason and brother Enoch was a graduate from Yale University and was the architectural engineer. The Childs brothers built many railroad and highway bridges throughout northeastern United States. The Childs brothers also created and patented their own truss design of which there are only seven examples still surviving. One is in Deleware County, Ohio (35-21-04) and the other six are found in Preble County, Ohio (American Society of Civil Engineers, 1976, p. 51)

Rowell's Bridge was constructed with a Long truss and has a single Burr arch sandwiched between the Long truss members. The exterior has dark plank siding halfway up the sides, exposing the upper half of the Long truss. The roof is corrugated galvanized tin. The single span rests on dry stone abutments. In 1930, a concrete pier was added but soon thereafter the supports were removed. The concrete pier is still there but it is not connected to the bridge.

The design of the bridge indicates that it once had walkways on either side which have since disappeared. In 1965, $9,521 was invested, refurbishing the bridge. The state spent another $9,000 in 1982 to restore it.

Rowell's Bridge is very attractive with its extended roof line. Because it was built by the Childs brothers, it makes the bridge a must for covered bridge enthusiasts.

WEST HOPKINTON

SR 127

DIRECTIONS: Hopkinton Township. In West Hopkinton, just north of SR 127 (American Society of Civil Engineers, 1976; Donovan, 1980; New Hampshire Department of Public Works and Highways; New Hampshire Department of Resources and Economic Development)

Merrimack County
29-07-09

Sulphite Railroad Bridge

The Sulphite Railroad Bridge spans the Winnepesaukee River and is 180 feet long.

Built in 1896, the three span structure is supported by huge cut stone abutments and two piers. Locally called the "Upsidedown Bridge," the tracks run on top of the bridge rather than through the bridge.

The Sulphite Bridge was burned by arson in 1981 and replacement costs would be as much as $500,000. The bridge was the only one of its kind. The bridge had a Pratt truss and was completely covered with a tin roof and plank siding. The ends had doors on them to allow access to the interior. Now all that remains is a charcoal shell, a sad reminder of a once spectacular and singular covered bridge.

To locate the remains of the Sulphite Railroad Bridge is difficult. You need to park in a warehouse parking lot south of US 5 and walk one-half mile east along the abandoned track site to find the bridge. Once you reach the bridge, access to the river bank is dangerous. To locate this covered bridge you must be extremely ambitious.

DIRECTIONS: Franklin Township. In Franklin, south of US 3 (SR 11). (Donovan, 1980; New Hampshire Department of Public Works and Highways; New Hampshire Department of Resources and Economic Development)

Photograph by Michael Krekeler

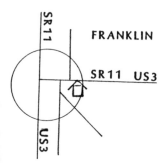

FRANKLIN

SR11 US3

Blacksmith Shop Bridge

Blacksmith Shop Bridge spans Mill Brook, which is a tributary of the Connecticut River. Their confluence is two miles west of the bridge site. The Connecticut River is the state boundary line between Vermont and New Hampshire.

James Tasker built the Blacksmith Shop Bridge in 1882 and was known as a construction genius. This bridge was only used by one family to have access to their home.

The 96-foot structure has its lower half covered with plank siding exposing the top half of the multiple kingpost truss. The roof is covered with rusted corrugated tin. The bridge rests on stone abutments that have concrete caps. In 1983, Milton Graton restored the bridge and raised the southern end two feet and the northern end one foot by installing the concrete caps. Graton also installed a new lengthwise floor and new siding. Prior to Milton Graton's restoration, Blacksmith Shop had been abandoned.

Access to the creek is difficult. The bridge is closed, open only to pedestrian traffic. Blacksmith Shop Bridge is listed on the National Register of Historic Places.

DIRECTIONS: Cornish Township. At Cornish City, two miles east of SR 12A. (Donovan, 1980; New Hampshire Department of Public Works and Highways; New Hampshire Department of Resources and Economic Development)

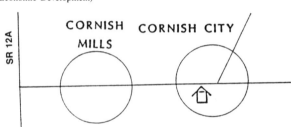

Dingleton Bridge

Dingleton Bridge spans Mill Brook one mile east of Blacksmith Shop Bridge (29-10-01). James Tasher built Dingleton Bridge in 1882.

Dingleton Bridge is a single span with 77 feet. The bridge is supported by one concrete abutment and one dry creek stone abutment. A camber is evident in the entire structure. The lower half of the bridge is covered with plank siding exposing the upper half of the multiple kingpost truss. The roof is rusted flat tin. The floor has lengthwise planking. Milton Graton refurbished the bridge in 1983.

The bridge site has easy access to the creek and is listed on the National Register of Historic Places. Dingleton Bridge is open to passenger cars only.

DIRECTIONS: Cornish Township. At Cornish Mills, one mile east of SR 12A. (Donovan, 1980; New Hampshire Department of Public Works and Highways; New Hampshire Department of Resources and Economic Development)

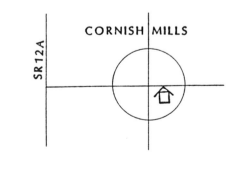

Pier Railroad/ Chandler Station Bridge

Pier Railroad Bridge is also known as the Chandler Station Bridge because it is located east of what was once called Chandler Station. Spanning Sugar River, the bridge is 228 feet long and abandoned. It is still owned by the Railroad. The first bridge at this site was built in 1871-1872. The present bridge was constructed in 1896 by the Sugar River Railroad.

The double span railroad bridge is supported by a cut stone pier and cut stone abutments with concrete facing. The exterior is covered with dark plank siding and a shake roof. The siding is missing planks and the roof is in sad repair. The shake is missing in spots, leaving gaping holes for water to get into the interior. This causes a covered bridge to deteriorate rapidly. The truss is a double Town lattice. The tracks have been removed. The floor consists of huge crosswise railroad ties.

This bridge is a beautiful old railroad bridge and is still in excellent shape structurally. The roof needs immediate attention or the truss will soon weaken and cause the bridge's eventual collapse. As so many covered bridges need repair, this one especially cries out for the attentions of Milton Graton.

The abandoned railroad track runs alongside the road, allowing easy access to the interior of the bridge. Because it is a railroad bridge, it is huge; 30 feet tall and 20 feet wide. There is no comparison to the traditional covered bridges. The railroad bridges use massive, tall beams. The U.S. only has six of the railroad bridges left. Hopefully, monies can be channeled into the repairs of the abandoned ones for restoration.

Pier/Chandler Station Railroad Bridge is a must for bridgers in New Hampshire.

DIRECTIONS: Newport Township. From Kellyville on SR 103, west along the south side of Sugar River for one and one half mile, on right. (Donovan, 1980; New Hampshire Department of Public Works and Highways; New Hampshire Department of Resources and Economic Development)

Wright Railroad Bridge

Wright Railroad Bridge is one mile west of Pier Railroad/Chandler Station Railroad Bridge (29-10-03) over Sugar River. Wright Bridge is in a similar situation as Pier Bridge in that it is railroad owned and abandoned. Wright Railroad Bridge is much more difficult to locate. It sits a considerable distance off the road. At the time of the photograph, the snow was melting but there was still a 24″ snow base which, unfortunately, prevented the hike to the bridge.

Wright Bridge is much shorter than Pier Bridge with only 122 feet. It is a single span bridge with an added laminated arch. The truss is a double lattice, the same as Pier's truss. Wright Bridge was built in 1895 by the Sugar River Railroad. The photo of Wright Bridge was taken from the road, which gives you some idea of the bridge's remote location. It was disappointing that we could not have access to the bridge.

Since the brige is abandoned, it probably is in need of repair just as the Pier Bridge.

DIRECTIONS: Newport Township. From Kellyville, west along the south side of Sugar River, two and one-half miles (easy to miss), on the right. (Donovan, 1980; New Hampshire Department of Public Works and Highways; New Hampshire Department of Resources and Economic Development)

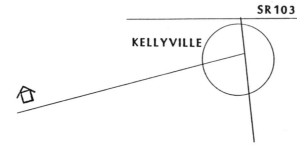

Corbin Bridge

Corbin Bridge spans the Croydon Branch of Sugar River, which is a tributary of Sugar River. Sugar River is one-half mile south of the bridge site.

The 105-foot structure was built in 1835. The exterior is covered with light brown plank siding, a shake roof, and rests on bedrock and mortar abutments that have partial concrete caps. The interior has a traditional Town lattice truss and lengthwise floor planking.

Corbin Bridge is open to traffic and offers easy access to the creek banks. Corbin Bridge is listed on the National Register of Historic Places.

DIRECTIONS: Newport Township. From North Newport, east one-half mile. (Donovan, 1980; New Hampshire Department of Public Works and Highways; New Hampshire Department of Resources and Economic Development)

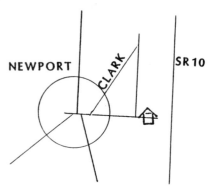

Meriden/Mill Bridge

Spanning Blood's Brook with 77 feet, Meriden Bridge was built by James Tasker in 1880 for $500.

In early 1950, Hurricane Carol damaged the bridge. The repairs cost $5,000. A heavy snow load collapsed the roof in the spring of 1977. The new roof was constructed by Neil Daniels, Inc. of Ascutny, Vermont for $8,296.

Today, Meriden Bridge has the lower two thirds covered with naturally weathered plank siding, exposing the top third of the multiple kingpost truss. The new steep roof is covered with shake. The single span rests on concrete abutments and one steel pier. The entire bridge exhibits a camber.

Meriden Bridge is open to traffic and offers easy access to the creek.

DIRECTIONS: Plainfield Township. At Meriden, (west of SR 120) northwest of Brook Road (the main street) left on Colby Hill. (Donovan, 1980; New Hampshire Department of Public Works and Highways; New Hampshire Department of Resources and Economic Development)

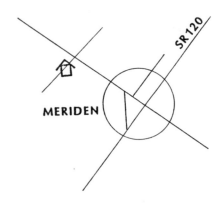

Sullivan County
29-10-09

Windsor County
45-14-14

Cornish/Windsor Bridge

Cornish/Windsor Bridge is the longest covered bridge in the U.S. with 460 feet. The bridge spans the Connecticut River and is the only covered bridge connecting two states, Vermont and New Hampshire. Built in 1866 by James Tasker and Bela Fletcher, it is the fourth bridge at this site. In 1796, a bridge was destroyed. In 1824 and 1848, the bridges were lost in floods.

Cornish/Windsor Bridge was a toll bridge until June 1, 1943. The states of Vermont and New Hampshire purchased the bridge in 1935 and renovated it in 1954. In March of 1977, the bridge experienced flood and ice damage and was repaired by the state for $25,000. There was an old Toll House located at the Windsor, Vermont portal that burned on July 18, 1982. Fortunately, the bridge survived and was not damaged.

Today Cornish/Windsor Bridge has only two spans. Supported by cut stone abutments, one faced in concrete, and one cut stone pier, Cornish/Windsor is covered by naturally weathered plank siding and a rusted, corrugated tin roof. Eighteen rectangular windows are on each side. The interior is 19 feet wide and allows two lanes of traffic. The truss is a Town lattice and the floor is lengthwise planking.

In 1977, Cornish/Windsor Bridge was designated as a National Historic Civil Engineering Landmark by the American Society of Civil Engineers. The bridge is also listed in the National Register of Historic Places.

Cornish/Windsor Bridge has easy access to the river banks. Because of its unique length, this covered bridge is a must when bridging in New Hampshire.

DIRECTIONS: Cornish Township, New Hampshire-Windsor Township, Vermont. From Cornish Mills, New Hampshire, west one mile, to SR 12A, north one-half mile, on left. (Donovan, 1980; New Hampshire Department of Public Works and Highways; New Hampshire Department of Resources and Economic Development)

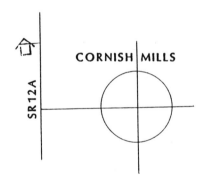

New York

At one time, New York had as many as 250 covered bridges (Allen, 1957, p. 80). Today, 23 of these historic structures remain.

The remaining covered bridges are as diverse in height and length as they are in the various trusses used in their construction. New York covered bridges have been well-maintained and each location offers an excellent opportunity to inspect the work of the crafts-men bridge builders. Almost every bridge site presents the occasion for a fine photograph.

New York State has six different truss designs and combinations in their covered bridges. The Town truss has the most representatives, with 10 examples. The Long, Howe, Burr, and King have three examples each, and there is one example of a queenpost truss. Although none of the trusses are rare, the Long truss used in the Blenheim Bridge (32-48-01) is fascinating because of its use of massive, tall beams, and its three trusses (one in the center dividing the two lanes).

The configuration of New York's covered bridges is where their unique character is exhibited. Many are long single span bridges with lengths such as 164 feet, (Buskirk, 32-58-04, 42-02), 174 feet, (Downsville, 32-13-01), and the longest at 228 feet, (Blenheim, 32-48-01). Both the Buskirk and Downsville Bridges are still in service. The Blenheim Bridge holds the distinction of being the longest single span covered bridge in the world. Blenheim Bridge is singularly distinctive because it is New York's only double bar-relled bridge and one of only five double barrelled bridges left in the United States. Blenheim was by-passed in 1931.

A number of New York's bridges have lateral sup-ports which protrude from the sides of the bridges in triangular boxes. These can be seen on Fitches, (32-13-02), Hamden, (32-13-03), Halls Mills, (32-53-01) and Beaverkill, (32-53-02). The supports give the bridges an added dimension.

Finding New York covered bridges is not difficult. The directions and map included with the text are to be used in conjunction with county maps available from the state of New York (please see chapter on "How To Find Covered Bridges and Obtain County Maps").

Historically, New York Bridges are excellent ex-amples of the covered structures. Most all of the covered bridges are well-maintained and offer pleasant surroundings. (Allen, 1957; Donovan, 1980; New York State Department of Transportation)

ACKNOWLEDGMENTS

I would like to thank the following people of New York for their suggestions, information and time:
Eileen J. O'Brien, Special Collections Librarian, New York State Historical Association
Dorothea Ives, Salisbury Historian, Town of Salisbury
James A. Kinley, Director, The Essex County Historical Society
Hank Messing, New York State Covered Bridge Society

BRIDGE NAME	COUNTY	NUMBER
Downsville	Delaware	32-13-01
Fitches	"	32-13-02
Hamden	"	32-13-03
Hyde Hall	Otsego	32-39-01
Blenheim	Schoharie	32-48-01
Halls Mills	Sullivan	32-53-01
Beaverkill	"	32-53-02
Van Tran Flat	"	32-53-03
Bendo/Willowemoc	"	32-53-04
Eagleville	Washington	32-58-01
Shushan	"	32-58-02
Rexleigh	"	32-58-03
Buskirk	"	32-58-04
	Rensselaer	32-42-02

Delaware County
32-13-01

Downsville Bridge

Downsville Bridge spans the East Branch of the Delaware River, which has a normal 150-foot bed width at the bridge site. The East Branch has its confluence with the West Branch of the Delaware River, twenty miles west of the village of Downsville, where they form the Delaware River. The Delaware River is the boundary between Pennsylvania and New Jersey.

Downsville Bridge, located in the village of Downsville, was built in 1854 by Robert Murray. With 174 feet, the bridge is the second longest in New York. The Downsville Bridge is the longest single span in service in New York.

The exterior has naturally weathered plank siding, a shake roof and rests on concrete abutments. The interior has a Long truss encasing a queen-post. The queenpost's vertical member is the vertical member of the Long truss. The floor has 2″ X 4″ boards set on edge.

The bridge is missing some siding, but otherwise appears in fair condition. Access to the river banks is easy and the bridge offers a picturesque location across the wide East Branch.

DIRECTIONS: Colchester Township. At Downsville, just south of SR 30. (Allen, "Covered Bridges existing in New York State in 1947-49"; Donovan, 1980; New York State Department of Transportation, 1983)

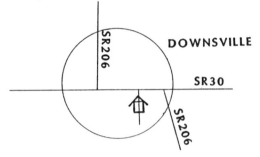

DOWNSVILLE

SR 30

SR 206

SR 206

Delaware County
32-13-02

Fitches Bridge

The 100 foot Fitches Bridge spans the West Branch of the Delaware River at a place known as Fitches Crossing. This bridge originally spanned the same river a few miles west of its current location, in Delhi, at Kingston Street. This bridge was replaced by an iron bridge in 1885, and moved to its present location by David Wright and a town crew.

Fitches Bridge was originally constructed by James Franzier and James Warren in 1870. The exterior has red plank siding, a corrugated tin roof, and a single span that rests on one concrete abutment and one round, creekstone abutment. The bridge has four lateral supports that appear as four enclosed triangles, extending out on each side of the bridge. The interior has a Town truss, 2″ X 4″ boards on edge for the floor, and a walkway consisting of two thick planks on one side of the floor.

Fitches crossing has an excellent creek bank and setting to inspect the bridge.

DIRECTIONS: Delhi Township. From Delhi, east on SR 10, two or three miles, just on the right. (Donovan, 1980; New York State Department of Transportation, 1983)

Photograph by Michael Krekeler

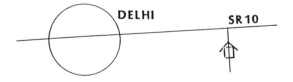

DELHI

SR 10

Photograph by Michael Krekeler

Delaware County
32-13-03

Hamden Bridge

Located in the village of Hamden, the Hamden Bridge spans the West Branch of the Delaware River with 125 feet.

Although Hamden Bridge is not as well-maintained as its cousin, Fitches Bridge (32-13-01), Hamden Bridge presents an impressive structure against the surrounding hills.

Robert Murray built Hamden Bridge in 1859. The exterior has a rusted, corrugated tin roof, faded red plank siding with batten and four lateral supports. The two center lateral supports are enclosed in full height, boxed triangles. The shorter lateral supports on either end are enclosed in a triangular box, but they only extend several feet up the side of the bridge. These lateral supports add a different perspective to the bridge. The abutments are bedrock without mortar, but concrete has been poured at the base of each one. The single span has steel pipes installed in the center as a pier. The interior of the bridge is much shorter than most covered bridges. The truss is a traditional Long. Two by four inch boards were stood on edge for the new floor.

The bridge is open to traffic and offers easy access to the river banks.

DIRECTIONS: Hamden Township. At Hamden, just south of SR 10. (Allen, "Covered Bridges Existing in New York State in 1947-49"; Donovan, 1980; New York State Department of Transportation, 1983)

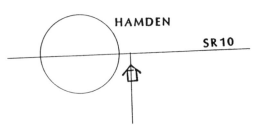

Otsego County
32-39-01

Hyde Hall Bridge

Hyde Hall Bridge spans Shadow Brook in Glimmerglass State Park.

Hyde Hall Bridge was built in 1823, which makes it the oldest covered bridge left in New York. The 53-foot structure has natural lap siding, a shake roof and a single span that is supported by concrete abutments. Although the exterior has new siding, roof, and abutments, the interior is the original hand-hewn beams. The truss has "X" panels with vertical beams at each panel encased in a double Burr arch. The floor has lengthwise planking. Hyde Hall Bridge sits in a secluded area of the park and has several trails.

DIRECTIONS: Springfield Township. At Glimmerglass State Park west of CR 31. (Donovan, 1980; New York State Department of Transportation, 1983)

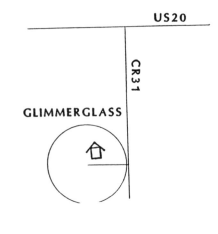

Blenheim Bridge

Blenheim Bridge is anything but ordinary. The bridge holds many distinctions. It is one of only five double-barrelled (two lanes separated by a truss) covered bridges left in the U.S. today. Of the five double-barrelled bridges left, Blenheim is the only one that has a Long truss. The other double-barrelled bridges use the multiple kingpost and Burr arch. Blenheim claims the honor of being the longest single span covered bridge in the world, with 228 feet. Blenheim is not only long, but, relative to other covered bridges, it is a huge bridge. The interior is extremely tall. The individual lanes are an average width, but the height of the trusses is striking.

Blenheim Bridge spans the Schoharie Creek, the largest drainage channel in Schoharie County.

Built in 1855 by Nicholas M. Powers, the bridge experienced a flood in 1869 which did not harm the bridge, but washed out a wider channel on the west side of the bridge. At that time, a wooden approach was added. In 1855, the wooden approach was replaced with an iron bridge. Blenheim Bridge was retired in 1931, which helps explain why the bridge is in such excellent condition. Presently, there is no approach ramp to the west side. Access to the interior of the bridge is limited to the east side portal.

The exterior of the bridge has natural plank siding with batten, a green tin roof, and a 24', full length ventilation panel on both sides. The extraordinarily long single span rests on bedrock abutments that have been encased in concrete.

The massive appearance of the interior is spectacular. A Long truss is used for the exterior trusses. The center truss has a three-foot Burr arch sandwiched between the Long truss members. The floor is unusual in that it has six-foot sections of planks laid one section at a time. The floor boards are original; they exhibit extreme wear, with raised grain.

The foresight that the local Board of Supervisors showed in 1931 by bypassing the Blenheim bridge and maintaining it, is sincerely appreciated today.

DIRECTIONS: Blenheim Township. Just south of SR 30 in North Blenheim (Allen, ''Covered Bridges Existing in New York State in 1947-49''; Donovan, 1980; New York State Department of Transportation, 1983)

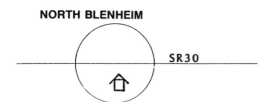

NORTH BLENHEIM

SR30

The floor boards in Blenheim Bridge exhibit years of use by the raised grain.

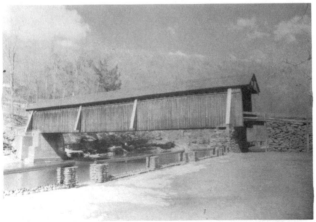

Photograph by Michael Krekeler

Sullivan County
32-53-01

Halls Mills Bridge

Halls Mills Bridge spans Neversink River, which supplies the water for Neversink Reservoir two miles west of the bridge site.

Halls Mills Bridge was built in 1906 by David Benton and John Knight. The 119-foot, single span has dark, natural plank siding and a flat, rusty tin roof. The bridge has five lateral supports which protrude from the bridge on either side, enclosed in siding. The bridge rests on two bedrock abutments, one encased in concrete and the other laid up without mortar. The interior has a Town lattice truss and crosswise floor planking with two runners. One end of the bridge has a 20-foot wooden approach.

The bridge has been bypassed and is being maintained. Driving north along CR 19, the bridge is visible on the left, in a valley. Just north of the bridge is a drive that allows easy access to the bridge's old road. It is a short walk from the parking area to the bridge site, where access to the creek is easy except in the winter months.

DIRECTIONS: Neversink Township. From Neversink, east on SR 55, two miles, left on CR 19, three miles, turn left on the first road after the bridge. (Allen, "Covered Bridge Existing in New York State in 1947-49"; Donovan, 1980; New York State Department of Transportation)

NEVERSINK   CR 19   SR 55

Sullivan County
32-53-02

Beaverkill Bridge

Beaverkill Bridge spans Beaverkill Creek, at Beaverkill State Campground, and is 98 feet long.

Built in 1865 by John Davidson, the bridge has naturally weathered plank siding with batten, a shake roof and a single span. The exterior exhibits four lateral supports that are covered with siding. One abutment is concrete. The other abutment is bedrock laid up without mortar. The approach is constructed with creek rock laid without mortar. The area surrounding the bridge is maintained by the state and has an entrance to the campgrounds. The bridge site has a rock wall along the river bank which blends in well with the bridge's rock supports. The interior has a Town truss and lengthwise floor planking.

Beaverkill Bridge presents a good opportunity for photographers.

DIRECTIONS: Rockland Township. West of CR 151 at Beaverkill State Campground. (Allen, "Covered Bridges Existing in New York State 1947-49"; Donovan, 1980; New York State Department of Transportation)

BEAVERKILL   CR 151

An excellent example of an abutment constructed of bedrock without mortar, referred to as dry stone.

Van Tran Flat Bridge

The Van Tran Flat Bridge spans Willowemoc Creek with 117 feet.

Built by John Davidson in 1860, Van Tran Flat Bridge has natural plank siding with batten, tin roof, and a single span. The abutments are concrete. Van Tran was closed in 1973 and reopened in 1984, after being restored under the supervision of Sullivan County Board of Supervisors. The work was performed by the Sullivan County Department of Public Works. The restoration had the technical assistance of Milton Graton from Ashland, New Hampshire.

The interior has a Town lattice truss with a 30-Ply, 12' wide arch that extends the full length of the bridge. One end of the bridge has a 25-foot wooden approach.

The creek has easy access.

DIRECTIONS: Rockland Township. From Livingston Manor, north on CR 179, first left just outside of the town limits, one-fourth mile. (Allen, "Covered Bridges Existing in New York State in 1947-49"; Donovan, 1980; New York State Department of Transportation, 1983)

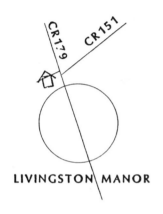

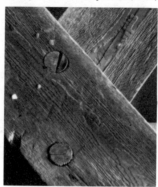

Treenails.

Bendo/Willowemoc Bridge

Bendo Bridge spans Willowemoc Creek and is 45 feet long.

The bridge was built in 1860 by John Davidson. Bendo Bridge has a single span and rests on cut stone abutments. The exterior has dark plank siding with batten and a tin roof. The interior has a Town truss and crosswise floor planking with two lengthwise runners.

Bendo Bridge was originally built in Livingston Manor and moved to its present location in 1913. The present bridge is only half of its original length.

The bridge is open to traffic and offers a picturesque location.

DIRECTIONS: Rockland Township. From Livingston Manor, four miles east on CR 81/CR 82, turn right, one and one-half mile, right, one-half mile. (Allen, "Covered Bridges Existing in New York State in 1947-49"; Donovan, 1980; New York State Department of Transportation, 1983)

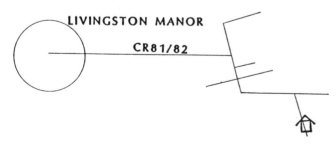

Photograph by Michael Krekeler

Eagleville Bridge

Eagleville Bridge crosses the Batten Kill River with a single span.

The Eagleville Bridge is 101 feet long and was built in 1858. The exterior has tongue and groove, dark brown plank siding, a shake roof and concrete abutments. The interior has a Town lattice truss. On one side of the bridge, in the center, (see photograph) there is a little door labeled, "inspection door" so any one can look out and "inspect" the river. The floor is different. It is laid lengthwise in 12-foot sections with a crosswise member between the sections.

The most impressive feature about Eagleville Bridge is its location. The bridge is open to traffic and has easy access to the creek.

DIRECTIONS: Jackson/Salem Township. At Eagleville, West of 313. (Donovan, 1980; New York State Department of Transportation)

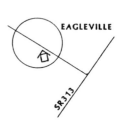

Centered in this bridge is a door that one can open to inspect the river.

Shushan Bridge

Shushan Bridge spans Batten Kill River with 160 feet. Built in 1858, Shushan Bridge has concrete abutments and steel pillars supported by concrete as a center pier. The exterior has dark brown plank siding, a shake roof and its portals have locked doors. The covered bridge houses a private museum and is open during the summer season for visitors.

A new, elevated bridge bypassed the Shushan Bridge and gives the Shushan Bridge the impression of being in a hole. It would have been better aesthetically if the new bridge had been placed at a more comfortable distance.

There is not any access to the creek, but the covered bridge can be viewed from upon the new bridge. The interior cannot be viewed off season or off hours. (Posted Hours 1-5 in season). The truss is listed in the *World Guide to Covered Bridges* as a Town.

DIRECTIONS: Salem/Jackson Township. In Shushan. (Donovan, 1980; New York State of Transportation)

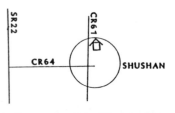

Washington County
32-58-03

Rexleigh Bridge

Rexleigh Bridge spans Batten Kill River with 98 feet.

The 1874 structure has dark brown, plank siding, a shake roof and a single span. There is one concrete abutment and one that has the bottom courses laid up in bedrock, and the upper courses laid in huge cut stone. The portals are painted white. The interior has a Howe truss and lengthwise floor planking.

Rexleigh Bridge has an attractive location.

DIRECTIONS: Jackson/Salem Township. From SR 29, south on SR 22, left on Rexleigh Road, one mile. (Donovan, 1980; New York State Department of Transportation)

Photograph by Michael Krekeler

**Washington County
32-58-04**

**Rensselaer County
32-42-02**

Buskirk Bridge

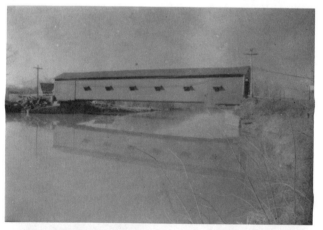

Buskirk Bridge spans the Hoosic River connecting Rensselaer and Washington Counties. This crossing was part of the Great Northern Turnpike, which had its beginning in 1799.

Buskirk Bridge was constructed in 1850. The present bridge was built to replace a previous covered bridge that was built in 1804.

With 164 feet and a single span, Buskirk rests on concrete abutments. The exterior is attractive with red plank siding, a shake roof and six small roofed windows on either side. The interior displays a Howe truss, lengthwise floor planking and the first 20 feet at each portal are paneled.

Buskirk Bridge is in fair condition but access to the river is difficult. The banks are cleared of vegetation, so the bridge is easily visible from the surrounding roads.

DIRECTIONS: White Creek Township in Washington County. At Buskirk, just north of SR 67. (Donovan, 1980; New York State Department of Transportation)

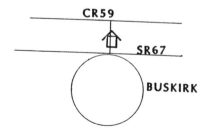

Ohio

A special thanks to the following people for their generous information, suggestions and materials while I was researching the covered bridges in Ohio:

John W. Smolen, Ashtabula County Engineer's Office
Dorthy Helton, Brown County Historical Society
Rhonda Curtis, Clinton County Historical Society
Lisbon Area Chamber of Commerce, Columbiana County
Gloria P. Schultz, Delaware County
James Walter, President of the Fairfield County Covered Bridge Association
Mrs. Emma Turner, Fairfield County District Library
Denny Jay, Franklin Historical Society
Lois Bell, Guernsey County District Public Library
County Engineer's Office, Lawrence County
Curtis W. Abbott, Newark, Ohio, Licking County
Mrs. Corinne M. Dixon, Logan County Historical Society
Mary Mathews, Carillon Historical Park, Montgomery County
Perry County's Engineer's Office
Angela R. Johnson, Pickaway County Historical Society
Ms. Kay Reeves, Preble County Historical Society
Gladys Riley, Otway, Ohio, Scioto County
Doris Falter, Scioto County Historical Society
Bonnie Banks, Amos Memorial Public Library, Shelby County
Rory L. Robinson, Cuyahoga Valley NRA, Summit County
Robert W. Parrott, Union County Historical Society
Roselle Hunter, Herbert Wescoat Memorial Library, Vinton County
Ray D. Gottfried, Upper Sandusky, Ohio, Wyandot County

I would also like to thank the Southern Ohio Covered Bridge Association, whose *Ohio Covered Bridge Guide* was extremely valuable in locating Ohio's covered bridges.

The World Guide to Covered Bridges, published by the National Society for the Preservation of Covered Bridges, was also helpful to locate the bridges and identify their lengths.

OHIO'S COVERED BRIDGES

At one time, there were over 60 different covered bridge trusses in existence throughout the United States. In 1986/87, the United States had only eighteen known different designs still in existence. Ohio has the greatest variety of trusses, with fourteen examples of the eighteen trusses left.

Ohio has three trusses that are unique to Ohio: the bowstring, Partridge, and Wernwag truss. The bowstring has two examples in Ohio. One is the John Bright Bridge (35-23-10) in Fairfield County. Built in 1881, the John Bright has an added Burr arch to the original bowstring construction. The second bowstring truss is located in Montgomery County (35-57-01), the Germantown Bridge, which is the only pure bowstring truss in the world.

The Partridge truss was designed by Reuben Partridge, native of Union County. Union County now has only five Partridge truss bridges left out of an original 200 built locally. There is also one Partridge truss located in the contiguous county of Franklin, for a total of six Partridge truss covered bridges left in the United States.

The third covered bridge truss singular to Ohio, is the only known Wernwag truss in the United States. Located in Butler County (35-09-02), the Governor Bebb Park Bridge was built in 1892.

Other trusses represented in Ohio as well as other states are the following: 1) Warren, 2) Pratt, 3) Long, 4) Smith, 5) Kingpost, 6) Queenpost, and 7) Child's.

The Warren truss has three examples in Ohio. Two are in Montgomery County; Carrillon Park (35-57-03) and Mud-Lick (35-57-36) Bridges. The other is geographically separated from these two and is found in Muskingum County (35-60-31), The Salt Creek Bridge. There are a total of only five Warren trusses left in the United States, and Kentucky has the other two examples.

The Pratt truss has two known examples in the United States. One is in California, and the second is located in Ashtabula, Ohio (35-04-59); the Cain Road Covered Bridge. This Pratt truss was built in 1986 and dedicated at Ashtabula's Covered Bridge Festival in October, 1986, and is one of two new covered bridges included in this book because it meets the definition of covered bridges used for this study. Cain Road Covered Bridge is 170 feet long, constructed of salt treated wood and galvanized connectors. It is an impressive bridge due to its size, rare truss, and the unparalleled construction.

The Smith truss is represented in Ohio with fourteen examples out of an estimated twenty-one in existence in the United States. Five Smith trusses can be found in Brown County, three in Jackson County, two in Greene County and one in each of Fairfield, Ross, Summit and Washington Counties.

The Long truss has an estimated twenty-nine examples in the United States. Ohio holds seven Long trusses in the following counties: Butler—1, Miami—1, Clinton—1, Shelby—1, and Washington—3. The Long truss in Miami County is the Eldean Bridge (35-55-01), which is 234 feet long, making it the longest Long truss today in America.

The pure kingpost truss is rare, usually used in combination with many vertical tension beams and attached diagonal compression beams, which transform the truss into a multiple kingpost truss. Using a pure kingpost as a truss, makes a short bridge. Ohio has one such example, the Church Hill Bridge in Columbiana County (35-15-08). This bridge also holds the distinction of being the shortest covered bridge in Ohio, with only 22 feet.

The queenpost truss is another uncommon truss. There are five examples of the queenpost truss in Ohio in the following counties: Fairfield—3, Hamilton—1, and Vinton—1. Although a popular truss used extensively throughout the United States, it was not a substantial structure and was susceptible to collapse. Consequently, there are not many queenpost trusses in existence today.

The Child's truss has seven examples in Ohio. Six are located in Preble County; one is found in Delaware. County. All of these Child's truss bridges were built by Evret S. Sherman between 1883 and 1896.

The remaining truss designs left in Ohio have numerous examples throughout the United States. Ohio

has: sixteen Howe trusses, twelve Town trusses, fifteen Burr trusses, and fifty-three multiple kingpost trusses.

The variety of truss designs exhibited in Ohio is unparalleled in any of the other 29 states that have covered bridges. One feature apparent when observing the geographic locations of various truss designs, is some are clustered in Union and Preble Counties, respectively, because of the location of the builders.

Another major influence in county clustering of trusses, was county engineers who decided what truss designs to use. Therefore, they often chose a certain design exclusively. Examples of such influences include: Ashtabula County, dominated by the Town truss, Columbus County, with mostly multiple kingpost, and Preble County's Child's trusses.

The Smith truss is found only in Ohio, Indiana and Pennsylvania, because the point of distribution for the prefabricated bridges was Toledo, Ohio. Bridge truss designs can also be found clustered by county or region depending on the builder's location, distribution centers, size of streams in a county or region, and funds available to build the bridges.

Ohio had a total of 142 covered bridges as of 1986/87. This figure is subject to change due to arson, dismantling and destruction. The figure of 142 is also relative because one of these bridges counted is the Roberts Bridge (35-68-05) in Preble County, which was burned by arson on August 5, 1986. Before and after pictures of the interior are included in this study. There is some discussion about restoring the Roberts Bridge at an estimated cost of $150,000. Roberts Bridge held two consequential records for Ohio's covered bridges. First, it was built in 1829, which made it the oldest covered bridge in Ohio. Secondly, it was the only double-barrelled covered bridge left in Ohio. Double-barrelled refers to a covered bridge that has two lanes divided by a truss, giving the bridge a total of three trusses. Fortunately, there are five other examples of double-barrelled covered bridges left in the United States: West Virginia—1, Vermont—2, New York—1, and Indiana—1.

Other covered bridges are being relocated or destroyed. For example, in Fairfield County, in 1987, there were 18 bridges. Of those 18, there are three slated to be moved or demolished. One of the 18 is in such poor condition that it could virtually collapse at any time. Due to attrition among covered bridges, and the fact that very few new covered bridges are being built, the number of bridges in Ohio continues to decrease.

Aside from the three extremely rare trusses that Ohio has: the bowstring, Partridge, and Wernwag, and apart from the variety of the fourteen different trusses represented in Ohio; many individual bridges have some interesting features, exceptional in their own right.

The Harpersfield Bridge in Ashtabula County (35-04-19), is the longest covered bridge in Ohio with 230 feet and two spans. Eagle Creek Bridge in Brown County (35-08-18), is the longest single span still in use and the only covered bridge on the state highway system. Lynchburg Bridge is the only bridge in Ohio that shares its existence with two counties: Clinton (35-14-11) and Highland (35-36-06). State Road Bridge (35-04-58), was built in 1983 and Cain Road Bridge (35-04-59), was built in 1987. Both of these bridges are in Ashtabula County, which makes them the newest covered bridges built to be functional. Buzzard Hill Bridge in Licking County (35-45-21), was moved to adjacent property from its original site in August, 1986, only to fall into a heap under the stress of its own weight and the crane's motion. Rock Mill Bridge, Fairfield County (35-23-48), is the only authentic location of a covered bridge and and existing mill combination left in the state of Ohio. There is one combination of mill and covered bridge in Columbiana County, but the bridge, Thomas J. Malone (35-15-96), was moved into Beaver Creek State Park next to Gaston's Mill in 1971. Carillon Park Bridge in Montgomery County (35-57-03), spans a now dry depression, which used to be part of the Miami and Erie Canal. Warner Hollow Covered Bridge in Ashtabula County (35-04-25), spans a deep gorge and has two immense piers. One pier is constructed of bedrock from the creek and the other is constructed with cut stone; optically, quite a contrast. Perry County's five covered bridges were all painted red, white and blue in 1976. Roberts Bridge in Preble County (35-68-05), Ohio's only double-barrelled bridge, was burned by arson in August 1986. The Roberts Bridge also held the distinction of being the oldest covered bridge in Ohio, built in 1829. Since its destruction, the oldest covered bridge today is located in Trumbull County (35-78-01), the Newton Falls Bridge, which was built in 1831. Newton Falls Bridge has another unique characteristic, as it is the only covered bridge in Ohio with an external walkaway. Summit County has the only authentically restored covered bridge, Everitt Road Bridge. The Everitt Road Bridge (35-77-01), was washed off its abutments in 1975 and restored by the Cuyahoga Valley National Recreation Area in 1986. Vinton County has a spectacular example of a humpback bridge, the Geer Mill/Ponn Humpback Bridge (35-82-06). This humpback bridge is 180 feet long, and has three spans. The Huffman Bridge in Noble County (35-61-57), located on an abandoned road, is privately owned and serving as a barn for cows. Eakin Mill Bridge in Vinton County (35-82-07), has a wooden dam near the bridge that was used as a mill race. Steel machinery left from the one-time mill can still be seen in the creek.

The list goes on and on with the individual, unique characteristics of each of the 142 covered bridges in Ohio. Whether a bridge is extremely picturesque, has an unusual truss or an interesting history; Ohio's covered bridges are available for everyone to enjoy.

BRIDGE NAME	COUNTY	NUMBER
Harshaville	Adams	35-01-02
Kirker	"	35-01-10
Dewey Road	Ashtabula	35-04-03
Creek Road	"	35-04-05
Middle Road	"	35-04-06
Root Road	"	35-04-09
Benetka Road	"	35-04-12
Graham Road	"	35-04-13
South Denmark Road	"	35-04-14
Doyle Road	"	35-04-16
Mechanicsville	"	35-04-18
Harpersfield	"	35-04-19
Riverdale Road	"	35-04-22
Warner Hollow	"	35-04-25
State Road	"	35-04-58
Cain Road	"	35-04-59
Palos	Athens	35-05-01
Kidwell	"	35-05-02
Blackwood	"	35-05-06
Belmont Campus	Belmont	35-07-05
Brown	Brown	35-08-04
New Hope Road	"	35-08-05
McCafferty	"	35-08-08
Eagle Creek	"	35-08-18
Scofield/Martin Hill	"	35-08-21
North Pole	"	35-08-23
George Miller Road	"	35-08-34
Governor Bebb Park	Butler	35-09-02
Black	"	35-09-03
Perintown	Clermont	35-13-02
Lynchburg	Clinton	35-14-11
	Highland	35-36-06
Martinsville	Clinton	35-14-09
Sells	Columbiana	35-15-01
McClellan	"	35-15-02
McKaig's Mill	"	35-15-03
Teegarden	"	35-15-05
Miller Road	"	35-15-07
Church Hill	"	35-15-08
Thomas J. Malone	"	35-15-96
Helmick	Coshocton	35-16-02
Hamilton Farm	"	35-16-07
Chambers Road	Delaware	35-21-04
John Bright	Fairfield	35-23-10
George Hutchins	"	35-23-13
Hannaway	"	35-23-15
Johnson	"	35-23-16
Zeller-Smith	"	35-23-19

BRIDGE NAME	COUNTY	NUMBER
Shade	Fairfield	35-23-20
McLerry	"	35-23-25
Shryer/Game Farm	"	35-23-27
Holliday	"	35-23-30
Ruffner	"	35-23-31
Baker	"	35-23-33
John Raab	"	35-23-37
Hartman #2	"	35-23-38
Hummel	"	35-23-40
Mink Hollow	"	35-23-43
Rock Mill	"	35-23-48
Roley School House	"	35-23-49
Smith-Carnes	"	35-23-51
Bergstresser	Franklin	35-25-03
Cemetery Road	Greene	35-29-01
Engle Mill	"	35-29-03
Stevenson Road	"	35-29-15
Charlton Mill Road	"	35-29-16
Ballard Road	"	35-29-18
Indian Camp	Guernsey	35-30-04
Armstrong	"	35-30-12
B & O Reservoir	"	35-30-33
Jediah Hill	Hamilton	35-31-01
Skull Fork	Harrison	35-34-19
Petersburg/Johnson	Jackson	35-40-06
Byer	"	35-40-08
Buckeye Furnace	"	35-40-11
Scottown	Lawrence	35-44-05
Belle Hall	Licking	35-45-01
Boy Scout/Rainrock	"	35-45-04
Girl Scout Camp	"	35-45-05
Gregg	"	35-45-06
Lobdell Park or McLain's	"	35-45-17
Buzzard Hill	"	35-45-21
Davis Farm	"	35-45-25
Hartford (Croton P.O.) Fairgrounds	"	35-45-80
McColly	Logan	35-46-01
Bickham	"	35-46-03
Eldean	Miami	35-55-01
Foraker	Monroe	35-56-14
Long/Old Camp	Monroe	35-56-18
Germantown	Montgomery	35-57-01
Carillon Park	"	35-57-03
Mud-Lick/Jasper Road	"	35-57-36
Barkhurst Mill	Morgan	35-58-15
McConnellsville Fairgrounds	"	35-58-32
Island Run	"	35-58-35

BRIDGE NAME	COUNTY	NUMBER
Adams/San Toy	Morgan	35-58-38
Saw Mill	"	35-58-41
Salt Creek	Muskingum	35-60-31
Manchester	Noble	35-61-33
Parrish	"	35-61-34
Park Hill Road	"	35-61-40
Danford	"	35-61-42
Huffman	"	35-61-57
Parks/South	Perry	35-64-02
Hopewell Church	"	35-64-03
Jacks Hollow	"	35-64-05
Bowman Mill	"	35-64-06
Bill Green	Pickaway	35-65-15
Harshman	Preble	35-68-03
Dixon's Branch	"	35-68-04
Roberts	"	35-68-05
Brubaker	"	35-68-06
Christman	"	35-68-12
Geeting	"	35-68-13
Warnke	"	35-68-14
Buckskin	Ross	35-71-02
Mull	Sandusky	35-72-01
Otway	Scioto	35-73-15
Lockington	Shelby	35-75-01
Everitt Road	Summit	35-77-01
Newton Falls	Trumbull	35-78-01
Upper Darby	Union	35-80-01
Spain Creek	"	35-80-02
Treacle Creek	"	35-80-03
Little Darby	"	35-80-04
Reed	"	35-80-05
Mt. Olive Road	Vinton	35-82-04
Bay	"	35-82-05
Geer Mill/Ponn/Humpback	"	35-82-06
Eakin Mill	"	35-82-07
Cox	"	35-82-10
Shinn	Washington	35-84-03
Henry	"	35-84-06
Root	"	35-84-08
Harra	"	35-84-11
Bell	"	35-84-12
Mill Branch	"	35-84-17
Schwenderman	"	35-84-20
Hills/Hildreth	"	35-84-24
Hune	"	35-84-27
Rinard	"	35-84-28
Parker	Wyandot	35-88-03
Swartz	"	35-88-05

Adams County
35-01-02

Harshaville Bridge

The Harsha family had a mill located next to the Harshaville Bridge which was built in 1860. The community and the bridge were named after this family. The bridge crosses Cherry Fork Creek, which is a tributary of Ohio Brush Creek. Ohio Brush Creek is the primary stream that drains Adams County. Cherry Fork has an average bed width of 75 feet and is a calm stream most of the year.

Originally, the Harshaville Bridge was a single span, but now it is supported by two concrete piers located at quarter points. The bridge rests on the original creek stone abutments. The exterior has a white tin roof and siding. The bridge was built in 1860 with a multiple kingpost truss encased by a double Burr arch. The truss in this bridge is particularly interesting because the center panel of the multiple kingpost truss is doubled. The bridge is open to traffic.

There is a pathway that leads down to the creek bed and if the water is low, one can walk down the creek to appreciate the bridge. This bridge is not one that lends itself to photography.

DIRECTIONS: SR. 32 East, SR. 247 south, left on T 292 (Graces Run), one and one-half miles. (Donovan, 1980; Ohio DOT; SOCBA)

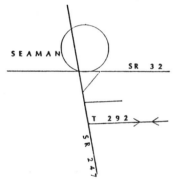

Adams County
35-01-10

Kirker Bridge

The Kirker Bridge was named after Governor Thomas Kirker who lived nearby. The bridge was built in 1867 and has a single span that crosses the East Fork of Eagle Creek, which is a tributary to the major drainage channel for southwestern Adams County.

Fifty-six feet long, the bridge is constructed with a multiple kingpost truss. The bridge had additional structural support installed in 1950. The interior has diagonal tie rods added to encase the truss. Steel head beams were also added that act as the bottom of the roof truss. The floor is blacktopped. The bridge is now bypassed and has a faded red tin roof and weathered white siding.

There is no access to the creek bed, but a park of sorts has been established around the bridge that allows pedestrian access to the bridge itself. The Kirker Bridge appears to have been bypassed and forgotten, fading away into the creek's foliage. The bridge is not colorful nor maintained and is not very impressive.

DIRECTIONS: Liberty Township. From West Union, SR. 41 south, right on SR. 136. (Donovan, 1980; Ohio DOT; SOCBA)

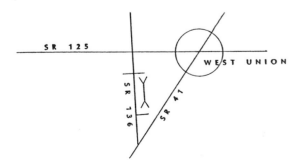

Dewey Road Bridge

The Dewey Road Bridge used to be named the Olin's Bridge after the Olin Family who have owned property south of the bridge since 1860. The Dewey Road Bridge is 127 feet long and spans the Ashtabula River, the major drainage channel in northeast Ashtabula. The Ashtabula River's bed averages 120 to 150 feet in width. During the spring and fall rains, it carries enormous amounts of water and in the winter the ice floes are huge.

The bridge was built in 1873 by a carpenter named, Potter, with a Town lattice truss. In 1981, a group of interested neighbors helped repair the bridge. A new shingle roof, some new side boards, repaired gables, painted portals and guardrails all helped restore the bridge. Steel I-beams were added to the underside of the bridge for additional support. The beams collected brush and trees. In 1985, ice floes tore some of the supports away from the bridge. The Ashtabula County Engineer's Department then installed a concrete pier. The bridge rests upon concrete abutments.

When the river is low, there is easy access to the creek bed. From the creek bed one can see the three sets of small windows exposing the lattice truss. The bridge's portals are painted white but the rest of the bridge is weathered and has a rough appearance. The bridge is located in a secluded valley and its massive structure is imposing against the large river and wooded terrain.

DIRECTIONS: Plymouth Township. From Ashtabula, SR. 84 East, right on Hadlock Road (T-335) South, left on Dewey Road (T-334). (Ashtabula County Engineer's Office, Bliss, 1968; Covered Bridge Festival Committee; Donovan, 1980; Ohio DOT Smolen; SOCBA)

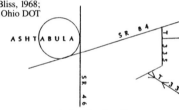

Creek Road Bridge

Creek Road Bridge is located on a lonely, narrow gravel road and appears suddenly around a bend. The 110 foot bridge spans the Conneaut Creek, which has an average bed of 100 feet and is the major drainage channel for northeast Ashtabula County.

The date of construction is not known. Creek Road Bridge has an asphalt shingled roof, white weathered wood siding and one long window on each side of the bridge exposing the Town lattice truss. It is supported by two cut stone abutments and a center support that has recently been added. The center support consists of a concrete wall to deflect ice floes (which is a persistent problem) and a steel bracing above the concrete pier which helps distribute the center support. The bridge looms twenty-five feet above the creek bed. The creek bed is easily accessible and allows for an excellent view of the bridge in any season.

DIRECTIONS: Liberty Township. From Kingsville, Creek Road (T-443) East, Northeast, four miles (Ashtabula County Engineer's Office; Bliss, 1968; Covered Bridge Festival Committee; Donovan, 1980; Ohio DOT; Smolen; SOCBA)

Middle Road Bridge

Middle Road Covered Bridge is located on Middle Road, spanning 152 feet across Conneaut Creek. Conneaut Creek is the largest river in northeastern Ashtabula County. The bridge is supported by stone abutments and two concrete piers at quarter points. The bridge is a Howe truss construction and was built in 1868. In 1984, the north end of the bridge dropped 18 inches. The County Engineer temporarily shored up the bridge until restoration was done. The County Engineer called for volunteers. Three men, four paid college students, and several county employees under the County Engineer's supervision, completed the restoration in six months. The refurbishment included constructing the piers, jacking up and straightening the bridge and strengthening the lower chords with treated lumber. The bridge originally only had an 8 inch overhang on the portals. This allowed water to drip inside, rotting the wood and causing serious problems which could have resulted in the loss of the bridge. The workers extended the portals by two feet to remedy the situation.

The bridge is 136 feet long. The exterior has an asphalt shingled roof and naturally weathered wood siding. A long narrow window stretches down each side of the bridge, exposing the Howe truss.

There is a driveway/path that leads down to the creek bed where one can obtain the view of the entire bridge. The Middle Road Covered Bridge is located in a remote, wooded valley and the Conneaut Creek provides the bridge with a dimensional and interesting composition.

DIRECTIONS: Conneaut Township. From Conneaut, SR. 7 south, three miles, left on 22, one mile right on Middle Road. (Ashtabula County Engineer's Office, Bliss, 1968; Covered Bridge Festival Committee; Donovan, 1980; Ohio DOT, Smolen; SOCBA)

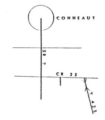

Root Road Bridge

Root Road Covered Bridge spans the east branch of the Ashtabula River. It was built in 1868 with a Town lattice truss and has creek stone abutments. It is 114 feet long.

In 1963 the bridge was in danger of collapse due to age and severe weather. Temporarily, guy wires were installed and the load limit was reduced. In 1982-1983, the bridge was restored. This restoration consisted of the following: 1) jacking up the bridge 18 inches, 2) building one concrete abutment, 3) adding a concrete center pier, 4) new floor beams and flooring, 5) new laminated girders, and 6) new siding and guardrails. The major advantage of the restoration was that the bridge can now carry large truck loads.

The bridge has a shingled roof and white painted portals. The white painted siding is fading. Each side has a long narrow window exposing the lattice truss.

The Root Road Bridge has severely limited access to the river bed. The physical location of the bridge limits the visual appreciation of it. A most unique aspect of this covered bridge is the new laminated girders that are exposed in the interior under the windows. The girders add a lineal effect interfacing with the lattice design. Even though the exterior view leaves something to be desired, the interior structure is an engineering aspect to be admired.

DIRECTIONS: Monroe Township. From Monroe Center, SR. 7 south, right on Root Road (T 414). (Ashtabula County Engineer's Office; Bliss, 1968; Covered Bridge Festival Committee; Donovan, 1980; Ohio DOT; Smolen; SOCBA)

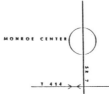

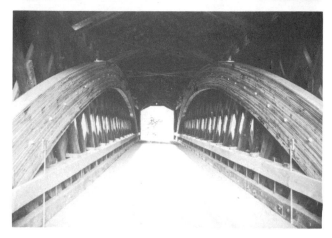

Benetka Road Bridge

Located two and one-half miles northeast of Sheffield, the Benetka Road Covered Bridge spans the Ashtabula River, the major drainage channel in Ashtabula County. Built in 1900, the bridge is 138 feet long and has a Town lattice truss.

Prior to restoration the bridge had problems that prohibited its use by daily traffic. It had a low flood clearance, a three ton load limit and low traffic height clearance. Creative expertise went into the restoration of this bridge. A nine inch wide, by 38 inch deep, arch was constructed out of one inch yellow poplar lumber. These one inch boards were dried and salt treated, then glued and spiked together. The result is a beautifully huge, multi-layer arch that enables the bridge to accept the heavy traffic necessitated by the local community. The enormous arches are also aesthetically very pleasing. Additional height clearance was obtained by attaching the floor beams under the chords rather than on the chords. The bridge was raised, which increased flood water clearance by two feet. The exterior was re-sided with redwood and has a shingled roof.

The interior of the bridge is geometrically exciting because of the massive arches combined with the lattice truss. There is easy access to the creek bed surrounding the bridge site. The bridge is extremely photogenic with a long narrow window and the redwood siding reflecting in the river pool.

DIRECTIONS: Sheffield Township. From Kingsville, SR. 193 south, right at Gageville on CR 325, one-half mile, right on Benetka Road (T 350). This section of Benetka Road does not appear on most maps. (Ashtabula County Engineer's Office; Bliss, 1968; Covered Bridge Festival Committee; Donovan, 1980; Ohio DOT; Smolen; SOCBA)

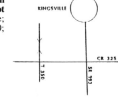

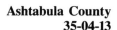

Graham Road Bridge

Graham Road Bridge used to cross one of the east branches of the Ashtabula River. In 1971, the Ashtabula Commissioners moved the bridge on to donated property just south of its original location. The bridge now rests on dry land and has a small park site that has a picnic table and a grill.

The bridge has a unique background. It was built on Graham Road in 1913 from pieces of the Callender Road Bridge (built in 1867) that had washed downstream during a flood of that same year. When Graham Road Bridge was rebuilt, steel beams were attached to the underside for additional structural support. Graham Road Bridge is 97 feet long and has a Town lattice truss. The bridge has a dark shingled roof and blackish-gray, naturally weathered wood siding. The siding has weathered in such a way as to expose the many knots in the wood.

DIRECTIONS: Pierpont Township. From Monroe Center, SR. 7, south, two miles, right on Graham Road (T 343). (Ashtabula County Engineer's Office, Bliss, 1968; Covered Bridge Festival Committee; Donovan, 1980; Ohio DOT; Smolen; SOCBA)

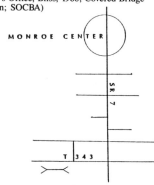

South Denmark Road Bridge

South Denmark Road Bridge spans Mill Creek with 94 feet. It was built in 1890 with a Town lattice truss. Years ago, it was called the Williams Corner Covered Bridge, after some local residents. It is rumored that this bridge was rebuilt from a bridge (built in 1863) that was washed away in the same location.

The bridge has a shingled roof and naturally weathered white siding. South Denmark Road Bridge has two small windows on both sides, disclosing the lattice truss. The floor has two wooden runners attached to horizontal floor planking. The grain of the wood has been raised from years of use. The portals are freshly painted white.

The County Engineer's Department bypassed the bridge in 1975 in order to preserve it. The bridge site has a small park but does not offer a picnic table or grill. There is not any access to the creek bed, but the exterior is easily visible from the surrounding park.

DIRECTIONS: Denmark Township. From Jefferson, SR. 167, east, one-half mile, right on South Denmark Road, two miles. (Ashtabula County Engineer's Office; Bliss, 1968; Covered Bridge Festival Committee; Donovan, 1980; Ohio DOT; Smolen; SOCBA)

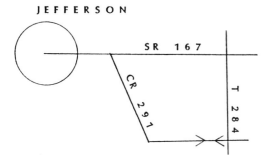

Doyle Road Bridge

The Doyle Road Covered Bridge has also been called the Mullen Bridge. It is 94 feet long and spans Mill Creek, a tributary of the Grand River. The Grand River is the principle drainage channel in the western half of Ashtabula County.

The bridge was built in 1868 by a carpenter from Vermont who designed it similar to one in his home town. The bridge is of Town lattice construction and has a long narrow window on both sides. It has a gray shingled roof and weathered, blackish wood siding. The portals are in poor condition, with some of the siding gone and the remaining siding rotting. Steel I-beams have been installed near the portals that prevent vehicles exceeding eight feet in height from crossing the bridge.

There is a path that leads down to the creek bed that has a vantage point of the entire bridge. The Doyle Road Bridge is attractive from the creek, but its portals are in great need of repair.

DIRECTIONS: Jefferson Township. From Jefferson, SR. 307 west, one-half mile, right on Doyle Road (T 287). (Ashtabula County Engineer's Office; Bliss, 1968; Ohio DOT; Smolen; SOCBA)

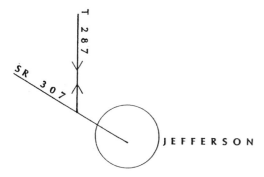

Mechanicsville Bridge

Mechanicsville Bridge crosses the Grand River and is the longest single span in Ashtabula County. The Grand River averages 150 to 200 feet wide and is the principle river that drains western Ashtabula County.

The Mechanicsville Bridge is 156 feet long and has a Howe truss and Burr arch construction. The arch is made of fifteen layers of two inch by eight inch lumber. This single massive arch is encased by the large beams in the "X" form of the Howe truss with vertical steel ties. Built in 1867, the bridge has a shingled roof, dark gray weathered wood siding and three small windows on each side. The siding around the portals is in poor condition. It is rotting and pieces are missing. The bridge rests on cut stone abutments and is about 40 feet above the river.

There is access down to the river bank and from there, the bridge is an impressive sight hanging above the Grand River.

DIRECTIONS: Austinburg Township. From Jefferson, SR. 307 west, four miles, left on Sexton Road (9). (Ashtabula County Engineer's Office; Bliss, 1968; Covered Bridge Festival Committee; Donovan, 1980; Ohio DOT; Smolen; SOCBA)

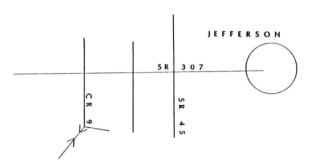

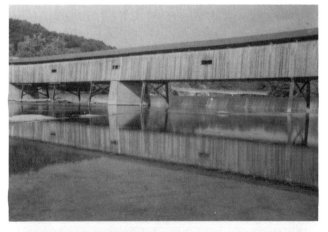

Harpersfield Bridge

Harpersfield Covered Bridge is the longest covered bridge in Ohio. It has two spans of 110 feet each and is a total of 230 feet long, including the eight foot overhang. The bridge was built in 1868 or 1873 by either Potter or Krieg. The bridge spans the Grand River and has a Howe truss construction. The 1913 flood changed the channel of the Grand River and a 140 foot steel bridge had to be added to the northern end of the covered bridge. The Grand River is the major channel in western Ashtabula County.

The bridge is in good condition and carries a considerable amount of local traffic. The Harpersfield Bridge has a green shingled roof and naturally weathered knotty pine siding. The bridge has three small windows on each side. Resting on concrete abutments, the bridge has one center concrete pier and five steel piers supporting the framework under the bridge.

The bridge has a dam to the west of it, and a new bridge beyond the dam to relieve the traffic burden from the Harpersfield Covered Bridge. The bridge has a beautiful location and is conducive to excellent photography. The Harpersfield Bridge's location once had a gristmill and a sawmill nearby. A waterworks is also in the proximity. The Ashtabula County Metropolitan Park Commission provides a 17 acre picnic and recreation area just north of the bridge.

DIRECTIONS: Harpersfield Township. From Jefferson, SR. 307 west, left on CR 154. At Harpersfield. (Ashtabula County Engineer's Office; Bliss, 1968; Covered Bridge Festival Committee; Donovan, 1980; Ohio DOT; Smolen; SOCBA)

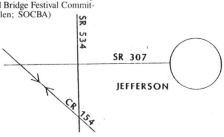

Riverdale Road Bridge

The Riverdale Road Covered Bridge spans the Grand River, which is the primary channel that drains the western half of Ashtabula County. The Grand River has an average bed width in this area of 120 to 150 feet.

The bridge was built in 1874 with a Town lattice truss. The bridge had a new roof and siding installed in 1965. In 1981, the floor was rebuilt using steel girders. Riverdale Road Bridge is 140 feet long and rests on cut stone abutments and a center steel bracing that rests on a concrete pier added in 1945. The bridge towers over the Grand River by 55 feet. The exterior has a shingled roof, knotty, weathered wood siding and one small window on either side.

Access to the creek bed is possible. The Riverdale Road Covered Bridge is located in a secluded valley and appears magnificently over the Grand River.

DIRECTIONS: Morgan Township. From Rock Creek, SR. 45 north, one-fourth mile, left on Riverdale Road (T 69). (Ashtabula County Engineer's Office; Bliss, 1968; Covered Bridge Festival Committee; Donovan, 1980; Ohio DOT; Smolen; SOCBA)

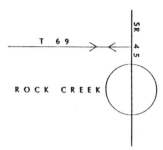

Photograph by Michael Krekeler

Warner Hollow Bridge

Warner Hollow Bridge has also been called Wiswell Road Covered Bridge. The Warner Hollow Bridge has three spans and is 121 feet long. It crosses Phelps Creek which is a deeply carved stream that is a tributary of the Grand River. The Grand River is the principle drainage channel in the western half of Ashtabula County.

The bridge was built in 1867 with a Town lattice truss. Warner Hollow Bridge was bypassed when Wiswell Road was a dirt/gravel road, which is evidenced by the existing path leading to either of the portals. This section of Wiswell Road has since been abandoned. The exterior of the bridge has a shingled roof, weathered siding with missing pieces, and is generally deteriorating. It has one small window on either side.

The sight of the bridge is very striking, as it hovers over Phelps Creek by 50 feet. The bridge rests on cut stone abutments. Warner Hollow bridge is distinctive because of the two stone piers supporting the bridge at quarter points. The one pier is huge pieces of cut sandstone quarried nearby at the historic Windsor Quarries. It is easy to notice that stone for the supports was also quarried from the side of the hill near the bridge. The other pier is constructed out of creek stone. The massive cut stone pier and the massive creek stone pier stand in great contrast.

A park surrounds the bridge site and access to the creek bed is available down a long hill. The area surrounding the bridge is thickly wooded and the creek bed is flat bedrock. The location is exceptional for hikers, photo buffs and nature lovers.

DIRECTIONS: Windsor Township. From Windsor Mills St SE 322, south on 537. (Covered Bridge Festival Committee; Donovan, 1980; Ohio DOT; Smolen; SOCBA)

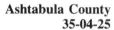

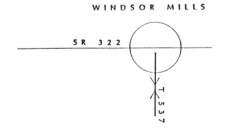

State Road Bridge

The State Road Bridge was built in 1983. It is included in this study of covered bridges because it was built for the express use of vehicles. Other new covered bridges have been built, but their purpose is solely decorative. State Road Bridge is one of two new bridges in Ashtabula County. The 175 foot State Road Bridge spans Conneaut Creek, which is a principle drainage channel for northeastern Ohio. Conneaut Creek has an average bed width of 150 to 200 feet in this area.

The building of a new covered bridge in Ashtabula was the result of funding provided by the Comprehensive Employment and Training Agency (CETA), and perseverance by the County Engineer's Department. County Engineer, John Smolen, designed the bridge in early 1983 and it was completed in October of that year. The bridge's construction is much different from the techniques used by craftsmen a hundred years ago. The abutments are sandstone and the bridge is reinforced by a center concrete pier. The lumber (97,000 board feet) is salt treated southern pine and oak. All of the connectors are hot dipped and galvanized to prevent rusting. The bridge was built by eight CETA workers, under the supervision of the County Engineer. It was built in five months on "dry land" and moved to the abutments in October of 1983. Even with the availability of modern equipment, the construction of the State Road Bridge is admirable. The workers must have wondered many times, ..."Just how did they build these covered bridges over 100 years ago?"

The State Road Bridge rests on cut stone abutments with poured concrete assistance. The bridge site has easy access to the creek bed, where the entirety of the bridge can be seen. The bridge has a dark shingled roof and salt treated, natural wood siding. A four foot tall window extends down the entire length of both sides of the bridge, exposing the Town lattice truss. The bridge is aesthetically appealing as it traverses the Conneaut Creek.

DIRECTIONS: Monroe Township. From Kingsville, SR. 193 South, one mile, left on SR. 84, one and one-quarter miles, left on CR 354 State Road), one-half mile. (Ashtabula County Engineer's Office; Covered Bridge Festival Committee; Donovan, 1980; Ellsworth, 1984; Ohio DOT; SOCBA)

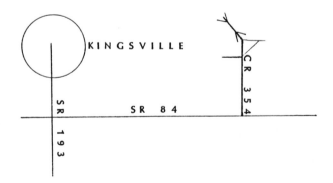

Cain Road Bridge

Cain Road Bridge spans a branch of the Ashtabula River. The branch has an average bed width of 125 feet. The Ashtabula River drains the northeast quarter of Ashtabula County.

Cain Road Bridge is rare because it is new. Finished in the fall of 1986, it has a Pratt truss, which is the only Pratt truss in Ohio. Estimated at 275 feet long, it has a long narrow window extending down both sides of the bridge. The bridge is a single span and rests on concrete abutments. The exterior has natural wood plank siding, is salt treated, and has galvanized connectors.

This is the most recent covered bridge built in Ashtabula County (Land of Covered Bridges). These two covered bridges are included in this study because they were designed and built to accommodate traffic. They were not built for decoration or promotional aspects.

The Cain Road Covered Bridge is fascinating because it is the only Pratt truss in Ohio and is one of only five in the United States. The Cain Road Covered Bridge was dedicated at the Ashtabula Covered Bridge Festival in Ashtabula County on October 11, 1986.

DIRECTIONS: Pierpont Township. From Pierpont, north on SR. 7, one mile, left on Caine Road (T 579). (Ohio DOT)

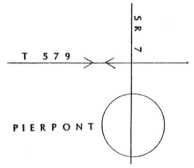

Palos Bridge

Built in 1875, the Palos Bridge was named after a town located nearby. The bridge spans Sunday Creek with 81 feet. Sunday Creek accepts the spillover from Burr Oak Lake, six miles north, and has an average bed width in the immediate vicinity of Palos Bridge of 60 to 70 feet. Sunday Creek is a third order tributary to Hocking River, which is the largest river coursing through Athens County.

The bridge has a variation multiple kingpost truss. The interior has been sided and the truss is not exposed except for about twelve inches at the roof. The exterior of Palos Bridge has a red tin roof and dark reddish-brown wood siding. The bridge has a steel pier for additional structural support. The original stone abutments are still supporting the bridge.

The Palos Bridge has been reasonably maintained and still serves the local community. The bridge is located in a broad, open valley and sits just off State Route 13, which allows visual access to numerous travelers even though they do not use the bridge. Palos Bridge is listed in the National Register of Historic Places.

DIRECTIONS: Trimble Township. From Glouster, one mile north on SR. 13 on the right. (Donovan, 1980; Ohio DOT; SOCBA)

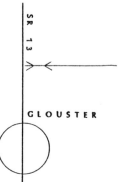

Kidwell Bridge

The Kidwell Covered Bridge was named for the town that used to be located at the junction of State Route 13 and State Route 685. It has also been known as the Monserrat Bridge. The bridge is 96 feet long and crosses the Sunday Creek which is a third order tributary of the Hocking River that is the largest river responsible for the drainage of Athens County.

Kidwell Bridge was built in 1880 with a Howe Truss. The exterior siding is painted reddish-brown and has a tin roof.

There is limited access to the creek bed and therefore it is difficult to appreciate the bridge in its totality. The bridge is closed to vehicular traffic. It has been painted recently, but appears to have been forgotten otherwise. The road has virtually been abandoned and the vegetation surrounding the bridge is so thick that it makes it difficult to observe the exterior. The interior is inviting because of the suspended steel wire supports and the diagonal floor planking. The Kidwell Bridge's physical location is not conducive for observation. The bridge is listed in the National Register of Historic Places.

DIRECTIONS: Dover Township. From Jacksonville, south on SR. 13, one mile, right on T 332. (Donovan, 1980; Ohio DOT; SOCBA)

Blackwood Bridge

The Blackwood Bridge was named after a local family and was built in 1881. The sixty-four foot bridge spans Pratts Fork, which is a tributary to Shade River, a significant drainage channel in this region. Pratts Fork is a shallow creek averaging 30 to 40 feet wide in the immediate area of the Blackwood Bridge.

The Blackwood Bridge has a multiple kingpost truss and is open for local traffic. It has a white tin roof and reddish-brown painted siding. The bridge has cut stone abutments and one added steel beam, which rests on two steel beam legs centered under the bridge.

Due to the physical location of the bridge and the foliage, it is difficult to see the exterior of the bridge completely. The Blackwood Bridge is listed in the National Register of Historic Places.

DIRECTIONS: Lodi Township. From Pratts Fork, east on T 71, two miles, right on T 76 which becomes T 78, one and one-half miles, left on CR 46. (Donovan, 1980; Ohio DOT; SOCBA)

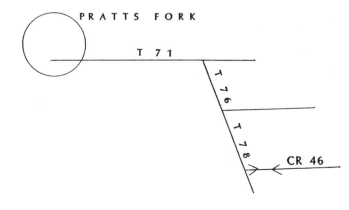

Belmont County
35-07-05

Belmont Campus Bridge

Formerly known as the Shaeffer-Campbell Bridge (35-23-46) while it served in Fairfield County, it crossed the Clear Creek in Clear Creek Township. It was moved in 1975 to Ohio University Branch Campus in Belmont County. County workers dismantled the bridge in Fairfield and numbered each piece of the bridge. A sketch was drawn to assist in the reconstruction of the bridge on Ohio University's Belmont Campus.

The old Shaeffer-Campbell Covered Bridge is 68 feet long and now sits over a small lake. Walkways have been built on either side of the bridge to allow foot traffic to cross the lake. Originally built in 1891, the bridge was constructed with a multiple kingpost truss. It has a reddish brown wood siding and is one of only a few bridges in Ohio that has a shake roof. The bridge has a beautiful setting and is in good condition.

Photograph by Michael Krekeler

DIRECTIONS: Richland Township. From Saint Clairsville, west on SR 40, three miles, right on SR 331, one mile, on right across from Belmont Campus. ("A Cool Place on a Hot Summer Afternoon"; "Covered Bridge Due at Belmont"; Donovan, 1980; Ohio DOT; "Reassembly Slated in Ohio"; "Rubber Neck Tour Stop"; SOCBA)

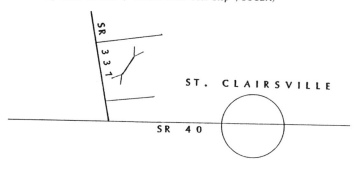

Brown County
35-08-04

Brown Bridge

The 129 foot Brown Bridge spans the Whiteoak Creek, which is the principle river draining central Brown County. The average width of the stream's bed is 130 to 150 feet in this immediate vicinity.

The bridge was built in 1878 with a Howe Truss. The floor is black-topped and open to vehicular traffic. Brown Bridge experienced a significant restoration in 1960 by the county highway department. The bridge is a single span resting on stone abutments. The exterior exhibits a white tin roof and naturally weathered wood siding that is in good repair.

Summer foliage makes it impossible to see the complete exterior of the bridge. Fall or winter is the season to visit the Brown Bridge.

DIRECTIONS: Washington Township. From New Hope, northeast on CR 5 (New Hope-White Oak Road), two miles. (Donovan, 1980; Ohio DOT; SOCBA)

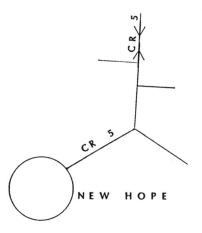

New Hope Road Bridge

The New Hope Road Bridge is a single span bridge that crosses the White Oak Creek with 173 feet. The White Oak Creek is the major drainage channel for central Brown County. The average width of the stream in this area is 160 feet.

The bridge was built in 1885 with a Howe truss. The interior of the New Hope Bridge is provocative. It has a massive eleven-ply laminated arch on each side of the bridge stretching the entire length. The floor has diagonal planking interfaced with two runners that have a raised grain from use. The bridge is enclosed by a white tin roof and a naturally weathered solid wood siding.

The bridge has been bypassed but is accessible to foot traffic. There is no access to the creek bed, but a park area is kept up in the vicinity of the bridge. A new bridge has been built adjacent to the covered bridge and one has a complete view from the new bridge or other areas in the park. The bridge is exciting to witness inside and out.

DIRECTIONS: Scott Township. From New Hope, just west of SR 68 on CR 5. (Donovan, 1980; Ohio DOT; SOCBA)

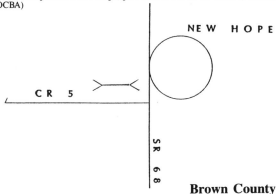

McCafferty Bridge

The McCafferty Bridge is located on McCafferty Road and spans the East Fork of the Little Miami River, which is the major river in this area. The East Fork of the Little Miami River is also the water supply for East Fork Lake in neighboring Clermont County.

The McCafferty Bridge is 157 feet long and was constructed with a Howe truss in 1895. The bridge is a clear single span resting on stone abutments. A white tin roof and naturally weathered, solid siding encloses the bridge.

The park-like area surrounding the bridge is mowed and the bridge has been well-maintained. Access to the river bed is difficult but the bridge is completely observable from the river banks.

DIRECTIONS: Perry Township. From Vera Cruz, southwest on SR 50, two miles, left on CR 105, (Donovan, 1980; Ohio DOT; SOCBA)

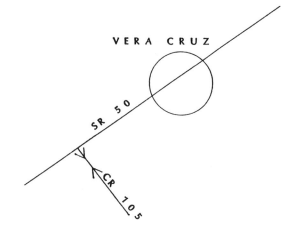

Eagle Creek Bridge

Once known as the Bowman Bridge and the Neel Bridge, the Eagle Creek Covered Bridge spans Eagle Creek. Eagle Creek is the principle river draining southeastern Brown County and southwestern Adams County. The stream's bed averages 175 to 200 feet.

Eagle Creek Bridge was built in 1872 with a Smith truss. The bridge is 174 feet long and is the longest single span bridge in Ohio. The floor has a thin coat of blacktop over wood planking. The exterior of the bridge has a gray tin roof and wooden plank siding, freshly painted white. Eagle Creek Bridge rests on limestone abutments reinforced by concrete. This bridge had a major renovation in 1952, and in 1963, the roof was replaced.

The observance of the bridge from a nearby hill is enjoyable. One can appreciate the entire bridge, the river and the wooded hills. The bridge is well-maintained by the State of Ohio Transportation Department, because Eagle Creek Covered Bridge has the distinction of being the only remaining covered bridge on the Ohio State Highway System. This bridge is the only covered bridge in Brown County that is listed on the National Register of Historic Places.

DIRECTIONS: Byrd Township. From Decatur, west on SR 125, one-half mile, left on SR 763, three and one-half miles at Neel. (Donovan, 1980; Greenberg, 1976; Ohio DOT; SOCBA)

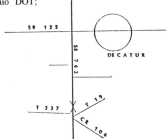

Scofield/Martin Hill Bridge

The Scofield Bridge is also called Martin Hill Covered Bridge and is located on Martin Hill Road at Scofield. Scofield once consisted of a general store and blacksmith shop, but today, only a few houses remain.

Scofield Bridge was built in 1882 by John Griffith, a local carpenter. This bridge has a unique backbone-type construction (a curved roof structure). Scofield Bridge has a multiple kingpost truss with a double arch encasing the multiple kingpost structure. The bridge is the shortest covered bridge in Brown County, with 96 feet; and spans Beetle Creek, which is a tributary of Eagle Creek. Eagle Creek is the area's major river.

Scofield Road winds around a hill above the covered bridge, allowing one to see the bridge from a most advantageous point of view. This bridge is one of the most picturesque covered bridges in Brown County because of the elevated vantage point and the curved backbone roof structure. The unique configuration of the Scofield Bridge adds perspective when observing the bridge.

DIRECTIONS: Huntington Township. From Ripley, east on SR 52, one-half mile, left on CR 49 (Scofield Road), three miles, right on Martin Hill Road (CR 31). (Donovan, 1980; Ohio DOT; SOCBA)

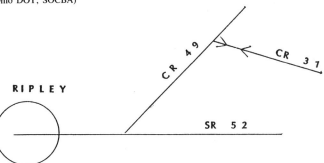

North Pole Bridge

The North Pole Bridge is located on North Pole Road three miles east of State Route 68 in southeastern Brown County. At one time, this bridge was called the Iron Bridge after Ripley Iron Pike Road. The North Pole Covered Bridge spans Eagle Creek. Eagle Creek carries tremendous amounts of water as it is the major drainage channel for southeastern Brown County.

The bridge was built in 1875 with a Smith truss. The 156 foot single span bridge rests on creek stone abutments. The bridge has been well-maintained. The floor has two wooden runners attached to opposing floor planking. The exterior has a white tin roof and naturally weathered wood siding.

Pictorially, the bridge is an impressive single span structure crossing a wide (125') stream bed, and is quite striking against the wooded setting.

DIRECTIONS: Huntington Township. From Ripley, north on SR 62, one mile, right on CR 15, three miles, right at North Pole Road. (Donovan, 1980; Ohio DOT; SOCBA)

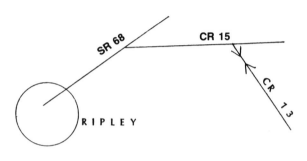

George Miller Road Bridge

The George Miller Bridge is located in a relatively remote part of southeastern Brown County. The 156 foot single span bridge crosses the West Fork of Eagle Creek, the bed of which averages 125 feet.

The George Miller Bridge has a white tin roof and black, weathered wooden siding. The bridge was built in 1875 with a Smith truss and now has a blacktop floor and is still open to traffic.

There is easy access to the creek bed down a path and from there, the bridge presents an impressive dark figure against the abundant surrounding foliage. Although there isn't a park located at the bridge, the area provides an excellent location for a picnic.

DIRECTIONS: Byrd Township. From Russellville, SR 62 south one-half mile, left on George Miller Road (CR 77), two miles. (Donovan, 1980; Ohio DOT; SOCBA)

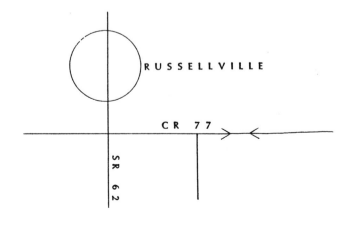

Governor Bebb Park Bridge

This covered bridge originally spanned Indian Creek on Fairfield Road, west of Oxford. It was relocated in Governor Bebb Park in 1970 by the Butler County Park District. It has two spans and is 118 feet long. Originally built in 1892, the bridge is constructed of white pine and has a Wernwag truss. This Wernwag truss is the only Wernwag left in the United States. Wernwag incorporated a double burr arch in this truss and it encases a version of a kingpost truss. The Governor Bebb Park Covered Bridge has been well preserved. The interior is in excellent condition and the wood plank flooring is the original floor. The bridge has a shake roof and naturally weathered siding that gives the bridge a nostalgic appearance. Even though this is not the bridge's original location, it looks quite at home.

DIRECTIONS: Morgan Township. From Okeana, northwest on SR 126, three miles, left into Bebb Park. (Donovan, 1980; Ohio DOT; SOCBA)

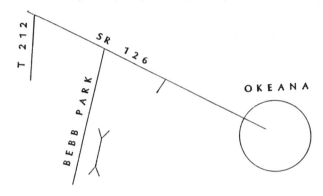

Black Bridge

Black Bridge was also known as Pugh's Mill Bridge and spans Dry Fork Creek. Dry Fork Creek accepts the spill over from Acton Lake at Hueston Woods State Park, three miles north. Built in 1870, Black Bridge is rapidly deteriorating. The bridge has two spans and is 206 feet long. The bridge rests on one stone pier and stone abutments.

The bridge is constructed with a variation of the Long truss. This truss has three members forming the "X" panel and two members forming the vertical that divides the panels. To look at the interior of Black Bridge with all of the huge timbers in the truss, it appears to be a structurally sound bridge. Further inspection of the floor reveals a ripple effect across the length of the bridge which is evidence that the bridge was used beyond the lifetime of a safe, sound bridge.

The exterior is naturally weathered and has not been painted, repaired or preserved in any manner. There is an eighteen inch tall horizontal ventilation panel extending the entire length of the bridge on both sides. The portals on either end are missing wood and, consequently, the water is destroying the wooden interior sides and the horizontal floor planking. A wire fence has been installed to prevent pedestrian passage on the bridge because its condition is so poor.

Black Bridge can easily be seen from an adjacent new bridge on State Route 732. The covered bridge strikes an imposing view across the Dry Fork Creek but if it is not repaired it will soon fall into the creek. As it is, it appears as if it has been bypassed and forgotten. Black Bridge is listed in the National Register of Historic Places.

DIRECTIONS: Oxford Township. From Oxford, north on SR 732, one-half mile. (Donovan, 1980; Greenberg 1976; Ohio DOT; SOCBA)

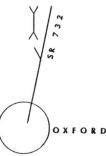

Perintown Bridge

The Perintown Bridge is also known as the Stonelick Bridge. Named after a nearby village, the bridge spans Stonelick Creek which has a bed width of 100 feet at the bridge site. Stonelick Creek is a tributary of the Little Miami River, a regional drainage channel.

The Perintown Bridge was built in 1878 with a Howe truss. The bridge is 140 feet long and is in excellent condition. Perintown Bridge is a single span and rests on stone abutments. The roof is tin, painted white, and the siding is in good repair and is painted red.

The bridge carries considerable local traffic. Large gas trucks, farm trucks and service trucks use the bridge daily. The bridge was repaired and reinforced in 1970-71 but has since had a truck fall through the floor, crushing the floor beams. The bridge was repaired, but if it continues to be treated in this manner, it will not last long. This is the only covered bridge left in Clermont County. Perintown Bridge is listed in the National Register of Historic Places.

DIRECTIONS: Stonelick Township. From Perintown, east on SR 50, two miles, left on CR 116, two miles. (Donovan, 1980; Ohio DOT; SOCBA)

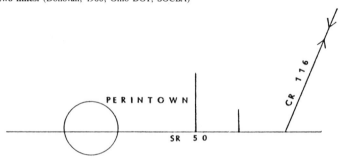

Clinton County
35-14-11

Highland County
35-36-06

Lynchburg Bridge

The 120 foot Lynchburg Bridge spans the East Fork of the Little Miami River. The bridge is located on the edge of Lynchburg and is geographically located half in Clinton County and half in Highland County. The Lynchburg Covered Bridge has a Long truss and was built in 1870. The bridge is bypassed. It is in fair condition except for some siding that has not been replaced. The bridge has a white tin roof and natural wood siding. The interior is in good condition but unless the siding is replaced, the weather will cause it to deteriorate.

The bridge site has a park area that is well-maintained but does not provide a picnic table or grill. Access to the creek bed is difficult but not really necessary because the park area allows for complete observation of the bridge.

DIRECTIONS: Clark Township in Clinton County. West side of Lynchburg. (Donovan, 1980; Ohio DOT; SOCBA)

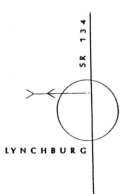

Martinsville Bridge

Martinsville Bridge spans Todd's Fork and is 80 feet long. Todd's Fork has a 50 foot bed width at the bridge site.

Martinsville Bridge was constructed in 1871 by the Champion Bridge Company of Wilmington, Ohio, which is still building bridges today. This bridge has a multiple kingpost truss, with crosswise floor planking and two attached lengthwise runners. The runners exhibit raised grain which occurs after much use.

The exterior of Martinsville Bridge has a rusting gray tin roof and rusty brown painted plank siding. The portals are square and trimmed with white paint. There is no projection of the portals from the bridge.

Martinsville Bridge has a country setting but is located at a busy intersection and accommodates numerous vehicles daily.

DIRECTIONS: Washington Township. From Martinsville, west on SR 28, one-half mile, right on CR 14, one-half mile. (Donovan, 1980; Greenberg, 1976; Ohio DOT; SOCBA)

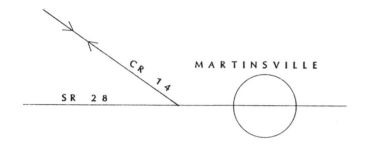

Sells Bridge

Sells Bridge is also refered to as Roller Mill Bridge. Charles Roller lived next to the bridge and owned a mill that was in the vicinity in the late 1800s.

The 48 foot Sells Bridge spans the West Fork of the Little Beaver Creek. The bridge, built in 1878, has a multiple kingpost truss. The bridge is in poor condition, with cut stone abutments falling into the creek; the siding is seriously deteriorated, and the floor is buckling at the ends in response to the crumbling abutments.

The original road the bridge served was abandoned long ago. Most recently, the bridge had served a now deserted farmhouse. The bridge is decrepit and can no longer function as a bridge for traffic but, somehow, maintains an alluring quality.

DIRECTIONS: Center Township. From Lisbon, west on SR 30, four miles, left on T 756, one mile. (Donovan, 1980; Lisbon Area Chamber of Commerce; Ohio DOT; SOCBA)

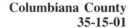

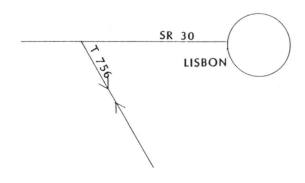

McClellan Bridge

Also known as Kinmuer Bridge, the McClellan Bridge was built in 1871. The bridge spans the West Fork of Little Beaver Creek, and is 53 feet long.

The McClellan Bridge has a multiple kingpost truss and is located on a dirt road that is used only for farm equipment. The old road is not passable by automobiles. Apparently, whoever used the bridge for local farming has repaired the siding. The floor is a little wobbly, but can sustain pedestrian traffic safely. The bridge has a tin roof and multicolored siding as a result of periodic replacement.

The only way to reach the bridge is to walk down a hill off of Little Trinity Church Road on the pathway and the bridge can be found at the bottom of the hill, nestled in the valley. Thick foliage prevents complete observation in the summer. Winter or fall would be the best time to see the entire bridge.

DIRECTIONS: Center Township. From Lisbon, west on SR 30, four miles, left on T 756, three miles, left down a hill. (Donovan, 1980; Lisbon Area Chamber of Commerce; Ohio DOT SOCBA)

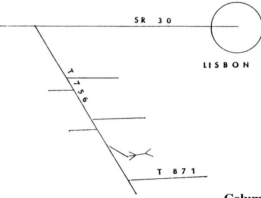

McKaig's Mill Bridge

McKaig's Mill Bridge, once known as Crosser Bridge, spans the West Fork of Little Beaver Creek with 53 feet. This bridge was built in 1870 with a multiple kingpost truss.

McKaig's Mill Bridge is open for local traffic and is in fair condition. The bridge has cut stone abutments. The roof is shake and is in need of repair. The wood siding is naturally weathered except for the pieces that have been replaced and were painted white. McKaig's Mill Bridge is located in an isolated, picturesque valley.

DIRECTIONS: Center Township. From Lisbon, west on SR 30, four miles, left on T 764 (Lisbon-Mellport Road). (Donovan, 1980; Lisbon Area Chamber of Commerce; Ohio DOT; SOCBA)

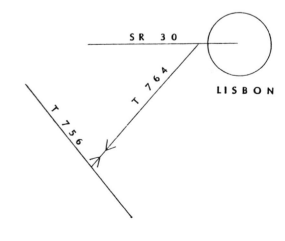

Teegarden Bridge

Teegarden Bridge is also known as the Centennial Bridge because it was built in 1876. The Teegarden Bridge has one 67 foot span and crosses the Middle Fork of Little Beaver Creek. The bridge has a multiple kingpost truss, concrete abutments, and a shake roof that needs some repair. The wooden siding is multicolored from sporadic replacements.

The bridge is next to a small park that has a carbonated spring. The park has an excellent vantage point to observe the bridge, as the creek bank is kept clear of brush and trees.

DIRECTIONS: Salem Township. From Lisbon, SR 45 north, two miles, left on T 761, two miles (bear left in Teagarden). (Donovan, 1980; Lisbon Area Chamber of Commerce; Ohio DOT; SOCBA)

Photograph by Michael Krekeler

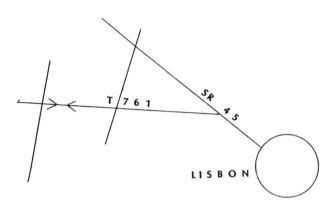

Miller Road Bridge

The Miller Road Bridge was built in 1860 and spans Millsite Creek with one span of 28 feet. The bridge has a multiple kingpost truss and was built by Perry Armstrong. The Miller Road Bridge has a tin roof and stone abutments. The wood siding is naturally weathered with no paint. This is the only covered bridge in Ohio that does not have access to one side or the other for one to take pictures from the stream. Each of the four corners has barb wire on its borders. This situation prevents anyone from being able to enjoy the aesthetic value that this covered bridge has to offer.

DIRECTIONS: Salem Township. From Lisbon, SR 45 north, two miles, right on T 862 (Miller Road) one mile. (Donovan, 1980; Lisbon Area Chamber of Commerce; Ohio DOT; SOCBA)

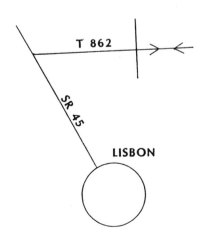

Columbiana County
35-15-08

Church Hill Bridge

The Elkton Historical Society says that Church Hill Bridge has the unique distinction of being the shortest covered bridge in the United States. The bridge is 19 feet 3 inches long, and has a multiple kingpost truss. Built in 1872, it has been relocated in Elkton next to the Lock 24 Restaurant, in a small park. Preserved by the local community, it has benches inside and has been the site of several weddings in the early 1980's. The Church Hill Bridge has a shingled roof, multicolored wood siding and stone abutments.

At the bridge site there is an abandoned lock and canal which is of historical interest. The Church Hill Bridge is listed in the National Register of Historic Places.

DIRECTIONS: Elk Run Township. From Lisbon, SR 154 east, three miles at Elkton. (Donovan, 1980; Lisbon Area Chamber of Commerce; Ohio DOT; SOCBA)

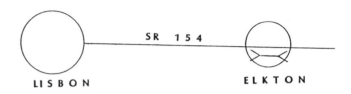

SR 154

LISBON   ELKTON

Columbiana County
35-15-96

Thomas J. Malone Bridge

The Thomas J. Malone Bridge is presently located in the Beaver Creek State Park east of State Route 7 in St. Clair Township. Built in 1870, it is 42 feet long and has a multiple kingpost truss. The Malone Bridge originally spanned Middle Run Creek on State Route 154 between Lisbon and Elkton. The bridge was moved twice by the Elkton Township Trustees and converted into a storage shed. Thomas J. Malone, a covered bridge researcher, discovered the converted bridge on Pine Hollow Road and recovered it. The restoration of the bridge was finished in 1971 and now has a shingled roof and dark brown stained wood siding. It sits beside Gaston's Mill on cut stone abutments.

Beaver Creek State Park is an interesting, historically restored area, worthy of a visit. It boasts of a restored mill, the covered bridge and an abandoned canal and lock. This site is one of only two locations in Ohio that has a covered bridge and mill combination.

DIRECTIONS: St. Clair Township. Near Williamsport, East of SR 7. (Donovan, 1980; Lisbon Area Chamber of Commerce; Ohio DOT; SOCBA)

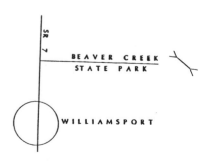

SR 7

BEAVER CREEK
STATE PARK

WILLIAMSPORT

Coshocton County
35-16-02

Helmick Bridge

The Helmick Bridge, once known as Doughty Bridge, was named after a fork of Killbuck Creek. Helmick Bridge spans Killbuck Creek, which carries a tremendous amount of water. Killbuck Creek is characteristic of most streams in the area in that it is prone to flooding.

Built in 1863, the bridge is 167 feet long with two spans. The truss is a multiple kingpost and has an extremely long span for this simplistic truss design. The bridge was closed long after it should have been, evidenced by the floor's condition. The flooring has a ripple effect, sagging from the stress of weight it was not designed to support. The Helmick bridge has a tin roof and naturally weathered wooden siding. It has not had paint, repair or any restorative action. The bridge is seriously deteriorated.

Restoration for this bridge is doubtful unless it was completely dismantled and the floor replaced, and most likely relocated over a stream that is not quite so violent.

The bridge is not easily accessible in the summer time because of foliage. Winter and fall would allow the entire bridge to be observed. The Helmick Bridge is listed in the National Register of Historic Places.

DIRECTIONS: Clark Township. From Blissfield on SR 60, turn right on CR 25, two miles at Helmick on left. (Donovan, 1980; Ohio DOT; SOCBA)

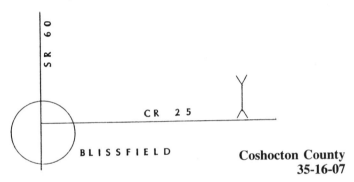

Coshocton County
35-16-07

Hamilton Farm Bridge

Also known as the Candels or Wills Creek Bridge, the Hamilton Farm Bridge was built in 1878. Built as a single span, it is 141 feet long. The construction is a double Burr arch encasing a multiple kingpost truss. Two wooden runners are interfaced on diagonal floor planking. The bridge rests on huge cut stone abutments. A steel pier of sorts has been installed. The bridge is currently being used as a shed for farm machinery. Hamilton Farm Bridge spans Wills Creek, which has an average 100 foot width. The bridge was closed before the floor started sagging and has been kept in good repair. The road has since been abandoned. The roof is red tin and the wooden siding is naturally weathered.

The bridge is long and ominous as it is elevated over Wills Creek and sits in the foreground of a wooded hill. The landscape is very photogenic but, unfortunately, a camper is stored in front of the bridge which serves to ruin the rustic scene.

DIRECTIONS: Franklin Township. From Wills Creek, south on CR 274, two miles. (Donovan, 1980; Ohio DOT; SOCBA)

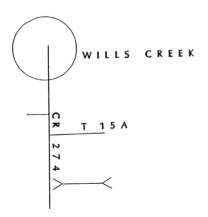

Chambers Road Bridge

The Chambers Road Bridge assumed its name after the Chambers family who lived just west of the bridge. The bridge spans Big Walnut Creek which has an average width of 60 to 70 feet and is the primary channel that supplies Hoover Reservoir, a lake 8 miles long and averaging a mile wide. The bridge was built in 1883 and is 73 feet long. Everett Sherman, a bridge builder in Delaware County, built the Chambers Road Bridge with a Childs truss and several other bridges in Delaware and Preble County, Ohio, with the same truss design.

In 1982, the commissioners of Delaware County assigned $18,300 for restoration of the bridge so that it could, when completed, support daily truck traffic. New concrete abutments and one concrete pier were poured. Originally the pier was constructed out of logs, then replaced by cut stone and with the recent restoration it is now concrete. The steel underframe was rebuilt and the floor was replaced. The white tin roof and natural wood siding were repaired. The interior of the bridge, after restoration, is in excellent condition. The Childs truss simulates the multiple kingpost truss with one added feature: there are steel braces used diagonally and in conjunction with the multiple kingpost beams.

The bridge site has easy access to the creek bed and allows one to appreciate the bridge in its entirety.

DIRECTIONS: Porter Township. From East Liberty, northeast on SR 656, one mile, left on Chambers Road, one mile.
(Donovan, 1980; Ohio DOT; SOCBA)

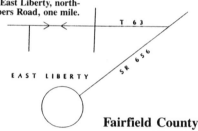

John Bright Bridge

Built in 1881, the John Bright Bridge spans Poplar Creek and is 85 feet long. Poplar Creek is a small stream with an average bed width of 70 feet.

The construction of this bridge is very interesting as well as unusual. It has an inverted steel bowstring and Burr arch. The opposing angles of the bowstring and the arch are pleasantly appealing and give this bridge its truly unique character. Built by A. Borneman and Sons, the John Bright Bridge's bowstring construction is distinctive because it is one of only two bowstring trusses in the United States.

As of the summer of 1986, the John Bright Covered Bridge was in poor condition. The sides of the bridge were gone and the roof had shotgun holes. What was left of the wood construction was deteriorating. Fortunately, there are plans to save the bridge. In 1987, the bridge was moved to the Ohio University Lancaster Campus on State Route 37. This relocation is the result of the efforts of local residents who are striving to preserve the covered bridges in Fairfield County.

DIRECTIONS: Liberty Township. From Baltimore, SR 158 south, one-half mile, right on Leonard Road (CR 15), left on Bader Road, one-quarter mile, right on Bish Road. (Donovan, 1980; Fairfield County Visitors and Convention Bureau; Greenberg, 1976; Goslin; Ohio DOT; SOCBA, SOCBA County Map)

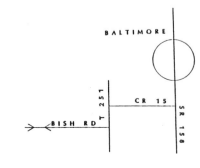

George Hutchins Bridge

Hutchins Bridge is 58 feet long and crosses Clear Creek. Clear Creek averages about 50 feet wide in the vicinity of the bridge and drains the southwestern portion of Fairfield County.

The Hutchins Bridge was built in 1904 with a multiple kingpost truss, a single span and stone abutments.

The summer of 1986 found the bridge in a deteriorating condition. Some of the white plank siding was missing, allowing the floor and interior to be exposed to the elements. The floor is planking laid lengthwise and would probably last for some years if the siding was repaired. The bridge has a rusted tin roof which seems to be preventing weather damage.

Hutchins Bridge is located on a country gravel road and serves the local traffic. The bridge is clearly visible from Amanda-Clearport Road, which is paved and carries more traffic. The bridge has a prominent location yet not much traffic, which makes this bridge an ideal candidate for preservation in its current, original location. However, the Hutchins Bridge was scheduled to be moved or demolished in 1987.

DIRECTIONS: Madison Township. From Clearport, west on CR 69 (Amanda-Clearport Road), two and one-half miles, left on T 137 (Strickler Road). (Donovan, 1980; Fairfield County Visitors and Convention Bureau; Goslin; Ohio DOT; SOCBA; SOCBA County Map)

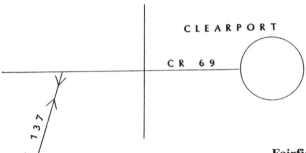

Hannaway Bridge

The Hannaway Bridge has a single span and crosses Clear Creek with 81 feet. Clear Creek averages 60 feet in the vicinity of Hannaway Bridge and drains the southwestern portion of Fairfield County.

Hannaway Bridge, built in 1901, has a multiple kingpost truss, a white tin roof and weathered white siding. The bridge rests on large cut stone abutments. The stone work is laid without any concrete assistance and its form is architecturally appealing. The floor boards are laid crosswise with plank runners laid lengthwise. The entire length of the bridge has a narrow window on both sides with an awning protecting the interior.

The bridge would be in good condition if some siding boards were replaced and the bridge painted. Hannaway Bridge is particularly impressive in its valley because of the angle it crosses Clear Creek. Unfortunately, the Hannaway Bridge was scheduled to be moved or demolished in 1987.

DIRECTIONS: Madison Township. From Clearport, south one-half mile on CR 24 (Clearport Road). (Donovan, 1980; Fairfield County Visitors and Convention Bureau; Goslin; Ohio DOT; SOCBA; SOCBA County Map)

Johnson Bridge

The Johnson Bridge spans Clear Creek with 92 feet. Clear Creek averages 80 feet wide in the area of the Johnson Bridge and drains southwestern Fairfield County.

Built in 1887, the Johnson Bridge has a rare combination of a Howe truss and two full length windows protected by awnings. Consequently, the Howe truss is exposed and can be easily seen from the exterior of the bridge. The roof is white tin and the floor planking is laid lengthwise. The bridge is in good repair and accommodates local traffic. The Johnson Bridge is a single span and rests on stone abutments with poured concrete assistance, over and around the stone.

Johnson Bridge is an excellent example of the Howe truss and is a well preserved covered bridge. This bridge should be one of the bridges Fairfield County preserves.

DIRECTIONS: Madison Township. From Clearport, east on CR 69, one and three-fourths miles. (Donovan, 1980; Fairfield County Visitors and Convention Bureau; Goslin Ohio DOT; SOCBA; SOCBA County Map)

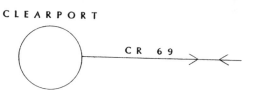

Zeller-Smith Bridge

Built in 1891, the 79 foot Zeller-Smith Bridge was constructed with a queenpost truss. It has white plank siding, tin roof and lengthwise floor planking.

Originally, the Zeller-Smith Bridge spanned Sycamore Creek, which is a tributary of Little Walnut Creek, the major drainage stream in northwestern Fairfield County. The bridge rested upon cut stone abutments and had only one span.

The summer of 1986, the village council of Pickerington helped finance the Zeller-Smith Bridge relocation to Sycamore Park in Pickerington.

DIRECTIONS: Violet Township. Relocated in Sycamore Park in Pickerington. Original Location: From Pickerington, south on CR 18 (Hill Road), one mile, left on T 216 (Busey Road) one-half mile. (Donovan, 1980; Fairfield County Visitors and Convention Bureau; Goslin; Ohio DOT; "Pickerington to Underwrite Cost of Moving Covered Bridge"; SOCBA; SOCBA County Map)

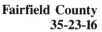
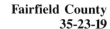

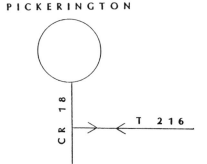

Shade Bridge

Built in 1871, the 122 foot Shade Covered Bridge originally spanned Walnut Creek. In 1980, the bridge was relocated at Pierson's Farm on private property. The bridge is visually accessible from Township Road 298. The 122 foot bridge is used as a shed and has doors securing it on both ends, preventing easy interior access. As with all covered bridges on private property, always request permission from the owners before entering. An interior photograph was not taken of this bridge because it was photographed at 7:00 one morning, and seemed too early to request permission.

The exterior of the bridge is in excellent condition with a gray tin roof and multicolored plank siding. The *World Guide to Covered Bridges* and the *Ohio Covered Bridge Guide* indicate that the Shade Bridge has a Burr arch.

In its original location, over Walnut Creek, the Shade Bridge had a shingled roof, rested on quarried stone abutments and had one span.

DIRECTIONS: Berne Township. From Sugar Grover, south on T 400 (Buckey) one mile, left on T 298, three-fourths mile, on right. (Donovan, 1980; Fairfield County Visitors and Convention Bureau; Goslin; Ketcham, 1969; Ohio DOT; SOCBA; SOCBA County Map)

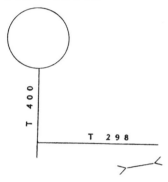

McLerry Bridge

Built in 1864, the McLerry Bridge spanned Walnut Creek and was 110 feet long. In 1983, the bridge was moved on to private property at the James Walter residence. Mr. Walter is the President of the Fairfield County Covered Bridge Association and was very helpful in assisting with locating the bridges and providing information on the Fairfield County covered bridges.

The McLerry Covered Bridge is easily visible from Pleasantville Road. If you wish to inspect the bridge closer, obtain permission from the owners first.

The McLerry Bridge has a tin roof, multiple kingpost truss and is now only 90 feet long because one end has rotted away.

DIRECTIONS: Liberty Township. From Baltimore, south on SR 158, one and one-half miles, right on Pleasantville Road, on left. (Donovan, 1980; Fairfield County Visitors and Convention Bureau; Goslin; Ketcham, 1969; Ohio DOT; SOCBA; SOCBA County Map)

Fairfield County
35-23-27

Shryer/Game Farm Bridge

The Shryer Bridge, named after a local resident, spans a tributary of the Paw Paw Creek which drains into Little Walnut Creek. The bridge, a single span, is 65 feet long and has a multiple kingpost truss. Shryer Bridge has a tin roof, white plank siding, and rests on cut stone abutments.

The interior is in excellent condition. The floor has lengthwise planking and the siding is complete. The Shryer Bridge was to be moved on to private property in 1987 to the Shryer Residence on County Road 17. The Shryer Bridge was located next to a Game Farm and has also assumed that name.

DIRECTIONS: Liberty Township. From Baltimore, North on SR 158, one mile, left on T 232 (Bickel), one and one-fourth miles. (Donovan, 1980; Fairfield County Visitors and Convention Bureau; Goslin; Ohio DOT; SOCBA; SOCBA County Map)

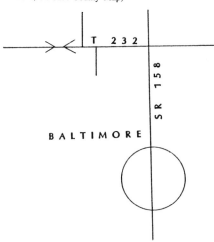

Fairfield County
35-23-30

Holliday Bridge

The Holliday Bridge originally spanned Walnut Creek with 110 feet. In 1982, the bridge was moved to the site of Millersport Lions Club Sweet Corn Festival, a permanent fairground. It currently spans a very small stream.

The bridge has a white tin roof and white plank siding. Built in 1899, the bridge has a queenpost truss, lengthwise planking and a painted white interior with graffiti.

Because of its new location it is prone to graffiti attacks and generally needs to be repainted. It is fortunate that the Lions Club was able to preserve the bridge instead of letting it disappear, as over 60 other covered bridges have in Fairfield County.

DIRECTIONS: Walnut Township. At Millersport on the Lions Club Sweet Corn Festival Fairgrounds. (Donovan, 1980; Fairfield County Visitors and Convention Bureau; Goslin; Ohio DOT; SOCBA; SOCBA County Map)

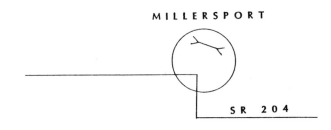

Fairfield County
35-23-31

Ruffner Bridge

Ruffner Bridge was built in 1875 with a Smith truss. The bridge is 82 feet long with a single span and rests on cut stone abutments. The bridge spans Little Rush River, which is a tributary of Rush Creek and drains eastern Fairfield County.

The summer of 1986 found this bridge to be in the poorest condition, yet still open to serve local traffic in Fairfield County. This bridge has received no maintenance in recent years. The portals are in extremely bad shape, half the siding is missing and the roof is leaking. The floor of the bridge is the bridge's single redeeming factor. The floor planking is laid diagonally and if the bridge was restored to its original condition, the floor would add to the bridge's aesthetic value. As is, the Ruffner Bridge's future is bleak.

DIRECTIONS: Richland Township. From Rushville, north on SR 664, one and one-half miles, left on T 368 (Bope Road) one mile, right on T 413 (Gun Barrell Road). (Donovan, 1980; Fairfield County Visitors and Convention Bureau; Goslin; Ketcham, 1969; Ohio DOT; SOCBA; SOCBA County Map)

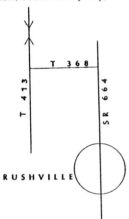

Fairfield County
35-23-33

Baker Bridge

Baker Bridge originally crossed a branch of Rush Creek and is 90 feet long. It had a shingled roof, a single span and rested on cut stone abutments. In 1981, Baker Bridge was moved to Fairfield Union High School Grounds. The bridge spans a small lake in a wooded area, far behind the high school building. Baker Bridge has a lovely setting and is well-maintained.

Built in 1871, the bridge was constructed with a queenpost truss. The floor planking is laid lengthwise. Baker Bridge has a tin roof and white plank siding.

Although Baker Bridge offers a captivating site, a long walk is required to reach the bridge.

DIRECTIONS: Richland Township. From West Rushville, southwest on SR 22, one mile, behind the Fairfield Union High School. (Donovan, 1980; Fairfield County Visitors and Convention Bureau; Goslin; Ketcham, 1969; Ohio DOT; SOCBA; SOCBA County Map)

Photograph by Michael Krekeler

WEST RUSHVILLE

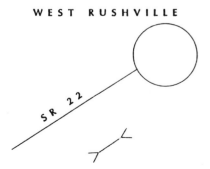

John Raab Bridge

The John Raab Bridge was built in 1891 with a queenpost truss. Fifty feet long, the bridge spanned a tributary of Raccoon Run. Raab Bridge was a single span and rested on cut stone abutments.

In 1974, the bridge was moved on to private property just west of its original location. It now sits on a splendid farm owned by Doid Raab, the son of John Raab, for whom the bridge was named. The bridge is visible from Ireland Road. As with all covered bridges on private property, obtain permission from the owner before inspection of the bridge.

Currently, the bridge is being used as a shed but the portals are open for easy interior observation. The roof is tin, the siding is white planking and the bridge is generally in excellent condition.

DIRECTIONS: Pleasant Township. From West Rushville, southwest on SR 22, three miles, left on T 344 (Ireland Road), one mile on right about 1/10 of a mile off the road. (Donovan, 1980; Fairfield County Visitors and Convention Bureau; Goslin; Ketcham, 1969; Ohio DOT; SOCBA; SOCBA County Map)

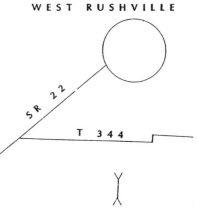

WEST RUSHVILLE

Hartman Bridge #2

Built in 1888 by Jacob Brandt, the Hartman Bridge was constructed with a queenpost truss and is 50 feet long. The Hartman Bridge was moved to Lockville Park in 1967, where it spans the old Ohio and Erie Canal bed. Lockville Park has preserved the locks of the old canal and maintains a portion of the old canal. The bridge sits just west of the park. It was repaired in 1967 when it was relocated. A shake roof, red plank siding and white paint on the interior were added at the time of relocation. The summer of 1986 found the Hartman Bridge with missing siding, steel bracing down the center of the bridge and a site that was grown over with weeds, making access to the bridge difficult. Apparently, either the interest or the funds for Lockville Park ran out.

DIRECTIONS: Violet Township. From Pickerington, CR 20 (Pickerington Road), south, three miles at Lockville in the Lockville Park. (Donovan, 1980; Fairfield County Visitors and Convention Bureau; Goslin; Greenberg, 1976; Ohio DOT, SOCBA; SOCBA County Map)

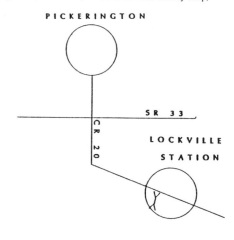

PICKERINGTON

SR 33

CR 20

LOCKVILLE
STATION

Hummel Bridge

Built in 1875, the Hummel Bridge crosses Rush Creek with a single span of 103 feet. Rush Creek averages a 90 foot width in the vicinity of the bridge and drains southeastern Fairfield County.

Hummel Bridge has a gray tin roof, weathered plank siding and rests on stone abutments. The interior is in excellent condition. The roof is in good repair and the floor's planking is laid lengthwise.

The bridge has been well-maintained, but the characteristic that is most striking about Hummel Bridge is the combination Smith truss and a single, ten-ply Burr arch that extends the entire length of the bridge. The arch is constructed of 2″ X 4″ timbers attached to form a 20″ thick arch. Hummel Bridge is one of two bridges in Fairfield County with a Burr arch. The other is the Shade Bridge which is privately owned. Shade Bridge is used as a shed, thus permission is required to see the interior. Hummel Bridge serves local traffic on Krile Hansley Road and is easily accessible for observers.

DIRECTIONS: Berne Township. From Sugar Grove, east on CR 50 (Sugar Grove Road) one-half mile, left on T-296 (Krile Hansley Road, two miles. (Donovan, 1980; Fairfield County Visitors and Convention Bureau; Goslin; Ohio DOT; SOCBA; SOCBA County Map)

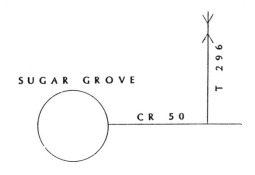

Mink Hollow Bridge

Mink Hollow Bridge spans Arney Mill Run with a single span of 51 feet. Arney Mill Run is an average 40 feet wide in this area and is a tributary of Clear Creek, which drains southwestern Fairfield County. Mink Hollow Bridge was built in 1887 with a multiple kingpost truss. The truss has an unusual configuration in that it has a double kingpost center panel. The floor planking is laid horizontally. The exterior has a gray tin roof and white plank siding. Characteristic of several other covered bridges in Fairfield County, there is a long window on both sides of the bridge, protected by a canopy. The bridge rests on cut stone abutments. The location of the bridge allows easy visual access from the road, but access to the creek bed is difficult because of fences and thick vegetation.

DIRECTIONS: Hocking Township. From Hamburg, south on T 289 (Hopewell Church Road) three-fourths mile, left on T 258 (Meister), one mile right on CR 28 (Crooks Road) one-fourth mile. (Donovan, 1980; Fairfield County Visitors and Convention Bureau; Goslin; Ohio DOT; SOCBA; SOCBA County Map)

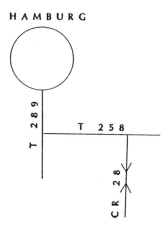

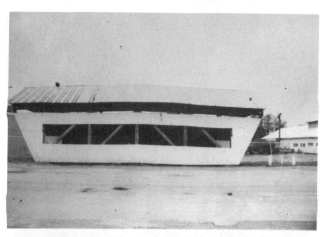

**Fairfield County
35-23-48**

Rock Mill Bridge

Rock Mill Bridge spans the Hocking River and is 50 feet long. The Hocking River is not a wide river at this point but it is deeply entrenched with bedrock. At the bridge site, the gorge drops forty to fifty feet. This area of the Hocking River drains the west-central section of Fairfield County.

The Rock Mill Bridge is located on Rock Mill Road next to the Rock Mill. Rock Mill has been abandoned and is sadly deteriorated. It is a huge building with five or six floors. This area of the Hocking River is its head waters and the water rushes through the gorge with tremendous power, supplying ample strength to power any mill.

Rock Mill Bridge was built in 1901. This bridge replaced another covered bridge at that location built in 1849. The Rock Mill Bridge was constructed with a queenpost truss. The bridge has been well-maintained with a shingled roof, white plank siding and white painted truss members. Characteristic of several Fairfield County covered bridges, Rock Mill Bridge has a long window, full length, with the sides of the bridge protected by a canopy. The bridge is a single span and is supported by cut stone abutments.

Rock Mill Bridge is listed on the National Register of Historic Places and is one of only two mill and covered bridge combinations left in Ohio.

DIRECTIONS: Bloom Township. From Lithopolis, southeast on CR 39 (Lithopolis Road), eight miles, left on CR 32 (Rock Mill Road) at Rock Mill. (Donovan, 1980; Fairfield County Visitors and Convention Bureau; Goslin; Greenberg, 1976; Ohio DOT; SOCBA; SOCBA County Map)

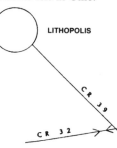

**Fairfield County
35-23-49**

Roley School Bridge

Roley School Bridge was built in 1899 or 1916, and spanned Paw Paw Creek with 60 feet. In 1972, the bridge was moved on to the Lancaster Fairgrounds. Roley School Bridge has a rusty gray tin roof and weathered white plank siding. The bridge was constructed with a multiple kingpost truss. The floor planking is laid lengthwise. The bridge has a long narrow window extending the length of one side of the bridge. At one time it had a canopy, but has since been removed. Other than the missing canopy and a need for paint, the Roley School bridge is in fair condition.

DIRECTIONS: Greenfield Township. On County Fairgrounds in Lancaster at Broad Street Entrance. (Donovan, 1980; Fairfield County Visitors and Convention Bureau; Goslin; Ketcham, 1969; Ohio DOT; SOCBA; SOCBA County Map)

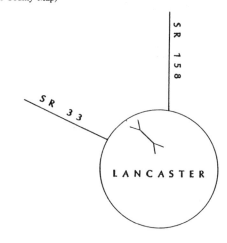

Carlton Bridge   29-03-07   New Hampshire

Johnson Powerhouse Bridge   45-08-08   Vermont

Ralston Freeman Bridge   38-63-27   Pennsylvania

Albany Bridge   29-02-06   New Hampshire

Shenk's Mill Bridge   38-36-30   Pennsylvania

Photograph by Michael Krekeler

Keefer Station Bridge   38-49-02   Pennsylvania

McConnell's Mill Bridge   38-37-01   Pennsylvania

Honeymoon Bridge   29-02-01   New Hampshire

Warner Hollow Bridge   35-04-25   Ohio

Dixon's Branch Bridge   35-68-04   Ohio

Governor Bebb Park Bridge 35-09-02 Ohio

Sunday River Bridge   19-09-04   Maine

Westport Bridge   14-16-01   Indiana

Geeting Bridge   35-68-13   Ohio

Fairfield County
35-23-51

Smith-Carnes Bridge

Also known as the Jackson Ety Bridge, the 80 foot Smith-Carnes Bridge spans Little Walnut Creek, which drains the northern third of Fairfield County.

The Smith-Carnes Bridge is located on an abandoned road on private property, the B.F. Fox Farms. To reach the Smith-Carnes Bridge, one must walk about a quarter of a mile down a hill (the old abandoned road). There is a fence surrounding the bridge entrance and the creek banks, to prevent anyone from viewing the bridge from the sides of the creek bed. The fence is understandable as the bridge is ready to collapse and the owners do not want anyone injured.

The bridge has red plank siding. The flooring was laid crosswise and was interfaced with two runners with planking running lengthwise. The abutments have heaved and, consequently, the flooring at the portals is raised and the center flooring sunken. The bridge itself has shifted in such a manner so that the portals resemble a trapezoid. The truss has an empty center panel. There is not even a head beam as used for the queenpost center panel, only the vertical and diagonal members pointing toward the empty center panel. Unfortunately, the bridge is beyond repair. The Smith-Carnes Bridge is doomed to collapse.

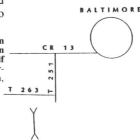

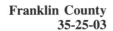

DIRECTIONS: Liberty Township. From Baltimore, west on CR 13 (Basil-Western Road) one and one-half miles, left on T 251 (Bader Road) one mile, right on Bish Road, one-half mile, left at Fox Farm, 3995 Bish Road. (Donovan, 1980; Fairfield County Visitors and Convention Bureau; Goslin; Ketcham, 1969; Ohio DOT; SOCBA; SOCBA County Map)

Franklin County
35-25-03

Bergstresser Bridge

The Bergstresser Bridge spans Little Walnut Creek, which is a primary stream draining the southeast corner of Franklin County. Little Walnut Creek has an average bed width of 130 feet in the vicinity of the Bergstresser Bridge.

The bridge is 134 feet long, single span, and is the second longest Partridge truss. The Little Darby Bridge in Union County is 155 feet. The Bergstresser Bridge is 16 feet wide and has a head clearance of thirteen feet, which makes it a large bridge. The exterior has red plank siding, a tin roof, and rests on cut stone abutments. The interior is in good condition. With no windows, the inside is dark. The floor has planking laid lengthwise.

The Bergstresser Bridge derived its name from a nearby neighbor who owned a farm just east of the bridge site, Daniel Bergstresser. The Bergstresser Bridge is the only covered bridge left in Franklin County in its original location. It is located on a country road and carries light traffic, and is kept in good repair by the Franklin County Engineering Department.

There is one dryland covered bridge listed in the *Ohio Covered Bridge Guide* for Franklin County north of Grove City, but after two hours of searching and talking to the local residents, the search was abandoned. It might be in existence, but it definitely is not accessible to the public.

Bergstresser Bridge was built in 1867 by the Columbus Bridge Company for $2,690. Reuben Partridge was an officer of the Columbus Bridge Company and, subsequently, the Partridge truss was used. There are only six located in Union County, which is Partridge's home county, and the sixth is the Bergstresser Bridge.

The Bergstresser Bridge is listed in the National Register of Historic Places.

DIRECTIONS: Madison Township. From Canal Winchester, south on SR 647, one mile, right on CR 224. (Architecture: Columbus; Donovan, 1980; Ketcham, 1969; Ohio DOT; SOCBA)

Cemetery Road Bridge

The 60 foot Cemetery Road Bridge was originally located about a mile east of New Burlington. Built in 1840, it was moved in 1979 and is now found in a small park-like area just south of Yellow Springs called, Glen Helen. The bridge spans Yellow Springs Creek, which is a tributary of the Little Miami River one-fourth of a mile from the bridge site. The Cemetery Bridge is only open to foot traffic. The covered bridge is the only point of interest at Glen Helen. The area is not kept up and is overgrown with weeds, but there are some identifiable trails near the bridge.

The Cemetery Bridge has a tin roof, gray-weathered siding and crosswise floor planking. The truss used in the construction of the bridge is an excellent example of a Howe.

DIRECTIONS: Miami Township. From Yellow Springs, southeast on CR 27, one-half mile, on right at Glen Helen. (Donovan, 1980; Ohio DOT; SOCBA)

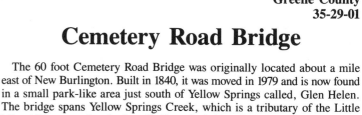

Engle Mill Road Bridge

Built in 1870, the Engle Mill Road Bridge is 145 feet long and spans Anderson Fork, which is one of two streams that feeds Caesar Creek Reservoir two miles west of the bridge site.

Engle Mill Road Bridge has a tin roof and weathered plank siding with traces of red paint around the portals, seams and knots on the eastern, less weathered side. The bridge has been maintained; siding has been replaced with multicolored planking, giving the bridge its novel charm.

The United States has approximately 21 Smith trusses left. Ohio has 13 of these trusses and the Engle Mill Road Bridge is a fine example of the Smith truss. Fortunately, the bridge has been bypassed for preservation. The floor planking is laid lengthwise. The bridge is a single span and rests on stone abutments.

DIRECTIONS: Caesar Creek Township. From Spring Valley, east on CR 75 (Spring Valley-Paintersville Road), five and one-half miles, right on Engle Mill Road, one mile, on right. (Donovan, 1980; Ohio DOT; SOCBA)

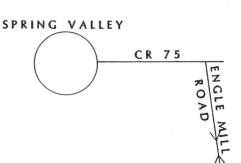

Stevenson Road Bridge

The Stevenson Road Bridge spans Massie Creek, which is a tributary to the Little Miami River which is about two miles from the bridge site. Massie Creek has an average bed width of 70 feet in the vicinity of the bridge.

The Stevenson Road Bridge was built in 1873 with a Smith truss. The floor planking is laid lengthwise. The bridge has a red tin roof, weathered red plank siding, and is 95 feet long. The bridge is a single span and rests on cut stone abutments with a steel pier on one creek bank to add support.

Open to local traffic, the bridge site has a junk yard adjacent to one side and no parking signs posted in a grassed area on the other side. One can easily park on the road and the grassy area is well-maintained, allowing easy visual access to the bridge.

DIRECTIONS: Xenia Township. From Xenia, north on SR 68, one mile, right of T 17 (Brush Row Road), two miles, left on CR 76 (Stevenson Road) one-half mile. (Donovan, 1980; Ohio DOT; SOCBA)

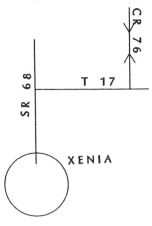

Charlton Mill Road Bridge

Charlton Mill Road Bridge spans Massie Creek, a tributary of the Little Miami River, which is about five miles west of the bridge site.

The date of construction for the 120 foot span is not known. It was constructed with a single span Howe truss and rests on cut stone abutments. In good condition, the bridge has a rusty-red tin roof, weathered plank siding and unusual floor planking. The floor boards are laid crosswise and additional floor planks were interfaced on top, running lengthwise, not as runners, but as a solid floor occupying three-fourths of the center part of the bridge floor. The bridge is open and serves local traffic.

DIRECTIONS: Xenia Township. From Xenia, northeast on SR 42, five miles, left on T 29 (Charlton Mill Road), one mile. (Donovan, 1980; Ohio DOT; SOCBA)

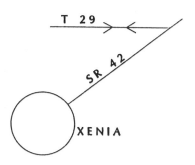

Greene County
35-29-18

Ballard Road Bridge

Ballard Road Bridge spans a north branch of Caesar Creek, which drains the south-central section of Greene County and feeds Caesar Creek Reservoir, which is eleven miles from the bridge site.

Ballard Bridge is 80 feet long. The date of construction is not known. The bridge was built with a Howe truss and the floor planking is laid lengthwise. The bridge has a red tin roof and multicolored, weathered siding. Ballard Bridge has a single span and rests on cut stone abutments.

The distinctively attractive bridge site can be attributed to a well-maintained bridge, the nature of the winding creek, local vegetation and a nearby farm.

DIRECTIONS: New Jasper Township. From Xenia, east on SR 35, six miles, right on Ballard Road, one mile. (Donovan, 1980; Ohio DOT; SOCBA)

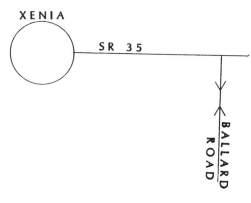

Guernsey County
35-30-04

Indian Camp Bridge

Indian Camp Bridge spans Indian Camp Run, a tributary of Wills Birds Creek that supplies water for Salt Fork Lake, which is a twelve mile long recreational lake, six miles north of Cambridge. Indian Camp Run averages 35 feet wide in the vicinity of the bridge site.

Restoration was complete in 1963, which consisted of strengthening the roof with I-beams, new siding, and the roof trusses required renovation. The date of construction is not known, but the timbers are hand-hewn. The bridge was constructed with a multiple kingpost truss and its floor planking is laid crosswise. Indian Camp Bridge is forty feet long and rests on cut stone abutments. The exterior has a tin roof and rusty red plank siding.

The Indian Camp Bridge takes its name from the fact that Indians lived in this area at one time. Indian Camp Bridge is the only covered bridge in its original location that is still serving local traffic in Guernsey County. At one time there were at least 87 covered bridges in Guernsey County. A compendium of them can be found in *Guernsey County, Ohio—A Collection of Historical Sketches and Family Histories* which was published by the Guernsey County Chapter 5, Ohio Genealogical Society, Cambridge, Ohio.

DIRECTIONS: Knox Township. From Indian Camp, north on SR 658, one mile, right on T 68. (Donovan, 1980; Goslin; Guernsey County Chapter 5 Ohio Genealogical Society; "Indian Camp Bridge"; "Indian Camp Span Improved"; Ketcham 1969; Ohio DOT; SOCBA)

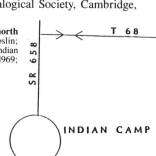

Armstrong Bridge

Of the three covered bridges previously located on the site of Salt Fork Lake, the Armstrong Bridge was the only one relocated and saved. The other two bridges were covered by the lake. As late as 1980, timbers of one of the covered bridges were slightly visible, sticking out of the lake. Guernsey County Historical Society formed a committee to save the Armstrong Bridge, and it was relocated in 1966-67 in the Cambridge City Park, where it spans a ravine. It now serves only foot traffic.

Armstrong Bridge is 70 feet long and was built in 1849 with a multiple kingpost truss. The floor planking is laid horizontally. The exterior has a white tin roof, dark red plank siding and rests on cut stone abutments with concrete assistance.

DIRECTIONS: Cambridge Township. In Cambridge at the Cambridge City Park. ("Armstrong Bridge All That Remains of Clio"; Donovan, 1980; "Finishing Touches"; Goslin; The Guernsey County Chapter 5 Ohio Genealogical Society; Ohio DOT; "Plan to Save Covered Bridge: ; "Public Invited to Covered Bridge Meeting")

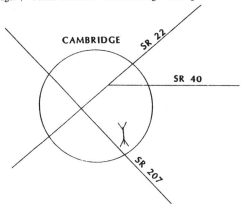

B & O Reservoir Bridge

The B & O Reservoir Bridge sits on an abandoned road that is now privately owned. At one time the bridge was used as a cow barn. The bridge was built in 1900 by the B & O Railroad Company to supply water from the reservoir to steam locomotives. After steam engines had become obsolete, the reservoir was used by Quaker City as their water supply and the bridge was abandoned.

The Reservoir Bridge spans Leatherwood Creek with 40 feet. Leatherwood Creek is a 30 foot wide stream that drains the southeastern most part of Guernsey County.

The B & O Reservoir Covered Bridge has a tin roof and weathered siding. It sits on the other side of a field and a railroad track, three-fourths of a mile off State Route 265. The abandoned road is not accessible by car and makes any kind of access difficult, at best.

DIRECTIONS: Millwood Township. From Quaker City, east on SR 265, one-half mile, on the right across a field and railroad tracks. ("B & O Reservoir Bridge"; Donovan, 1980; Goslin; The Guernsey County Chapter 5 Ohio Genealogical Society; Ohio DOT; SOCBA)

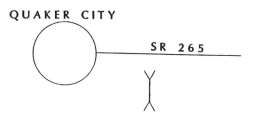

Hamilton County
35-31-01

Jediah Hill Bridge

The 45 foot Jediah Hill Bridge is also known as the Groff Mill Bridge. Jediah Hill Bridge spans the West Fork of Hill Creek and is one of several sources that supplies water for Hill Creek Lake at Winton Woods, a recreational area. The creek bed at the bridge site is 40 feet wide.

Built in 1850, the Jediah Hill Bridge has been refurbished in the last ten years. It was dismantled, new stone abutments were built and the bridge was reconstructed. New plank siding and a shake roof were added. The interior has horizontal floor planking and a queenpost truss with an "X" support in the center panel.

Listed on the National Register of Historic Places, Jediah Hill Bridge is the only covered bridge left in Hamilton County.

Jediah Hill Bridge is located on a picturesque stream that offers waterfalls and easy access to the creek.

DIRECTIONS: Springfield Township. From New Burlington, south on SR 127, one-half mile, left on CR 229, one-tenth mile, right on CR 228. (Donovan, 1980; Greenberg, 1976; Ohio DOT; SOCBA)

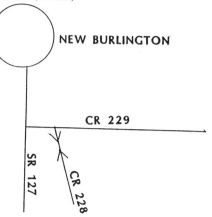

Harrison County
35-34-19

Skull Fork Bridge

Skull Fork Bridge spans Skull Run with 45 feet. Skull Run supplies the water for Piedmont Reservoir which is three miles east of the bridge site.

Date of construction is not known. The truss used for construction is similar to that of a queenpost, but it does not have the horizontal top member in the center panel; the center panel is empty.

Skull Fork Bridge has a shake roof, gray weathered plank siding and floor boards laid crosswise. The bridge is a single span and rests on stone abutments with some poured concrete assistance.

Skull Fork Bridge has been bypassed for preservation and has a park at the bridge site.

DIRECTIONS: Freeport Township. From Freeport, south on SR 800, three miles, right on T 123, one and one-half miles. (Donovan, 1980; Ohio DOT; SOCBA)

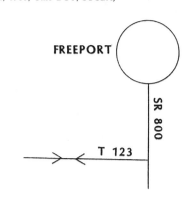

Petersburg/Johnson Bridge

The 80 foot Petersburg/Johnson Bridge spans the Little Scioto River. The Little Scioto River averages 70 feet wide in the vicinity of the bridge site.

Built in 1869, the Petersburg Bridge was constructed with a Smith truss. The floor planking is laid on a diagonal and, aside from the graffiti, the interior is in fair repair. The exterior has a tin roof, weathered white plank siding and rests on stone abutments with a single span. Access to the creek is impossible due to thick vegetation in the spring and summer months. Accordingly, fall and winter offer better visual access to the exterior of the bridge.

DIRECTIONS: Scioto Township. From Petersburg, southwest on SR. 776, five miles, left on T 291 (Johnson Road). (Donovan, 1980; Ohio DOT; SOCBA)

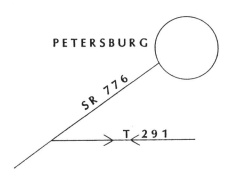

Byer Bridge

Byer Bridge spans Pigeon Creek with 70 feet and is located on the edge of a small village called, Byer, from which the bridge gets its name. Pigeon Creek has an average creek bed of 60 feet in the vicinity of the bridge site.

Byer Bridge was built in 1872 by W. H. Connery. The bridge was constructed with a Smith truss from a prefabricated kit prepared by the Smith Bridge Company. Because of the diagonal floor planking and the "X" panels of the Smith truss, the interior of Byer Bridge is geometrically very interesting. The exterior has a tin roof and weathered wood siding. The bridge is a single span and rests on stone abutments that have poured concrete assistance.

During the spring and summer months, the bridge and creek banks are thick with vegetation and prevent access to the creek bed. Winter and fall allow greater visual access to the exterior of the bridge.

Byer Bridge is listed in the National Register of Historic Places.

DIRECTIONS: Washington Township. At Byer just off SR 327. (Donovan, 1980; Ohio DOT; SOCBA)

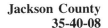

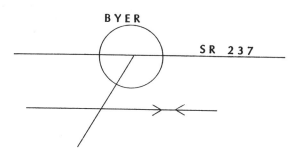

Buckeye Furnace Bridge

Buckeye Furnace Bridge takes its name from a huge furnace in the immediate vicinity. Buckeye Furnace is a reconstruction of a charcoal iron furnace complex with its original huge stack. The furnace was used to smelt iron. The entire operation has been preserved by the Ohio Historical Society and is an extremely striking, towering historical structure.

Built in 1872, Buckeye Furnace Covered Bridge spans Little Butter Run with 58 feet. Little Butter Run averages 50 feet wide in the vicinity of the bridge site. Access to the creek is reasonably easy, but not really necessary to view the bridge's exterior.

The bridge has a tin roof, dark red plank siding and green portals. It is a single span and rests on stone abutments.

The interior of the bridge is fascinating. A Smith truss was used in the construction. The floor planks were laid on a diagonal and two runners were interfaced on the floor planking, which runs lengthwise.

DIRECTIONS: Milton Township. From Middleton, east on SR 124, one mile, right on CR 58 (Buckeye Furnace Road), one mile, right on T 165, one-half mile, at Buckeye Furnace. (Donovan, 1980 Greenberg, 1976; Ohio DOT; SOCBA)

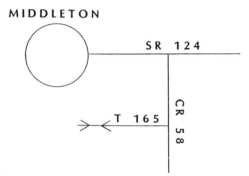

Scottown Bridge

Built in 1874, the 85 foot Scottown Bridge spans Indian Guyan Creek, which drains the southeastern corner of Lawrence County with an average bed width of 70 feet.

The Scottown Bridge is open to local traffic. The bridge rests on cut stone abutments and is a single span. The exterior has a gray tin, rusting roof and corrugated, rusting tin sides. The bridge is constructed with a version of a multiple kingpost truss, an added Burr arch and in 1934, iron rods were added, encasing the truss. The rods are visible on the exterior of the bridge. The bridge's floor beams are in poor condition. The roof was replaced in 1971.

The Scottown Bridge is the only covered bridge in Lawrence County and is listed in the National Register of Historic Places. When the bridge can no longer support the local traffic, it will be bypassed.

DIRECTIONS: Windsor Township. From Platform, SR 217 west, one and one-half miles, left on T 86. (Donovan, 1980; Ohio DOT; SOCBA)

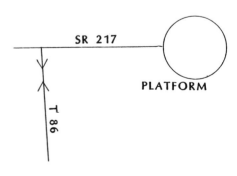

Belle Hall Bridge

Belle Hall Bridge spans Otter Fork with 60 feet. Otter Fork is a tributary of the Licking River, which drains the northeastern portion of Licking County. Otter Creek is 50 feet wide at the bridge site.

Belle Hall Bridge was built in 1887 with a multiple kingpost truss. The bridge is a single span and rests on cut stone abutments. The exterior has a tin roof and red plank siding. The floor planking was laid horizontally and is the only part of the bridge that is even partially complete. The floor has loose boards but they are all in place.

It is difficult to believe that a bridge in such a decrepit condition is still open to serve local traffic. Immediately, one notices the lack of any siding except for some damaged boards around the portal. The multiple kingpost truss has virtually disappeared. Only the vertical tension members remain and one diagonal compression member. The roof has shotgun holes and gaping separations between the tin sections. Remarkably enough, Belle Hall Bridge is listed in the National Register of Historic Places. This is possibly the reason the county has not dismantled this bridge.

Belle Hall Bridge receives the notation as being the covered bridge in the worst condition in Ohio, and was still open for traffic as of the summer of 1986.

DIRECTIONS: Bennington Township. From Hartford (Croton P.O.), east on CR 2 (Bennington Chapel), two miles right on T 56 (Dutch Cross), one-fourth mile. (Donovan, 1980; Ohio DOT; SOCBA)

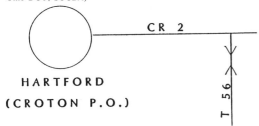

Boy Scout/Rainrock Bridge

Boy Scout/Rainrock Bridge is located in a boy scout camp just off of Rocky Fork Road in Eden Township. The 50 foot long bridge sits over a ravine, back in the woods on a trail behind the fishing lake. Moved here in 1974, the bridge looks like it has been there forever because the foliage is thick around the bridge.

The interior has a truss that has an empty center panel, with two sets of tension and compression beams pointing toward the center on either side of the empty center panel. The floor has horizontal planking. There is one small window centered in each of the empty center panels. The exterior has a tin roof and handsomely weathered plank siding. A gravel walking trail leads into each portal.

Originally, the bridge was located one mile south of its current location over Rainrock Creek on Rocky Fork Road. At its original location, the bridge had a single span and rested on cut stone abutments. The date of construction is unknown.

DIRECTIONS: Eden Township. From Rocky Fork on SR 79, north on CR 210 (Rocky Fork Road) one mile, on left at Boy Scout Camp. (Donovan, 1980; Ketcham, 1969; Ohio DOT; SOCBA)

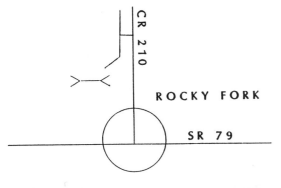

Licking County
35-45-05

Girl Scout Camp Bridge

The Girl Scout Bridge spans the Wakatomika Creek with 68 feet. The Wakatomika Creek drains a small portion of the far northeastern section of Licking County.

The bridge was built in 1882 with the same truss design as the Boy Scout Bridge. In the covered bridge guides, the truss is identified as a multiple kingpost, but Girl Scout Bridge does not have the traditional kingpost center panel. Instead, the center panel is empty. The floor is laid horizontally. The exterior has a part red and part white tin roof and red plank siding with one small window on one side. The bridge was found to be in fair condition in the summer of 1986, but was missing several pieces of siding. Girl Scout Bridge is a single span resting on cut stone abutments.

The Girl Scout Bridge has also been known as the Mercer Bridge and as the Shoults Bridge.

DIRECTIONS: Fallsburg Township. From Fallsburg, northwest on SR 586, two miles right on T 255 (Girl Scout Road) one mile. (Donovan, 1980; Ohio DOT; SOCBA)

Licking County
35-45-06

Gregg Bridge

Once known as the Handel Bridge, the Gregg Bridge spans the Wakatomika Creek. The Wakatomika Creek drains a small portion of the far northeastern corner of Licking County and has a 70 foot bed width at the bridge site.

Built in 1882, Gregg Bridge is 126 feet long, which makes it the longest covered bridge in Licking County. This bridge is also the most striking covered bridge in the county. Constructed with a traditional multiple kingpost truss, the bridge was built with a camber which is evidenced in the roof and floor. The interior is exciting because of the clean, massive timbers used in the truss and the lengthwise flooring with the obvious curvature, which accommodates the camber.

The exterior is not quite so dramatic but has a rustic appeal in a country setting. Gregg Bridge has a rusty tin roof, blackened weathered siding and a single span. Resting on cut stone abutments, the bridge has a wood and steel pier installed on the creek bank to add support to the bridge.

DIRECTIONS: Fallsburg Township. From Fallsburg, northwest on SR 586, one mile, right on CR 201 (Frampton) one mile. (Donovan, 1980; Ohio DOT; SOCBA)

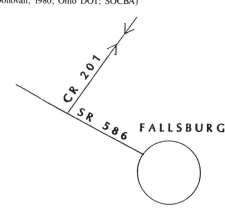

Lobdell Park or McLain's Bridge

The 47 foot Lobdell Park Bridge was moved into Fireman's Park in Alexandria in 1977. This covered bridge was built in 1891 with a multiple kingpost truss and the floor planking was laid crosswise. The exterior has a shake roof and gray weathered siding. The bridge rests on flat dry land and is in good repair. Firemen's Park is a well-maintained recreational area.

Lobdell Park Bridge's original location was two miles north of its current site at the intersection of Township Road 116 and Lobdell Road, spanning Lobdell Creek. The bridge was a single span and rested on stone abutments. The Lobdell Park Bridge's history indicates that at its original location it was subjected to extensive vandalism. Fortunately, the bridge was moved and restored before it disappeared.

DIRECTIONS: St. Albans Township. In Alexandria at the Fireman's Park on SR 37. (Donovan 1980; Ketcham, 1969; Ohio DOT SOCBA)

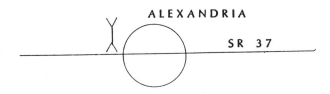

Buzzard Hill Bridge

Buzzard Hill Bridge spans Brushy Fork Creek with 50 feet. Brushy Fork is a shallow creek with a 30 foot creek bed at the bridge site.

Buzzard Hill Bridge was built in 1872. The interior of the bridge is appealing. The truss is identified in the covered bridge guides as a multiple kingpost, but it is typical of other covered bridges in Licking County in that it has an empty center panel. It lacks the traditional kingpost center panel. The truss was given additional reinforcement with an interior bowstring suspension added after the original construction. The floor planking was laid horizontally and had two lengthwise runners attached. Sadly, the floor was in dilapidated condition. The floor dropped two feet below the road level. I drove across the bridge trying to locate a parking spot. One soon learns just because a covered bridge is open for traffic does not mean it is safe! Subsequently, I observed all other traffic driving through the creek on a gravel/dirt trail off to one side of the bridge. That was my route to leave!

The exterior of the bridge was as broken-down as the floor. The siding was all intact but badly weathered and rotted. The roof was excessively damaged. The rusty tin had been blown off in many places and the roof boards were falling and rotting away.

The week of August 18, 1986, the county began to dismantle Buzzard Hill Bridge. A crane was brought in to move the structure onto the adjacent property so that local residents could have the opportunity to preserve the bridge. Unfortunately, the bridge collapsed under the stress of the crane's motion and its own weight and fell into a pile. There is some discussion as to the reconstruction of the bridge, but the extent of the damage to the timbers is not known nor the feasibility of the preservation project.

DIRECTIONS: Hanover Township. From Claylick, southeast on CR 277 (Brushy Texas Road), two miles, right on T 290 (Jeffries). (Donovan 1980; Ohio DOT; ''Residents May Restore Former Covered Bridge.'' ; SOCBA; ''Township Residents Lament Loss of Covered Bridge'')

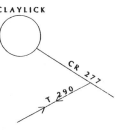

Davis Farm Bridge

Davis Farm Bridge spans Rocky Run with 50 feet. Rocky Run is usually a shallow stream with a 40 foot bed width at the bridge.

The Davis Farm Bridge has the same truss construction that is typical of many of the covered bridges in Licking County. The truss has an open center panel. The truss has two sets of tension and compression members pointing toward the center on either side of the empty center panel. The floor has the crosswise planking with two lengthwise runners attached.

The exterior has a gray tin roof and attractively weathered gray siding. The bridge is a single span and rests on stone abutments.

The Davis Farm Bridge has tragically aged and is skewed out of shape. The portal facing Hickman Road resembles a trapezoid. If steps to restore the bridge are not taken soon, the bridge will disappear. Records indicate that Davis Farm Bridge was built in 1947. It is difficult to believe that the bridge is only over 40 years old given its state of severe deterioration.

DIRECTIONS: Mary Ann Township. From Hickman on SR 79, south on CR 210 (Hickman Road) one and one-half miles, on right on private road. (Donovan, 1980; Ohio DOT; SOCBA)

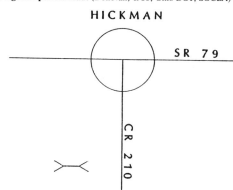

Hartford (Croton P. O.) Fairgrounds Bridge

This covered bridge was moved onto the fairgrounds in Hartford in 1975. Not much information was available on this bridge, not even the date of construction or where it was originally located.

At its current site, the bridge has a shingled roof that sags a little in the center. The siding is blackened, weathered planking. The bridge is constructed with a multiple kingpost truss. The Fairgrounds Bridge is only 22 feet long and has a single kingpost center panel for a truss, and vertical members to frame the portals. The bridge has lengthwise floor planking.

The Hartford Fairgrounds Bridge is on dry land and sits on well-maintained fairgrounds.

DIRECTIONS: Hartford Township. From Hartford (Croton P.O.), north on CR 44 (Fairgrounds Road) three-fourths mile, on right at Fairgrounds. (Ohio DOT; SOCBA)

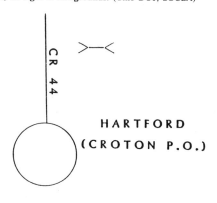

Logan County
35-46-01

McColly Bridge

The 136 foot McColly Bridge spans the Great Miami River six miles south of Indian Lake. The North Fork Miami River and South Fork Miami River supply the water for Indian Lake. The overflow from Indian Lake is the head waters for the Great Miami River. In the area of McColly Bridge, the Great Miami has a 120 foot bed width.

Named after a local family, the McColly Bridge was built in 1876. The truss used in this structure is a splendid example of the Howe truss. The bridge was built by the Anderson-Green Company of Sidney, Ohio for $3,103.

The interior of the bridge has horizontal floor planking and the steel tie-rods are painted silver. There is a full length metal guardrail on either side of the interior of the bridge, which is evidence that the bridge is maintained. The exterior has a white tin roof and weathered white plank siding. The bridge is a single span and rests on stone abutments faced with concrete.

McColly Bridge is listed in the National Register of Historic Places.

DIRECTIONS: Bloomfield Township. From Bloom Center, east on CR 60, one mile, right on CR 59, one mile, left on CR 13, one-tenth mile. (Associate Membership of the Indian Lake Chamber of Commerce (McColly); Donovan, 1980; Greenberg, 1976; Ohio DOT; SOCBA)

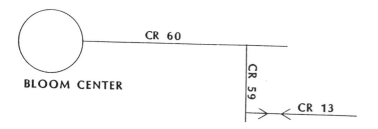

Logan County
35-46-03

Bickham Bridge

The 96 foot Bickham Bridge takes its name from a family who owned land adjacent to the bridge. The bridge spans the South Fork of the Miami River which, along with the North Fork of the Miami River, supplies water for Indian Lake. Indian Lake is less than one mile from Bickham Bridge site. Indian Lake was known as the Lewistown Reservoir in the 1800s. The South Branch of the Miami River and the reservoir supplied water for the Miami-Erie Canal System which operated from the 1850s through 1896. The South Fork of the Great Miami River in the vicinity of Bickham Bridge, has an 80 foot bed width.

The Bickham Bridge was constructed in 1877 by the Smith Bridge Company for $2,335. The structure has an excellent example of a Howe truss and horizontal floor planking. The steel tie-rods are painted silver and there is a full length metal guardrail on both sides of the interior of the bridge. The exterior has a gray tin roof and white plank siding. The bridge is a single span and rests on stone abutments with formed concrete poured over the stone.

DIRECTIONS: Richland Township. From Russells Point, east on SR 366, two and one-half miles, left on CR 38A, one-fourth mile. (Associate Membership of the Indian Lake Chamber of Commerce (Bickman); Donovan, 1980; Ohio DOT; SOCBA)

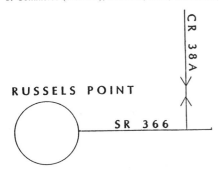

Eldean Bridge

The Eldean Bridge spans the Great Miami River two miles north of Troy. The Great Miami River has a 210 foot bed width at the bridge site and is the major drainage river for southwestern Ohio.

The Eldean Bridge is the second longest covered bridge in Ohio, with a 234 foot span. The Eldean Bridge was built in 1860 with a Long truss. This covered bridge has the singular distinction of being the longest covered bridge in the United States with a Long truss in existence today.

The exterior has a white tin roof, faded red plank siding and four small windows on each side of the bridge. Eldean Bridge has two spans with the one pier, and abutments made of cut stone.

Eldean Bridge has been bypassed for preservation but is still open and traffic does use the bridge as a secondary entrance/exit for a small park. To maintain the bridge's longevity, vehicles should be prevented from traversing the bridge. Eldean Bridge is a favorite of covered bridge enthusiasts because of the nature of the river, length of the bridge and truss, and its general location.

Eldean Bridge is listed in the National Register of Historic Places.

DIRECTIONS: Staunton Township. From Troy, north on CR 14 (Troy-Sidney Road), two miles, left on CR 33 (Eldean Road), one-half mile. (Donovan, 1980; Ohio DOT; SOCBA)

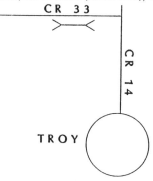

Photograph by Michael Krekeler

Foraker Bridge

Foraker Bridge spans the Little Muskingum River with 92 feet. Little Muskingum River is a major drainage channel which drains the lower southwestern corner of Monroe County. Little Muskingum River has a primary drainage bed of 50 feet at the bridge site.

Built in 1886, the Foraker Bridge has a multiple kingpost truss and lengthwise floor planking. The bridge has undergone some major renovations. The interior has had diagonal steel tie-rods installed in the last three panels at each end of the truss on both sides of the bridge. The tie-rods form an "X" against each compression member of the panel. Steel rods were also installed vertically at the floor level and incorporated into the truss. All of these adjustable steel tie-rods are attached to exterior steel floor beams that encase the entire bridge's floor. A steel pier was also added to sustain the structure.

The exterior has a gray rusting roof and becomingly weathered gray siding. The abutments are cut stone.

Foraker Bridge is listed on the National Register of Historic Places.

DIRECTIONS: Perry Township. From Graysville, east on CR 12 (Trail Run) three miles, left on CR 40, three-fourths mile. (Donovan, 1980; Ohio DOT; SOCBA)

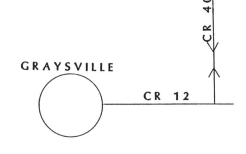

Monroe County
35-56-18

Long/Old Camp Bridge

The Long or Old Camp Bridge crosses the Little Muskingum River with 192 feet. The Little Muskingum River drains the lower southwestern quarter of Monroe County and has a 100 foot normal bed width at the bridge site.

This covered bridge has numerous characteristics that make it extraordinary. The exterior of the bridge offers a spectacular sight. Two immense piers and abutments are constructed of huge cut stones supporting the bridge's three spans. There is a trail that leads down to the river bank and from there, the bridge looms 30 feet over the river. The piers are built well into the upper river bank and the bridge appears as if suspended in air. The rustic gray weathered siding is so thin and shrunken in places, that the upper portion of the Burr arch is visible from the exterior. The red tin roof is in fair condition, but the level of the roof is wobbly at best.

One must climb a tall fence to investigate the interior, but it is well worth the effort.

Each span has a separate truss. The spans on either end of the bridge are much shorter than the center truss (the section that hovers over the river). The shorter trusses are multiple kingpost with two sets of tension and compression panels pointing toward the center kingpost. The center trusses (one on each side of the bridge) are 120 feet long and are multiple kingpost trusses encased by four-ply, double Burr arches. The interior has six multiple kingpost trusses and immense double Burr arches in the center span. The diagonally laid floor planking only adds to the enchanting nature of the bridge. Unfortunately, the date of construction is not known.

Long Bridge is located in a small park that has minimal upkeep. The bridge is closed and it does not appear to have had any maintenance. The bridge is still capable of being salvaged for preservation, but if it continues to decay, in another five to ten years it will be beyond repair. Because it is such a captivating old covered bridge, it would be a shame to lose it.

DIRECTIONS: Washington Township. From Rinard Mills, north on CR 88, one and one-fourth miles, just off Old Camp Road. (Donovan, 1980; Ohio DOT; SOCBA)

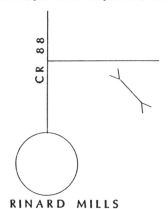

CR 88

RINARD MILLS

Montgomery County
35-57-01

Germantown Bridge

Built in 1870, the Germantown Bridge crosses the Little Twin Creek in Germantown. Little Twin Creek drains a small portion of southwestern Montgomery County and has a bed width at the bridge of 80 feet. Little Twin Creek is usually a shallow stream and mostly dries up in the summer. Germantown Bridge was originally located on the Dayton Pike. It was moved in 1911 to its present location. Presently the bridge is closed, but is accessible for pedestrian traffic.

The Germantown Bridge is one of the more famous covered bridges in Ohio and the United States because it is one of only two bowstring suspension bridges left in the world. The other bowstring is the John Bright Bridge in Fairfield County, Ohio, which also has a Burr arch. The Germantown is the only one that has a strictly bowstring truss without any additional supports added.

The covered bridge in Germantown is quite spectacular. It is 105 feet long and has no siding, so the entire truss can be viewed externally. Accordingly, the curve of the bowstring combined with the wooden/steel compression/tension members, and the crisscrossed steel tie rods form enticing geometrical configurations. The floor planking is laid crosswise and the roof is shingled. The bridge has one span and rests on cut stone abutments.

In the early 1980s, the bridge was washed off its abutments and carried downstream. The community rallied and, piece by piece, the bridge was reconstructed. Germantown is an historic village which celebrates its heritage with festivals such as an Octoberfest and a Pretzel Festival.

The Germantown bridge is listed in the National Register of Historic Places.

DIRECTIONS: German Township. In Germantown on the eastern side on Little Twin River. (Donovan, 1980; Greenberg, 1976, Ketcham, 1969, Ohio DOT, SOCBA)

Montgomery County
35-57-03

Carillon Park Bridge

The Carillon Park Covered Bridge was known as the Feedwire Road Covered Bridge. Built in Sugar Creek Township, Green County, just north of Ballbrook in 1870, the bridge's construction has a special triangular framing system called a Warren truss. The Smith Bridge Company was contracted to build the bridge. Smith's local agent used the Warren truss instead of Smith's truss design. The 42 foot long Carillon Park Covered Bridge has the distinction of being one of only five Warren truss covered bridges left in the United States.

The covered bridge was moved to Carillon Park in 1948. It received a new wooden arch to increase the strength of the bridge. A new roof was extended over the portals for increased protection. The bridge rests on stone abutments and spans a dry ditch which used to be a canal. The bridge has a black shake roof and red plank siding.

Carillon Park has many historical points of interest. A restored mill is close to the covered bridge's location.

DIRECTIONS: Dayton Township. In Kettering at Carillon Park. (Carillon Historical Park; Donovan, 1980; Ohio DOT: Shannon; SOCBA)

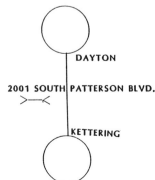

Montgomery County
35-57-36

Mud-Lick/Jasper Road Bridge

Mud-Lick Bridge crosses Mud-Lick Creek, which is a small stream that has a 40 foot bed width.

The 55 foot long Mud-Lick Bridge is located on a private road, surrounded by a fence which makes access to the bridge difficult. This bridge was moved to this location in 1964. Originally constructed in 1877, the bridge can be somewhat observed from the road. The exterior has brown weathered siding, a shake roof and six small windows on each side of the bridge.

The interior is what is most alluring about Mud-Lick Bridge. Constructed with a Warren truss, it is encased with a double Burr arch. The Warren truss is so unique because there are only five of them left in the United States (three in Ohio, two in Kentucky).

The floor planking is laid lengthwise. Mud-Lick Bridge is a single span and rests on stone abutments.

DIRECTIONS: German Township. From Germantown, west on Mud-Lick Road and one-fourth mile on right. (Donovan, 1980 Ohio DOT; SOCBA)

Morgan County
35-58-15

Barkhurst Mill Bridge

Barkhurst Mill Bridge assumes its name from a mill that sits adjacent to the bridge. The mill has been closed for years. Standing three stories tall, the mill is boarded up and has dark brown, weathered siding. The mill towers rather ominously over the bridge site, which appears as if forgotten in time. Barkhurst Mill Bridge spans Wolf Creek with 81 feet. Wolf Creek is usually a shallow stream with a 70 foot wide bed at the bridge.

Barkhurst Mill Bridge was built in 1872 with a multiple kingpost truss and a Burr arch. The bridge has lengthwise floor planking, a red tin roof and weathered gray siding. Originally there were horizontal ventilation panels open on the bridge, but plank siding was installed to cover the opening on the west side to prevent water and snow from blowing into the bridge. The bridge has an ever so slight camber visible in the floor and roof. The single span bridge rests on cut stone abutments with formed concrete poured to one side of the abutments to prevent the stream from washing out behind the abutments.

The north portal of the bridge has a gravel road but the south portal has a dirt road. The Barkhurst Mill Bridge seems to have been neglected for many years. The siding is in poor condition. Where the siding has shrunken, water can get in through the seams between the planks and pieces are missing. If Barkhurst Mill does not receive some attention, its future is doomed to non-existence.

DIRECTIONS: Marion Township. From Todds, south on CR 52, one and one-half miles, left on T 19, one-half mile, at Barkhurst Mill. (Donovan, 1980; Ohio DOT, SOCBA)

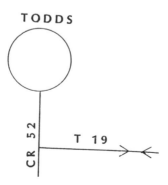

TODDS

CR 52

T 19

Morgan County
35-58-32

McConnellsville Fairgrounds Bridge

The McConnellsville Fairground Bridge is on dry land on the Fairgrounds amidst numerous Fairground buildings. The original construction date is unknown. The bridge was moved to the Fairgrounds in 1953.

McConnellsville Bridge is 58 feet long. Constructed with a multiple kingpost truss, the bridge has a red tin roof and weathered gray plank siding. Concrete steps lead into the bridge where there are benches.

DIRECTIONS: Morgan Township. At McConnellsville on SR 376. (Donovan, 1980; Ohio DOT; SOCBA)

MCCONNELLSVILLE

SR 376

Morgan County
35-58-35

Island Run Bridge

Also known as the Helmic Bridge, the Island Run Bridge spans Island Run, a deeply engorged stream about 60 feet wide at the bridge. Island Run Bridge hovers over the stream by 25 feet, near waterfalls.

Built in 1867, the Island Run Bridge was constructed with a multiple kingpost truss. The bridge is 73 feet long and located on a gravel road. The exterior has a gray tin roof and gray weathered siding. Access to the creek bed is easy.

DIRECTIONS: Deerfield Township. From Eagleport, west on SR 669, one and one-half miles, left on T 201, one and one-half miles, left on T 269. (Donovan, 1980; Ohio DOT; SOCBA)

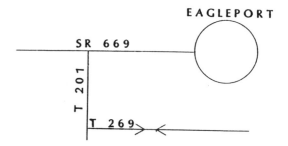

EAGLEPORT

SR 669

T 201

T 269

Adams/San Toy Bridge

The Adams Bridge spans a branch of Sunday Creek with 58 feet. Sunday Creek supplies the water for Burr Oak Lake, a recreational area which is four miles south of the bridge site. Sunday Creek has a bed width of 50 feet at the bridge.

Built in 1875, the Adams Bridge was constructed with a multiple kingpost truss. The floor has planking laid crosswise and two runners are attached running lengthwise.

The exterior has a rusty-red/white tin roof and weathered gray siding that has many pieces missing. Adams Bridge is a single span and is supported by cut stone abutments. Adams Bridge is located on a remote gravel road and receives little traffic. It is in poor condition. The portals are skewed out of square, the tin roof has major separations and is allowing water in to decay and weaken the floor.

If the bridge were to be preserved it would need to be done as soon as possible.

DIRECTIONS: Union Township. From Ringgold, northwest on SR 555, four miles, right on CR 16, one-fourth mile. (Donovan, 1980; Ohio DOT; SOCBA)

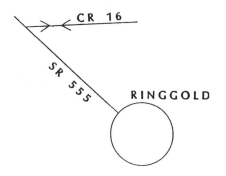

**Morgan County
35-58-41**

Saw Mill Bridge

Built in 1915, Saw Mill Bridge spans Brannans Fork which is a small stream with a normal creek bed five feet wide at the bridge site. Saw Mill Bridge was moved to its current location in 1965. The bridge rests on stone abutments at Campsite D of the Ohio Power Company.

Saw Mill Bridge has a red tin roof, gray weathered siding and is only 40 feet long. The interior is constructed with a multiple kingpost truss and the floor planking is laid crosswise with two lengthwise runners.

The Saw Mill Bridge's location is well-maintained and offers a pleasant campground. The stream is choked with cattails and offers a picturesque background for the bridge.

DIRECTIONS: Manchester Township. From Bristol, east on SR 78, one-fourth mile, north on SR 83, three and one-half miles, on right at Campsite D of Ohio Power Company. (Donovan, 1980; Ohio DOT; SOCBA)

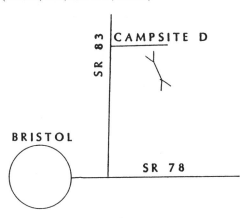

Muskingum County
35-60-31

Salt Creek Bridge

Salt Creek Bridge crosses Salt Creek with 87 feet. Salt Creek has a normal bed width of 50 feet at the bridge site.

Built in 1870, the Salt Creek Bridge was constructed with a Warren Truss. The Warren truss is very rare. There are only five of them still in existence (three in Ohio, two in Kentucky). With the inverted "V" Warren truss and the diagonal planking, the interior is optically pleasing.

The exterior has a white tin roof and weathered black siding with several replaced planks painted white. Salt Fork Bridge is a single span and rests on cut stone abutments.

When the Salt Fork Bridge was bypassed in the 1960s, the Southern Ohio Covered Bridge Association bought the covered bridge and has since preserved it. The bridge presently has a well-maintained park area.

DIRECTIONS: Salem Township. From Sonora, east on CR 64, two miles, right on T 109, one mile, right on T 261A, one mile, left on T 82, one fourth mile. (Donovan, 1980; Ohio DOT; SOCBA)

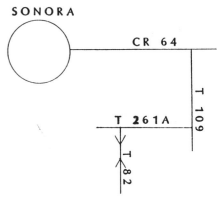

Noble County
35-61-33

Manchester Bridge

Manchester Bridge spans Manchester Creek and is 49 feet long. Manchester Creek is a small stream with a 25 foot bed width at the bridge.

Built in 1914, the Manchester Bridge was constructed with a multiple kingpost truss. The floor planking is laid crosswise. The exterior of the bridge has a red tin roof and red weathered plank siding. The bridge sits on a gravel road with a single span and rests on cut stone abutments.

DIRECTIONS: Sharon Township. From Olive Green, south on T 3, two miles. (Donovan, 1980; Ohio DOT; SOCBA)

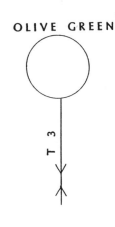

Parrish Bridge

The Parrish Bridge is named after Isaac Parrish, who had a flour mill near the covered bridge. The Parrish Covered Bridge was built in 1914 with a multiple kingpost construction and is 85 feet long. The bridge spans Olive Green Creek which has a bed width of 70 feet.

The Parrish Bridge has a white tin roof and a new coat of bright red paint on its wooden siding.

Parrish Bridge has been bypassed for preservation. A new bridge is now adjacent to Parrish Bridge. Access to the creek is difficult but not really necessary because the bridge can easily be viewed from many different angles around the bridge site.

DIRECTIONS: Sharon Township. From Caldwell, SR 78, west, two miles, left on CR 8, three miles. (Donovan, 1980; Ohio DOT; SOCBA)

Photograph by Michael Krekeler

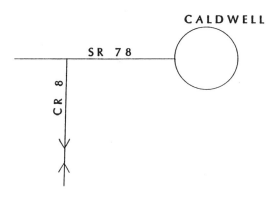

Park Hill Road Bridge

The Park Hill Road Bridge was relocated to the Caldwell Fairgrounds in 1970. This bridge has also been known as Otter Slide Bridge and Guerst Bridge.

The original location of Park Hill Road Bridge crossed Middle Fork Duck Creek on Township Road 295, just south of SR 564, four miles northwest of Middleburg in Enoch Township. At Middle Fork Duck Creek, the Park Hill Road Bridge had a single span and rested on cut stone abutments.

Presently the bridge rests on cut stone abutments on dry land at the Fairgrounds. The bridge is isolated from the other buildings and has an attractive location.

Park Hill Bridge is 44 feet long, has a gray tin roof and bright red siding. The truss is a multiple kingpost. Date of construction is not known.

DIRECTIONS: Olive Township. At Fairgrounds in Caldwell. (Donovan 1980; Ketcham 1969; Ohio DOT; SOCBA)

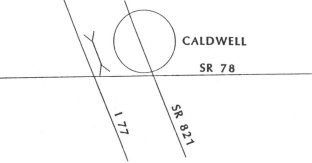

Danford Bridge

Danford Bridge spans Keith Fork with 57 feet. Keith Fork is a small stream with a 40 foot bed width at the bridge site.

Built in 1875 with a multiple kingpost truss, the floor has crosswise planking with two lengthwise runners. Periodically, there are some crosswise planks laid through the runners. So much dirt and gravel has accumulated that the runners are barely visible at one end of the bridge.

The exterior has blackened weathered siding that hints of previous red paint and a gray tin roof. Danford Bridge has one span and rests on stone abutments on a gravel road.

Access to the creek is difficult during summer months because of thick vegetation. Winter months offer better exterior visual access.

DIRECTIONS: Jackson Township. From Keith, southwest on CR 7 one mile. (Donovan, 1980; Ohio DOT; SOCBA)

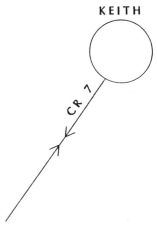

KEITH

CR 7

Huffman Bridge

The Huffman Bridge was built in 1914. The bridge is now on private property on an abandoned road, but is visible from State Route 564.

The bridge is 50 feet long with a multiple kingpost truss and spans Duck Creek, a small stream about 30 feet wide.

Huffman Bridge is currently serving as a barn for cows. The summer of 1986 found vegetation enclosing much of the exterior of the bridge. The exterior of the bridge has a tin roof and red, wood plank siding.

Duck Creek is small but deeply entrenched and allows no access to its creek bed, but it really is not necessary because the bridge can be viewed from the surrounding area. Huffman Bridge is listed in the National Register of Historic Places.

DIRECTIONS: Jefferson Township. From Middleburg, SR 564, southeast, one and one-half miles on left. (Donovan, 1980; Ohio DOT; SOCBA)

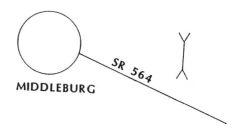

MIDDLEBURG

SR 564

Parks/South Bridge

Parks or South Bridge spans Brother Jonathon Creek and is 58 feet long. Jonathon Creek is a small stream with a 40 foot bed width at the bridge.

Parks Bridge was built in 1882 with a multiple kingpost truss by Dean Builders. The floor planking is laid horizontally and there is a wooden guardrail that extends the entire length of the bridge on both sides.

Perry County celebrated our Bicentennial in 1976 by painting the county's four covered bridges red, white and blue. The exterior has a gray tin roof and plank siding that is painted in three horizontal strips of red, white and blue. The portals are painted in the same scheme.

The tin roof, truss and floor are in fair condition. Unfortunately the siding and portals are seriously deteriorated, with several planks missing and the existing planks rotting.

The most imposing feature about the Parks Bridge is its conspicuous camber. The floor exhibits a prominent arc as well as the roof.

Parks Bridge is listed in the National Register of Historic Places.

DIRECTIONS: Hopewell Township. From Somerset, north on SR 668, two miles, left on CR 33 (Gower Road), one-fourth mile. (Donovan, 1980; Ohio DOT; SOCBA)

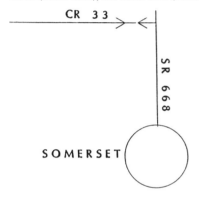

Hopewell Church Bridge

Hopewell Church Bridge traverses Brother Jonathan Creek with 55 feet. Jonathan Creek is a small stream with a 40 foot bed width at the bridge.

Built in 1882 with a multiple kingpost truss, Hopewell Church Bridge has a tin roof, and red, white and blue plank siding. The floor planking is laid lengthwise. As is the case with the other three covered bridges in Perry County, the exterior is in poor condition. The tin roof is decrepit and the siding is rotting.

DIRECTIONS: Hopewell Township. From Chalfant, south on CR 33, one-fourth mile, left on CR 51, one-fourth mile. (Donovan, 1980; Ohio DOT; SOCBA)

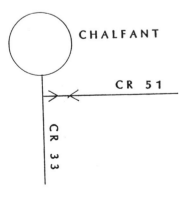

Perry County
35-64-05

Jacks Hollow Bridge

Jacks Hollow Bridge is 60 feet long and crosses Kents Run in the far northeast corner of Perry County. Kents Run is a normally shallow stream with a 55 foot bed width at the bridge site. Jacks Hollow Bridge is located at the bottom of a very deep valley.

Jacks Hollow Bridge was built in 1881 with a multiple kingpost truss. The bridge has a gray tin roof, a white painted truss, crosswise floor planking and red, white and blue plank siding. Of the four bridges in Perry County, this one was the most vandalized. Panels of siding had been knocked into the river and graffiti was scrawled on the interior. Jacks Hollow Bridge is a single span and is supported by cut stone abutments.

DIRECTIONS: Madison Township. From Mt.Perry, north on CR 55, one-fourth mile, right on CR 34, one mile, straight on CR 67 (Kroft) one and one-half miles, left on T 108, three-fourths mile. (Donovan, 1980; Ohio DOT; SOCBA)

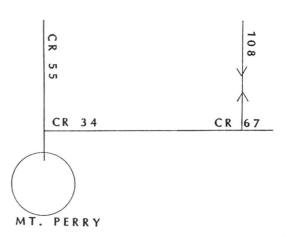

Perry County
35-64-06

Bowman Mill Bridge

Named for the Bowman Mill that was nearby, the covered bridge is 98 feet long and spans the Little Rush Creek. Little Rush Creek drains the local area and has an average bed width of 70 feet.

Although the date of construction is unknown, the Bowman Mill Bridge has its own unique characteristics. The bridge has a multiple kingpost design with a center stone pier, but no additional supports. The 98 foot length is extremely long for a multiple kingpost design. The bridge has a hump in its center and it is quite evident on its roof and the interior floor.

Access to the creek bed is difficult, but the bridge can be viewed effortlessly from the road on either side of the bridge. Bowman Mill Bridge is typical of many covered bridges in that the road follows the creek on one side and makes a right angle curve onto the bridge. The road makes a right angle turn off of the bridge in the opposite direction and continues to follow the creek.

This bridge appears in the National Register of Historic Places, however, the bridge is in poor condition. The bridge is now closed to vehicle traffic and there is no indication of what the future holds for the bridge.

DIRECTIONS: Reading Township. From Somerset, SR 22, southwest one-fourth mile, right on Winegardner Road (CR 86), three miles. (Donovan, 1980; Ohio DOT; SOCBA)

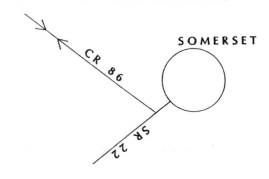

Bill Green Bridge

The Bill Green Bridge spans a portion of a lake on private property in Scioto Township. It is the only covered bridge in Pickaway County. Bill Green restored the bridge and provides a private, but accessible road to visit the covered bridge near the fishing lake. The area is well maintained and presents a pictorial setting for the bridge.

The Bill Green Bridge was originally named the Valentine Bridge. The bridge's original location was in Hocking Township and crossed the Muddy Prairie Run. The bridge was originally constructed in 1887. In 1971, the bridge was moved to a nearby farm. In 1978, William Green acquired the bridge, and moved it to its present location and restored it.

The Bill Green Bridge is 36 feet long and was built with a multiple kingpost truss. The bridge has lengthwise floor planking, a gray tin roof and rusty-red plank siding. The bridge is easily accessible and offers an intriguing landscape.

DIRECTIONS: Scioto Township, From Orient, east on SR 762, two and one-half miles, right on T 152 (Thrailkill), one-half mile, turn left into private drive. ("Covered Bridges"; Donovan, 1980; Ohio DOT; SOCBA)

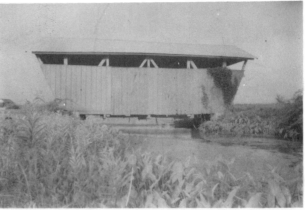

Photograph by Michael Krekeler

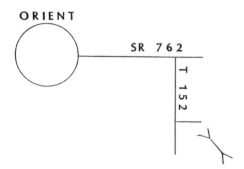

Harshman Bridge

Harshman Bridge was built in 1894 by Evret S. Sherman for $3,184. Sherman built 14 Child's truss bridges and one multiple kingpost bridge in Preble County between 1886 and 1896. At one time there was a total of 29 covered bridges in Preble County.

Harshman Bridge traverses Four Mile Creek with 109 feet. Four Mile Creek has a normal bed width of 40 feet at the bridge site and drains the western half of Preble County. Four Mile Creek supplies the water for Acton Lake, which is eight miles south of the bridge site.

Harshman Bridge is constructed with a Child's truss. There are only seven examples of the Child's truss left in the United States. Six are in Preble County and one is in Delaware County, Ohio.

Harshman Bridge has a single span and rests on cut blue limestone abutments. The exterior has a red tin roof, white plank siding and one small window on each side. Each portal has an extended roof. The interior has a low wooden guardrail and vertical floor planking. Harshman Bridge was closed for repairs in January, 1987. The floor beams and planking were renovated at each portal.

The Harshman Bridge is listed on the National Register of Historic Places.

DIRECTIONS: Dixon Township. From Eaton, SR 732 south, two miles, right on Consolidated Road, five miles, left on T 218 (Fairhaven Road), one-half mile. (Donovan, 1980; Ohio DOT; Schlotterbeck, 1976; SOCBA)

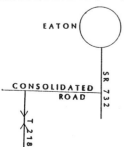

Dixon's Branch Bridge

Located in Lewisburg Village Park, in Lewisburg, the Dixon's Branch Bridge is on dry land. The bridge was moved here in 1964 after it lost its roof in a windstorm. The Civitan Club dismantled the bridge and restored it, and now the bridge acts as a shelter housing several picnic tables.

Built in 1887, the bridge has one of Preble County's rare Child's trusses. The truss has an open center panel and the floor consists of horizontal planking. The exterior has a rusty white tin roof and white plank siding, with a small window on each side. The bridge is 50 feet long and only serves pedestrian traffic. Dixon's Branch Bridge served from 1887 through 1963 on Concord Road where it spanned Dixon's Branch.

The park is well-maintained and offers a selection of facilities.

DIRECTIONS: Harrison Township. In Lewisburg at the Lewisburg Village Park, east side of town. (Donovan, 1980; Ohio DOT; Schlotterbeck, 1976; SOCBA)

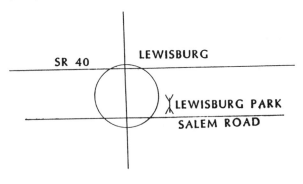

Roberts Bridge

Roberts Bridge spans Seven Mile Creek with 80 feet. Seven Mile Creek is a stream with an average bed width of 70 feet and drains central Preble County. The bridge was built by Orlistus Roberts in 1829, which makes the Roberts Bridge the oldest in Ohio. The bridge rests on stone abutments. The stone was cut nearby at the Halderman Quarry.

Roberts Bridge is exceptional because it is the only double-barrelled covered bridge in Ohio and is one of only six left in the United States. The Roberts Bridge has three trusses, one in the center and one on each side of the bridge. Each truss has a multiple kingpost truss encased by two Burr arches. The interior is spectacular with runners on either side and the three double Burr arches. The exterior has rusty-red wood siding. The portals are also painted with the top-half red and bottom-half white.

Unfortunately, on August 5, 1986, the bridge was burned by arson. The fire destroyed most of the bridge. There is some discussion of sandblasting the remaining timbers and restoring the bridge at a cost of $150,000.

The fire was a great tragedy because it not only ruined the oldest bridge in Ohio, but the only double-barrelled bridge in Ohio.

DIRECTIONS: Gasper Township. From Eaton, south on SR 127, two miles, left on Consolidated Road, immediately, turn right on Consolidated. First right. (Donovan, 1980; Ohio DOT; Schlotterbeck, 1976; SOCBA)

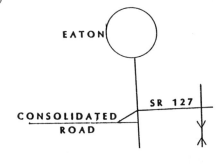

Brubaker Bridge

The Brubaker Bridge is located on Brubaker Road and crosses Sam's Run Creek with 90 feet. Sam's Run is a small creek with an average bed width of 50 feet.

The Brubaker Bridge is one of the seven remaining Child's truss covered bridges in the United States. Of the six Child's truss covered bridges in Preble County, this is one of three that has an open center panel. The other three have a kingpost center panel. The Brubaker Bridge is distinctive because the upper two-thirds of the sides of the bridge have been removed to allow visual access for traffic and exposes the Child's truss.

The Brubaker Bridge was built in 1887. The bridge has a charcoal gray shake roof and fresh white plank siding. The floor has lengthwise runners interfaced on crosswise floor planking. The bridge site has easy access to Sam's Run Creek. The location of the bridge lends itself to photography.

The Brubaker Bridge is listed in the National Register of Historic Places.

DIRECTIONS: Gratis Township. From Gratis, SR 122, northwest, one-fourth mile, left on TR 328 (Aukerman Creek Road/Brubaker Road). (Donovan, 1980; Ohio DOT; SOCBA)

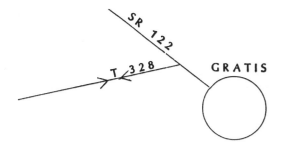

Christman Bridge

Christman Bridge was named after Solomon Christman, who had a farm south of the bridge site. Solomon Christman also had a water powered sawmill and remnants of the mill trace can still be seen near the road, 200 yards west of the bridge. Christman Bridge spans Seven Mile Creek, which drains central Preble County and has a normal bed width of 70 feet at the bridge.

Evret S. Sherman constructed the 100 foot Christman Bridge in 1895. The total cost of the bridge was $2,452. Of the six covered bridges in Preble County built by Sherman, all are constructed with the Child's truss. The Christman Bridge, Dixon's Branch Bridge and the Brubaker Bridge have open center panels. The other three, Harshman, Geeting and Warnke, have kingpost center panels. The interior of Christman Bridge has horizontal floor planking with two lengthwise runners. The exterior has a red/white tin roof and white plank siding with projected portals. With a single span, the bridge rests on stone abutments with concrete assistance. The bridge was reinforced in 1920 and again in 1960.

Christman Bridge is open to local traffic and is listed on the National Register of Historic Places.

DIRECTIONS: Washington Township. From Eaton, north on CR 11, left on T 142 (Eaton-New Hope Road). (Donovan, 1980; Ohio DOT; Schlotterbeck, 1976; SOCBA)

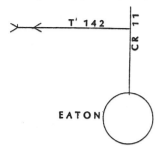

Geeting Bridge

Built in 1894, the Geeting Bridge was named after Dave Geeting, who had a farm southwest of the bridge site.

Geeting Bridge spans Prices Creek and is 100 feet long. Prices Creek drains the northeastern corner of Preble County and has a normal 50 foot bed width at the bridge.

Geeting Bridge is the most distinctive covered bridge Preble County has, due to the bridge's configuration and its physical location. The bridge has a shake roof, handsomely gray weathered siding and has a small window on both sides. The interior is as distinctive as the exterior. The Child's truss has a kingpost center panel and crosswise floor planking with two lengthwise runners that exhibit raised grain from so much use.

Geeting Bridge is one of the six remaining covered bridges in Preble County. All six have the Child's truss and were constructed by Evret Sherman. This bridge was constructed for a cost of $2,691.

Geeting Bridge has had its share of damage. In 1914, a windstorm tore the roof off the bridge. In 1969, a truck that was loaded too high, ripped some roofing out of the bridge. On several occasions, the floor was crushed from heavy trucks. However, each time the bridge was damaged, it was repaired and is still serving the local traffic.

Geeting Bridge is listed on the National Register of Historic Places.

DIRECTIONS: Monroe Township. From Lewisburg, west on T 436 (Western Road) three miles, straight on Price Road, one-tenth mile, (Donovan, 1980; Ohio DOT Schlotterbeck, 1976; SOCBA)

LEWISBURG

PRICE ROAD — T 436

Warnke Bridge

Warnke Covered Bridge was the last bridge Evret Sherman built. Sherman's health was failing and he moved to Richmond, Indiana, where he died soon after.

Built in 1896, Warnke Covered Bridge spans Swamp Creek with 51 feet. Swamp Creek has an average bed width of 45 feet at the bridge site. Swamp Creek drains a small portion of northeast Preble County.

The Warnke Covered Bridge has a gray tin roof and white plank siding that is rotting at the lower chords. Each side has a small window which is characteristic of all covered bridges in Preble County. This bridge has a Child's truss with a kingpost center panel. Each side has a wooden guardrail. The floor is horizontal planking interfaced with two lengthwise runners.

The bridge is a single span and rests on cut stone abutments. Reinforced in 1913 and wing walls added, the Warnke Bridge is listed on the National Register of Historic Places and is still open to local traffic.

DIRECTIONS: Harrison Township. From Lewisburg, east on SR 40, one-fourth mile, left on T 404 (Euphemia Road) one and one-fourth mile, right on T 403 (Swamp Creek Road), one-third mile. (Donovan, 1980; Ohio DOT; Schlotterbeck, 1976; SOCBA)

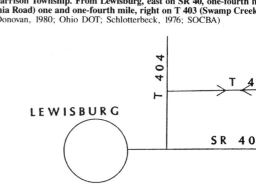

T 404

T 403

LEWISBURG

SR 40

Buckskin Bridge

Buckskin Bridge spans Buckskin Creek with 100 feet. Buckskin Creek has a 70 foot bed width at the bridge and is responsible for draining the far western section of Ross County.

Buckskin Bridge is the only covered bridge in Ross County. It was built in 1872 with a Smith Truss by the Smith Bridge Company. The interior is in good repair. The interior siding and truss members are painted red and the floor planking is laid lengthwise. The exterior has a gray tin roof and multicolored weathered siding. Buckskin Bridge is a single span and rests on cut stone abutments.

The bridge sits in a pleasant valley and is listed on the National Register of Historic Places.

DIRECTIONS: Buckskin Township. From Greenfield, east on SR 28, three and one-half miles, right on CR 46 (Lyndon-Salem Road) one mile, right on CR 54 (Lower Twin Road) one-fourth mile. (Donovan, 1980; Ohio DOT; SOCBA)

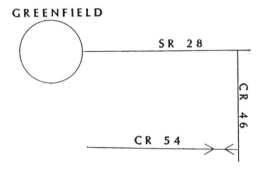

Mull Bridge

Mull Bridge was named after Amos Mull, a nearby resident, and was built in 1842. Mull Bridge is a very old bridge, yet it is still in fair condition. The bridge has been bypassed for preservation.

Mull Bridge has two spans and traverses the East Branch of Wolf Creek with 100 feet. The East Branch of Wolf Creek is a tributary of the Sandusky River. Their confluence is two miles from the bridge site.

The bridge was constructed with a Town truss that had wooden pegs to attach the diagonal members. The floor planking is laid crosswise. The interior is dark because of the lack of windows, but the lattice truss offers a symmetrically pleasing effect.

The exterior has a red tin roof, beautifully weathered, gray-knotted siding and a long narrow opening for ventilation under the gable on both sides of the bridge that exposes the lattice truss on the exterior. The one pier is concrete but both abutments are large quarried stones, laid without any concrete. Some of the stones are shifting out of position. The old bridge presents a spectacular sight both on the interior and exterior.

DIRECTIONS: Bellville Township. From Bettsville, northeast on SR 12 one mile, right on T 7, one and one-fourth mile, right on T 118, one-tenth mile, left on T 9, one-tenth mile. (Donovan, 1980; Ketcham, 1969; Ohio DOT; SOCBA)

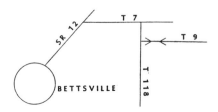

Scioto County
35-73-15

Otway Bridge

Otway Bridge spans Scioto Brush Creek with 128 feet. Scioto Brush Creek has a normal bed width of 120 feet at the bridge. Scioto Brush Creek is the drainage channel for northwestern Scioto County and drains into the Scioto River 10 miles east of the bridge site.

Otway Bridge was constructed in 1874 by the Smith Bridge Company, Toledo, Ohio. At one end of the bridge was an attached open bridge that spanned the mill race for a saw mill. The open wooden bridge was replaced in 1923 with a steel bridge 81 feet long.

Otway Covered Bridge was constructed with a Smith truss and crosswise floor planking. In 1896, a six-ply, double Burr arch was installed encasing the Smith truss. Subsequently, steel tie-rods were added corresponding with the "X" members, tying the upper chord and lower chord. Also, tie-rods connecting the arch to the lower chord were added. A wooden guardrail extends the length of the bridge.

The exterior of the bridge has a red tin roof and dark brown weathered siding. The roof extends three feet beyond the portals.

Otway bridge is located on the edge of the town of Otway in a park-like area. The bridge is open, but it appears that only bikers and pedestrians use the bridge.

Otway Bridge is listed on the National Register of Historic Places.

DIRECTIONS: Brush Creek Township. West side of Otway off SR 348 on T 344. (Donovan, 1980; Ohio DOT; Riley, 1986; SOCBA)

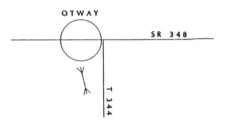

Shelby County
35-75-01

Lockington Bridge

Lockington Bridge spans the west channel of the Great Miami River and is 178 feet long. The Great Miami drains southwestern Ohio. Lockington Bridge assumes its name from the nearby village, where six sets of locks are found that were a part of the Miami and Erie Canal.

Lockington Bridge was built in 1870 with a Long truss. The bridge has two spans. The one pier and abutments are cut stone. The exterior has a shake roof and gray/brown weathered siding. Steel has been added to reinforce the chords and floor beams. The floor boards are rotted, the abutments are crumbling, the roof is leaking and siding is missing. The bridge is closed and will be demolished when funds are available.

The east side of the bridge has a steel bridge that spans the east channel of the Great Miami. Both of these bridges, the covered and the steel, are in extremely poor condition. No pedestrian traffic is suggested. The Lockington Bridge is listed in the National Register of Historic Places.

DIRECTIONS: Washington Township. From Lockington, east on CR132, one mile. ("Closed to Traffic"; Donovan, 1980; Greenberg, 1976; Ohio DOT; SOCBA)

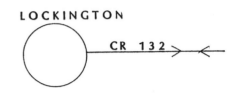

Everitt Road Bridge

Built in 1873, the Everitt Road Covered Bridge is located in the Cuyahoga Valley National Recreation Area. The bridge spans Furnace Run, which is a tributary of the Cuyahoga River. The Cuyahoga River is the major river for the northern half of Summit County. Furnace Run has an average bed width of 75 feet.

The Everitt Road Bridge is 100 feet long and is a clear span. The bridge rests on cut stone abutments. In 1975, the bridge was washed off its abutments by a flood. It was dismantled and stored at Hale Farm, in a restored historic village. In July of 1984, preservation specialists from the National Park Service started reconstruction. Photographed on October 7, 1986, the bridge was almost complete. About two-thirds of the siding on one side was missing and the roof was almost shingled.

The Everitt Road Covered Bridge has been exquisitely restored. The rotted timbers have been replaced with new timber. The Smith truss, rare in northeastern Ohio, has been painted white. The plank siding is painted red and the roof is finished with shake.

The Everitt Road Bridge is an authentic restoration. The Cuyahoga Valley National Recreation Area should be proud of their endeavors.

DIRECTIONS: Boston Township. From Everitt, west on CR 47 (Everitt Road). (Cuyahoga Valley National Recreation Area; Donovan, 1980; National Park Service, D. S. Department of the Interior; Ohio DOT; SOCBA)

Newton Falls Bridge

The Newton Falls Covered Bridge spans the East Branch of the Mahoning River, which is the major river in southwestern Trumbull County. The East Branch, in the area of Newton Falls Bridge, has an average bed width of 120 feet.

The Newton Falls Bridge is located in the town of Newton Falls and is the only covered bridge in Trumbull County. The bridge was built in 1831 and was constructed with a Town lattice truss. The bridge is 124 feet long with no windows, making it very dark inside.

The Newton Falls Covered Bridge is unusual because it is the only covered bridge in Ohio that has an outside walkway. This covered bridge now has the distinction of being the oldest covered bridge in Ohio. Previously, before it was burned by arson, Roberts Bridge in Preble County held that distinction. The Roberts Bridge was built in 1829. Newton Falls Bridge was built in 1831, making it over one hundred and fifty years old.

The exterior of the bridge has a white tin roof and reddish-brown plank siding. The bridge has two steel piers that were installed in 1943. The bridge is open to local traffic and is in fair condition, but the walkway needs repair.

Because the bridge is out of the ordinary, with its outside walkway, efforts have been made to maintain the bridge. The bridge site is kept attractive and there is easy access to the river bank to view the bridge.

The bridge carries too much traffic and in order to preserve the structure, it needs to be bypassed.

Newton Falls Covered Bridge is listed in the National Register of Historic Places.

DIRECTIONS: Newton Township. At Newton Falls. (Donovan, 1980; Ohio DOT; SOCBA)

Upper Darby Bridge

Upper Darby Bridge spans Big Darby Creek with 100 feet. Big Darby Creek has a 70 foot bed width at the bridge site and drains the southwest corner of Union County. Upper Darby Bridge was once known as Beltz Mill Bridge and Pottersburg Bridge.

Built in 1873, Upper Darby Bridge is a magnificent example of the Partridge Truss. Reuben Partridge designed and built 200 Partridge truss covered bridges in Union County. The summer of 1986 found five still in existence in Union County. There is only one other Partridge truss in the United States and that is the Bergstresser Bridge in the contiguous county of Franklin.

Upper Darby Bridge has a shake roof, and white plank siding. There is a three foot window that stretches the entire length of the bridge that is protected by a tin roofed canopy. The interior is even more striking, with the five member "X" panels assisted with corresponding steel tie-rods, and vertical tie-rods between the panels. The interior is painted white and has been well-maintained. The floor planking is laid lengthwise. Upper Darby Bridge is a single span and rests on concrete abutments. The bridge is open and serves local traffic.

DIRECTIONS: Allen Township. From Marysville, west on SR 245, seven miles, right on CR 163 (Cratty Road), two miles, right on CR 164 (Lewisburg Road). ("Covered Bridges are Charming Links to the Past"; Donovan, 1980; Ohio DOT; SOCBA)

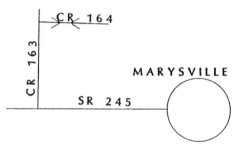

Spain Creek Bridge

Spain Creek Bridge crosses Spain Creek and is 65 feet long. This is the shortest of the six existing Partridge truss bridges. Spain Creek is a tributary of Big Darby Creek and has a 50 foot normal bed width at the bridge site.

Spain Creek Bridge was built in 1870. The exterior has a tin roof and white plank siding, with long windows extending the full length of the bridge, protected by a tin roofed canopy. As with all of the five, in use, covered bridges in Union County, the interior is in excellent condition. All of the wood is painted white. Spain Creek Bridge is unusual not only because it is the shortest Partridge truss, but also because it only has three wooden members in the "X" panels as opposed to the normal five, but maintains the steel tie rods diagonally and vertically. The floor has crosswise floor planking interfaced with two lengthwise runners.

As with all of the Union County bridges, Spain Creek is well-maintained and open for local traffic.

DIRECTIONS: Allen Township. From Marysville, west on SR 245, seven miles, right on CR 163 (Cratty Road). ("Covered Bridges are Charming Links to the Past"; Donovan, 1980; Ohio DOT; SOCBA)

Treacle Creek Bridge

Also known as the Culberson Bridge and the Winget Road Bridge, the Treacle Creek Bridge traverses Treacle Creek, a tributary of Big Darby Creek, which has a normal bed width of 90 feet at the bridge site. The bridge is 96 feet long.

Another spectacular Union County bridge, the Treacle Creek Bridge has a black shingled roof, white plank siding and two full length windows protected by canopies. Built in 1868, the Partridge truss has five member ''X'' panels painted white. The floor planking is laid crosswise. With a single span, Treacle Creek Bridge rests on concrete abutments and is open to traffic.

Located on a dead-end road, the bridge does not receive much traffic. Situated in farm country, as with all of Union County's bridges, the Treacle Creek Bridge has an impressive physical location and lends itself to be photographed.

DIRECTIONS: Union Township. From Milford Center, two and one-half miles south on SR 4, left on CR 86 (Homer Road) left on T 82 (Winget Road) one-fourth mile. (Donovan, 1980; Ohio DOT; SOCBA)

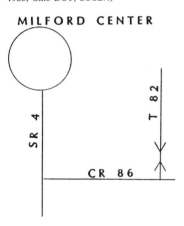

MILFORD CENTER

SR 4

T 82

CR 86

Little Darby Bridge

The Little Darby Bridge was also known as the Bigelow Bridge, named after the Bigelow family who owned the land around the bridge site.

Little Darby Bridge is the longest of the usable covered bridges in Union County and is 102 feet long. The bridge crosses Little Darby Creek, which has a 90 foot creek bed.

Built in 1873, it was one of more than 200 bridges built in Union County by Reuben L. Partridge. He designed and patented this diagonal truss and supporting brace.

Little Darby Covered Bridge has a single span, supported on either end with stone abutments. The bridge has a tin roof and white painted side boards. It has a window that runs the full length of the bridge on both sides, with a tin roofed canopy to protect the interior.

Access to the creek is difficult but not necessary. Visual access is easy from the surrounding area.

DIRECTIONS: Union Township. From Chuckery, SR 161, west two miles, right on Axe Handle Road (CR 87). (''Covered Bridges are Charming Links to the Past''; Donovan, 1980; Ohio DOT; SOCBA)

CR 87

CHUCKERY

SR 161

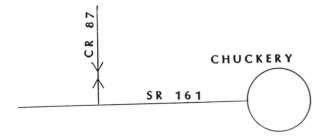

Reed Bridge

Reed Bridge is a single span and crosses Big Darby Creek with 155 feet, making it the longest Partridge Truss in existence. Big Darby Creek has a creek bed width of 150 feet at the bridge site and drains the southwestern corner of Union County.

Built in 1870, the Reed Bridge has sixteen Partridge "X" panels in each truss, with each panel having five members, assisted by corresponding tie-rods and vertical tie-rods between the panels. The floor is laid lengthwise. The bridge has a gray tin roof and weathered white siding.

The bridge is now bypassed and has virtually been abandoned. The canopies are gone, little siding remains, and many truss members are missing. The bridge was bypassed in 1968 and has since fallen apart. The bridge has not seen any maintenance since 1968 or before.

It is sad that a once majestic bridge has been left to the destructive forces of nature and vandalism. There is some discussion about restoring the bridge, but if it is not done soon, it will be lost forever.

The Reed Bridge is listed on the National Register of Historic Places.

DIRECTIONS: Darby Township. From Plain City, west on SR 161, six miles, right on SR 38, three miles, on right. ("Covered Bridges are Charming Links to the Past"; Donovan, 1980; Ohio DOT; SOCBA)

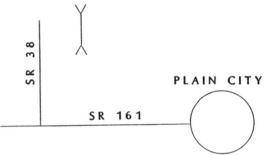

Mt. Olive Road Bridge

Mt. Olive Road Bridge crosses Salt Creek and is 48 feet long. Salt Creek is a small stream with an average bed width of 35 feet at the bridge site.

Mt. Olive Bridge was built by George Washington Pilcher in 1875 with a queenpost truss. It has been reinforced with steel on the diagonals. The floor planking was laid crosswise and two runners are attached lengthwise.

The exterior has a gray tin roof and weathered gray plank siding, with several planks missing. The roof is extended two feet over the portals. Access to the creek is impossible. Fences prevent access to the creek bed and, consequently, one has difficulty in viewing the sides.

Mt. Olive Bridge is a single span and rests on cut stone abutments. The bridge is open and serves local traffic. Mt. Olive Road Bridge is listed in the National Register of Historic Places.

DIRECTIONS: Jackson Township. From Allensville, north on CR 18 one mile, right on T 8. (Donovan, 1980; "Five Covered Bridge in Vinton County"; Ohio DOT; SOCBA)

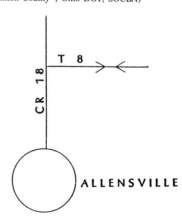

Bay Bridge

Bay Bridge was moved to its present location, over a pond at the Fairgrounds in Elk Fork, in 1966.

Built in 1876, the Bay Bridge has been weathered by time. The 63 foot single span rests on poured concrete abutments. The exterior has a red tin roof with several pieces blown off, exposing the roof sheeting. The siding is intact and is handsomely weathered, gray planks. The roof extends two feet over each portal.

The most exciting feature about the bridge is not its nostalgic location, but rather the interior truss design. Bay Bridge has a double multiple kingpost truss. The floor has horizontal planking with two lengthwise runners. The combination of the truss and the flooring make this covered bridge an interesting architectural structure.

DIRECTIONS: Elk Township. At Elk Fork west side of SR 93 on Fairgrounds. ("Covered Bridge, Park of the Past"; Donovan, 1980; "Five Covered Bridges in Vinton County"; Ohio DOT; SOCBA; "Vinton County Has Bridge, But Lake Will Come Later")

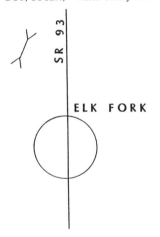

Geer Mill/Ponn/Humpback Bridge

Ponn or Humpback Bridge is also known as the Geer Mill Bridge after a local mill. Humpback Bridge spans Raccoon Creek, which is a major drainage channel for this area. The creek has a 170 foot bed width at the bridge site.

This covered bridge is one of a kind in Ohio and one of the best examples of a humpback bridge left in the United States. The Humpback Bridge was built in 1874 by Martin E. McGrath and Lymar Wells.

Humpback Bridge is 180 feet long and has three spans. The center and longest span has a single huge arch encased in a double multiple king post truss. One end span has a double queenpost truss and the other end span has a double multiple kingpost structure.

The Humpback Bridge has a significant camber noticeable on its roof and the interior floor. The entire bridge exhibits the arched design. The bridge rests on stone abutments and on two stone piers located almost at quarter points. The bridge's unique design is thought to have increased the structural soundness of the bridge and to have given greater clearance for flood waters.

Access to the creek is fairly easy and the view of the backbone bridge looming over the creek is spectacular. The Ponn/Humpback Bridge was listed in the National Register of Historic Places in 1973.

DIRECTIONS: Wilkesville Township. From Wilkesville, SR 124 west, three miles, left on T 4, three miles. (Donovan, 1980; "Five Covered Bridges in Vinton County"; Greenberg, 1976; "More Research Shows Ponn Bridge was Burned in 1874 and Restored"; Ohio DOT; SOCBA; "Unique Hump-Backed Covered Bridge at Geer's Mill In Good Condition, Vinton Engineer Says"; "Vinton's Humpback Bridge Goes Down in History")

Eakin Mill Bridge

Eakin Mill Bridge spans Raccoon Creek with 111 feet. Raccoon Creek has a bed width at the bridge site of 50 feet. Eakin Mill Bridge was built in 1870 by contractor A. L. Hunter for $2,200. Eakin Hill Bridge has a double multiple kingpost truss encasing a Burr arch that extends the entire length of the bridge. The double truss and massive arch are symmetrically enticing. The floor planking is unusual. The floor planks are laid on a diagonal but change direction every so often. Interfaced on the diagonal floor planking is a lengthwise floor planking covering the center three-fourths of the floor. Steel tie-rods have been anchored into the arch, connecting the arch to the upper and lower chords. Additional tie-rods were placed in conjunction with the diagonal truss members.

The exterior of the bridge has a rusty tin roof that is missing pieces, and gray weathered plank siding that is also missing pieces. The roof extends three feet beyond the portals. The bridge is in desperate condition. Wooden piers have been installed to support the bridge.

In the creek, there is part of a wooden dam and parts of steel machinery that is evidence of the existence of the Eakin Mill.

There was controversy for years over the continued existence of the Eakin Mill Bridge. It appears that neither the county who owned the bridge, nor the township that now owns it, had the funds to maintain it.

The Eakin Mill Bridge, accessible only by foot, is still standing only because the local residents would not allow it to be torn down. Due to the bridge's unique interior and physical location, Eakin Mill Bridge would be an ideal candidate for restoration.

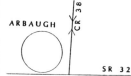

DIRECTIONS: Vinton Township. At Arbaugh. Off SR 32 on CR 38, one-half mile. ("A Bridge Without a County"; Donovan, 1980; "Five Covered Bridges in Vinton County"; "Letter to the Editor" (Eakin Hill Bridge); Ohio DOT; "Save our Bridge"; SOCBA)

Cox Bridge

Cox Bridge was also known as Woodgard Bridge. This covered bridge is only 40 feet long and spans Brushy Fork Creek. Brushy Fork is a little stream whose bed is only 30 feet wide.

Cox Bridge was built in 1884 with a queenpost truss construction. The bridge has a tin roof that is in good repair. The siding is multi-colored because pieces have been replaced with used painted planks. The effect is twofold. First the bridge is protected from the weather and, second, the dimensional colors of the siding add distinctly to the charm of the covered bridge. The maintenance of the covered bridge is credited to the local community.

Access to the creek is difficult and with summer vegetation it is hard to see the entire bridge.

DIRECTIONS: Swan Township. From Mt. Pleasant, SR 93, south, two miles, right on CR 20. (Donovan, 1980; "Five Covered Bridges in Vinton County"; Ohio DOT; SOCBA)

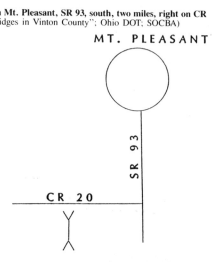

Shinn Bridge

Shinn Bridge is named after its builder, Charles T. Shinn, who lived nearby. The Shinn Bridge spans a branch of Wolf Creek that has a 45 foot bed width at the bridge.

The 98 foot Shinn Bridge was built in 1886 with a multiple kingpost truss and Burr arch. The bridge is a single span and rests on cut stone abutments. The floor has lengthwise planks. The exterior has a red tin roof and red plank siding with white portals.

Shinn Bridge is open and serves the local traffic and is listed on the National Register of Historic Places.

DIRECTIONS: Palmer Township. From Wolf Creek, west on SR 676, two miles, left on CR 206 one mile, left on T 129, one mile, right on T 1, one mile, at T 447. (Donovan, 1980; Greenberg, 1976; Ohio DOT; SOCBA)

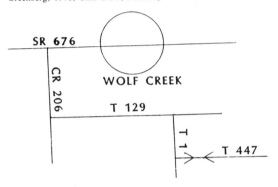

Henry Bridge

Henry Bridge spans West Branch, a small stream with a 30 foot bed width at the bridge site.

Henry Bridge was built in 1892 with a truss similar to that of a kingpost but with an empty center panel (no center kingpost). The interior is in fair condition with horizontal floor planking. The exterior has weathered plank siding and one window centered in the empty center panel. The roof is green tin. The 45 foot single span bridge rests on cut stone abutments.

This bridge has been bypassed for preservation. Although there is access to the bridge, the area is overgrown. What could be an ideal location for a small park, is full of shrubs and thickets. Access to the creek is impossible, but the bridge can be easily viewed from the adjacent bridge.

DIRECTIONS: Fairfield Township. From Bartlett, SR 555 south, four miles left on T 61, one-half mile. (Donovan, 1980; Ohio DOT; SOCBA)

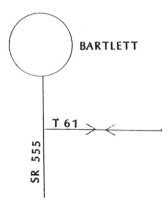

Root Bridge

Root Bridge is also known as Qualey Bridge and spans West Branch. West Branch has a 40 foot normal bed width at the bridge.

Built in 1888, the 65 foot Root Bridge was constructed with a Long truss by Alta and Charles Meredith Builders. The floor has horizontal planking with two lengthwise runners. The exterior has a tin roof, red plank siding and white, arched portals.

Root Bridge has been bypassed for preservation. The seventy-foot long structure is a single span and rests on stone abutments.

There is a small park area next to the bridge that offers picnic facilities. Access to the creek bed is easy and the bridge, although nothing out of the ordinary, offers many picturesque angles.

Root Bridge is listed on the National Register of Historic Places.

DIRECTIONS: Decatur Township. From Decaturville, one-half mile north on CR 6, one-fourth mile. (Donovan, 1980; Greenberg, 1976; Ohio DOT; SOCBA)

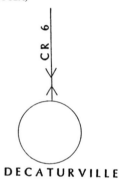

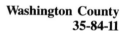

DECATURVILLE

Harra Bridge

Harra Bridge spans the South Branch of Wolf Creek, which has a 90 foot bed width at the bridge site.

This bridge was built in 1870/71 with a Long truss. The summer of 1986 found the exterior in poor condition. The once slate roof has been replaced by tin and was all intact, but rusting. Many planks of the siding were missing. The bridge has been bypassed for preservation and it is sad that it has been so vandalized.

The single span, 95 foot structure, rests on cut stone abutments. Directly under the bridge is a poured concrete dam.

Harra Bridge offers a picturesque location and, since it has been bypassed, deserves to be properly maintained. Harra Bridge is listed in the National Register of Historic Places.

DIRECTIONS: Watertown Township. From Watertown, north of SR 339, two miles, left on T 172, one-fourth mile. (Donovan 1980; Greenberg, 1976; Ohio DOT; SOCBA)

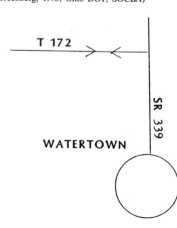

T 172

SR 339

WATERTOWN

Bell Bridge

Bell Bridge spans the South Fork of Wolf Creek with 63 feet. The South Fork of Wolf Creek has a 40 foot bed width at the bridge.

Built in 1880, the Bell Bridge has a truss similar to that of a multiple kingpost, but is missing the center kingpost panel. This center panel is empty. The floor planking is crosswise with two lengthwise runners. The roof is gray tin and the siding is red planking. The portals are painted white except where planks were replaced. Bell Bridge has had extensive reinforcing with steel beams added to the underside of the floor for support. This single span structure rests on stone abutments and is still open to traffic.

DIRECTIONS: Barlow Township. From Barlow, north on SR 339, one-tenth mile, north on T 39, two miles. (Donovan, 1980 Ohio DOT; SOCBA)

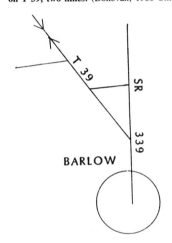

Mill Branch Bridge

Built in 1885, Mill Branch Bridge was moved onto the Barlow Fairgrounds in 1979/80 from Belpre Township.

Mill Branch Bridge currently spans a small stream with 40 feet. Listed in the *Ohio Covered Bridge Guide* as a multiple kingpost truss, the bridge has a red tin roof and multicolored plank siding with many pieces missing. The bridge's location is accessible but has been overgrown with weeds.

In its original location in Belpre Township, the Mill Branch Bridge spanned the Little Hocking River two miles northeast of Porterfield on T 289.

DIRECTIONS: Barlow Township. At Barlow on the Fairgrounds. North side of SR 550. (Donovan, 1980; Ketcham, 1969; Ohio DOT; SOCBA)

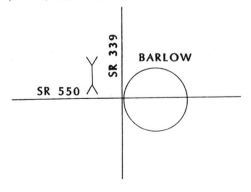

Schwenderman Bridge

Moved to Jackson Hill Park in Marietta in 1967, the 44 foot Schwenderman Bridge was originally built in 1887 with a multiple kingpost truss, with an empty center panel. The floor has crosswise floor planking and no runners. The exterior has a shake roof and weathered plank siding. This bridge spans a dry depression and rests on cut stone abutments.

Jackson Hill Park offers picnic facilities and is well-maintained.

DIRECTIONS: In Marietta, north on SR 60 north on Washington Street, top of the hill the road becomes Cisler Street. At Jackson Hill Park. (Donovan, 1980; Ohio DOT; SOCBA)

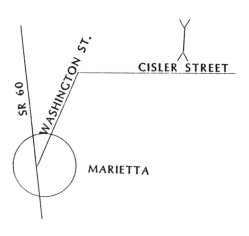

Hills/Hildreth Bridge

Hills/Hildreth Bridge spans the Little Muskingum River with 112 feet. The Little Muskingum River has a normal bed width of 50 feet, but exhibits a large channel at the bridge, which characterizes a stream that is prone to flooding.

Hills Bridge was built in 1881 with a Howe truss. The interior is interesting because of the Howe truss in conjunction with the diagonal floor planking and two lengthwise runners. The exterior is spectacular. Either side of the covered bridge has a 30-foot, open steel bridge approach that rests on stone abutments. Hills Bridge is suspended on two huge cut stone piers. The exterior of the bridge has a gray tin roof, red plank siding and white portals. The bridge has a head railing, limiting traffic solely to automobiles. Hopefully, the bridge will be bypassed and preserved. Hills Bridge is listed on the National Register of Historic Places.

DIRECTIONS: Newport Township. From Marietta, SR 26, northeast, three miles, right on T 333, one-fourth mile. (Donovan, 1980; Greenberg, 1976; Ohio DOT; SOCBA)

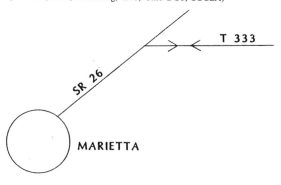

Washington County
35-84-27

Hune Bridge

Hune Bridge spans the Little Muskingum River with 112 feet. The Little Muskingum River is a major drainage channel for northeastern Washington County and has a 50 foot normal bed width at the bridge site.

Built in 1877, the Hune Bridge was constructed with a Long truss. The exterior has a gray tin roof and weathered, dark gray plank siding. The single span bridge rests on cut stone abutments and has ten foot approach ramps on either side. Hune Bridge is open to automobiles only and is listed in the National Register of Historic Places.

DIRECTIONS: Lawrence Township. From Lawrence, SR 26, south, one-fourth mile, left at T 34. (Donovan, 1980; Ohio DOT; SOCBA)

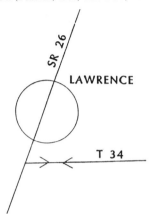

Washington County
35-84-28

Rinard Bridge

Rinard Bridge spans Little Muskingum River and is 128 feet long. Little Muskingum River is a major drainage channel for northeastern Washington County and has a 50 foot bed width at the bridge, with an elevated, wider channel, indicating that the stream is prone to flooding its normal banks periodically.

Bypassed, Rinard Bridge was built by the Smith Bridge Company with a Smith truss in 1874. The interior is exceptional. With eight windows erratically located throughout the bridge, the interior is well illuminated. The floor has diagonal planking with two lengthwise runners. Steel tie-rods have been added vertically between the panels periodically throughout the bridge. A steel bowstring cable has also been added inside and outside to aid in reinforcing the bridge. The exterior has a tin roof and brown weathered siding. The single span rests on cut stone abutments and has 15-foot open steel approach ramps at either end. The bridge has a park area and is listed in the National Register of Historic Places.

DIRECTIONS: Ludlow Township. From Wingett, northeast on SR 26, one mile, right on CR 406. (Donovan, 1980; Greenberg, 1976; Ohio DOT; SOCBA)

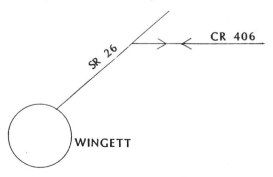

Photograph by Michael Krekeler

Parker Bridge

Parker Bridge spans the Sandusky River with 172 feet. The Sandusky River is a major drainage channel for eastern Wyandot County and has a 125 foot normal bed width at the bridge site.

Parker Bridge was built is 1873 with a Howe truss. The floor is lengthwise planking. The exterior has a tin roof and red plank siding with many pieces missing. The single span structure rests on cut stone abutments and is open to traffic.

Parker Bridge is listed in the National Register of Historic Places.

DIRECTIONS: Crane Township. From Upper Sandusky, SR 67, northeast, three miles, left on CR 37, one and one-fourth miles, right on T 40, one-tenth mile. (Donovan, 1980; Greenberg; 1976; Ohio DOT; SOCBA)

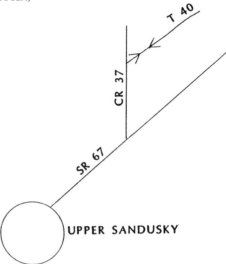

Swartz Bridge

Located in relatively flat terrain in northeastern Ohio, Swartz Bridge is visible for quite a distance. It spans the Sandusky River with 110 feet. The Sandusky River has a bed width of 90 feet.

This covered bridge has a Howe truss and was built in 1878. The exterior's red paint has faded, enhancing the knots in the plank siding. The wooden shake roof is in poor condition and has virtually disappeared around the peak. The interior of the bridge is still sound and the graffiti is acting as a temporary wood preservative. Unless the roof receives immediate attention, the wooden floor boards will soon rot.

Access to the river bed is difficult but not necessary to view the bridge. There are open fields surrounding the bridge, allowing it to be viewed from many advantageous angles.

DIRECTIONS: Antrim Township. From Upper Sandusky, SR 23, south, left on CR 62, two miles, right on CR 130. (Donovan, 1980; Ohio DOT; SOCBA)

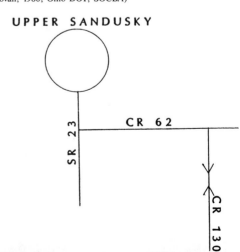

Pennsylvania

ACKNOWLEDGMENTS

I would like to extend my personal appreciation to the following people of Pennsylvania for their time and the generous information they provided:
Lancaster County Library
Gerald Bruce, Reference Librarian
Chester County Historical Society
Bucks County Historical Society
Dwight E. Copper
Marguerite Foster
Treva Lawyer, Library Staff, Kittochtinny Historical Society, Franklin County
Beth Goodwin Glass, Greene County Historical Society
Chester County Library and District Center
Washington County Tourism

INTRODUCTION

Pennsylvania today has 229 historic covered bridges, more covered bridges than any other state, for two reasons. First, Pennsylvania originally had more covered bridges than any other state, and secondly, because state-wide, counties and townships decided to maintain and preserve their historic structures.

The state of Pennsylvania has a diverse landscape. From the southeastern rolling hills in Lancaster, Bucks and Chester Counties; to the mountainous terrain of Perry, Mountour, Columbia and Northumberland Counties; all are landscapes that demanded covered bridges.

PENNSYLVANIA'S TRUSSES

Pennsylvania has ten different examples of trusses or combination of trusses. Of the 229 bridges, 129 have multiple kingpost trusses encased with a double Burr arch. This truss design is the most popular and has more examples than any other truss design in Pennsylvania. The second most popular truss in existence today in Pennsylvania is the queenpost. Found in six counties, the queenpost truss has 40 examples. The truss with the third greatest number of examples is the Town, with 19 examples in five counties. Twelve Town trusses are found in Bucks County alone.

The balance of the trusses have the following examples: kingpost—12, Multiple kingpost and queenpost combination—11, Multiple kingpost—9, Howe—4, Multiple kingpost—1, Childs—2, Town and queenpost combination—1, and Smith—1.

PENNSYLVANIA'S LONGEST AND OLDEST

Pennsylvania's longest covered bridge is Academia Bridge (38-34-01). Spanning the Tuscarora Creek in Juniata County, it has 305 feet and two spans. Academia Bridge was built in 1901 with a Burr truss.

Determining the oldest covered bridge existing in the United States is difficult. Both New Hampshire and Vermont have exceptional contenders for that position. However, it is just as likely Pennsylvania could have the oldest covered bridge. We will probably never know because any records kept in the early 1800s are not accurate, and most do not even exist.

Pennsylvania has some viable contenders for the oldest covered bridge in America. There are two that could have been built as early as 1812. They include Rishel (38-49-05) in Northumberland County, and Wagoner's Mill (38-50-15) Bridges in Perry County. There are two other antique bridges that should be mentioned. The Hassenplug Bridge (38-60-03) in Union County, was built in 1827 and the Uhlerstown Bridge (38-09-08) in Bucks County, was built in 1830. The dates of construction in the early 1800s are extremely difficult to pin down. The only thing we can be sure of is that this group does represent some of the oldest covered bridges in the United States.

SOME COUNTIES AND
THEIR COVERED BRIDGES

As with all covered bridges found in counties throughout the United States, Pennsylvania's covered bridges within each county's boundaries, are very similar. For example, Bucks County has 13 covered bridges, all of them constructed with a Town lattice truss and one has a combination Town and queenpost. Lancaster has 28 remaining covered bridges. All, except one kingpost, were built with a multiple kingpost and double Burr arch. All of Lancaster's covered bridges are painted red and have a tin roof. Perry County has 14 bridges; four are excellent examples of a multiple kingpost and queenpost combination truss, and ten have Burr arch trusses. With all of these examples, it is apparent that the reason each county has the same style truss is because the decision of what type of truss to use was determined by county officials. Whether the county engineer's office (people who make the decisions today), or another appropriate county official made the decisions; the construction of covered bridges, county by county, was homogenous. Many counties only had one person who built their bridges. Other counties had more than one builder, but the truss design and style of the bridge was held consistent.

BEDFORD COUNTY

Bedford County has 15 covered bridges. Thirteen have a Burr arch and two have a multiple kingpost truss. In most cases, Bedford County's bridges are painted white on the interior as well as the exterior and trimmed in red.

Six of the covered bridges are bypassed or closed. Three of those are impossible to reach because of fencing: Felton's Mill (38-05-03), Heirline (38-05-11), and Jackson's Hill (38-05-25).

Over half of Bedford's bridges have only partial siding, usually only the lower third is covered with vertical planks. Felton's Mill (38-05-03) is unusual because one side is completely sided while the other only has the lower third sided.

Claycomb Bridge (38-05-12) is particularly unique. It is the only bridge in Bedford County that has one external walkway.

The date of construction for the Colvin Bridge (38-05-24) is not known, but it must be very old. The beams of the multiple kingpost truss are all hand-hewn. Another striking characteristic of this bridge is the half-size multiple kingpost truss. One diagonal of each panel extends to the upper half. This is the only example of this half-size multiple kingpost design in Bedford County.

BUCKS COUNTY

Bucks County has 13 covered bridges. All of these have a Town lattice truss. Most of the bridges are covered with red plank siding and a shake roof. These bridges are all similar in design and character. One that is unique is the Uhlerstown Bridge (38-09-08) because it spans the Delaware Canal. Bucks County has preserved miles of the Delaware Canal system. Uhlerstown Bridge is the only covered bridge left in the United States that spans a canal. This bridge was also built in 1830, making is one of Pennsylvania's oldest bridges.

COLUMBIA COUNTY

With 22 covered bridges, Columbia County has 12 queenpost trusses and 10 Burr arch trusses. Columbia County's bridges are covered with red plank siding and tin roofs.

What makes Columbia County's bridges especially impressive is the character of the streams. Most of the creeks are mountain streams; they flow fast and have a lot of rapids, which adds a dramatic nature to each bridge. Since all covered bridges are found in valleys, the mountainous terrain provides a great background for the photographer and a wonderful landscape to search for covered bridges.

All of Columbia's bridges are special, but one location provides the only existing example of twin covered bridges left in America today. East and West Paden (38-19-11,12) are preserved in a park. County representatives had the foresight to bypass the twins and preserve them. They are well-maintained and a delight for any covered bridge enthusiast.

LANCASTER COUNTY

Lancaster County has 28 covered bridges, second only to Parke County, Indiana, which has 34. Characterized by dark red, plank siding with batten, cut stone wingwalls at each approach, and a multiple kingpost truss with a double Burr arch; all of Lancaster's bridges have white portals and diagonal black and white lines on the portals to identify the sides of the bridges.

Locating Lancaster County's Covered Bridges

Lancaster County has a tremendously well-developed road system in a densely populated, rural area. This presents problems when bridging because there are so many roads, and many of the roads are not identified. Some of the roads have names and/or numbers. Invariably, if you have the number, the road will be identified with a name. My suggestion is to obtain the county map available from the state, a local county map and an atlas. Hopefully, with these maps and my directions, you will be able to locate the bridges. Discovering where Lancaster has its covered bridges is half the fun.

None of Lancaster's bridges are a disappointment. They all have attractive locations and the bridges are well-maintained.

The Amish

Bridging in Lancaster County is a unique experience. The landscape is beautiful with rolling hills, farm houses and barns dotting the countryside. What makes the countryside particularly interesting; the area is densely populated by the Amish. Their white farm houses, multiple barns and distinctive way of life permeate the environment. Numerous black carriages drawn by horse, travel the highways along with automotive traffic. People bicycling and walking are also very prominent. The Amish methods of transportation require traveling Lancaster roads carefully. The average speed is 40 mph, everyone drives slowly, and things generally move at a gentle pace.

The landscape at many of the bridges is also characterized by the Amish lifestyle. The fields,

plowed by horse drawn plows, the sound of a horse whinny in a nearby barn, and the clop, clop of the horses as they pull the carriages across a covered bridge take you back a hundred years in time. The experience is exciting; a whole different reality.

Summary For Lancaster

Bridging in Lancaster County is fun because there are so many covered bridges and each one has an attractive location. The county is rich in history. Many mills still exist near the covered bridges. Some of these mills were built in the early 1720s. Pennsylvania has a rich supply of covered bridge and mill combinations. Lancaster County is no exception.

Each bridge site offers the bridger an opportunity to glimpse back in time. The bridges, mills and the Amish lifestyle give us an idea of how the landscape appeared in the United States over a hundred years ago. Lancaster County is unique, and a must when bridging in Pennsylvania.

PERRY COUNTY

Perry County has some of the most picturesque covered bridges in the United States. Many of the bridges once had mills nearby. One in particular, Wagoner's Bridge (38-50-15), stands near a three-story stone gristmill that was used into the 1940s. The mill, dam and bridge combine to form a spectacular setting.

There are eight covered bridges within fourteen miles of each other that span Shermans Creek. Shermans Creek drains a long valley between two mountains and produces a strikingly scenic location for the bridges. These eight bridges are all south of SR 274 in the western half of Perry County.

Perry County has one of the most magnificent groups of covered bridges. A day in Perry County will reward the bridger with many valued memories.

SOMERSET COUNTY

Somerset County has ten covered bridges. Six of these bridges have a Burr truss, two have a multiple kingpost truss and two have a Child's truss using a multiple kingpost center. I previously believed that Ohio had the only example of a Child's truss. While Ohio has the only queenpost center panel used with the Child's truss, Somerset County can boast of two Child's truss bridges; the Trostletown (38-56-10), and the Barronvale (38-56-03) Bridges, both of which are bypassed. When I saw the Barronvale truss, I could not believe my eyes. The information I was able to obtain about this bridge, prior to my visit, indicated that the truss was simply a multiple kingpost with a Burr arch. The discovery of its existence in the Barronvale Bridge was exciting because the Child's truss is so rare.

What is even more spectacular about the truss is that there are two spans, consequently, there are a total of four individual Child's trusses. Each truss also has a Burr arch. To my knowledge, this is the only Child's truss with a Burr arch—What a Find! The Child's design was extremely popular during the late 1800s on highway and railroad bridges. Unfortunately, it is one of those trusses which has only a few examples left. The Trostletown Bridge (38-56-10), the other Child's truss in Somerset County is impossible to locate. It has been closed and the one road that leads to it is overgrown and prevents any reasonable access.

Needless to say I was extremely disappointed when I gave up the search after an hour of hunting. I finally determined exactly what road it was on but I was by myself and I was not sure how far through the dense vegetation I would have to walk. I knew that it was a rare Child's truss which made the decision to abandon the search more difficult.

Somerset County was probably the county that presented the greatest difficulty in locating covered bridges. Consequently, I only found three out of a possible ten, which was frustrating.
(Donovan, 1980; Pennsylvania County Maps; Pennsylvania Department of Transportation; Zacker)

WASHINGTON COUNTY

Washington County has 25 covered bridges. Each bridge is covered with red plank siding, a tin roof and has several windows. The single most obvious feature about Washington County's covered bridges is that they are all short. The longest is 77 feet, but most of them are between 40 and 50 feet long. The shortest is only 24 feet long.

Most of the bridges are open, serving traffic and in excellent condition. One is preserved at Meadowcroft Village, Pine Bank Bridge (38-63-35). Meadowcroft Village preserves old historic structures and has them available to the public in season.

One feature about Washington County is some of their covered bridges are found on roads made out of crushed coal. It is an unusual sight to see a road surface glimmering black coal.

BRIDGE NAME	COUNTY	NUMBER
Felton's Mill	Bedford	38-05-03
Heirline/Kinton	"	38-05-11
Claycomb/Reynoldsdale	"	38-05-12
Knisley	"	38-05-16
Ryot	"	38-05-17
Cupperts/New Paris	"	38-05-18
Diehl's/Turner's/Raystown	"	38-05-19
McDaniels	"	38-05-20
Bowser/Osterburg	"	38-05-22
Snook's	"	38-05-23
Colvin	"	38-05-24
Jackson's Mill	"	38-05-25
Erwinna	Bucks	38-09-04
South Perkasie	"	38-09-05
Mood	"	38-09-07
Uhlerstown	"	38-09-08

BRIDGE NAME	COUNTY	NUMBER
Frankenfield	Bucks	38-09-09
Cabin Run	"	38-09-10
Loux	"	38-09-11
Rapps	Chester	38-15-14
Shoemaker	Columbia	38-19-06
Sam Eckman	"	38-19-08
Josiah Hess	"	38-19-10
East & West Paden Twin	"	38-19-11
		38-19-12
Davis	"	38-19-16
Stillwater	"	38-19-21
Jud Christie	"	38-19-25
Paar's Mill	"	38-19-29
Krickbaum	Columbia	38-19-32
	Northumberland	38-49-12
Rupert	Columbia	38-19-33
Hollingshead	"	38-19-34
Creasyville	"	38-19-36
Johnson	"	38-19-37
Richards	"	38-19-41
Lehman/Port Royal	Juniata	38-34-04
Pool Forge/Wimer	Lancaster	38-36-01
Weaver Mill/White Hall	"	38-36-02
Pinetown/Nolt's Point/Bushongs Mill/Shand's	"	38-36-05
Hunsecker's Mill	"	38-36-06
Oberhaltzer's Mill/Red Run/ Red Bank/Red River Mill	"	38-36-10
Bucher's Mill	"	38-36-12
Zook's Woolen Mill/Rosehill/Wenger's	"	38-36-14
Eshelman's Mill/Leaman Place	"	38-36-20
Herr's Mill/Soudersburg	"	38-36-21
Neff's Mill	"	38-36-22
Lime Valley	"	38-36-23
Baumgardner's Mill	"	38-36-25
Colemanville/Martic Forge	"	38-36-26
Forry's Mill	"	38-36-28
Shenk's Mill	Lancaster	38-36-30
Erb's	"	38-36-34
Horst Mill/Risser's Mill/Sam Hopkins	"	38-36-36
Seigrist Mill/Moore's Mill	"	38-36-37
Willows	"	38-36-43
McConnell's Mill	Lawrence	38-37-01
Sam Wagner	Montour	38-47-01
	Northumberland	38-49-11
Old Keefer	Montour	38-47-03
Keefer Station	Northumberland	38-49-02
Rishel	"	38-49-05
Flickinger's Mill/Bistline	Perry	38-50-03

BRIDGE NAME	COUNTY	NUMBER
Cisna Mill/Adair's	Perry	38-50-04
Saville	"	38-50-07
Kochendefer	"	38-50-09
Landisburg/Rice	"	38-50-10
New Germantown	"	38-50-11
Mount Pleasant	"	38-50-12
Book's/Kaufman	"	38-50-13
Enslow/Turkey Tail	"	38-50-14
Wagoner's Mill/Roddy's Mill/Thompsons	"	38-50-15
Barronvale	Somerset	38-56-03
King's	"	38-56-06
Lower Humbert/Faidley	"	38-56-12
Devil's Den/McClurg	Washington	38-63-13
Jackson's Mill	"	38-63-18
Lyle	"	38-63-21
Ralston/Freeman	"	38-63-27
Wilson's Mill	"	38-63-28
Pine Bank	"	38-63-35

Felton's Mill Bridge

Felton's Mill Bridge spans Brush Creek with 100 feet. The bridge sits just behind the old Felton's Mill, which is structurally still intact, but is closed and appears abandoned.

Felton's Mill Bridge is bypassed and has fencing and overgrowth blocking the entrance. The bridge is also closed and appears abandoned.

Built in 1892, the bridge has white plank siding and a tin roof. The truss is a multiple kingpost with a double Burr arch. Members of the truss are also painted white. A different aspect of Felton's Mill Bridge is that one side is completely sided and the other is open. The side that faces the new bridge is the open side.

Access to the stream is impossible. Access to the bridge is also prevented.

DIRECTIONS: East Providence Township. From Breezewood at the intersection of US 30 and CR 05021, go southwest on CR 05021, four and one-half miles, on left as you cross over Brush Creek. (There are signs directing you to each of three bridges clustered in the immediate vicinity, this one, 38-05-25 and 38-05-20). (Donovan, 1980; Pennsylvania County Maps; Pennsylvania Department of Transportation; Zacker)

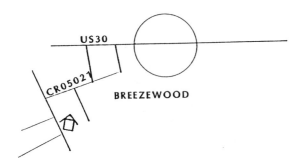

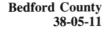

Heirline/Kinton Bridge

Heirline Bridge spans Juniata River with 136 feet. This is the longest covered bridge in Bedford County.

Built in 1902, this single span is supported with dry stone abutments (no mortar). Protected by faded dark red plank siding and a tin roof, the multiple kingpost truss is encased with a double Burr arch. The floor has crosswise planking interfaced with a solid lengthwise runner occupying two-thirds of the floor space.

Access to the creek is difficult. Heirline Bridge is closed and is leaning to one side. The bridge is guy-wired to keep it from collapsing. The bridge site is not appealing and the portals are blocked because the structure is unsafe for walking.

DIRECTIONS: Harrison and Napier Townships. From SR 31 at Manns Choice, west on CR 05097, one-half mile. (Donovan, 1980; Pennsylvania County Maps; Pennsylvania Department of Transportation)

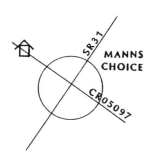

Claycomb/Reynoldsdale Bridge

The 126 foot Claycomb Bridge was relocated at its present location in 1975. Spanning Raystown Branch of the Juniata River, Claycomb Bridge is found at the entrance of Old Bedford Village, which preserves old historic structures.

Originally, Claycomb Bridge was built in 1884 in Reynoldsdale on CR 05099. Today, Claycomb Bridge is covered with naturally dark plank siding and a shake roof. The truss is the characteristic Pennsylvanian multiple kingpost with a double Burr arch.

The single span is the only Bedford County bridge with an external walkway on one side. With a shake roof, the walkway was added in 1975 at the time it was reconstructed at the entrance to Old Bedford Village.

The bridge is open, well-maintained and the stream has easy access.

DIRECTIONS: Bedford Township. Two miles north of Bedford on US 220, on right at Old Bedford Village. (Donovan, 1980; Pennsylvania County Maps; Pennsylvania Department of Transportation; Zacker)

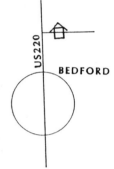

Knisley Bridge

Knisley Bridge crosses Dunning Creek with 87 feet and is one of four covered bridges clustered in the immediate vicinity, all of which span Dunning Creek. The date of construction is unknown for the Knisley Bridge.

A common characteristic of Bedford County's covered bridges is not to cover the entire sides with planking. Knisley Bridge is sided only on the lower third, with faded white planks. The roof is corrugated tin. The multiple kingpost truss members are painted white and the double Burr arch is painted red on the exterior. The floor is laid with one crosswise and five lengthwise sections of eight-foot planking.

Knisley Bridge is privately owned, but is not fenced. The bridge allows easy access to the stream. The bridge is open, but not used for traffic.

DIRECTIONS: St. Clair Township. From the intersection of SR 56 and SR 96, east on SR 56, two miles, right on CR 05098, one-half mile, on right. (Donovan, 1980; Pennsylvania County Maps; Pennsylvania Department of Transportation)

Ryot Bridge

Ryot Bridge, named after the local community, spans Dunning Creek one and one-half mile southwest of Knisley Bridge. Date of construction is unknown. Ryot Bridge is 81 feet long.

Exhibiting a slight camber, the single span is supported by cut stone abutments with mortar and protected by white plank siding and a corrugated tin roof. The interior multiple kingpost truss and double Burr arch are painted white. The floor has crosswise planking with two lengthwise runners.

The bridge site is attractive and offers easy access to the stream, Ryot Bridge is open to traffic.

DIRECTIONS: St. Clair Township. From the intersection of SR 56 and SR 96, take SR 56 east, two miles, turn right on CR 05098, three miles, on right. (Donovan, 1980; Pennsylvania County Maps; Pennsylvania Department of Transportation)

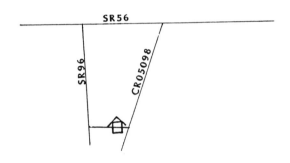

Cupperts/New Paris Bridge

The 71 foot Cupperts Bridge is just north of the community of New Paris. Spanning Dunning Creek, two miles south of Ryot Bridge (38-05-17), Cupperts Bridge has a single span. Date of construction is not known

Characteristic of Bedford County's covered bridges, the structure only has the lower third sided with natural dark planks that follow the contour of the low, double Burr arch, which encases the multiple kingpost truss. Cupperts Bridge rests on cut stone abutments with mortar that is crumbling. The tin roof is rusting. The interior of the bridge houses firewood and a tractor. Crosswise planking forms the floor.

Privately owned, Cupperts Bridge has been bypassed. The bridge site does allow easy access to the creek, or inspection of the bridge.

DIRECTIONS: Napier Township. From New Paris on SR 96, north one mile, on right. (Donovan, 1980; Pennsylvania County Maps; Pennsylvania Department of Transportation)

Diehl's/Turner's/Raystown Bridge

Diehl's Bridge spans the Raystown Branch of the Juniata River with 87 feet. Built in 1892, the bridge has a single span.

Supported by concrete abutments, Diehl's Bridge has its lower third covered by white plank siding and the roof is protected by tin. Its multiple kingpost truss and double Burr arch are also painted white. The portals are trimmed in red. Crosswise planking with two lengthwise runners form the floor.

Open to traffic, Diehl's Bridge has difficult access to the stream during the summer months because it is densely vegetated.

DIRECTIONS: Harrison Township. From Manns Choice, west on SR 31, five miles right on CR 05097, one-fourth mile. (Donovan, 1980; Pennsylvania County Maps; Pennsylvania Department of Transportation; Zacker)

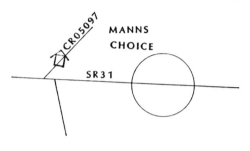

McDaniels Bridge

Spanning Brush Creek with 110 feet, McDaniels Bridge has a single span.

Built in 1873, the bridge is supported by concrete abutments. Fully sided by white planking, the bridge has a corrugated tin roof. The multiple kingpost truss and double Burr arch are painted white. The interior has experienced much graffiti. The floor has crosswise planking with two lengthwise runners.

McDaniels Bridge is open to traffic. One corner of the bridge site offers easy access to the stream.

DIRECTIONS: East Providence and West Providence Townships. From Breezewood at the intersection of US 30 and CR 05021, southwest on CR 05021, four miles, right, one-half mile, right, one-half mile on TR 419. (Donovan, 1980; Pennsylvania County Maps; Pennsylvania Department of Transportation; Zacker)

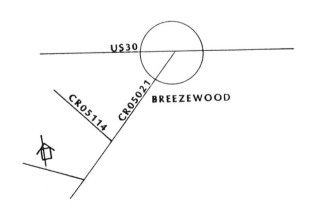

Bedford County
38-05-22

Bowser/Osterburg Bridge

Bowser Bridge, located just west of the village of Osterburg, crosses Bob's Creek with 98 feet. Date of construction is unknown.

Supported by concrete abutments, the single span has its lower third sided with white planks. The roof is covered with rusting tin. The multiple kingpost truss and double Burr arch are also painted white.

The floor has lengthwise planking with an open 12″ center that exposes crosswise planking. The portals are trimmed in red.

Bowser Bridge is bypassed. Access to the stream is easy and the bridge site is well maintained.

DIRECTIONS: East St. Clair. From Osterburg at the intersection of SR 869 and US 220, west on SR 896, two miles, on left. (Donovan, 1980; Pennsylvania County Maps; Pennsylvania Department of Transportation)

Bedford County
38-05-23

Snook's Bridge

Snook's Bridge, named after a local family, spans Dunning Creek. This is one of four covered bridges that crosses Dunning Creek within 5 miles of each other. Date of construction is unknown.

The 81-foot structure is supported by cut stone abutments and added steel piers for support. The single span is covered with white plank siding and a tin roof. The interior members of the multiple kingpost truss and double Burr arch are painted white. The exposed side of the Burr arch is painted red. The exterior and portals are also trimmed in red. The floor has crosswise planking with two lengthwise runners.

Snook's Bridge is open to traffic and access to the creek is easy.

DIRECTIONS: East Saint Clair Township. From the intersection of SR 96 and SR 56, east on SR 56, one and one-fourth mile, left CR 05073, one and one-half mile, second right, one-half mile, right, one-half mile on TR 578. (Donovan, 1980; Pennsylvania County Maps; Pennsylvania Department of Transportation; Zacker)

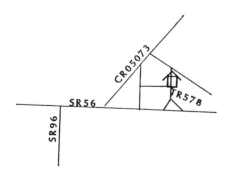

Colvin Bridge

Colvin Bridge spans Shawnee Creek with 72 feet. Date of construction is not known. The bridge is obviously very old because the truss members are hand hewn. The lower fourth of the sides are encased in planking, outside and inside, surrounding the truss. The truss is peculiar. The lower half of the truss is a multiple kingpost and the upper portion is constructed with a solid diagonal member that is part of the lower multiple kingpost truss. The upper portion also has vertical bracing. The roof is corrugated tin. The truss, interior and exterior of the bridge are painted dark red and trimmed in white. The abutments are concrete. There are two concrete piers with wooden piles supporting the bridge.

The Colvin Bridge is open to traffic. The bridge site has difficult access to the creek, especially in the summer months due to heavy vegetation.

DIRECTIONS: Napier Township. From Schellsburg, at the intersection of US 30 and SR 96, west on US 30, one-tenth mile, first left in town on TR 443, one and one-fourth miles. (Donovan, 1980; Pennsylvania County Maps; Pennsylvania Department of Transportation; Zacker)

Jackson's Mill Bridge

Jackson's Mill Bridge spans Brush Creek and is 91 feet long. Built in 1889 by Karns Rohm, the bridge site is next to the old mill building. The mill is closed, as is the bridge. The bridge is barricaded by fencing, preventing any access. The one photo shows the mill building. The close-up of the bridge was done with a zoom lens because I could not get any closer.

Jackson's Mill Bridge is protected by white plank siding and a tin roof. The portals are trimmed in red. The interior has a multiple kingpost truss and a half-size Burr arch.

Locating the bridge is easy, but because you cannot get to it, the discovery is a disappointment.

DIRECTIONS: East Providence Township. From Breezewood at the intersection of US 30 and SR 05021, southwest on 05021, two miles, left, one mile, left, one-tenth mile, on TR 412. (Donovan, 1980; Pennsylvania County Maps; Pennsylvania Department of Transportation; Zacker)

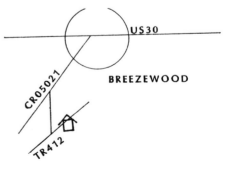

Erwinna Bridge

Built in 1871, Erwinna Bridge spans Roaring Rocks Creek with 56 feet. This is the shortest covered bridge in Bucks County.

Resting on cut stone with mortar abutments with some concrete assistance, the single span Erwinna Bridge is protected by a shake roof, solid dark brown plank siding, and white portals. The bridge has rock wingwalls at both of the approaches, which is a characteristic of Bucks County's covered bridges and Eastern Pennsylvania's covered bridges. The interior has a Town lattice truss and the floor has crosswise floor planking that has been blacktopped.

Erwinna Bridge is open to traffic. Access to the creek is easy.

DIRECTIONS: Tinicum Township. At Erwinna. (Donovan, 1980; Pennsylvania Department of Transportation; Zacker)

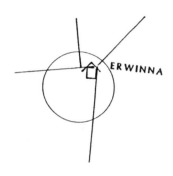

South Perkasie Bridge

The 98 foot South Perkasie Bridge is now dryland at Lenape Park in the village of South Perkasie. Originally, this bridge spanned Pleasant Spring Creek. It was condemned at that location and closed. The local historical society moved the bridge into Lenape Park and restored it in 1958.

South Perkasie Bridge was originally built in 1832, which makes it the oldest covered bridge in Bucks County. The single span structure now rests on cut stone abutments over flat dryland. Protected by a shake roof and dark brown plank siding, the bridge has a Town truss. The floor has an unusual character in that it is laid lengthwise, but the six-foot long planks are placed erratically, forming six-foot long sections of lengthwise planking.

Located in a well-maintained park, South Perkasie Bridge has found a safe home.

DIRECTIONS: In South Perkasie at Lenape Park. (Donovan, 1980; Pennsylvania Department of Transportation; Zacker)

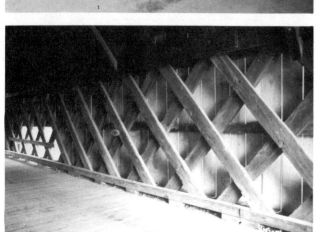

Mood Bridge

Mood Bridge spans the Northeast Branch of Perkiomen Creek with 126 feet.

Built in 1873/1874, the single span is covered with a shake roof and red plank siding. Supported by stone and mortar abutments that are extended to form long wingwalls at each approach, the bridge's portals are painted white. The truss is a Town and the floor is crosswise planking.

In 1962, Mood Bridge was repaired. Today, the bridge is well-maintained and serves traffic. The site allows convenient access to the stream. The bridge presents an impressive figure as it hovers over the Northeast Branch.

DIRECTIONS: East Rockhill Township. East of SR 563 and south of SE 313. (Donovan, 1980; Pennsylvania Department of Transportation; Zacker)

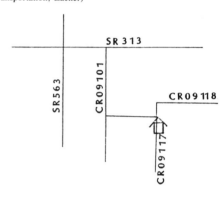

Uhlerstown Bridge

Uhlerstown Bridge spans the Delaware Canal and is the only bridge left in the United States that crosses a canal. In Bucks County, miles of the historic canal have been restored and preserved which functioned until the late 1800s, until the advent of the railroad. When the photograph was taken (April, 1987), the canal was almost dry. A stone lock can be viewed on the right under the bridge. The dirt road on the right of the photo is where horses walked, pulling the canal boats.

Once known as Mexico, Uhlerstown was renamed after Michael Uhler, who built and operated canal boats.

The Uhlerstown Bridge was built in 1830/1832 and is the only covered bridge in Bucks County with a window. Covered with a shake roof and red plank siding, the 110-foot bridge is supported by stone and mortar abutments. The interior has a Town truss and crosswise floor planking.

The bridge site is extremely interesting because it is the only covered bridge that spans a canal in the United States. The bridge is well-maintained and has an attractive location. Uhlerstown Bridge is open to traffic and access to the canal is easy.

DIRECTIONS: Tinicum Township. At Uhlerstown, just west of SR 32. (Donovan, 1980; Pennsylvania Department of Transportation; Zacker)

Frankenfield Bridge

Frankenfield Bridge crosses Tinicum Creek with 136 feet. Built in 1872, the bridge has two spans.

Each abutment is constructed with stone and mortar and has extended wingwalls at each approach. The center pier is concrete. The exterior has a shake roof and solid red plank siding. The interior has a Town lattice truss and crosswise floor planking.

Restored by the county in the early 1980s, Frankenfield Bridge has an attractive location and easy access to the stream. The bridge is open to traffic.

DIRECTIONS: **Tinicum Township. In Sundale, west of SR 32.** (Donovan, 1980; Pennsylvania Department of Transportation; Zacker)

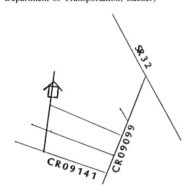

Cabin Run Bridge

Spanning Cabin Run Creek with 86 feet, the Cabin Run Bridge was built in 1874.

Covered with a shake roof and red plank siding, the single span rests on stone and mortar abutments that are extended to form wingwalls at each approach. The interior has a Town truss and lengthwise floor planking. The portals are painted red and white and the first six feet at the portals are paneled in the interior and painted white. Each entrance is fashioned so that the portal opening is four feet wider than the width of the bridge.

Cabin Run Creek is very interesting. Many of the creek stones are slate. Pink, green, and gray pieces of the slate make the creek bed very colorful. The stream has easy access and the bridge is open to traffic.

DIRECTIONS: **Plumstead Township. Southwest of Point Pleasant, two and one-half miles.** (Donovan, 1980; Pennsylvania Department of Transportation; Zacker)

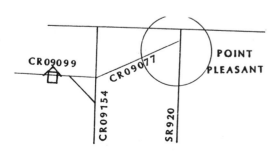

Loux Bridge

Loux Bridge crosses Cabin Run Creek one mile south of Cabin Run Bridge (38-09-10). The single span bridge was built in 1874 and is 90 feet long.

Supported by stone and mortar abutments with the Bucks County traditional extended wingwalls at the approaches, Loux Bridge is covered with a shake roof and white plank siding. The interior has a Town lattice truss and lengthwise floor planking laid in six-foot sections.

The stream is impossible to reach because it is completely fenced, preventing any access. There is a mill race near the bridge site. The bridge is open to traffic.

DIRECTIONS: Bedminster-Plumstead Townships. At Pipersville, on TR 09060. (Donovan, 1980; Pennsylvania Department of Transportation; Zacker)

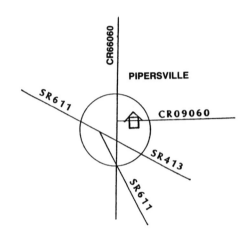

Rapps Bridge

Rapps Bridge spans French Creek with 106 feet. Built in 1866 for $3,595 by a local carpenter, Rapps Bridge has one span. Rapps Bridge is named after George A. Rapp and Sons, who operated a saw mill and grist mill south of the bridge site.

Supported by stone and mortar abutments with extended wingwalls, the bridge has a long narrow window on both sides, roofed with shake. Exhibiting a camber, the structure is covered with a shake roof and brown lap siding. The truss is a multiple kingpost with a double Burr arch composed of two separate beams. The floor has crosswise planking.

Access to the creek is easy and the bridge is open and carries much traffic.

DIRECTIONS: East Pikeland Township. Southwest of Phoenixville on TR 463. (Donovan, 1980; Pennsylvania Department of Transportation; Zacker)

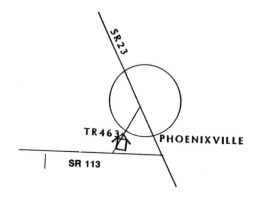

Columbia County
38-19-06

Shoemaker Bridge

Shoemaker Bridge crosses Branch Run, a tributary of Little Fishing Creek. Their confluence is one-fourth mile east of the bridge site. Little Fishing Creek drains western Columbia County. The bridge was named after a local farmer and lumberman, Joseph Shoemaker.

T.S. Christian built the Shoemaker Bridge in 1881. The single span, 54-foot structure rests on dry stone abutments (no mortar) with concrete facing. The dry stone abutments are extended to form wingwalls at each approach. One portal is skewed, where the bridge meets the creek bank at an angle. The bridge sits in a valley at the bottom of a mountain. The exterior of the bridge consists of faded red plank siding with batten and a tin roof. The interior displays a queenpost truss with bracing and crosswise floor planking.

Shoemaker Bridge is open to traffic. The valley provides a beautiful setting for the old bridge. The stream is easily accessible.

DIRECTIONS: Pine Township. From Iola on SR 42, west CR 19054, one-fourth mile, right on CR 19053, one-half mile. (Donovan, 1980; Pennsylvania County Maps; Pennsylvania Department of Transportation; Zacker)

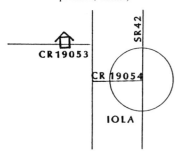

Columbia County
38-19-08

Sam Eckman Bridge

The Sam Eckman Bridge was named after a local farmer who owned a shingle mill and burch-oil factory near this site. Built in 1876 by Joseph Redline, the construction costs of the bridge were $498. The single span, 71-foot structure spans Little Fishing Creek, which drains northern Columbia County.

Supported by stone abutments, the bridge is covered with faded red plank siding with batten and a tin roof. The truss is queenpost with bracing. Diagonal planks form the floor with two lengthwise runners.

Sam Eckman Bridge is open to traffic. The area is dense with vegetation, but the site offers easy access to the stream.

DIRECTIONS: Pine and Greenwood Townships. From Sereno on SR 42, northeast on CR 19061, two and one-half miles, left, at TR 548. (Donovan, 1980; Pennsylvania County Maps; Pennsylvania Department of Transportation; Zacker)

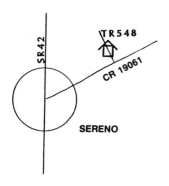

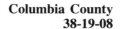

Josiah Hess Bridge

Named after a local farmer who operated a sawmill nearby, the Josiah Hess Bridge spans Huntington Creek with 110 feet. Huntington Creek is a tributary of Fishing Creek, which winds around the northern half of Columbia County. The Hess Bridge was constructed by Joseph Redline in 1875 for $1,349.50.

Displaying an obvious camber, the single span rests on bedrock and mortar abutments. Covered by faded red planking with batten and a tin roof, the structure was built with a multiple kingpost truss encased with a double Burr arch. The interior and truss members are painted red. The floor has crosswise planking and two lengthwise runners.

Open to traffic, Josiah Hess Bridge poses an impressive structure over the fast flowing, cold waters of a most picturesque mountain stream. Access to the creek is easy.

DIRECTIONS: **Fishing Creek Township. From Forks on SR 487, east on CR 19068 one and one-half miles.** (Donovan, 1980; Pennsylvania County Maps; Pennsylvania Department of Transportation; Zacker)

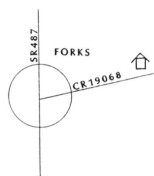

East and West Paden Twin Bridges

Once a common site, East and West Paden Bridges are the only set of twin covered bridges left in the United States today. They are not identical twins. West Paden is 103 feet long and spans the main channel of Huntington Creek. East Paden is only 79 feet long and spans the upper river bed; Huntington Creek's flood plain, which is dryland most of the time and houses a park with picnic tables and gym sets. The twin bridges were named after John Paden, who owned a nearby sawmill. W.C. Pennington built the Paden Twins in 1884.

Resting on stone abutments, each twin has a three-foot tall, full length window on each side. They are both covered with red plank siding and a tin roof. Both bridges are trimmed in white. West Paden exhibits a camber and is constructed with a multiple kingpost truss encased with a full-size double Burr arch. East Paden (the shorter one) was built with a queenpost truss that has bracing. East and West Paden's interior and truss members are painted red and their floors have lengthwise planking.

Bypassed, the Paden Twins are exquisitely preserved and well-maintained. The surrounding park is also superbly maintained. Fortunately, Columbia County had the foresight to preserve the last remaining twin covered bridges in America.

DIRECTIONS: **Fishing Creek Township. At Forks, at SR 487, east on CR 19068 on right.** (Donovan, 1980; Pennyslvania County Maps; Pennsylvania Department of Transportation; Zacker)

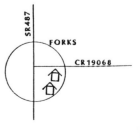

Columbia County
38-19-16

Davis Bridge

Named after a nearby family, the Davis Bridge spans Roaring Creek with 95 feet. Built in 1875 by Daniel Kostenbauder, the bridge's construction costs were $1,248.

Exhibiting a very slight camber, Davis Bridge is covered by red plank siding and a tin roof. A multiple kingpost truss with a double Burr arch supports the bridge. All of the truss members are hand-hewn beams. The interior and the truss members are painted red. The floor has crosswise planking with two lengthwise runners.

Davis Bridge is open to traffic and the site offers easy access the stream.

DIRECTIONS: Cleveland Township. From Slabtown on SR 42, west on TR 356 one mile. (Donovan, 1980; Pennsylvania County Maps; Pennsylvania Department Transportation; Zacker)

Columbia County
38-19-21

Stillwater Bridge

Named after the local village, Stillwater Bridge spans Fishing Creek with 168 feet. The single span was built in 1849 by James McHenry for $1,124.

Exhibiting a camber, Stillwater Bridge rests on stone abutments with concrete facing. The exterior has faded red plank siding with batten and a tin roof. The truss is a multiple kingpost encased with a double Burr arch. This bridge has a most fascinating floor. It is laid diagonally, but out from the center of the floor. It is most unusual. The planks are dried and severely worn and are thought to be the original floor.

Open to traffic, Stillwater Bridge has an attractive location and offers easy access to the stream. The area is heavily vegetated, which prevents good visual access during the summer months.

DIRECTIONS: Fishing Creek Township. In Stillwater east of SR 487. (Donovan, 1980; Pennsylvania County Maps; Pennsylvania Department of Transportation; Zacker)

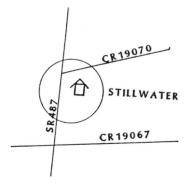

Jud Christie Bridge

Jud Christie Bridge was named after a local farmer and lumberman. The bridge was built in 1876 by William L. Manning for $239. The 60-foot structure crosses Little Fishing Creek.

Supported by bedrock and mortar abutments, the single span has a camber and is covered by red plank siding with batten and a tin roof. The truss is a queenpost with bracing. The floor has diagonal planking interfaced with two lengthwise runners.

The creek is a bubbling, fast flowing stream that presents an impressive setting for the Jud Christie Bridge. Open to traffic, the bridge site provides easy access to the stream.

DIRECTIONS: Pine and Jackson Townships. From Sereno, on SR 42, northeast on CR 19061, four miles, right at TR 685. (Donovan, 1980; Pennsylvania County Maps; Pennsylvania Department of Transportation; Zacker)

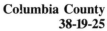

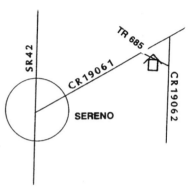

Paar's Mill Bridge

Paar's Mill Bridge was named after a nearby gristmill. The bridge crosses Roaring Creek with 92 feet. F. L. Shuman built Paar's Mill Bridge in 1865.

Resting on cut stone and mortar abutments, the single span displays a slight camber. The exterior of the bridge is different. One side is covered with horizontal planking (in photo), but the other side has vertical planking, making each side look like a different bridge. The roof is tin. A multiple kingpost truss encased with a Burr arch supports the structure. Diagonal planking forms the floor with two lengthwise runners.

Access to the stream is easy, but from the angle the exterior photo was taken, permission is required from the bridge's neighbors. The bridge is open to traffic.

DIRECTIONS: Franklin Township. From Paar's Mill on SR 487, south one mile, left on CR 19004, one-fourth mile, right on TR 371. (Donovan, 1980; Pennsylvania County Maps; Pennsylvania Department of Transportation; Zacker)

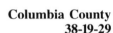

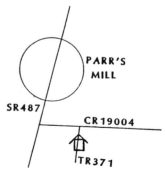

Columbia County
38-19-32

Northumberland County
38-49-12

Krickbaum Bridge

Krickbaum Bridge spans the South Branch of Roaring Creek with 68 feet. George W. Keefer built this bridge in 1876. Krickbaum Bridge connects Northumberland County and Columbia County on TR 459.

Supported by bedrock abutments, the single span is protected by red plank siding with batten and a tin roof. The interior has a queenpost truss with bracing and crosswise floor planking with two lengthwise runners.

Open to traffic, Krickbaum Bridge has easy access to the stream, but the area has thick foliage.

DIRECTIONS: Cleveland Township in Columbia County and Ralpho Township in Northumberland County. In Ralpho Township at Elysburg at the intersection of SR 487 and SR 54, take SR 54 southeast, two and one-fourth miles, turn left across from CR 49037, one-half mile, turn right, one half mile, turn right, one-tenth mile on TR 459. (Donovan, 1980; Pennsylvania County Maps; Pennsylvania Department of Transportation; Zacker)

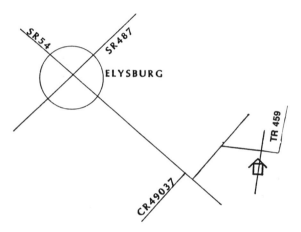

Columbia County
38-19-33

Rupert Bridge

Rupert Bridge is located in the village of Rupert. The bridge spans Fishing Creek. Jesse M. Beard built this bridge in 1847. The single span is 205 feet long, making it the longest covered bridge in Columbia County.

Resting on cut stone abutments, Rupert Bridge is covered with a tin roof and red plank siding. The interior has a multiple kingpost truss encased by a massive double Burr arch. The interior walls and truss members were painted red but have since faded. The floor has runners laid on crosswise floor planking.

Access to the river is easy. The bridge is open to traffic.

DIRECTIONS: Montour Township. At Rupert just east of SR 42 on TR 449. (Donovan, 1980; Pennsylvania County Maps; Pennsylvania Department of Transportation; Zacker)

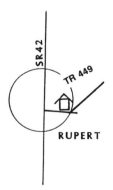

Columbia County
38-19-34

Hollingshead Bridge

Located in a mountain valley spanning Catawissa Creek, Hollingshead Bridge has 128 feet. The single span was built in 1850 by Peter Ent for $1,180. The bridge was named after a local miller.

Supported by cut stone and mortar abutments with a concrete base, Hollingshead Bridge is protected by red plank siding with batten and a tin roof. With a slight camber, the structure was built with a multiple kingpost truss and a single Burr arch. The interior walls and truss members are painted red. The floor is composed of crosswise planking and two lengthwise runners.

The bridge is open to traffic and is visually accessible from the surrounding roads.

DIRECTIONS: Catawissa Township. From the northern junction of SR 42 and SR 487, south, one-half mile, left on CR 19014, right on TR 405, one-tenth mile. (Donovan, 1980; Pennsylvania County Maps; Pennsylvania Department of Transportation: Zacker)

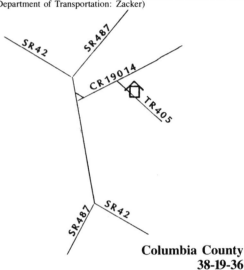

Columbia County
38-19-36

Creasyville Bridge

Creasyville Bridge crosses Little Fishing Creek with 49 feet. R. S. Christian built this bridge in 1881 for $301.25.

Supported by concrete abutments, the single span is covered with red plank siding with batten and a tin roof. The interior has a queenpost truss with bracing. The floor, similar to the one in Stillwater Bridge (38-19-21) is laid diagonally from the center with two lengthwise runners.

Open to traffic, Creasyville Bridge has easy access to the stream and the surrounding area is free of dense vegetation.

DIRECTIONS: Pine and Jackson Townships. From Sereno on SR 42, northeast on CR 19061, five and one-half miles, left on TR 683. (Donovan, 1980; Pennsylvania County Maps; Pennsylvania Department of Transportation; Zacker)

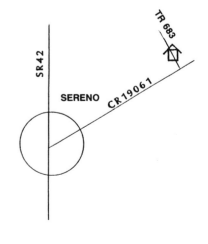

Johnson Bridge

Johnson Bridge spans Mugser Run with 66 feet. In 1882, Daniel Stine built this bridge for $799.

Supported by stone abutments, the single span is covered with red plank siding with batten and a tin roof. With a slight camber, the bridge was built with a queenpost truss with bracing. The floor consists of crosswise planking interfaced with two lengthwise runners.

Open to traffic, Johnson Bridge allows easy access to the stream and offers an attractive location.

DIRECTIONS: Cleveland Township. From Pensyl's Mill on SR 487, take SR 487 south, two and one-half miles, left one and one-half miles, right on TR 320. (Donovan, 1980; Pennsylvania County Maps; Pennsylvania Department of Transportation; Zacker)

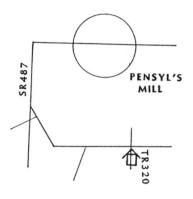

Richards Bridge

Richards Bridge spans the South Branch of Roaring Creek with 69 feet. Obediah S. Campbell built this bridge in 1875.

With a slight camber, this single span rests on stone and mortar abutments and is covered with red plank siding with batten and a tin roof. The interior has an unusual combination truss using a queenpost and a multiple kingpost. The floor has crosswise planking.

Open to traffic, Richards Bridge does not have any access to the stream because of fencing.

DIRECTIONS: Cleveland Township in Columbia County and Ralpho Township in Northumberland County. From Elysburg in Ralpho Township, northeast on SR 487, two miles, right on TR 804, one mile. (Donovan, 1980; Pennsylvania County Maps; Pennsylvania Department of Transportation; Zacker)

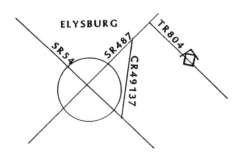

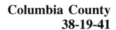

Juniata County
38-34-04

Lehman/Port Royal Bridge

Originally built in 1888, the Lehman Bridge was seriously damaged during the Hurricane Agnes flood of 1972. The bridge was reconstructed with as many of the original timbers as possible. The bridge spans Licking Creek.

The 120-foot double span structure is supported by stone and mortar abutments and one stone pier. The Lehman Bridge is protected by naturally weathered plank siding and a red tin roof. Over the pier there are two kingpost center panels. Also over each span is a single half-size Burr arch. The bridge is supported by steel beams under the bridge. What truss members are left, no longer support the bridge. Lengthwise planking forms the floor.

Lehman Bridge is privately owned but allows easy access to the stream. The bridge is well-maintained and has a picturesque location.

DIRECTIONS: At Port Royal. One-fourth mile, northwest on SR 333 from SR 75. (Donovan, 1980; Pennsylvania County Maps; Pennsylvania Department of Transportation; Zacker)

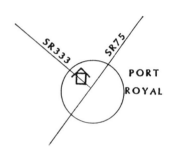

Lancaster County
38-36-01

Pool Forge/Wimer Bridge

Spanning the Conestoga River, Pool Forge Bridge is located near the site of an old iron works plant. The site has a mill race, but it was destroyed by a flood from a hurricane in 1955. Conestoga River has its headwaters east of the bridge site. The river soon develops into a major drainage channel as it flows southwest through Lancaster, the county seat of Lancaster County.

The 99-foot Pool Forge Bridge rests on cut stone abutments with mortar. The single span structure is protected by a corrugated tin roof and faded red plank siding with batten. The bridge was built in 1859 by Elias McMellen, with a multiple kingpost truss encased with a double Burr arch.

Still in its original location, Pool Forge Bridge has been bypassed for almost 20 years. This bridge was saved due to the efforts of many people so the public could continue to enjoy this historic landmark. Unfortunately, the bridge has fallen into private ownership and can only be viewed from the new bridge. The area surrounding the bridge is fenced off and is used as a pasture.

DIRECTIONS: Caernarvon Township. From Churchtown, SR 23, west one-half mile, left on CR 36053, one-fourth mile, left, on left. (Caruthers, 1974; Donovan, 1980; Pennsylvania County Maps and Recreational Guide; Pennyslvania Department of Transportation)

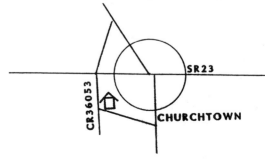

Lancaster County
38-36-02

Weaver Mill/White Hall Bridge

The 88-foot Weaver Mill Bridge spans Conestoga River one and one-half miles northwest of Pool Forge Bridge (38-36-01). This site once had a saw mill and mill race. The dam has since disappeared. One of the mill buildings still exists as part of a nearby farm.

The 1878 structure was built by Carter and the mason work was done by J. F. Stauffer. The single span is supported by stone abutments with mortar that extend to form long wingwalls at each approach. Exhibiting a slight camber, the bridge is covered with a corrugated tin roof and dark red plank siding with batten. The interior has Pennsylvania's traditional multiple kingpost truss encased with a double Burr arch and lengthwise floor planking.

The bridge site has a beautiful location and the bridge is in superb condition. Access to the stream is convenient and the area is free of vegetation allowing easy visual access.

DIRECTIONS: Caernarvon Township. From Churchtown on SR 23, north on CR 36053, one and one-half miles, left one-half mile. (Caruthers, 1974; Donovan, 1980; Pennsylvania County Maps and Recreational Guide; Pennsylvania Department of Transportation)

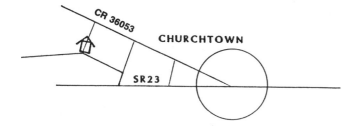

Lancaster County
38-36-05

Pinetown/Nolt's Point Bushongs Mill/Shand's Bridge

A bridge with many names, Pinetown Bridge has an exciting recent history. On June 22, 1972, a flood carried the bridge over one and one-half miles before it stopped almost unharmed on a road. The amazing phenomena is that before the bridge finally stopped, it floated around another covered bridge, the Hunsecker (38-36-06). Unfortunately, the Hunsecker was raised off its abutments soon thereafter, floated a mile down the Conestoga River and crashed into a concrete bridge at SR 23. Hunsecker Bridge was damaged beyond repair. The Pinetown Bridge was dismantled and reconstructed by Amish carpenters. Two cranes set the bridge back on its abutments on May 2, 1975. Reconstruction costs were $40,000.

Today, Pinetown Bridge spans the Conestoga River with 152 feet. Originally constructed in 1867 by Elias McMellen, the single span is covered with dark red plank siding and a shake roof. The abutments are made of bedrock and mortar which are extended to form rock wingwalls at each portal. The interior exhibits a multiple kingpost truss encased with a double Burr arch and has lengthwise flooring.

Pinetown Bridge is open and access to the creek is easy but, as so often is true, the area is heavily vegetated and visual access is poor during the summer months.

DIRECTIONS: Upper Leacock Township. From Leacock on SR 23, northwest on CR 36009 two and one-half miles. (Caruthers, 1974; Donovan, 1980; Pennsylvania County Maps and Recreational Guide; Pennsylvania Department of Transportation; Zacker)

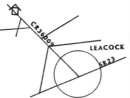

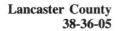

Lancaster County
38-36-06

Hunsecker's Mill Bridge

The original Hunsecker's Mill Bridge was built in 1848 and was destroyed in the 1972 Hurricane Agnes flood. It was this bridge, hours before it was destroyed, the Pinetown Covered Bridge (38-36-05) floated around. When the Hunsecker Bridge rose off its abutments, it floated a mile downstream and crashed into the SR 23 bridge, which damaged it beyond repair. The local residents almost lost their bridge in 1961 when it was scheduled for demolition. The residents rallied and saved their bridge. With the advent of Hurricane Agnes, the residents would not accept any bridge other than a wooden covered structure. The new Hunsecker Bridge was finished in 1975 for $321,000.

The new Hunsecker Bridge is a single span with 180 feet. Protected by natural plank siding with batten and a shake roof, the Hunsecker rests on stone abutments with mortar that extend to form wingwalls at each approach. The truss is a multiple kingpost encased by a double Burr arch constructed with two separate beams. The beams in the arches are attached with steel plates and bolts. The vertical members of the multiple kingpost truss are constructed with two beams instead of the normal one. The floor has crosswise planking.

The bridge site is attractive and there is access to the stream on one side of the bridge. The best angle the bridge has to offer is fenced.

DIRECTIONS: Upper Leacock and Manheim Townships. From Leacock, west on SR 23, one and one-half miles, right on 36011, one mile. (Caruthers, 1974; Donovan, 1980; Pennsylvania County Maps and Recreational Guide; Pennsylvania Department of Transportatiion)

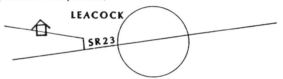

Lancaster County
38-36-10

Oberhaltzer's Mill/Red Run/Red Bank/Red River Mill Bridge

Oberhaltzer's Mill Bridge spans Muddy Creek near the community of Red Run. Muddy Creek is a tributary of the Conestoga River. About three miles southwest of the bridge site is their confluence.

Built in 1866 by Elias McMellen, Oberhaltzer's Mill Bridge is 104 feet long. The single span is supported by cut stone abutments with mortar. One end has a crumbling abutment. Protected by faded red plank siding with batten and a tin roof, the bridge houses carriages for the owners, who repair wagons. Privately owned, the bridge has a gate to prevent entrance. The truss is a multiple kingpost encased with a double Burr arch. An interesting feature is that the kingpost center panel is doubled. There are two kingpost panels, side by side.

Bypassed in 1961, Oberhaltzer's Mill Bridge is deteriorating. Inspection of the bridge is limited to the view from the adjacent new bridge.

DIRECTIONS: Earl and Brecknock Townships. From Murrell at the intersection of US 222 and US 322, northeast on CR 36050 four miles, right on CR 36013, one and one-half miles (at Red Run Park, a campground). (Caruthers, 1974; Donovan, 1980; Pennsylvania County Maps and Recreational Guide; Pennsylvania Department of Transportation)

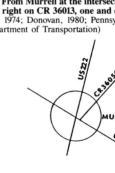

Bucher's Mill Bridge

Bucher's Mill spans Cocalico Creek with 63 feet. Originally built by Elias McMellen in 1891, the bridge was destroyed by a flood in 1892 and had to be completely reconstructed, also done by McMellen. In 1966, the bridge was in such a dilapidated condition, demolition was discussed. The local residents fought the removal of their bridge and instead, their bridge received a new roof and general repairs.

Today, Bucher's Mill Bridge rests on stone with mortar abutments that have a concrete base. The stone abutments are extended at the approaches to form wingwalls. Covered with a shake roof and dark red plank siding with batten, the single span is constructed with a multiple kingpost truss encased with a double Burr arch, which extends only two-thirds the height of the center kingpost panels. The center kingpost panel has two kingposts side by side. Some steel tie rods have been added to the bridge for additional support. The floor has lengthwise planking.

Access to the creek is easy and Bucher's Mill Bridge is open to traffic.

DIRECTIONS: East Cocalico and West Cocalico Townships. From Erbs Corner at the intersection of SR 272 and US 322, northeast on SR 272, three and one-half miles, right, on right. (Caruthers, 1974; Donovan, 1980; Pennsylvania County Maps; Pennsylvania Department of Transportation)

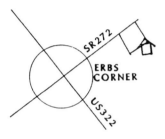

Zook's Woolen Mill/Rosehill/ Wenger's Bridge

Zook's Woolen Mill Bridge spans Cocalico Creek with 89 feet. The single span was built in 1849, making it one of Lancaster County's oldest covered bridges. Henry Zook built the bridge for $700. He also had a flour mill and a woolen mill near the bridge site. In 1972, the bridge was filled with six feet of water during the flood produced by Hurricane Agnes.

Today, Zook's Mill Bridge is supported by stone and mortar abutments with concrete bases. The stone work extends to form Lancaster's identifiable wingwalls at each approach. Covered with a shake roof and dark red plank siding with batten, the structure has a multiple kingpost truss encased with a double Burr arch. The arch is half the height of the two center kingpost panels. The floor has lengthwise planking.

Access to the creek is easy. The location is attractive. Zook's Mill Bridge is open to traffic.

DIRECTIONS: Warwick and West Earl Townships. From Brownstown at the intersection of CR 272 and CR 772 and CR 722, north on CR 772, one mile, left, one mile, right. (Caruthers, 1974; Donovan, 1980; Pennsylvania County Maps; Pennsylvania Department of Transportation)

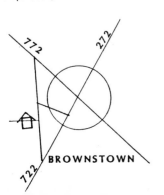

Eshelman's Mill/ Leaman Place Bridge

Eshelman's Mill Bridge spans Pequea Creek near the community of Leaman Place.

Built in 1894, the 118-foot structure is supported by stone abutments faced with concrete. Each approach has long stone wingwalls. The bridge is a typical Lancaster County covered bridge. Dark red plank siding with batten, white portals and a multiple kingpost truss with a double kingpost center panel encased with a Burr arch characterize the bridge.

Eshelman's Mill Bridge has a well-maintained, easily accessible bridge site. The bridge is open for traffic.

DIRECTIONS: Leacock and Paradise Townships. From Leaman Place on US 30, north on TR 36030, one half mile. (Donovan, 1980; Pennsylvania Department of Transportation)

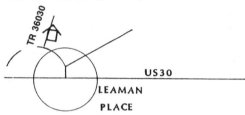

Herr's Mill/Soudersburg Bridge

Herr's Mill Bridge crosses Pequea Creek three miles west of Eshelman's Mill Bridge (38-36-20). Herr's Mill Bridge is located at an Amish Village. The Village offers historical buildings and features aspects concerning Amish life. Herr's Mill, built in 1728, has been restored and has a museum.

Herr's Mill Bridge was constructed in 1885 with two spans and 186 feet. The one pier and abutments are made of cut stone and mortar. The creek's channel normally only flows under one of the spans. Protected by a tin roof and dark red plank siding, the bridge has a multiple kingpost truss over each span and two sets of double Burr arches, one over each span. Each Burr arch has two separate beams. The floor has lengthwise planking.

The bridge has restricted access to the creek because it is privately owned by the Amish Village. The bridge was bypassed in the 1970s. The bridge and site are well-maintained and the bridge is used by the Amish Village when they take tourists on carriage rides.

DIRECTIONS: East Lampeter and Paradise Townships. From Soudersburg at the intersection of US 30 and CR 36029, west on US 30 one and one-tenth mile, left, one mile, left on TR 696 (follow the signs to Amish Village). (Caruthers, 1974; Donovan, 1980; Pennsylvania County Maps; Pennsylvania Department of Transportation; Zacker)

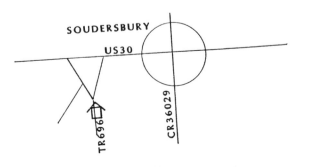

Neff's Mill Bridge

Neff's Mill Bridge spans Pequea Creek with 102 feet. The 1875 structure was built by James C. Carpenter with a single span.

Neff's Mill Bridge is supported by stone abutments with mortar and concrete facing. The approaches have extended stone wingwalls. Exhibiting a slight camber, the bridge is protected by dark red plank siding with batten and a tin roof. The interior has a multiple kingpost truss encased by a double Burr arch and lengthwise floor planking.

The area is fenced off with barbed wire, preventing any access to the creek on one side. Neff's Mill Bridge is open to traffic.

DIRECTIONS: Strasburg and West Lampeter Townships. At the intersection of SR 741 and CR 36027, south on 36027, one mile, left on TR 559, one mile (Caruthers, 1974; Donovan. 1980; Pennsylvania County Maps; Pennsylvania Department of Transportation; Zacker)

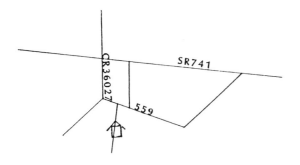

Lime Valley Bridge

Lime Valley Bridge spans Pequea Creek one and one-fourth mile south of Neff's Mill Bridge (38-36-22). Lime Valley Bridge was built in 1871 by Joseph Cramer.

The single span structure is 104 feet long and supported by stone and mortar abutments that extend to form long wingwalls at the approaches. Lime Valley Bridge is a standard Lancaster County covered bridge with a tin roof, dark red plank siding with batten, a Burr arch truss and lengthwise flooring.

Access to the creek is easy and the bridge is open to traffic.

DIRECTIONS: West Lampeter and Strasburg Townships. At Lime Valley at the intersection of CR 36028 and TR 498, on TR 498. (Caruthers, 1974; Donovan, 1980; Pennsylvania County Maps; Pennsylvania Department of Transportation; Zacker)

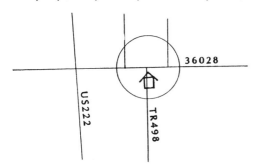

Baumgardner's Mill Bridge

Named after the nearby mill, Baumgardner's Mill Bridge crosses Pequea Creek with 120 feet.

The 1860 structure was built by Davis Kitch. June, 1987, found the bridge under major reconstruction. The old abutments have been replaced with concrete and the approaches are being completely replaced. Although many of our covered bridges have received renovation in the U.S., it is unusual to be able to witness the skeleton of a bridge without its siding.

Baumgardner's Mill Bridge presently has a tin roof, but that might be replaced during this restoration project. The truss is a multiple kingpost encased with a double Burr arch.

At the time of this photograph, it was impossible to reach the creek due to the excavation, but once the bridge work has been completed, access should be no problem.

DIRECTIONS: Pequea and Providence Townships. From Lancaster, SR 324 south, from its departure with US 222, six or seven miles south on SR 324, one mile after you cross the Pequea Creek, turn left, one-half mile, turn left, one-half mile on TR 427. (Caruthers, 1974; Donovan, 1980; Pennsylvania County Maps; Pennsylvania Department of Transportation; Zacker)

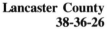

Colemanville/Martic Forge Bridge

Once the site of an iron works plant, Colemanville Bridge spans Pequea Creek with 183 feet, which makes it the longest single span bridge in Lancaster County.

Built by James C. Carpenter in 1856, this long structure is protected by faded red plank siding and a shake roof. The abutments are constructed with stone and mortar with a concrete base. Each of the abutments are extended to form long wingwalls at the approaches. The interior has a multiple kingpost truss sandwiched between a double Burr arch. Each arch consists of two separate beams. The floor has lengthwise planking.

The Colemanville Bridge site has easy access to the creek and offers a pleasant location. The bridge is open to traffic.

DIRECTIONS; Conestoga and Martic Townships. From Lancaster, south on SR 324, two miles from where US 222 departs, one mile after you cross the Pequea Creek for the second time, turn left on TR 408, one-fourth mile. (Caruthers, 1974; Donovan, 1980; Pennsylvania County Maps; Pennsylvania Department of Transportation; Zacker)

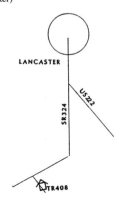

Lancaster County
38-36-28

Forry's Mill Bridge

Forry's Mill Bridge spans Chickies Creek with 103 feet.

Built in 1869 by Elias McMellen, Forry's Mill Bridge is covered with dark red plank siding with batten and a shake roof. One abutment is concrete and the other is cut stone with mortar. The interior has a multiple kingpost truss encased with a double Burr arch. The arch has steel tie rods anchoring it to the lower chord. The floor has lengthwise planking laid in sections, eight feet long.

Forry's Mill Bridge site is attractive, but the corner that offers the most attractive angle has barbed wire preventing access to the stream and further inspection of the bridge. The bridge is open to traffic.

DIRECTIONS: Rapho and West Hempfield Townships. From the intersection of SR 230 and SR 141, east on SR 230, one-fourth mile, right on CR 36067, three and one-half miles, left on TR 362, one-mile. (Caruthers, 1974; Donovan, 1980; Pennsylvania County Maps; Pennsylvania Department of Transportation; Zacker)

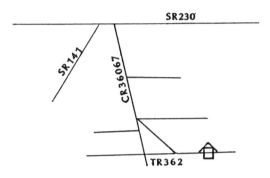

Lancaster County
38-36-30

Shenk's Mill Bridge

Shenk's Mill Bridge spans Chickies Creek with 96 feet. The bridge was built in 1855 by Charles Malhorn.

Exhibiting a camber, the single span structure rests on cut stone abutments with mortar that are extended to form long wingwalls at each approach. Shenk's Mill Bridge is protected by a shake roof and faded red lap siding, which is out of character for Lancaster's covered bridges. The bridge also has windows on both sides at one end, which is also unusual for Lancaster's bridges, most, do not. The interior has a multiple kingpost truss encased with a double Burr arch. The arch's height is only half that of the center kingpost panel. The floor has lengthwise planking.

This bridge has a particularly attractive location. The site is well-maintained and allows easy access to the stream. The bridge is open to traffic.

DIRECTIONS: Rapho and East Hempfield Townships. From the intersection of SR 283 and SR 230 over Chickies Creek, east on SR 283, one mile, exit, left, another immediate left, one mile, on left on TR 372. (Caruthers, 1974; Donovan, 1980; Pennsylvania County Maps; Pennsylvania Department of Transportation; Zacker)

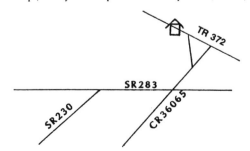

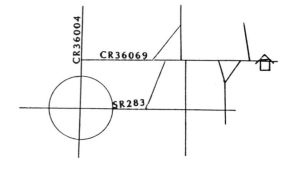

Erb's Bridge

Named after a nearby family, Erb's Bridge is one of the few bridges in Lancaster which was not built next to a mill site. Spanning Hammer Creek, named after a nearby, noisy forge, Erb's Bridge is 80 feet long. This 1887 bridge was built by John G. Bowman.

Exhibiting a camber, this single span is supported by cut stone abutments with mortar and extended to form tall wingwalls at each approach. Erb's Bridge has the traditional Lancaster covered bridge character. Covered by dark red plank siding with batten and a tin roof, the multiple kingpost truss is encased with a double Burr arch extending two-thirds the height of the kingpost center panel. The floor has lengthwise planking laid in eight foot sections.

Erb's Bridge site is especially attractive, but is fenced and entry to the creek is prevented. The bridge is open to traffic.

DIRECTIONS: Warwick and Ephrata Townships. From the intersection of SR 272 and SR 772, northwest on SR 772, two and one-half miles, right on CR 36060 one mile, left on 36061, three-fourths mile. (Caruthers, 1974; Donovan, 1980; Pennsylvania County Maps; Pennsylvania Department of Transportation)

Horst Mill/Risser's Mill/ Sam Hopkins Bridge

Horst Mill Bridge spans Little Chickies Creek with 82 feet. Built in 1872 by Elias McMellen, the bridge has a single span.

Supported by cut stone abutments with mortar and concrete poured at each base, the bridge has a new protective shell. The roof is tin and the plank siding with batten is freshly painted dark red. The multiple kingpost truss is encased with a double Burr arch that extends three fourths the height of the center kingpost panel. The floor has crosswise planking.

The bridge site is most attractive, which is characteristic of Lancaster County's covered bridges. The bridge is open to traffic. Access to the creek is difficult because the area is overgrown and one corner is fenced. The bridge, however, is easily visible from the surrounding roads.

DIRECTIONS: Rapho and Mount Joy Townships. From an exit off of SR 283 at CR 36004, north on CR 36004, one-half mile, right on CR 36069, three miles. (Caruthers, 1974; Donovan, 1980; Pennsylvania County Maps; Pennsylvania Department of Transportation)

Lancaster County
38-36-37

Seigrist Mill/Moore's Mill Bridge

Seigrist Mill Bridge spans Chickies Creek with 82 feet. James Carpenter built this structure in 1885. Seigrist Mill is only one-half mile north of Forry's Mill Bridge (38-36-28). In 1972, Seigrist Bridge experienced the wrath of Hurricane Agnes with over five feet of water in the bridge. Suffering only minor damage, the bridge remained structurally sound.

With a slight camber, Seigrist Mill Bridge is supported by concrete abutments. Stone with mortar forms wingwalls at each approach. Protected by a shake roof and dark red plank siding with batten, the multiple kingpost truss is encased by a double Burr arch. Eight-foot sections of lengthwise planking form the floor.

The bridge setting is attractive and also allows easy access to the creek. This bridge is open to traffic.

DIRECTIONS: Rapho and West Hampfield Townships. From Mariettaboro at the intersection on SR 23 and SR 441, east on SR 23, four miles left on CR 36065, one mile, first left on TR 360, one mile. (Caruthers, 1974; Donovan, 1980; Pennsylvania County Maps; Pennsylvania Department of Transportation; Zacker)

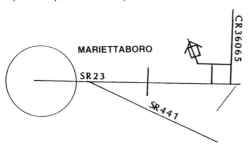

Lancaster County
38-36-43

Willows Bridge

Willows Bridge is an historic covered bridge displayed on US 30 at the Willows Restaurant. Preserved by Adolph Neuber, owner of the Willows, the bridge was restored in 1962, by Roy Zimmerman of Strasburg. Zimmerman used two bridges to complete this one. Most of the materials came from the Miller's Farm Bridge which was built in 1871 by Elias McMellen. The other materials came from the Goods Fording Bridge which was built in 1855.

Willows Bridge is an excellent example of a restored bridge. Presently, spanning a tributary of Mill Creek, the single span structure has a slight camber. The bridge is supported with concrete abutments and each approach has cut stone and mortar wingwalls. Protected with dark red plank siding with batten and a shake roof, the multiple kingpost truss is encased with a double Burr arch. The floor has crosswise planking.

Willows Bridge is open and invites autos to drive through. It sits right next to US 30 and offers a high degree of visibility. The Willows Bridge is distinctive because it is privately owned yet shared with the public for all to enjoy. The bridge has an attractive location and the area is well maintained.

DIRECTIONS: East Lampeter Township. US 30 at the Willows Restaurant, one mile west of SR 896. (Caruthers, 1974; Donovan, 1980; Pennsylvania County Maps; Pennsylvania Department of Transportation)

McConnell's Mill Bridge

One of the few covered bridge and mill combinations left in the U.S., the McConnell's Mill Bridge is part of a 2,500 acre State Park that has been restored and maintains the old mill.

Spanning Slippery Rock Creek, the bridge is 110 feet long. Slippery Rock Creek is a fast flowing, rocky stream.

Built in 1874, McConnell's Mill Bridge is protected by an asphalt roof and red plank siding with batten. The long single span is supported by cut stone abutments with concrete icebreakers. The underside of the bridge has massive steel I-beams installed for support. The interior is constructed with a Howe truss and crosswise floor planking. The wooden roof, truss and floor are painted white.

McConnell's Mill was in business until 1928. The McConnell Family sold the mill to maintain its historic value and today, the mill is state owned, restored and producing cornmeal in season with original equipment.

The mill, bridge, creek and valley compose a beautiful scene. The creek's access is extremely difficult, but the bridge can be viewed from the surrounding roads. McConnell's Mill and Bridge are a must to see when bridging Pennsylvania.

DIRECTIONS: South of US 422, at McConnell's Mill. (Donovan 1980; Pennsylvania Department of Transportation)

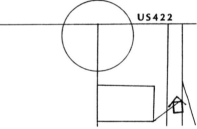

Montour County
38-47-01

Northumberland County
38-49-11

Sam Wagner Bridge

Sam Wagner Bridge spans Chillisquaque Creek with 95 feet. This bridge was built in 1881 by George W. Keefer for $939.

Supported by cut stone abutments with mortar, the bridge is covered with new plank siding with batten and a tin roof. The interior has a multiple kingpost truss with a half-size double Burr arch and crosswise floor planking.

At the time of the photograph, November, 1986, it was extremely foggy. Access to the stream is easy and the bridge site is very picturesque. Sam Wagner Bridge is open to traffic.

DIRECTIONS: Liberty Township in Montour County and East Chillisquaque Township in Northumberland County. From Milton in Northumberland County at the intersection of SR 147 and SR 642, SR 642 east four miles, left on CR 49057, just before you cross over Chillisquaque Creek, one and one-half miles. (Donovan, 1980; Pennsylvania County Maps; Pennsylvania Department of Transportation; Zacker)

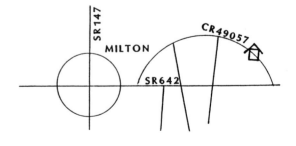

Old Keefer Bridge

The Old Keefer Bridge crosses Chillisquaque Creek with 81 feet. Built in 1853 by William Butler, the construction costs were $498.

Supported by stone and mortar abutments with concrete facing, the bridge is covered with red plank siding with batten and a shake roof. Exhibiting a slight camber, Old Keefer Bridge has a multiple kingpost truss encased with a double Burr arch and lengthwise floor planking.

November, 1986, found the Old Keefer Bridge fogged in, but the structure was still quite imposing with its peculiar square portals.

Old Keefer Bridge was restored in 1983 by the county. Access to the creek is easy. The bridge is in excellent condition and has an attractive location and is open to traffic.

DIRECTIONS: Liberty Township. From Mexico, CR 47003 east, two miles, right on TR 346, one-half mile. (Donovan, 1980; Pennsylvania County Maps; Pennsylvania Department of Transportation; Zacker)

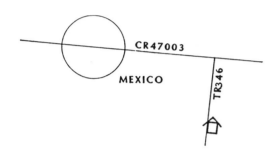

Keefer Station Bridge

Named after the local community's railroad stop, Keefer Station Bridge spans Shamokin Creek with 100 feet. This bridge was built in 1888 by George W. Keefer for $882.

Resting on cut stone abutments with mortar, the single span has new plank siding and a tin roof. The multiple kingpost truss is encased with a double Burr arch. Some of the multiple kingpost members have been replaced. The floor has lengthwise planking.

Access to the creek is easy. The bridge is open and offers a picturesque location.

DIRECTIONS: Upper Augusta Township. From Sunbury, SR 61 east, five miles, left on CR 49032, left on CR 49125, one and one-fourth miles, right on TR 698, one-tenth mile. (Donovan, 1980; Pennsylvania County Maps; Pennsylvania Department of Transportation; Zacker)

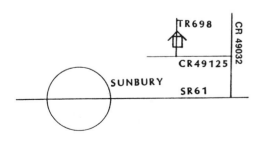

Northumberland County
38-49-05

Rishel Bridge

Rishel Bridge, photographed on a very foggy morning in November, 1986, spans Chillisquaque Creek with 121 feet. Built by John Shriner, Jr. and Zacheus Braley, Rishel Bridge was constructed between 1812 and 1830. This is one of the oldest covered bridges in Pennsylvania and one of the oldest left in the United States.

Supported by stone and mortar abutments, Rishel Bridge has a slight camber. Covered with red plank siding and a tin roof, the single span structure has a multiple kingpost truss encased with a halfsize double Burr arch. The floor has crosswise planking with two lengthwise runners.

Rishel Bridge is open to traffic and has easy access to the stream.

DIRECTIONS: East Chillisquaque and West Chillisquaque Townships. From Montandon at the intersection of SR 45 and SR 147, SR 45 east, one mile, second right one-half mile, left, three-quarters mile. (Donovan, 1980; Pennsylvania County Maps; Pennsylvania Department of Transportation; Zacker)

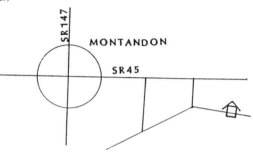

Perry County
38-50-03

Flickinger's Mill/Bistline Bridge

Flickinger's Mill Bridge spans Shermans Creek. This is one of seven covered bridges that span Shermans Creek just south of SR 274 within twelve miles of each other. The single span structure has two added steel piers. Built in 1871, Flickinger's Mill Bridge is 100 feet long.

Supported by cut stone and mortar abutments, the structure is covered with faded red plank siding with batten and a brown shingled roof. The interior has a multiple kingpost truss encased by a double Burr arch. The floor has crosswise planking with three-fourths of the floor space covered with lengthwise planking.

Flickinger's Mill Bridge is open to traffic and the creek has easy access, but is thick with vegetation which prevents good visual accessibility. Of all the seven clustered covered bridges over Shermans Creek, this has the least attractive location, solely due to the many trees surrounding the bridge site.

DIRECTIONS: Southwest Addison Township. From Blain on SR 274, east on SR 274, two and one-half miles, right on CR 50008, one and one-half miles. (Donovan, 1980; Pennsylvania County Maps; Pennsylvania Department of Transportation; Zacker)

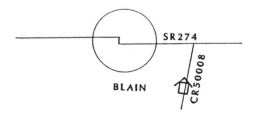

Cisna Mill/Adair's Bridge

Cisna Mill Bridge crosses Shermans Creek with 176 feet, making it the longest bridge in Perry County.

Built in 1884, the bridge was reconstructed in 1919. Today, Cisna Mill Bridge is supported by cut stone and mortar abutments that extend to form wingwalls. The two span structure has one concrete pier. Two steel piers have been added at quarter points to support the bridge. Covered with faded red plank siding and a tin roof, the bridge was built with a multiple kingpost truss encased by a full-size double Burr arch. The floor has lengthwise planking.

Access to the creek is easy and the bridge is open to traffic.

DIRECTIONS: Southwest Madison Township. From Cisna Run at the intersection of SR 274 and CR 50009, south on CR 50009, one-half mile. (Donovan, 1980; Pennsylvania County Maps; Pennsylvania Department of Transportation; Zacker)

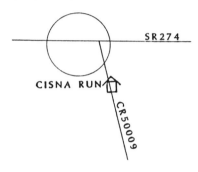

Saville Bridge

Saville Bridge, named after the local community, spans Buffalo Creek with 79 feet. This single span was constructed in 1903 by L. M. Wentzel.

Resting on cut stone and mortar abutments, the structure has a slight camber. Three steel piers have been added to support the bridge. Covered by faded red plank siding with batten and a tin roof, the bridge was constructed with a multiple kingpost truss and a double Burr arch. The beams used in the arch are bolted together. The floor is composed of crosswise planking with three-fourths of the floor space occupied by lengthwise runners laid in ten-foot sections.

Saville Bridge is open to traffic and has easy access to the creek.

DIRECTIONS: Saville Township. From Ickesburg on SR 17, west on CR 50012, two and one-half miles, left on CR 50037, two miles. (Donovan, Pennsylvania County Maps; Pennsylvania Department of Transportation; Zacker)

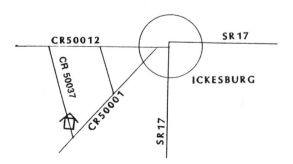

Kochendefer Bridge

Kochendefer Bridge spans Buffalo Creek three-quarters mile south of Saville Bridge (38-50-07). The Adair Brothers built Kochendefer Bridge in 1919 for $2,380.

Supported by concrete abutments, the 77 foot Kochendefer Bridge is covered with bright red plank siding and a tin roof. The single span has a camber and was constructed with an interesting combination queenpost and multiple kingpost truss. The floor has crosswise planking.

Open to traffic, Kochendefer Bridge is a striking structure. The surrounding area is free of trees and the bridge can be fully appreciated.

DIRECTIONS: Saville Township. From Ickesburg on SR 17, southwest on CR 50012, one-half mile, left on CR 50011, two and one-half miles, left on TR 332 across from CR 50037, one-half mile. (Donovan, 1980; Pennsylvania County Maps; Pennsylvania Department of Transportation; Zacker)

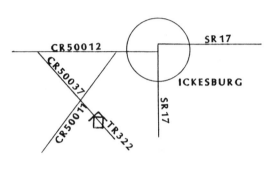

Landisburg/Rice Bridge

Named after the local village, Landisburg Bridge spans Shermans Creek with 123 feet.

Built in 1869, the two span structure is supported with cut stone and mortar abutments faced with concrete and a concrete center pier. The stone abutments extend at each approach to form wingwalls. Covered by red plank siding with batten, the bridge has a rusting tin roof. The interior has a unique example of a queenpost truss and a single Burr arch. The arch extends over both spans. Under the arch, over each span is a queenpost truss that is only one-fourth the average height of a truss. The combination of the single Burr and the queenpost truss is very unusual. The floor has lengthwise planking.

Access to the river is easy and the bridge, which is well-maintained, presents an attractive sight.

DIRECTIONS: Tyrone Township. From Landisburg at the intersection of SR 233 and SR 850, south on TR 333, one-half mile. (Donovan, 1980; Pennsylvania County Maps; Pennsylvania Department of Transportation; Zacker)

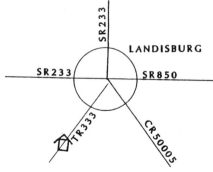

Harpersfield Bridge   35-04-19   Ohio

Belmont Campus Bridge   35-07-05   Ohio

Parrish Bridge   35-61-34   Ohio

290

Little Darby Bridge   35-80-04   Ohio

State Road Bridge   35-04-58   Ohio

Rock Mill Bridge   35-23-48   Ohio

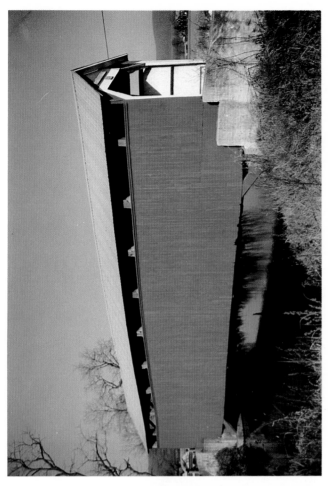

Kochendefer Bridge   38-50-09   Pennsylvania

Hayward/Noble/Mill Bridge   45-09-09   Vermont

Swanton Railroad Bridge   45-06-10   Vermont

Landisburg/Rice Bridge   38-50-10   Pennsylvania

Bull's Bridge   07-03-01   Connecticut

Eagle Creek Bridge   35-08-18   Ohio

Cox Bridge   35-82-10   Ohio

Hectorville Bridge   45-06-06   Vermont

Cilley/Lower Bridge   45-09-08   Vermont

Upper/Morgan Bridge   45-08-07   Vermont

East Johnson/Scribner/Mudget Bridge   45-08-09   Vermont

Clark's Railroad Bridge 29-05-14 New Hampshire

Rutland Railroad Bridge   45-01-05   Vermont

Cornish/Windsor Bridge 29-10-09/45-14-14 New Hampshire/Vermont

Germantown Bridge   35-57-01   Ohio

Benetka Road Bridge   35-04-12   Ohio

Station Bridge   45-01-01   Vermont

Fuller/Black Falls/Post Office Bridge
45-06-05   Vermont

Lumber Mill/Lower/Montgomery Bridge
45-08-06   Vermont

Danford Bridge   35-61-42   Ohio

Swartz Bridge   35-88-05   Ohio

Newton Falls Bridge   35-78-01   Ohio

Perry County
38-50-11

New Germantown Bridge

Just south of New Germantown Village, the New Germantown Bridge crosses Shermans Creek with 74 feet. John W. Fry built this bridge in 1857.

Exhibiting a camber, the single span rests on cut stone abutments with mortar. The stone abutments extend along the approach to form wingwalls. Covered by bright red plank siding with batten, the bridge has a tin roof. The interior has a combination multiple kingpost and queenpost truss and lengthwise floor planking.

The stream is inaccessible because of fencing. Open to traffic, New Germantown Bridge is well-maintained.

DIRECTIONS: Toboyne Township. From New Germantown on SR 274, south, one-fourth mile on TR 302. (Donovan, 1980; Pennsylvania County Maps; Pennsylvania Department of Transportation; Zacker)

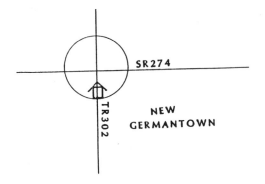

Perry County
38-50-12

Mount Pleasant

Mount Pleasant Bridge, named after the local village, spans Shermans Creek with 60 feet.

Built in 1918 by L. M. Wentzel, Mount Pleasant Bridge rests on cut stone and mortar abutments with two added concrete piers placed close to the abutments. The abutment stone work extends at each approach, forming wingwalls. Covered with red plank siding and a tin roof, the bridge was constructed with the characteristic Perry County combination multiple kingpost and queenpost truss. The floor has crosswise planking with two lengthwise runners.

The bridge site is fenced and prevents entry to the stream, but the bridge is easily viewed from the surrounding area. Mount Pleasant Bridge is open to traffic.

DIRECTIONS: Jackson Township. At Mount Pleasant on SR 274, south, one-tenth mile on TR 304. (Donovan, 1980; Pennsylvania County Maps; Pennsylvania Department of Transportation; Zacker)

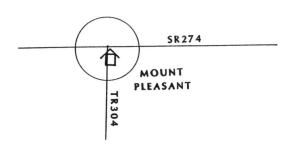

Book's/Kaufman Bridge

Book's Bridge spans Shermans Creek with 75 feet.

Built in 1884, the single span is supported by cut stone and mortar abutments with concrete facing. The stone work of the abutments is extended at each approach to form wingwalls. Red plank siding with batten covers the bridge but is rotting at the bottom from high water exposure. The roof is tin. A multiple kingpost truss and double Burr arch support Book's Bridge. Lengthwise floor planks comprise the floor.

The stream is easily accessible. Shermans Creek winds around at the bridge site, presenting a spectacular location for the covered bridge. Book's Bridge is open to traffic.

Book's Bridge is one of eight covered bridges that spans Shermans Creek in this valley. The eight bridges are within fourteen miles of one another. Consequently, the scenery at each of the bridges as well as the drive between the bridges is nothing but spectacular!

Perry County is one of my favorite bridging locations in the country.

DIRECTIONS: Jackson Township. From Mount Pleasant on SR 274, east on SR 274, one and one-half miles right on CR 50054, one-fourth miles. (Donovan, 1980; Pennsylvania County Maps; Pennsylvania Department of Transportation; Zacker)

Enslow/Turkey Tail Bridge

Enslow Bridge spans Shermans Creek with 110 feet. Built in 1904, the bridge was constructed at a cost of $2,250.

Resting on cut stone and mortar abutments and one concrete pier, Enslow Bridge is covered by faded red plank siding with batten and a rusting tin roof. With a slight camber, the bridge is constructed with a multiple kingpost truss and a double Burr arch. The floor has crosswise planking which also displays a camber.

Open to traffic, Enslow Bridge has easy access to the stream.

DIRECTIONS: Jackson Township. From Blainboro south on CR 50001, one and one-fourth mile, left on TR 312, one-tenth mile. (Donovan, 1980; Pennsylvania County Maps; Pennsylvania Department of Transportation; Zacker)

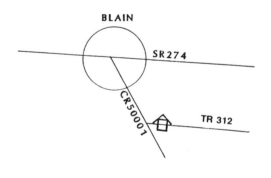

Wagoner's Mill/ Roddy's Mill/Thompsons Bridge

Wagoner's Mill Covered Bridge has also been known as Roddy's Mill Bridge and Thompsons Bridge. Wagoner's Mill Bridge has one span and crosses Bixler Run, which is a tributary of Shermans Creek. Shermans Creek drains northwestern Perry County.

Alex Roddy built the first mill at this site in 1762. The grain mill was of log construction and served Perry and Juniata Counties. The present stone building was built by F. Bryner and was purchased in 1839 by Benjamin Wagoner. The Wagoner Family operated the mill until the 1940s. Wagoner's Mill Bridge was built as early as 1812 and is thought to be one of two oldest covered bridges in the United States.

Wagoner's Mill Bridge has been bypassed, but it is still open. The bridge has a tin roof and red plank siding. A multiple kingpost truss with a double Burr arch supports the structure. The bridge has a camber built into it and is evidenced by a slight hump in the floor and roof. The floor has lengthwise planking.

The Wagoner's Bridge has a sensational setting. Next to the three story stone gristmill is a dam that was originally laid up in stone and has since been poured in concrete. The old gristmill, the dam and the bridge make an extraordinary landscape.

DIRECTIONS: Tyrone Township. From Loysville, west on SR 274, two miles, left, on TR 579. (Donovan, 1980; Pennsylvania County Maps; Pennsylvania Department of Transportation; Zacker)

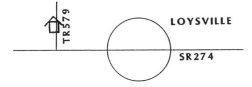

Barronvale Bridge

Named after the local community, Barronvale Bridge spans Laurel Hill Creek with 162 feet, the longest covered bridge left in Somerset County.

Built in 1902 by Cassimer Cramer, the two span bridge is supported by abutments and one pier made of cut stone and mortar. The lower half of the bridge is sided with red planks. The roof is red tin. The truss is a Child's encased with a double Burr arch over each span. The shorter span's Burr arch is only one-fourth the height of the kingpost center panel. The longer span's Burr arch is half the height of the kingpost center panel. The upper three-fourths of the truss is painted white. Steel tie-rods are placed diagonally across the wooden diagonal members of the multiple kingpost truss. The discovery of this Child's truss was very exciting because I had previously thought that the bridge was simply a multiple kingpost.

Bypassed, Barronvale Bridge sits next to an old mill building that is closed and appears abandoned. The bridge site allows easy access to the stream, but it is not necessary to appreciate the bridge because it is visually accessible from the new bridge and the surrounding area.

DIRECTIONS: Middlecreek Township. From New Lexington, SR 653, west, one mile, right on CR 55048, one mile, left on CR 55118, one mile, right on CR 55149 one-tenth mile, on right. (Donovan, 1980; Pennsylvania County Maps; Pennsylvania Department of Transportation; Zacker)

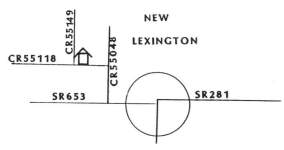

King's Bridge

King's Bridge spans Laurel Hill Creek with 128 feet. Built in 1906, the bridge has a single span.

Supported by cut stone abutments with mortar, King's Bridge is protected by dark red plank siding with batten and a dark brown shingled roof. The interior has gates at the accessible portal. The multiple kingpost truss is encased by a multi-layered, full size Burr arch. Some steel tie-rods have been added to the truss. The lower third of the truss has been paneled on the interior.

Bypassed, King's Bridge has an attractive location.

DIRECTIONS: Middlecreek Township. From New Lexington, west on SR 653, two miles, left on CR 55118, one-tenth mile on right. (Donovan, 1980; Pennsylvania County Maps; Pennsylvania Department of Transportation; Zacker)

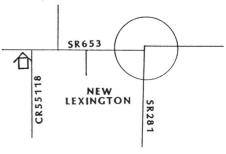

Lower Humbert/Faidley Bridge

Lower Humbert Bridge spans Laurel Hill Creek with 125 feet. Built in 1891, the structure has one span.

Lower Humbert Bridge rests on cut stone abutments with mortar. The lower two-thirds of the trusses are protected by red plank siding and the roof is corrugated tin. The multiple kingpost truss is encased by a double Burr arch. The truss members are painted white. The lower third of the truss is paneled inside and painted red. The floor has lengthwise planking.

Lower Humbert Bridge is open to traffic. The site allows easy access to the stream, but due to dense vegetation, visual access is poor.

DIRECTIONS: Turkeyfoot Township. From Ursinaboro at the intersection of CR 55115 and SR 281, north on SR 281, one mile, left on TR 393, one and one-half miles on left. (Donovan, 1980; Pennsylvania County Maps; Pennsylvania Department of Transportation; Zacker)

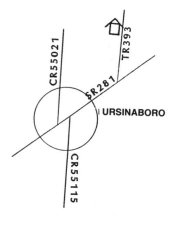

Washington County
38-63-13

Devil's Den/McClurg Bridge

The Devil's Den Bridge spans Aunt Clara's Fork of Kings Creek with 32 feet. Date of construction is unknown.

The single span structure is supported by cut stone abutments with concrete facing at the stream level to protect the abutments from ice damage. A wooden pier has been installed in the creek to support the center of the bridge. Even with the support, the center still sags. Devil's Den Bridge is protected by a corrugated tin roof and red plank siding. The interior has a kingpost truss with some bracing. The truss members and interior walls are painted red. Each side of the bridge has four windows. The floor sags in the middle and is made of crosswise planks.

Devil's Den Bridge is open to traffic and offers a scenic location.

DIRECTIONS: **Hanover Township. From Boyd, south one mile, on TR 346.** (Donovan, 1980; Pennsylvania Department of Transportation; Washington-Greene County Covered Bridge Map; Zacker)

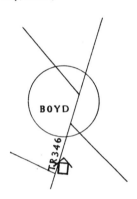

Washington County
38-63-18

Jackson's Mill Bridge

Jackson's Mill Bridge crosses Kings Creek with 46 feet. Date of construction is unknown because construction records of the bridges in Washington County were not kept.

The single span structure rests on cut stone abutments with some concrete assistance. Two wooden piers have been added to support the bridge. Protected by a rusting tin roof and red plank siding, the bridge has two windows on each side. The truss is a queenpost with bracing. The truss members and interior are painted red. The floor is crosswise planking.

The bridge is open, serving traffic and access to the creek is easy.

DIRECTIONS: **Hanover Town** 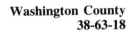 **p. From Boyd, south, one mile on TR 853.** (Donovan, Pennsylvania DOT; Washington-eene County Covered Bridge Map; Zacker)

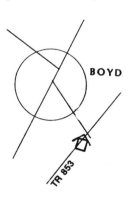

Lyle Bridge

Lyle Bridge spans Brush Run of Raccoon Creek with 39 feet. Date of construction is unknown.

Supported by cut stone abutments with concrete, the single span structure has two added steel piers. A traditional Washington County covered bridge, it is covered with a rusting tin roof and red plank siding. Each side of the bridge has three large windows. The queenpost truss, interior walls and roof are painted red. Crosswise planking composes the floor.

Lyle Bridge is open to traffic. A most interesting character of the area is that the road is made of coal, black crushed coal, and can be seen in the foreground of the exterior's photograph.

DIRECTIONS: Hanover Township. From Five Points, east, two miles on Route 861. (This is the best directions I can provide. I remember, though, that I made some turns somewhere. I asked a local resident and he had me follow him a while and then he gave me directions for the rest of the distance. My suggestion is to ask someone for directions once you get in the area of the bridge. (Donovan, 1980; Pennsylvania Department of Transportation; Washington-Greene County Covered Bridge Map; Zacker)

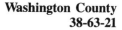

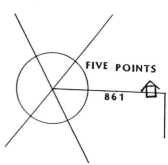

Ralston/Freeman Bridge

Ralston Bridge crosses Aunt Clara's Fork of Kings Creek with 36 feet. Date of construction is unknown.

Protected by a corrugated, rusting tin roof and red plank siding the bridge has two windows on each side. The single span rests on cut stone abutments with concrete. The abutments are starting to crumble. The kingpost truss has some additional bracing and the truss members, interior walls and roof truss are also painted red. The floor is made of crosswise planking.

Ralston Bridge has an attractive location. February of 1987 found the bridge closed. Access to the creek is easy.

DIRECTIONS: Hanover Township. From Boyd northwest on TR 352. There is a short walk required to reach the bridge. (Donovan, 1980; Pennsylvania Department of Transportation; Washington Greene County Covered Bridge Map; Zacker)

Wilson's Mill Bridge

Wilson's Mill Bridge spans Cross Creek with 40 feet. Cross Creek had recently been ditched and cleaned out at the time of the photograph. (February, 1987).

Wilson's Mill Bridge was moved to its present location in 1978 as a result of a flood control project. The single span rests on cut stone abutments that have been capped with concrete. Covered with a corrugated tin roof and red plank siding, the bridge has a queenpost truss. The interior is painted red and the floor is made of crosswise planks. The entire structure is two to three feet taller than the other Washington County bridges. It appears that the walls, truss and roof (shell of the bridge) were set on top of an existing three-foot wall of an another bridge, which creates the additional height evidenced in Wilson's Mill Bridge.

The bridge is open to traffic and access to the creek is easy.

DIRECTIONS: Cross Creek and Hopewell Townships. From Woodrow on SR 50, south on 62039, two miles, right, immediately on the left. (Donovan, 1980; Pennsylvania Department of Transportation; Washington-Greene County Covered Bridge Map; Zacker)

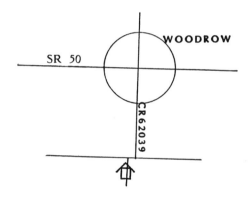

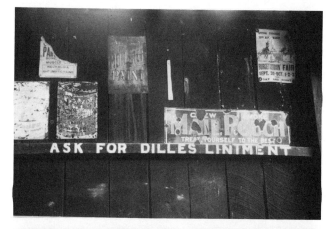

Pine Bank Bridge

Presently located in Meadowcroft Village, the Pine Bank Bridge was moved here in 1961 by Albert Miller. Originally, Pine Bank Bridge spanned Tom's Run in Gilmore Township, Greene County, Pennsylvania.

The 1870 structure now crosses a branch of Cross Creek. Pine Bank Bridge rests on bedrock abutments with concrete. The abutments are starting to crumble. Covered with a shake roof and dark plank siding with batten, the 50-foot bridge is built with a kingpost truss and crosswise floor planking. The interior is decorated with many excellent examples of antique advertisements. Two photos of the advertisements are shown on this page.

The bridge is well-maintained and located in the privately owned Meadowcroft Village, which displays many historic structures such as old churches and log cabins. During season there is an admittance fee.

DIRECTIONS: Jefferson Township. From Avella, west on SR 50 two miles, turn right and follow the signs to Meadowcroft Village. (Donovan, 1980; Pennsylvania Department of Transportation; Washington Green County Covered Bridge Map; Zacker)

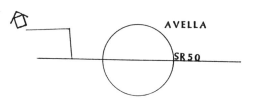

Vermont

ACKNOWLEDGMENTS

To the following people of Vermont, thank you for the information you provided me:

Anita Danigalis, Reference Librarian, Fletcher Free Library

Evelyn Keefe, Secretary, Lising History Association, Inc.

Sally G. Reed, Director, Ilsley Public Library

Karen A. Stites, Reference Specialist, The University of Vermont, Bailey/Howe Library

INTRODUCTION

Vermont once had over 500 covered bridges; today, 98 of these historical structures remain. This is a remarkable number, given the relative size of Vermont compared to other states which have a great number of covered bridges such as: Indiana, Ohio, and Pennsylvania. The old covered bridges that Vermont has maintained and restored, represent a wealth of fine examples.

TRUSSES

Seven of the eighteen existing trusses in the United States are represented in Vermont. The Town truss has the greatest number, with 42. There are 12 Burr arch trusses, 3 Paddleford trusses, two Howe trusses and one Haupt. The Haupt truss, seen in Orange County (45-09-06) on the Sayres Bridge is extremely rare. There are only two left in the U.S. The other Haupt truss is found in Catawba County, North Carolina (33-18-01). The rest of Vermont's trusses are queenposts, multiple and singular kingposts and combinations of various trusses. One of the most unusual trusses found in Vermont is at the Scott Bridge (45-13-13) in Windham County. The original 166-foot length has a Town lattice truss with a Burr arch. A flood washed out the west river bank and a 110-foot covered section was added; however, the trusses used

in this two span addition were kingposts, one over each span. The result is that one end of the bridge is constructed with kingposts and the other end with a Town truss.

Other most unusual trusses are the multiple kingposts found in Orange County on the Gifford (45-09-03) and Blaisdell (45-09-04) Bridges. The multiple kingpost truss is only half as tall as the usual height for such a truss. Gifford Bridge has the upper half braced but the Blaisdell Bridge's upper portion is empty except for basic framing, which makes the walls and roof look almost like an afterthought.

THE LONGEST AND OLDEST OF VERMONT'S COVERED BRIDGES

Vermont's longest covered bridge holds the distinction of being the longest covered bridge in the United States. The Cornish/Windsor Bridge (45-14-14) is shared with New Hampshire as the 460-foot structure spans the Connecticut River. The Cornish/Windsor Bridge's text and photographs are included with New Hampshire bridges categorized as 29-10-09. Cornish/Windsor was included with New Hampshire because Sullivan County, New Hampshire was studied. Windsor County, Vermont was, unfortunately, not included in this book because of a time constraint.

Vermont's longest covered bridges that are solely within the state are found in Windham County. Each of these long bridges span West River. Scott Bridge (45-13-13) is 290 feet long and its northern neighbor, West Dummerston Bridge (45-13-02), is 280 feet long.

The oldest recognized covered bridge in Vermont is the Pulpmill Bridge (45-01-04) located in Addison County. It is thought to have been built as early as 1808, but no later than 1820. More than several covered bridges vow to be the oldest in America, but, unfortunately, records are not available to confirm the dates.

RAILROAD COVERED BRIDGES

Vermont has three railroad covered bridges, Rutland Railroad (45-01-05) in Addison County, Swanton Railroad (45-06-10) in Franklin County, and Fisher Railroad (45-08-16) in Lamoille County. Rutland and Swanton are included in this book and both are excellent, well-preserved structures.

The Swanton Bridge is the longest railroad covered bridge left in America with 381 feet. Swanton is constructed with a double Town lattice truss. The bridge is huge; 22 feet wide and 36 feet tall. The rail still remains in the bridge, but the line has long since been abandoned. Swanton Railroad Bridge was burned by arson in 1987. The abutments are the only evidence left of the once majestic railroad bridge. I consider myself fortunate in that I was able to visit the bridge, but it is sad to think that Swanton Railroad Bridge no longer exists for everyone else to enjoy. The photographs included in this text of Swanton Railroad Bridge were taken in late March of 1987.

Rutland Railroad Bridge in Addison County is 108 feet long and is also impressively huge. Well-preserved, the Rutland Bridge spans a pond in its original location. Also located on an abandoned railroad line, the bridge is a spectacular example of turn of the century engineering and craftsmanship.

Vermont is one of only two states that still has railroad bridges. New Hampshire with four, two of which are abandoned and will not last long unless repaired, and Vermont with now only two, make up the only six examples of the once common, railroad covered bridges.

VERMONT'S DOUBLE-BARRELLED BRIDGES

Two double-barrelled bridges remain in Vermont. The Museum Bridge (45-04-06) in Chittenden County and the Pulpmill (45-01-04) in Addison County. Pulpmill is also the oldest covered bridge in Vermont. A double-barrelled covered bridge is characterized by two lanes divided by a truss. In both of Vermont's double-barrelled covered bridges, a multiple kingpost and Burr arch combination are used.

An excellent example of a two-lane covered bridge is the Cornish/ Windsor (45-14-14) over the Connecticut River. This bridge is wide enough for two lanes, but the lanes are not divided by a truss. It is the truss between the two lanes that defines a double-barrelled bridge.

There are only five double-barrelled bridges left in the United States today. Vermont is fortunate to have these two examples.

COVERED BRIDGES AND MILL SITES

The combination of covered bridges and mills was once a common sight throughout the midwestern and eastern United States. Vermont was no exception. The fast flowing streams provided ample power to operate the gristmills, flour mills, papermills and miscellaneous factories.

The Hayward Bridge (45-09-09) in Orange County still has several mill buildings at the bridge site which have been preserved. The most common element left from the old mills is the mill race; a dam built to hold back water to supply energy. These mill races can be seen at many of our covered bridge locations today. Some of these sites in Vermont include the Pulpmill Bridge (45-01-04) in Addison County, the Papermill Bridge (45-02-03) in Bennington County, and Henry Bridge (45-02-02), also in Bennington County. The Henry Bridge's mill race is particularly impressive because it has an original wooden dam. Many other bridges had mills in their proximity. If you look around the bridge sites, you will find many remnants of the old mills which include the mill race, collapsed buildings, portions of rock walls and old machinery. Vermont has many such sites because of the powerful streams.

Another characteristic commonly found at Vermont's covered bridges is the existence of waterfalls. One waterfall or a series of falls can be found at many bridge site locations.

COUNTIES AND THEIR BRIDGES

ADDISON COUNTY has five historic covered bridges left. Each one is unique and individually charming. Station Bridge (45-01-01) is located on Swamp Road, which is appropriately named. The road is two feet above the surrounding swamp. The area has abundant wildlife and is especially beautiful. Spade Farm (45-01-02) is privately owned, but is superbly maintained and displays antique advertisements. Halpin

Bridge (45-01-03), once used to service a nearby mill, hovers 30 feet over a gorge formed by the Muddy Branch of the New Haven River. This bridge has the distinction of having the highest elevation over its stream. Pulpmill Bridge (45-01-04), is a double-barrelled structure and is the oldest covered bridge in Vermont. Addison County's last covered bridge is the Rutland Railroad Bridge (45-01-05). Preserved, the Rutland Bridge is an excellent example of the old Railroad Covered Bridges.

ORANGE COUNTY has maintained eleven historic covered bridges. All are located on beautiful streams in lush valleys, and many are near mill sites. The day we were in Orange County, March of 1987, it rained, not just a little, a deluge! It rained—all day. The snows were melting and these conditions created dense fog. I was naturally concerned about the quality of my photographs because I knew it was a one-shot situation. Fortunately, the bridges' presence and their configuration shined through the fog and heavy rains and the photographs turned out reasonably well, to my relief. Given a sunny day, Orange County's bridges would be fabulous.

LOCATING VERMONT'S COVERED BRIDGES

Finding covered bridges in Vermont is reasonably easy. The directions and maps included with the text are suggested to be used in conjunction with county maps available from the state (please see the chapter on ''How to Find Covered Bridges and Obtain County Maps''). Another suggestion is to locate a Vermont Atlas or a Gazetteer. Whenever you are bridging, helpful tools are a compass, maps and a full tank of gas. Remember, just because a map shows a road, does not necessarily mean it really is there. In Vermont, as in many states, you can travel on a well-paved road for miles in a rural setting when, suddenly, the road becomes dirt and soon ends without warning. Helpful hints: be prepared, and don't forget your sense of adventure. (A sense of humor also helps, especially when lost!)

SUMMARY

Vermont has an abundance of covered bridges and all of them are well-maintained. Most of the bridges are open and none of them are a disappointment. The State of Vermont has a natural wealth of beautiful valleys, fast flowing, rocky streams, enchanting hills and spectacular mountains, all of which form a fabulous background for historic covered bridges. (Allen, 1969; Donovan, 1980; Lovell, 1951; Morse, 1960; Northern Cartographic; Royes, 1947)

BRIDGE NAME	COUNTY	NUMBER
Station	Addison	45-01-01
Spade Farm	"	45-01-02
Halpin	"	45-01-03
Pulpmill	"	45-01-04
Rutland Railroad	"	45-01-05
Henry	Bennington	45-02-02
Papermill	"	45-02-03
Locust Grove/Silk	"	45-02-04
Hills Bay/Lake Shore	Chittenden	45-04-01
Upper/Sequin	"	45-04-02
Lower/Quinlan	"	45-04-03
Museum	"	45-04-06
Hopkins	Franklin	45-06-01
Comstock	"	45-06-04
Fuller/Black Falls/Post Office	"	45-06-05
Hectorville	"	45-06-06
Hutchins/Levis	"	45-06-07

BRIDGE NAME	COUNTY	NUMBER
Longley/Harnois	Franklin	45-06-08
Swanton Railroad	"	45-06-10
Jeffersonville/Grist Mill/Scott/Bryant	Lamoille	45-08-01
Poland/Station/Junction	"	45-08-02
Lumber Mill/Lower/Montgomery	"	45-08-06
Upper/Morgan	"	45-08-07
Johnson/Powerhouse	"	45-08-08
East Johnson/Scribner/Mudget	"	45-08-09
Village/Meat Market	"	45-08-13
Guy/Moxley	Orange	45-09-01
Gifford/C.K. Smith	"	45-09-03
Blaisdell/Braley/Upper	"	45-09-04
Union Village	"	45-09-05
Sayres	"	45-09-06
Howe	"	45-09-07
Cilley/Lower	"	45-09-08
Hayward/Noble/Mill	"	45-09-09
Larkin	"	45-09-10
Flint/North Tunbridge	"	45-09-11
Station/Northfield Falls	Washington	45-12-08
Slaughterhouse	"	45-12-09
Newell/Lower	"	45-12-10
Upper	"	45-12-11
Creamery Bridge	Windham	45-13-01
West Dummerston	"	45-13-02
Scott Bridge	"	45-13-13

Addison County
45-01-01

Station Bridge

Station Bridge is so named because it is located at Salisbury Station, an old railroad stop. Station Bridge spans Otter Creek with 136 feet.

The two span structure was built in 1865. In 1970, Station Bridge was restored. The bridge is supported by cut stone abutments with mortar and one concrete pier that was added in 1970. The bridge is covered with a brown corrugated tin roof and naturally weathered plank siding. A Town lattice truss was used for construction and the floor has diagonal planking with two lengthwise runners.

Station Bridge is located on Swamp Road, which is appropriately named. The entire road is elevated two feet above the surrounding swamp. This is a rare example of a road runing through such a swamp. The area is full of wildlife and produces a feeling of isolation. Going east from SR 30 on Swamp Road, just when you are convinced you are lost, Station Bridge appears.

Majestically spanning Otter Creek, the bridge has a unique character because of its isolation and location. Access to the creek banks is easy and the bridge, as with most all of Vermont's bridges, presents a poignant picture. Station Bridge is open to traffic.

DIRECTIONS: Cornwall/Salisbury Township. From Middlebury, south on SR 30, six miles, left on Swamp Road, one and three-fourths miles. (Donovan, 1980; Northern Cartographic; Vermont Agency of Transportation)

Photograph by Michael Krekeler

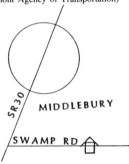

MIDDLEBURY

SR 30

SWAMP RD

Addison County
45-01-02

Spade Farm Bridge

Photograph by Michael Krekeler

Spade Farm Bridge was moved in 1958 and placed over a pond and is privately owned, but accessible to the public.

Dates of construction range from 1820 to 1850. The single span is 85 feet long and is supported by concrete abutments. A shake roof and naturally weathered plank siding cover the bridge. A Town lattice truss is used for the construction. Multiple width planking laid lengthwise comprise the floor covering. The boards on the floor exhibit extremely raised grain, which is a characteristic of much wear. The interior of the bridge is well-preserved and boasts of several antique signs that were commonly displayed in all covered bridges for advertisement purposes. These old relics are a real novelty. Two examples can be found in this book. One of the signs provides toll information and another sign advertises tobacco.

Spade Farm Bridge has been well-preserved at the Spade Farm and is easily accessible so the public can enjoy their efforts.

DIRECTIONS: Ferrisburg Township. From North Ferrisburg, west one mile to US 7, south on US 7 about one mile, on the right at Spade Farm. (Donovan, 1980; Northern Cartographic; Vermont Agency of Transportation)

NORTH FERRISBURG

US 7

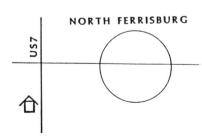

Halpin Bridge

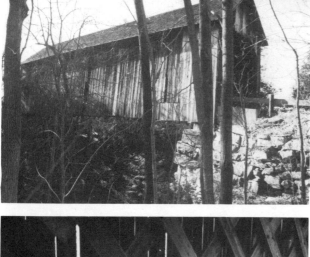

Halpin Bridge spans the Muddy Branch of New Haven River with 65 feet. Halpin Bridge has the distinction of being the highest elevated bridge over its stream in Vermont, some 30 feet. Muddy Branch is a deeply entrenched stream at the Halpin Bridge site. The stream has numerous waterfalls, creating a dramatic series of cascades. Halpin Bridge is seldom used today. It sits on a road that is now virtually abandoned, but once served a marble mill.

Halpin Bridge was built in 1840 with dry stone abutments that presently have a concrete cap. What is so different about the Halpin abutments is the construction with all sizes and all kinds of stones, from large cut stones to small, round creek stones. These abutments are most unusual, especially since they are still in good condition.

The bridge is protected by a shake roof and naturally weathered plank siding that needs some pieces replaced. The interior has a Town truss and a new floor made of 2″ X 6″ boards set on edge.

Access to the stream is difficult and the surrounding area is dense with vegetation, but the bridge is still scenic as it looms over the gorge formed by the Muddy Branch. Halpin Bridge is open but is not often used.

DIRECTIONS: Middlebury/New Haven Townships. From Middlebury, north on US 7, two miles, right on River Road, one mile, right on Halpin Road, three-quarters mile, left, one-fourth mile. (Donovan, 1980; Lovell; Northern Cartographic; Vermont Agency of Transportation)

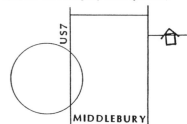

Pulpmill Bridge

Pulpmill Bridge crosses Otter Creek with three spans. The date of construction is thought to be as early as 1808, but no later than 1820, making Pulpmill the oldest covered bridge in Vermont. Built for the Waltham Turnpike, the three span structure is 195 feet long. The bridge is located on the township line of Middlebury and Weybridge.

Pulpmill Bridge is most famous because it is one of only five double-barrelled covered bridges left in the United States. Sitting next to a recently abandoned paper mill, a dam (mill race) creates a waterfall at the bridge site.

Covered with a corrugated tin roof and natural plank siding, the structure is supported by concrete abutments and two concrete piers. The underside of the bridge has structural steel added to support the weight of modern traffic. The interior of the bridge is fascinating with the two lanes and three trusses. The outside trusses are multiple kingpost with one 10-ply Burr arch. The center truss which divides the two lanes is a multiple kingpost truss sandwiched between two 10-ply Burr arches. All three of the trusses have bracing, which makes the truss resemble "X" panels, but the bracing is not mortised into the members as is the case for the Philippi "double-barrelled" Bridge (48-01-01) in Barbour County, West Virginia. The floor has crosswise planking with two lengthwise runners on each lane.

Pulpmill Bridge carries a lot of traffic and is located in an urbanized area. Access to the creek is impossible. Opportunities to photograph the bridge from an attractive angle are very few.

DIRECTIONS: Middlebury/Weybridge Townships. In Middlebury, west of US 7 and east of SR 23, northwest portion of town. (Donovan, 1980; Lovell, p. 13; Northern Cartographic; Vermont Agency of Transportation)

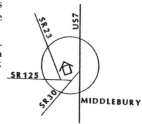

Rutland Railroad Bridge

Rutland Railroad Bridge was restored in 1982. In its original location, it spans Richville Pond with 108 feet.

The 1897 Rutland Railroad Bridge has one span, but the bridge is excessively tall, which is characteristic of all railroad covered bridges. Rutland Bridge is 30 feet tall and 18 feet wide. It is an immense structure. The Howe truss uses three or four steel rods vertically between the "X" panels. The beams used for the "X" members are much thicker and, accordingly, much taller than ones used in a Howe truss for a traditional covered bridge. The tracks have been removed from the bridge as the bridge site is on a long since abandoned rail line. A walking platform has been installed on top of the pre-existing railroad ties.

Rutland Railroad Bridge is structurally sound, well-maintained and preserved. Covered with a new shake roof and natural plank siding, the bridge is supported by huge cut stone abutments with mortar.

Rutland Bridge's physical location is breathtaking. Vermont's Green Mountains to the east border the skyline. The massive bridge hovers over the finger of the pond, creating a spectacular setting. Rutland Railroad Bridge is a must when visiting and bridging in Vermont.

DIRECTIONS: Shoreham Township. From Whiting on SR 30, west on Shoreham Road, two and one-half miles, left on East Shoreham Road, one-half mile. Parking on the right. A short walk is required down a trail that used to be the rail line. (Donovan, 1980; Northern Cartographic; Vermont Agency of Transportation)

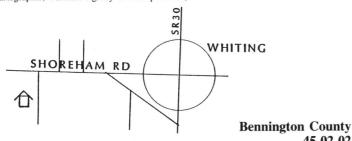

Henry Bridge

Henry Bridge spans the Walloomsac River and is 127 feet long.

Built in 1840, the Henry Bridge is a single span structure resting on concrete abutments. The exterior has tongue and groove lap-type siding covering the lower half of the bridge. The roof is covered with shake. With some pieces doubled, a Town lattice truss supports the bridge. A new floor is constructed with 2″ X 6″ boards laid on edge.

The bridge site is quite impressive. There is an original wooden dam at the site where once a mill stood. The Walloomsac is a wide river. Surrounding the bridge is a well-maintained area with little vegetation to block the view of the bridge and stream. Henry Bridge is open and serving traffic.

DIRECTIONS: Bennington Township. From North Bennington, south on SR 67A, one and one-half miles, right on Murphy Road, one and one-half miles. (Donovan, 1980; Vermont Agency of Transportation)

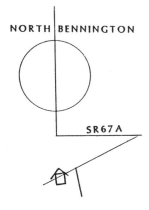

Papermill Bridge

Papermill Bridge assumed its name from the adjacent mill recently closed. The single span crosses Walloomsac River with 131 feet.

Built by Charles F. Sears around 1840, the bridge is covered with freshly painted red tongue and groove, lap-type siding and a shake roof. The portals are red trimmed in white. The interior has the first six feet at either portal paneled. A most rare example of a Town lattice truss is the one displayed in Papermill Bridge. Almost each plank of the lattice has an added plank. These additional members were added to the original truss to strengthen the bridge. A new floor is constructed of 2″ X 8″ boards laid on edge.

The bridge is bypassed with a temporary bridge, and it is not known if or when Papermill Bridge will be reopened to traffic.

Resting on concrete abutments, a pool created by a dam at the site reflects the bridge's image. There is a mechanical lock that opens to drain the pool above the mill race, to work on the dam and the mill area.

Access to the bridge and riverbanks is easy.

DIRECTIONS: Bennington Township. From North Bennington, south on SR 67A one and one-half miles, right on Murphy Road, one-tenth mile. (Donovan, 1980; Vermont Agency of Transportation)

Locust Grove/Silk Bridge

Built in 1840, Locust Grove Bridge crosses the Walloomsac River with a single span and 92 feet.

Concrete forms one abutment, the other abutment is a combination of various kinds, sizes and types of dry stones capped with concrete. Shake covers the roof and red plank siding covers the lower two-thirds of the sides. The portals are trimmed in white. A Town truss supports the bridge with a new floor made out of 2″ X 8″ boards laid on edge.

The bridge is open to traffic and access to the creek is easy. As with all of Bennington County's covered bridges, Locust Grove Bridge is well-maintained and in an attractive location.

DIRECTIONS: Bennington Township. From North Bennington, south on SR 67A two miles, right on Silk Road. (Donovan, 1980; Vermont Agency of Transportation)

Hills Bay/Lake Shore Bridge

Hills Bay Bridge spans Holmes Creek with 39 feet. Holmes Creek drains into Lake Champlain at the bridge site. Located on Lake Road, Hills Bay Bridge is named after its geographic location on the bay. Hill Point is one mile north of the bridge site. Date of construction is unknown. Hills Bay Bridge was built by Leonard Sherman.

Hills Bay Bridge is characterized by its elevation. It is the only covered bridge close to Lake Champlain and is, consequently, the closest to sea level. Lake Champlain and New York's Adirondack Mountains form a breathtaking background for Hills Bay Bridge.

Covered with a corrugated tin roof and naturally weathered plank siding, the bridge rests on cut stone abutments with some concrete assistance. The interior has a kingpost truss with a 5-ply Burr arch, a unique combination. The new floor is constructed with 2″ X 6″ boards laid on edge.

The little covered bridge is open and serving traffic. Hills Bay Bridge is a dramatic covered bridge because of its fabulous geographic location.

DIRECTIONS: Charlotte Township. From Charlotte on US 7, west on Ferry Road, one and one-half miles, right on Lake Road, two miles. (Donovan, 1980; Northern Cartographic; Vermont Agency of Transportation)

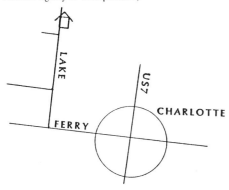

Upper/Sequin Bridge

Upper Bridge spans Lewis Creek and is 71 feet long.

Upper Bridge exhibits a very slight camber in its 71-foot length. The single span structure rests on concrete abutments. Built in 1849, the bridge is covered with a tin roof and creosoted plank siding. The interior has a multiple kingpost truss encased with a double Burr arch. The new floor is made of 2″ X 4″ boards set on edge.

Access to the creek is very difficult.

DIRECTIONS: Charlotte Township. From Prindle Corners, south on Prindle Road, one and one-fourth miles, right on Roscoe Road, one-tenth mile. (Donovan, 1980; Vermont Agency of Transportation)

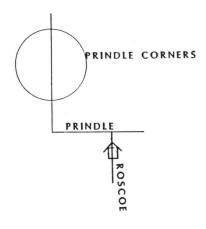

Lower/Quinlan Bridge

Lower Bridge spans Lewis Creek almost two miles southwest of Upper Bridge with 86 feet. The single span structure was built in 1849.

Resting on concrete abutments, Lower Bridge is covered with a corrugated tin roof and naturally weathered plank siding with two windows on either side. The multiple kingpost truss is encased with a double Burr arch and the new floor is made of 2″ X 6″ boards set on edge.

The creek has easy access and Lower Bridge is open to traffic.

DIRECTIONS: Charlotte Township. From Scott Pond, west on Creek Road, one and one-fourth miles. (Donovan, 1980; Vermont Agency of Transportation)

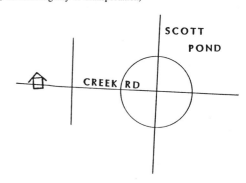

Museum Bridge

Museum Bridge spans Burr Pond at the entrance of Shelburn Museum. Shelburn Museum has a unique display of many historic structures including a round barn, an old church and antique airplanes.

Built in 1845 by Farewell Wetherby, Museum Bridge was moved to its present location from Cambridge, Vermont in 1951. Museum Bridge was then restored by Walter B. Hill.

At the time of this photograph, it was off season and we were not permitted to enter the grounds. Consequently, the construction of the abutments is unknown. The 168-foot structure is covered with black plank siding and a shake roof. The bridge is so unique because it is one of only five remaining double-barrelled bridges left in the U.S., of which Vermont has two. The other double-barrelled bridge is Pulpmill (45-01-04) in Addison County.

Museum Bridge has three multiple kingpost trusses and each is encased with a double Burr arch. One lane is used for storage of carriages and other vehicles during the off season and, as a result, it is impossible to appreciate the impact of the bridge's double-barrelled character. Access off season is impossible except for a portal view, due to blind fencing. In season there is a charge to enter the museum.

DIRECTIONS: Shelburn Township. At Shelburn. (Donovan, 1980; Northern Cartographic; Vermont Agency of Transportation)

Franklin County
45-06-01

Hopkins Bridge

Hopkins Bridge crosses Trout River with 84 feet. Hopkins Bridge was built by Sheldon and Savannah Jewett in 1875.

The single span structure is supported by one cut stone abutment and one bedrock abutment with a concrete cap. Covered with a corrugated tin roof and naturally weathered plank siding, the bridge's superstructure is a Town lattice truss. The floor has crosswise planking and two lengthwise runners.

Hopkins Bridge is open to traffic. Access to the creek is easy and the bridge site is well-maintained, allowing good visual access of the bridge.

DIRECTIONS: Enosburg Township. From East Berkshire at the junction of SR 105 and SR 118, take SR 118 southeast, two miles, turn right. (Donovan, 1980; Northern Cartographic; Vermont Agency of Transportation)

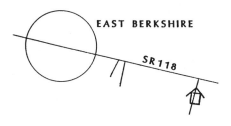

Franklin County
45-06-04

Comstock Bridge

Comstock Bridge spans Trout River with 70 feet. Built in 1883, the bridge was constructed by Sheldon and Savannah Jewett.

The Comstock Bridge's exterior has a corrugated tin roof and black plank siding with the portals freshly painted white. Supported by a Town lattice truss, the bridge has lengthwise floor boards. The first six feet of the interior is paneled and painted white. The single span rests on bedrock abutments.

Open and serving traffic, Comstock Bridge has difficult access to the creek, but the bridge can be viewed from the surrounding road.

DIRECTIONS: Montgomery Township. In Montgomery, just south of SR 118. (Donovan, 1980; Northern Cartographic; Vermont Agency of Transportation)

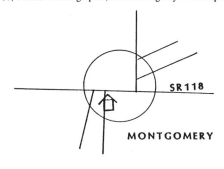

Fuller/Black Falls/
Post Office Bridge

Fuller Bridge crosses Black Falls Brook with a single span. The 50-foot structure was built in 1890 by two brothers, Sheldon and Savannah Jewett.

Spanning a fast flowing little stream, Fuller Bridge rests on bedrock abutments with a concrete cap and some concrete facing to prevent ice damage. The approaches are built up and walled with bedrock. Covered with a corrugated tin roof and naturally weathered plank siding, the bridge's portals are painted white. The first six feet of the interior at the portals is paneled and also painted white. A well-maintained covered bridge, as are all of Franklin County's, Fuller Bridge is constructed with a Town lattice truss and presently has a new floor composed of 2″ X 4″ boards laid on edge.

The bridge is open and the site offers easy access to the creek. The bridge is a short structure but more often than not, the shorter bridges offer the best opportunities for the photographer. Fuller Bridge is no exception.

DIRECTIONS: Montgomery Township. In Montgomery, just north of SR 118 South Richford Road. (Donovan, 1980; Northern Cartographic; Vermont Agency of Transportation)

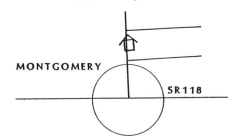

MONTGOMERY SR 118

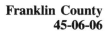

Hectorville Bridge

Spanning the South Branch of Trout River, Hectorville Bridge is located at a place called Hutchins, but is named after the small village of Hectorville, which is one and one-half miles south of the bridge site on SR 118. The 54-foot, single span structure was built in 1883 by Sheldon and Savannah Jewett, two brothers who built many covered bridges in Franklin County.

Hectorville Bridge exhibits a very slight camber and sits on concrete abutments that were poured over naturally located, huge boulders in the creek bed. Not in as fine repair as most of Franklin County's covered bridges, Hectorville Bridge has suffered vandalism, with some of the naturally weathered plank siding missing. Corrugated tin covers the roof and the portals are Franklin County's traditional white with the first six feet of the interior at the portals paneled and painted white. The bridge is constructed with a Town truss but has a kingpost combination. The vertical member of the kingpost is composed of adjustable steel tie-rods. The entire floor has steel reinforcing.

Access to the creek is very difficult, but the bridge can be viewed from the surrounding area. Open to traffic, Hectorville Bridge is still in service.

DIRECTIONS: Montgomery Township. At Hutchins, just west of SR 118. (Donovan, 1880; Northern Cartographic; Vermont Agency of Transportation)

HUTCHINS SR 118

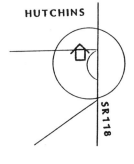

Hutchins/Levis Bridge

Hutchins Bridge, located at Hutchins, spans the South Branch of Trout River with 54 feet. Built in 1883 by Sheldon and Savannah Jewett, Hutchins Bridge is a single span.

Supported by one concrete abutment and one bedrock abutment, the bridge has a red tin roof, natural plank siding and red portals. One side of the bridge has the lower quarter sided horizontally and the upper three-quarters sided in the traditional vertical direction. The other side is sided vertically, which may indicate that the bridge once had an external walkway. A Town lattice truss supports the bridge and crosswise floor planks are interfaced with two lengthwise runners.

Access to the creek is impossible and the surrounding area is heavily vegetated. Hutchins Bridge is open to traffic.

DIRECTIONS: Montgomery Township. From Hutchins, south one-half mile, turn right on Gibbo Road, one-tenth mile. (Donovan, 1980; Northern Cartographic; Vermont Agency of Transportation)

Photograph by Michael Krekeler

Longley/Harnois Bridge

The Longley Bridge crosses Trout River with a single span. The 89-foot structure was constructed in 1863 by two brothers, Sheldon and Savannah Jewett.

Presently supported by concrete abutments, the exterior has a tin roof, naturally dark plank siding and white portals. The interior has the first six feet at the portals sided and painted white, which helps protect the truss. A Town truss supports the bridge and the new floor is composed of 2″ X 4″ boards laid on edge.

The river has convenient access to the banks at the bridge site. Longley Bridge is still in service.

DIRECTIONS: Montgomery Township. From Montgomery, west on SR 118, one mile, left at Longley Flat Road. (Donovan, 1980; Northern Cartographic; Vermont Agency of Transportation)

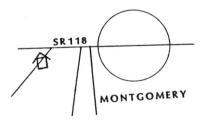

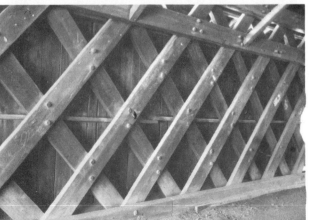

Franklin County
45-06-10

Swanton Railroad Bridge

On an abandoned rail line of the St. Johnsbury and L. C. Railroad, stands the longest remaining railroad covered bridge left in the United States. With 381 feet, the Swanton Railroad Bridge crosses the wide Missisquoi River with three spans, in the village of Swanton.

Resting on concrete abutments and two concrete piers, the structure is covered with naturally dark plank siding and a tin roof. The roof has several vents that allowed the smoke from the trains to escape.

Swanton Railroad Bridge is singularly impressive. The structure is 36 feet tall, 22 feet wide and 381 feet long. The track still remains inside the bridge and a walkway has been installed between the rails.

The truss is astonishing because of its size. It is the tallest, longest Town lattice known to this author. Over and above the 30-foot length of each truss member, the construction uses a double truss on each side. Not two planks set side by side, but two trusses, one in front of the other.

Preserved, Swanton Railroad Bridge has a small park at the site which offers easy visual access. Located in Swanton close to Lake Champlain, the Swanton Bridge is a real treasure and a must to visit when in Vermont.

The photographs shown in this text were taken in March of 1987. That same year, Swanton Railroad Bridge was burned by arson and now the only evidence that this once fabulous bridge existed is the abutments and two piers. When I received this information, I almost cried. It was one of the most beautiful bridges I had seen. The local residents must have been sickened by their loss. I was.

DIRECTIONS: Swanton Township. In Swanton, from SR 36, on Old County Road, one-half mile. (Donovan, 1980; Northern Cartographic; Vermont Agency of Transportation)

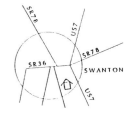

Lamoille County
45-08-01

Jeffersonville/Grist Mill/ Scott/Bryant Bridge

Jeffersonville bridge spans Brewster River with 80 feet. The date of construction in unknown.

Resting on cut stone and bedrock abutments with a concrete cap, the single span is covered with naturally weathered plank siding and a green, corrugated tin roof. A multiple kingpost truss is encased by a double Burr arch that is half as tall as the kingpost center panel. The floor has lengthwise planking.

Open for traffic, the bridge site has easy access to the creek. The creek has an excellent setting and provides an attractive background for the bridge.

DIRECTIONS: Cambridge Township. From Jeffersonville, south on SR 108, one-half mile, left on Canyon Road. (Donovan, 1980; Northern Cartographic; Vermont Agency of Transportation)

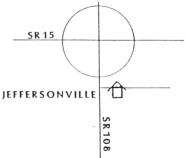

Poland/Station/Junction Bridge

Poland Bridge, located at Cambridge Junction, spans the Lamoille River with 152 feet. Built in 1887 by George W. Holmes, the structure is a single span.

Resting on bedrock abutments with concrete caps, Poland Bridge is covered with a corrugated green tin roof and naturally weathered plank siding. An unusual character about Poland Bridge is that the siding follows the contour of the interior Burr arch and covers it so it is not exposed to the elements. The span is constructed with a multiple kingpost truss encased with a double Burr arch. The floor has lengthwise planking with two lengthwise runners.

Unfortunately, Poland Bridge might not survive much longer. The center of the bridge sags two feet below the road surface. At the very least, the bridge should be closed to traffic because it is unsafe. To preserve this bridge, it would take considerable time and investment because it suffers from age and over use.

Access to the river bank is easy and as of March 1987, Poland Bridge was open.

DIRECTIONS: Cambridge Township. At Cambridge Junction south of SR 109 north of SR 15. (Donovan, 1980; Northern Cartographic; Vermont Agency of Transportation)

CAMBRIDGE JUNCTION

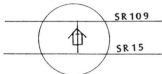

SR 109

SR 15

Lumber Mill/Lower/ Montgomery Bridge

Lumber Mill Bridge crosses the North Branch of Lamoille River with 70 feet. The single span was built in 1895.

Lumber Mill Bridge is supported by bedrock abutments capped with concrete. Covered with a rusting, gray tin roof and dark, naturally weathered plank siding, the bridge is constructed with a queenpost truss with bracing. The new floor is made of 2" X 4" boards set on edge and crosswise with two lengthwise runners made of planks. The most striking feature about Lumber Mill Bridge is that its eaves extend 18" beyond the sides of the bridge.

Access to the creek is impossible, but the bridge site offers visual accessibility. Lumber Mill Bridge is open.

DIRECTIONS: Waterville Township. From Waterville, north one mile on SR 109, on left. (Donovan, 1980; Vermont Agency of Transportation)

WATERVILLE

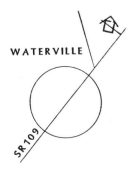

SR 109

Upper/Morgan Bridge

Upper Bridge crosses the North Branch of the Lamoille River with a single span and 63 feet. Lewis Robinson, Fred Tracy and Charles Leonard built Upper Bridge in 1895.

Resting on concrete abutments, the bridge is covered with a corrugated tin roof and naturally weathered plank siding. Some of the planks were once painted white and the effect is multidimensional. A queenpost truss with bracing supports the structure. The floor has crosswise planking and two lengthwise runners.

Upper Bridge has an incredible location. In an isolated valley surrounded by hills, the picturesque bridge presents an imposing structure

DIRECTIONS: Belvidere Township. At Belvidere Junction, just north of SR 109, on Back Road. (Donovan, 1980; Northern Cartographic; Vermont Agency of Transportation)

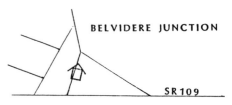

Johnson/Powerhouse Bridge

Johnson Bridge spans Gihon River, a swift flowing stream full of rocks and rapids. Just east of the bridge site is an old building that generates electricity using the power supplied by the stream.

Originally built in 1870, Johnson Bridge was repaired in 1960 by Wilmer Locke. Supported by concrete abutments, the single span, 62-foot structure is covered with naturally weathered plank siding with batten and a shake roof that is showing its age. The interior is constructed with a queenpost truss with bracing and crosswise floor planking and two lengthwise runners.

Gihon River is quite picturesque because of a rapid flow and a series of waterfalls east of the bridge site. Access to the actual river bank is impossible, but the bridge is easily viewed from the surrounding roads. Johnson Bridge is open to traffic.

DIRECTIONS: Johnson Township. In Johnson, just north of SR 15 on SR 100C, one-half mile, left. (Donovan, 1980; Northern Cartographic; Vermont Agency of Transportation)

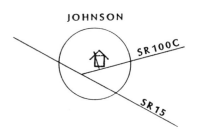

Lamoille County
45-08-09

East Johnson/Scribner/ Mudget Bridge

East Johnson spans Gihon River with 60 feet. Date of construction is unknown. In 1960, Wilmer Locke repaired the bridge.

The single span structure is supported by concrete abutments. Covered with a tin roof and natural gray plank siding, East Johnson Bridge was constructed with a queenpost truss. The queenpost structure in this bridge is unusual because it is only half the height of a normal queenpost truss and the traditional wooden vertical members are steel tie rods. The floor has crosswise planking with two lengthwise runners.

East Johnson Bridge has an excellent location. The bridge site allows easy access to the creek. The bridge is well-maintained and the stream, surrounding hills and valley present a good opportunity to photographers.

DIRECTIONS: Johnson Township. From Johnson on SR 15, northeast on SR 100C, one and one-half miles, right, one-fourth mile, on right. (Donovan, 1980; Northern Cartographic; Vermont Agency of Transportation)

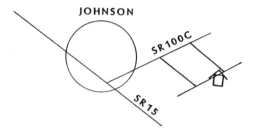

Lamoille County
45-08-13

Village/Meat Market Bridge

Village Bridge spans the North Branch of the Lamoille River with 61 feet.

Built in 1895, Village Bridge is covered with a rusted, corrugated tin roof and naturally weathered plank siding. The single span rests on bedrock abutments with a concrete cap. The new floor is composed of 3″ X 6″ boards laid on edge. The queenpost truss has some bracing. One portal is skewed to fit the curvature of the rocky river bank.

Village Bridge also has a picturesque location over a rapidly flowing stream. At the bridge site there is a series of waterfalls that are quite spectacular.

DIRECTIONS: Waterville Township. At Waterville, just west of SR 109. (Donovan, 1980; Vermont Agency of Transportation)

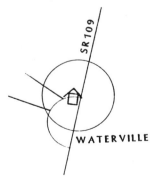

Guy/Moxley Bridge

Built in 1886 by Arthur Adams, Guy Bridge spans the First Branch of the White River with 59 feet.

The single span structure is supported by one concrete abutment and one bedrock abutment. Covered with a corrugated tin roof and natural plank siding, Guy Bridge was built with a queenpost truss. Presently, the truss has additional bracing and a kingpost placed in the center panel, with the vertical member made of steel. Lengthwise planking composes the floor.

Guy Bridge is open to traffic. The bridge site has easy access to the creek and the surrounding hills/mountains create a beautiful setting.

DIRECTIONS: Chelsea Township. From Chelsea at the junction on SR 110 and SR 113, south on SR 110 two and one-half miles, left one-tenth mile. (Donovan, 1980; Northern Cartographic; Vermont Agency of Transportation)

Photograph by Michael Krekeler

Gifford/C.K. Smith Bridge

Gifford Bridge crosses the Second Branch of the White River with 55 feet and a single span.

Built in 1904, Gifford Bridge has some rare characteristics. The roof is corrugated tin but one half of it is new and the other half is rusted. The plank siding has faded red paint and is in a deteriorated condition. The interior construction is the most striking. The truss is a multiple kingpost, but is only half the normal height of a truss. The lower portion has 15 panels with a kingpost center panel. The upper half appears to have been an addition consisting of bracing in the form of a kingpost center panel, and only two multiples, one on either side of the kingpost. A 24″ steel I-beam has been placed on the interior's floor and tied into the lower chord to support the bridge. The floor has crosswise floor planking.

Gifford Bridge does not have an attractive exterior but the interior truss is fascinating. The bridge site has easy visual access and the bridge is open to traffic.

DIRECTIONS: Randolph Township. From East Randolph at the junction on SR 66 and SR 14, take SR 14 south, one and one-half miles, left on Hyde Road. (Donovan, 1980; Northern Cartographic; Vermont Agency of Transportation)

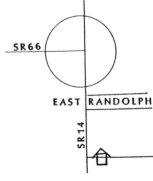

Orange County
45-09-04

Blaisdell/Braley/Upper Bridge

Blaisdell Bridge spans the Second Branch of the White River with 48 feet and a single span.

Built in 1904, Blaisdell Bridge was restored in 1977 by an organization called Bridges, Inc. Today, the bridge is covered with a galvanized corrugated tin roof and freshly painted red plank siding. The interior has the same truss as the Gifford Bridge (45-09-03) in that the truss is a multiple kingpost but is only one-half the height of a normal truss. It appears as if the walls and roof were added to the existing structure, which consisted of the truss and floor. The new floor is made of 2″ X 6″ boards set on edge and laid crosswise.

The most interesting feature about the bridge is its unique multiple kingpost truss design. The bridge is open but is located on a short dead end road and is not used very much.

DIRECTIONS: Randolph Township. From East Randolph, south on SR 14, one and one-half miles, right. (Donovan, 1980; Northern Cartographic; Vermont Agency of Transportation)

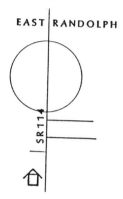

EAST RANDOLPH

SR 14

Orange County
45-09-05

Union Village Bridge

Union Village Bridge spans the Ompompanoosuc River with 119 feet. Built in 1867, the bridge has one span.

Union Village Bridge is covered with a corrugated tin roof and naturally gray plank siding. The interior is constructed with a multiple kingpost truss and an added, inverted "V" arch. The new floor has lengthwise 2″ X 6″ boards set on edge.

Access to the river is impossible. The bridge is open.

DIRECTIONS: Thetford Township. At Union Village just east of SR 132. (Donovan; Northern Cartographic; Vermont Agency of Transportation)

UNION VILLAGE

SR 132

Sayres Bridge

Sayres Bridge crosses the Ompompanoosuc River with 134 feet. Over one hundred and forty-eight years old, Sayers Bridge was built in 1839. In 1963, the bridge received major repairs.

The single span structure is covered with a corrugated tin roof and natural plank siding. The portals are painted red. Resting on huge cut stone abutments, the concrete pier was probably added in 1963. The most interesting feature about the Sayres Bridge is it is one of only two Haupt trusses in existence in the United States today. The other Haupt is located in Catawba County, North Carolina (33-18-01), which was built in 1894 and is 85 feet long. Sayres Bridge's Haupt truss is encased with a double Burr arch. Sayres floor has crosswise planking.

Although the exterior is not very attractive, and access to the stream is impossible, the interior Haupt truss is fascinating, especially since there are only two left. Sayres Bridge is open and serving a tremendous amount of traffic. The roadway is straight and the local traffic speeds through the bridge. I seriously doubt that the motorists who use the Sayres Bridge realize its rare character or it would not be so harshly abused.

DIRECTIONS: Thetford Township. At Thetford Center, just west of SR 113. (Donovan, 1980; Northern Cartographic; Vermont Agency of Transportation)

THEDFORD CENTER

Howe Bridge

Howe Bridge spans the First Branch of the White River with 78 feet. Ira Mudget, Edward Wells and Chauncey Tenney built Howe Bridge in 1879.

A tin roof and deteriorated plank siding cover the multiple kingpost truss and lengthwise plank flooring. The bridge exhibits a slight camber and rests on large cut stone abutments with no mortar.

Access to the creek banks is easy. The site is well-maintained and allows a full view of the bridge. Howe Bridge is open.

DIRECTIONS: Tunbridge Township. From Tunbridge on SR 110, south two miles, left on Hill Road. (Donovan, 1980; Northern Cartographic; Vermont Agency of Transportation)

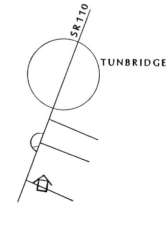

TUNBRIDGE

Orange County
45-09-08

Cilley/Lower Bridge

Cilley Bridge crosses the First Branch of the White River with 68 feet.

Built in 1883, Cilley Bridge exhibits a slight camber and is covered with a tin roof and natural plank siding. Resting on huge cut stone abutments, the single span was built with a multiple kingpost truss and now has lengthwise plank flooring.

Access to the stream is easy. The stream, surrounding hills and bridge present a beautiful location. Cilley Bridge is open.

DIRECTIONS: Tunbridge Township. From Tunbridge, south on SR 110, three-fourths mile, right on Russell Road, one-fourth mile. (Donovan, 1980: Vermont Agency of Transportation)

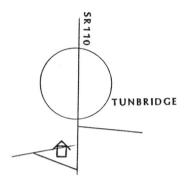

Orange County
45-09-09

Hayward/Noble/Mill Bridge

Spanning the First Branch of the White River, Hayward Bridge is 76 feet long.

Built in 1883, the bridge is covered with a gray tin roof and naturally weathered plank siding. Resting on concrete abutments, the single span is constructed with a multiple kingpost truss. The lengthwise plank flooring has raised grain, indicative of much use.

The bridge site has a spectacular location. The First Branch of the White River is rocky and fast flowing, creating alot of white water. There are several buildings at the bridge site that are restored and were once part of an operating mill. The mountain stream, bridge and mill create an impressive setting. Hayward Bridge is open for traffic.

DIRECTIONS: Tunbridge Township. At Tunbridge, west of SR 110. (Donovan, Vermont Agency of Transportation)

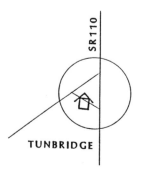

Larkin Bridge

Larkin Bridge spans the First Branch of the White River with 71 feet. The single span structure was built in 1902 by Arthur Adams.

Today, Larkin Bridge rests on concrete abutments and is covered with a tin roof and natural plank siding. The roof is very steep to avoid collapse from the abundant snows. The interior is built with a multiple kingpost truss and lengthwise flooring.

Although access to the creek is difficult, the surrounding scenery makes Larkin Bridge interesting. Larkin Bridge is open to traffic.

DIRECTIONS: Tunbridge Township. From North Tunbridge, north on SR 110, one and one-fourth miles, right on Larkin Road, one-tenth mile. (Donovan, 1980; Northern Cartographic; Vermont Agency of Transportation)

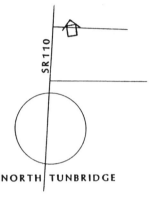

NORTH TUNBRIDGE

Flint/North Tunbridge

The Flint Bridge spans the First Branch of the White River with 92 feet. Built in 1845, the structure has one span.

Flint Bridge displays a camber and rests on bedrock abutments with concrete caps. Covered with a gray tin roof and gray plank siding, the bridge is supported by a queenpost truss with bracing. Lengthwise planking covers the floor.

Access to the stream is difficult, but the bridge is visible from the roads or the surrounding hills. The valley gives the bridge a beautiful background. Flint Bridge is open for traffic.

DIRECTIONS: Tunbridge Township. From North Tunbridge, north on SR 110, three and one-half miles, right one mile. (Donovan, 1980; Vermont Agency of Transportation)

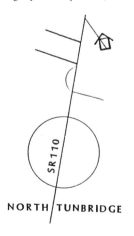

NORTH TUNBRIDGE

Station/Northfield Falls Bridge

Spanning Dog River with 138 feet, Station Bridge was built in 1872.
The original single span structure is now supported by bedrock abutments with some concrete assistance and an added concrete pier. Covered by a corrugated tin roof and red plank siding, the bridge is constructed with a Town lattice truss that is also painted red. The floor is made of 2″ X 8″ boards set on edge and laid crosswise.

It is at this location two covered bridges can be seen together. They are not twins and do not span the same stream, but it is the only place in Vermont where there are two covered bridges visually present. The second covered bridge viewed through the portal of Station Bridge, is the Newell Bridge (45-12-10).

Station Bridge is open and access to the stream is impossible.

DIRECTIONS: Northfield Township. At Northfield Falls, just west of SR 12. (Donovan, 1980; Northern Cartographic; Vermont Agency of Transportation)

Slaughterhouse Bridge

Slaughterhouse Bridge spans Dog River with 55 feet. Built in 1872, the structure has a single span. No doubt there was a slaughterhouse nearby.

Resting on huge cut stone abutments without mortar, Slaughterhouse Bridge is covered with a corrugated tin roof and red plank siding with batten. Constructed with a queenpost truss, the bridge floor has crosswise planking interfaced with two lengthwise runners. The interior is painted red, but has experienced much graffiti.

Access to the creek is impossible though the bridge can be viewed from the surrounding roads. The road is dirt and a dead end. The bridge is not used much, yet it is open.

DIRECTIONS: Northfield Township. From Northfield Falls, south on SR 12 one-half mile, first right, one-fourth mile. (Donovan, Vermont Agency of Transportation)

Newell/Lower Bridge

Spanning Cox Brook with 54 feet, Newell Bridge sits only one-tenth mile from Station Bridge (45-12-08). This is the only place in Vermont that two covered bridges can be seen together. They are not twins and do not span the same stream. The date of construction for Newell Bridge is unknown.

The single span structure rests on concrete abutments and is covered with a tin roof and red plank siding with batten. The interior has a queenpost truss that is painted red and a crosswise floor made of 2″ X 8″ boards set on edge.

The bridge is open but access to the creek is difficult.

DIRECTIONS: Northfield Township. At Northfield Falls just west of SR 12. (Donovan, 1980; Northern Cartographic; Vermont Agency of Transportation)

Upper Bridge

Upper Bridge spans Cox Brook with 45 feet. The single span bridge was built in 1899.

Today, Upper Bridge has red plank siding with batten and a tin roof. The queenpost truss and interior is painted red. The floor has 2″ X 8″ boards set on edge and laid diagonally across the bridge.

Access to the brook is difficult but not necessary because the bridge can be viewed from the surrounding area. Upper Bridge is open to traffic.

DIRECTIONS: Northfield Township. From Northfield Falls, west on SR 9 one-half mile. (Donovan, 1980; Vermont Agency of Transportation)

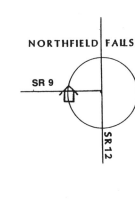

Creamery Bridge

A creamery once stood near this historic bridge, but has since disappeared. Spanning the Whetstone Brook, the Creamery Bridge is 84 feet long.

Built in 1879, the bridge was constructed by thirteen men. The single span structure is most striking because of its external walkway and pink and green slate roof. The walkway is an addition and is covered with corrugated green tin. The use of the slate roof over the bridge is rare and is the only one known to this author. The sides are covered with red planking. The structure rests on one concrete abutment and one abutment that is a combination of concrete and cut stone. The interior is interesting because only the lower third of the sides are covered, exposing the upper two-thirds of the Town lattice truss. The walkway and bridge floor are relatively new and are covered with 2″ X 8″boards set on edge and laid lengthwise. The bridge floor has two thick lengthwise runners.

In the summer, the Creamery Bridge has a beautiful location; however, during the winter and early spring months, the bridge site is used to deposit excess snow from the roads, giving the site a scarred appearance. Creamery Bridge is open and carries heavy traffic.

DIRECTIONS: Brattleboro Township. From Brattleboro, west on SR 9, one-half mile west of I-91. (Donovan, 1980; Northern Cartographic; Vermont Agency of Transportation)

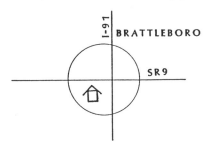

West Dummerston Bridge

West Dummerston Bridge is recognized as being the second longest covered bridge solely in Vermont, with 280 feet. Vermont shares the longest covered bridge in the U.S. with New Hampshire; the Cornish/Windsor Bridge (45-14-14), found in Windsor County, Vermont, over the Connecticut River.

Built in 1872 by Caleb B. Lamson, West Dummerston Bridge crosses the West River with two spans and is supported by abutments and one pier constructed with cut stone. Covered with natural plank siding and a tin roof, the bridge is supported by a Town truss.

West Dummerston Bridge has an excellent location across a wide river and surrounded by beautiful hills. The bridge is open to traffic.

DIRECTIONS: Dummerston Township. At West Dummerston, just east of SR 30. (Donovan, 1980; Northern Cartographic; Vermont Agency of Transportation)

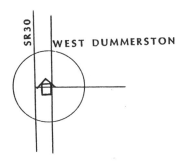

Scott Bridge

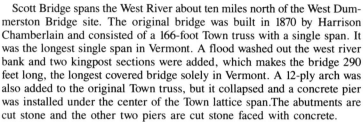

Scott Bridge spans the West River about ten miles north of the West Dummerston Bridge site. The original bridge was built in 1870 by Harrison Chamberlain and consisted of a 166-foot Town truss with a single span. It was the longest single span in Vermont. A flood washed out the west river bank and two kingpost sections were added, which makes the bridge 290 feet long, the longest covered bridge solely in Vermont. A 12-ply arch was also added to the original Town truss, but it collapsed and a concrete pier was installed under the center of the Town lattice span.The abutments are cut stone and the other two piers are cut stone faced with concrete.

The two added kingpost spans are constructed with hand-hewn timbers, and the vertical member is made of two steel rods. The 12-ply collapsed arch has formed a peculiar curve from the excess use and is tied to the lower chord with steel rods.

Scott Bridge is covered with natural plank siding and a green tin roof. In 1970, Scott Bridge was restored by the Vermont Division for Historic Places.

Scott Bridge is most unusual because of the distinctively different types of trusses used on one bridge. March of 1987 found the bridge closed. The river valley location offers a good opportunity to view the bridge. The Townshend Dam is located just north of the bridge site.

DIRECTIONS: Townshend Township. From Townshend, west on SR 30, one mile. (Donovan, 1980; Northern Cartographic; Vermont Agency of Transportation)

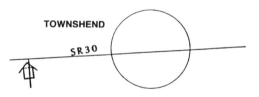

An excellent example of a hand hewn bean is found in the Scott Bridge.

Virginia

ACKNOWLEDGMENTS

I would like to extend my appreciation to the following individuals in Virginia for their generous information, time and effort.

Sandra V. Robertson, Librarian, Town of Pearisburg

Mike Hatchett, Patrick County Branch Library

Joanna F. Keck, Administrative Assistant, The Charles Pinckney Jones Memorial Library

Nick Whitmer, Assistant Librarian, Rockingham Public Library

Frances Fugate, Reference Librarian, Virginia Historical Society

Liz Hamilton, Campbell County Public Library

VIRGINIA

Virginia has nine historic covered bridges left out of what was once almost 100 (Allen, 1959, p. 80). As of 1936, 50 were still in use (Presbrey, 1980). Today only one covered bridge is used by traffic, Meem's Bottom Bridge (46-86-01). Of the other seven bridges, four have been bypassed and three are located on private property.

Virginia's covered bridges offer some unique examples. The most famous bridge is the "Old Humpback." This bridge has an eight foot elevation at its center which gives the bridge its unique backbone structure. Giles County has three covered bridges that have unusual trusses. Various sources classify them as a modified Howe or a multiple queenpost truss. To me, they resemble Haupt trusses without the diagonal supports. No matter what the designation, they are unique to Giles County, Virginia.

Finding Virginia's covered bridges is not difficult. The maps and directions included in the text should be used in conjunction with county maps available from the State of Virginia (see chapter on "How to Find Covered Bridges and Obtain County Maps").

Locating covered bridges in Virginia is exciting because they are found in the beautiful valleys of Virginia.

(Allen, 1959; Aritt, 1982; "Covered Bridge Attracts Visitor, Vandals"; "Covered Bridge Still in Use"; "Covered Bridge Still Stands"; Donovan, 1980; Department of Highways, 1963; "Few Covered Bridges Still Remain As Reminders of Virginia's Past"; "Historical Landmarks Serve Patrick County"; Jackson River Vocational Center; "Last In County"; Presbrey, 1980; Virginia Department of Highways (a))

BRIDGE NAME	COUNTY	NUMBER
Old Humpback	Allegheny	46-03-01
Sinking Creek	Giles	46-36-01
Link Farm	"	46-36-02
Craig	"	46-36-03
Biedler	Rockingham	46-83-01
Meem's Bottom	Shenandoah	46-86-01

Photograph by Michael Krekeler

The underside of Old Humpback Bridge.

Allegheny County
46-03-01

Old Humpback Bridge

Old Humpback Bridge acquired its name from its unusual configuration. The bridge spans Dunlop Creek with 100 feet from abutment to abutment. The actual length of the bridge is closer to 120 feet, because the center of the floor rises eight feet above its portals. This rise is exemplified in the interior photograph. The floor blocks two-thirds of the far portal and this was taken with the camera 24″ off the floor.

Old Humpback Bridge was built in 1835. This is the oldest covered bridge in Virginia and the only one left built prior to the Civil War. There were three such "Humpback" bridges in the immediate vicinity. All three were part of a toll road, the James River and Kanawha Turnpike. One of the humpbacks was burned in the Civil War, and the other was lost in a flood in 1913 (Allen, 1959, p. 84; Jackson River Vocational Center, 1976).

The craftsman who designed and constructed Old Humpback was Captain Thomas McDowell Kincaid. Kincaid used a multiple kingpost truss, oak timbers, and fashioned pins out of locust trees to hold the beams together. Although the siding, floors and roof have been repaired and portions replaced, the truss and chords are made of the original hand-hewn oak timbers that Kincaid fashioned.

For ninety-four years the Humpback Bridge served travelers. In 1929 the bridge was bypassed and a nearby farmer assumed it and used it for storing hay. In 1954, twenty five years later, the bridge and the surrounding five acres were purchased by the Covington Chamber of Commerce, the Covington Business and Professional Woman's Club, and the Virginia State Highway Department. The bridge was purchased, resided and repaired for $10,000.

Fondly referred to as the "Granddaddy of covered bridges", Old Humpback can be seen today in a well-maintained park. The exterior has black lap siding, a shake roof and rests on stone abutments that have had concrete pointing in the cracks. The interior has an eight-foot rise, a multiple kingpost truss and dry, worn crosswise floor planking.

Access to the creek is convenient because the park incorporates the river banks into the bridge site. Old Humpback is a must for all bridgers.

DIRECTIONS: From Covington, three miles west on US 60, turn left under a railroad trestle. (Allen, 1959; Arritt, 1982; Donovan, 1980; Department of Highways, 1963; "Few Covered Bridges Still Remain"; Jackson River Vocational Center; Presbrey, 1980; Virginia Department of Highways (a); Virginia Department of Highways (b))

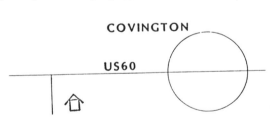

**Giles County
46-36-01**

Sinking Creek Bridge

Sinking Creek Bridge spans Sinking Creek with 70 feet.

Built in 1916, Sinking Creek Bridge has a flat, green tin roof, red lap siding, and rests on stone abutments that have been faced with some concrete. The single span sags in the center. The interior has a crosswise floor and the truss is perplexing. Virginia Department of Highways and Transportation, 1985, refers to the truss as a modified Howe. *The World Guide to Covered Bridges* has it listed as a multiple queenpost truss. To me, it resembles a Haupt without the multiple, diagonal braces. Whatever its classification, it is a distinctive truss. This truss design is in all three of the remaining Giles County Covered Bridges.

Sinking Creek Bridge was bypassed in 1963. The creek is easily accessible.

DIRECTIONS: From Newport at US 460 and SR 42, take SR 42 northeast, three-quarters mile, left on Route 601, one-half mile. (Donovan, 1980; Department of Highways, 1963; Virginia Department of Highways and Transportation (a); Virginia Department of Highways and Transportation (b))

Photograph by Michael Krekeler

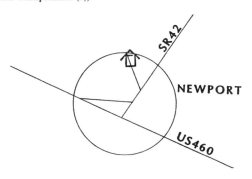

**Giles County
46-36-02**

Link Farm Bridge

Link Farm Bridge spans Sinking Creek one-half mile west of Sinking Creek Bridge (46-36-01).

Built in 1912, Link Farm Bridge was bypassed in 1949 and sits on private property. The exterior has a flat, lapped, rusted tin roof, dark red lap siding and creek stone abutments almost entirely encased with concrete. The 50-foot structure has the same design truss as Sinking Creek (46-36-01). The trusses identity is bewildering. Virginia Highways Department (1985) identifies it as a modified Howe. *The World Guide to Covered Bridges* lists it as a multiple queenpost. To me it is a Haupt variation. It has the same structure as a Haupt but without the diagonal braces. The interior's floor has crosswise planking with two runners that are four inches thick.

Located on private property, attempts have been made to preserve the bridge. Some of the siding has been knocked off but, generally, the bridge is in fair condition.

DIRECTIONS: From Newport at US 460 and SR 42, take US 460 west, one and one-half miles, right on Route 700 one-fourth mile, on left. (Donovan, 1980; Department of Highways, 1963; Virginia Department of Highways (a); Virginia Department of Highways (b))

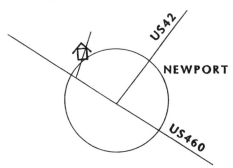

Giles County
46-36-03

Craig Bridge

The Craig Bridge is located in a beautiful valley. Spanning Sinking Creek, as do all three of Giles County's remaining covered bridges, the Craig Bridge is only 36 feet long. The road that leads down to the bridge from US 42 is a private road secured with a fence. Viewing of this bridge has to be done from up on the hill.

Craig Bridge was built in 1919 and is thought to have the same truss construction as the other two Giles County covered bridges. The exterior appears to have a red tin roof and gray tin siding.

Access to the creek is impossible as the bridge is part of a private drive with a gate.

DIRECTIONS: From Newport, three miles, northeast on SR 42, on right. (Donovan, 1980; Virginia Department of Highways (b))

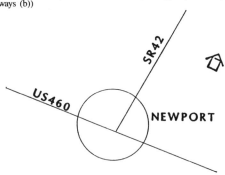

Photograph by Michael Krekeler

Rockingham County
46-83-01

Biedler Bridge

The 95 foot Biedler Bridge is named after its builder, Daniel W. Biedler, who built the bridge in 1880 over Smith Creek.

The exterior has creosoted lap siding, a flat tin roof and cut stone abutments with mortar. The interior has diagonal floor planking with two runners. The truss is a Burr. The arch only comes halfway up the height of the kingpost center panel, and the arch itself encases and surrounds the multiple kingpost truss with wood pieced together to give the impression of a solid arch.

Biedler Bridge is located on a private drive.

DIRECTIONS: Plains Township. From Mauzy at SR 259 and US 11, north about two miles on the right between Route 796 and 798 on a private road, one-half mile. (Donovan, 1980; Department of Highways, 1963; "Last In County"; Virginia Department of Highways and Transportation (a); Virginia Department of Highways (b))

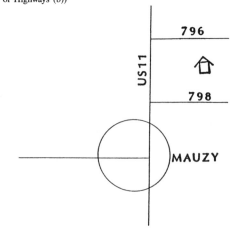

Shenandoah County
46-86-01

Meem's Bottom Bridge

Meem's Bottom Bridge spans the North Fork of the Shenandoah River with 191 feet. The bridge's name comes from the river site, which was named after a Civil War officer, General G. S. Meems.

Meem's Bottom Bridge was built in 1893. The bridge was burned by arson on Halloween of 1976. All but some framework was destroyed. County and State funds were used to rebuild the bridge at a cost of $250,000. In 1982-1983, the bridge was closed due to a broken floor beam. Repairs at a cost of $140,000 were done at that time that consisted of placing steel beams under the bridge and installing three concrete piers.

Today, Meem's Bottom Bridge has a tin roof, treated lap siding, and is supported by cut stone abutments and three concrete piers. The interior has a Burr arch encasing and surrounding the members of a multiple kingpost truss. All of the wooden members of the truss have been coated with plastic sealant. The floor has crosswise planking and two lengthwise runners.

The west side of the creek is easily accessible, which makes the afternoon a better time to photograph the bridge.

DIRECTIONS: Ashly Township. From Mount Jackson, south on US 11, one mile, right on Route 720, one-fourth mile. (Donovan, 1980; Department of Highways, 1963; Presbrey, 1980; Virginia Department of Highways (a); Virginia Department of Highways (b))

Photograph by Michael Krekeler

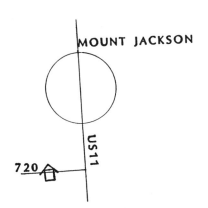

MOUNT JACKSON

US 11

720

West Virginia

ACKNOWLEDGMENTS

I appreciate the time, efforts and materials provided by the following people of West Virginia:

Mr. Ed Rauh, County Librarian, Jackson County Library

Cabell County Public Library

Doddridge County Public Library

Barbara V. Stewart, Acting Director, New Martinsville Public Library

Susan E. Swanson, Reference Librarian, Morgantown Public Library

Elizabeth B. Wiseman, Genealogist, Greenbrier Historical Society

Melanie Wetzel, Reference Librarian, Marion County Public Libraries

Mrs. Carol Hassig, Secretary, The Wetzel County Genealogical Society

Vera S. Crum, Treasurer, Jackson County Historical Society

INTRODUCTION

West Virginia at one time had hundreds of covered bridges. Today only 17 remain.

The Philippi Bridge is West Virginia's most unusual covered bridge. One of only five double-barrelled covered bridges left in the U.S., the structure is the longest with 304 feet. Philippi Bridge is also the longest covered bridge in the state of West Virginia.

There are eight different truss designs represented in West Virginia: "X" panel with Burr arch—1, Multiple kingpost truss with Burr arch—2, Long truss—2, Long truss with arch—1, Howe—1, Howe and queen combination—2, Multiple kingpost truss—2, queenpost—3, Kingpost truss—2, and Smith truss—1.

West Virginia has three covered bridges that survived the Civil War. Philippi (48-01-01) and Carrollton (48-01-02) Bridges in Barbour County, built in 1852 and 1862, respectively, and the Barrackville Bridge (48-25-02) in Marion County, built in 1852. Many covered bridges were burned during the Civil War. Many that survived the Civil War were destroyed in a devastating flood in 1888.

The most famous bridge builder in West Virginia was Lemuel Chenoweth. He was a carpenter who built furniture and cabinets. Chenoweth built several covered bridges near his home town and was eventually hired by the state of West Virginia to construct the covered spans on state roads.

The state of West Virginia has an unusual distribution of its covered bridges as compared with the distribution of covered bridges in other states. In most states, covered bridges are concentrated in certain counties. In West Virginia there are twelve counties holding the seventeen bridges, and the twelve counties are erratically dispersed throughout the state, thus requiring at least three days to see them all. Ten West Virginia covered bridges are studied in this book and it seemed to me a good representation of the covered bridges in West Virginia today.

Finding covered bridges in West Virginia is not difficult and the scenery is wonderful. The maps and directions provided with the text for each bridge are to be used in conjunction with county maps available from the state. (Please see the chapter on "How to Find Covered Bridges and Obtain County Maps".)

West Virginia's covered bridges offer a variety of truss designs, the impressive Philippi Bridge and simply beautiful scenery.

(Allen, 1959; Donovan, 1980; West Virginia Department of Highways)

BRIDGE NAME	COUNTY	NUMBER
Carrollton	Barbour	48-01-02
Milton/Sink's Mill/Mudd River	Cabell	48-06-01
Center Point	Doddridge	48-09-01
Philippi	Barbour	48-01-01
Fletcher	Harrison	48-17-03
Simpson Creek	"	48-17-12
Odaville/Sandyville/New Era	Jackson	48-18-01
Staats Mill	"	48-18-04
Barrackville	Marion	48-25-02
Laurel Point/Dents Run	Monongalia	48-31-03

Carrollton Bridge

Carrollton Bridge spans the Buckhannon River, which is a tributary of the Tygart Valley River. Their confluence is three-quarters mile northeast of the bridge site.

Built in 1862, Carrollton Bridge is 156 feet long. In 1962, the state and county built a new bridge for $50,000 and placed the covered bridge on it. Carrollton was fortunate to be able to retain their old covered bridge and yet receive a safe bridge to carry all traffic. At the time of this construction, two concrete piers were installed and structural steel supports the newly poured concrete floor. The interior has a multiple kingpost truss encased by a double Burr arch. The exterior has a shake roof that needs repair at the peak, and beautiful, naturally weathered plank siding.

Access to the river is extremely difficult because of an existing railroad track. The Carrollton Bridge is very picturesque and worth the effort.

DIRECTIONS: At Carrollton on SR 36, three-quarters mile southeast of US 119. (Auvil, 1977; Donovan, 1980; West Virginia Department of Highways)

Photograph by Michael Krekeler

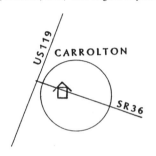

Milton/Sink's Mill/ Mud River Bridge

Milton Bridge spans the Mud River with 112 feet in the village of Milton.

The single span structure was built in 1875 by R.K. Baker, the local postmaster. Resting on cut stone abutments and steel piers added near the abutments, the exterior has red plank siding and a shake roof. The interior has a Howe truss with a thick 4-ply Burr arch and diagonal floor planking. The floor joist are also built on a diagonal, which is a peculiar technique.

The river banks have easy access. The bridge is closed and gives the impression that it has been abandoned. It seems to be a favorite party spot with broken glass and debris at the site.

DIRECTIONS: At Milton, off of US 60, south, close to the west end of town. (Donovan, 1980; West Virginia Department of Culture and History; West Virginia Department of Highways)

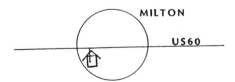

Doddridge County
48-09-01

Center Point Bridge

Center Point Bridge spans Pike Fork of McElroy Creek with 43 feet.

Built in 1890, Center Point Bridge rests on dry cut stone abutments (no mortar). The short bridge was constructed with a Long truss and has crosswise floor planking. The exterior has a rusty-gray tin roof and naturally weathered plank siding.

The bridge is open and used as part of a private driveway.

The bridge is visually accessible.

DIRECTIONS: At Center Point, just north of SR 25. (Donovan, 1980; West Virginia Department of Highways)

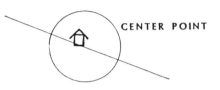

Barbour County
48-01-01

Philippi Bridge

The longest double-barrelled covered bridge left in the United States, Philippi Bridge spans the Tygart Valley River with 304 feet. Tygart Valley River is a major regional drainage channel that almost equally dissects Barbour County from north to south. The Philippi Bridge assumes its unique name from the town in which it is located.

Built in 1852, Philippi Bridge was constructed by Lemuel Chenoweth, a bridge architect, who was one of West Virginia's famous bridge builders. The cut sandstone and mortar abutments and pier were built by Emmet O'Brien. Completed in 1852, Philippi was opened as a toll bridge and is famous for its participation in the Civil War.

Today Philippi is supported by the cut stone abutments, one cut stone pier in the center and two added concrete piers at quarter points. The center of the bridge, over the original cut stone pier, exhibits a camber. The most striking features are the double lanes and an external walkway on one side. The roof is green shingles and the siding is faded white lap.

The bridge was reinforced in 1934 to support modern traffic.

The underside of the bridge has structural steel supporting a poured concrete floor in the bridge and walkway. The wooden truss and roof have been kept intact. Each of the three trusses is encased with a double Burr arch. The truss is uncommon today, but found in some very old covered bridges. It is an "X" panel divided by a vertical beam.

Philippi Bridge is on U.S. 250 and is heavily traveled. The bridge site offers easy access to the river banks and convenient parking.

Philippi is a must when visiting West Virginia.

DIRECTIONS: At Philippi on US 250. (Auvil, 1977; Donovan, 1980; McCallum, 1983; West Virginia Department of Highways)

Harrison County
48-17-03

Fletcher Bridge

Fletcher Bridge crosses Ten Mile Creek with 62 feet and was named after a nearby family.

The single span structure was built in 1892 and rests on cut stone abutments that were quarried from a hill just south of the bridge site. The exterior has faded red plank siding and a green tin roof, The interior has a multiple kingpost truss and diagonal floor planking.

The bridge is open and serving local traffic. The site allows easy access to the creek and offers a beautiful location.

DIRECTIONS: From Wolf Summit on US 50, west, one and one-half miles, right on SR 5, one mile, on left. (Auvil, 1977, Donovan, 1980; West Virginia Department of Highways)

Photograph by Michael Krekeler

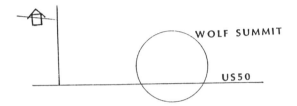

Harrison County
48-17-12

Simpson Creek Bridge

Simpson Creek Bridge spans Simpson Creek, at the northern edge of Bridgeport, with 75 feet. Built by A.S. Hugill, the Simpson Creek Bridge was constructed for $1,483. Built on land owned by John Lowe in 1881, the bridge originally stood one-half mile upstream. In 1899, it was washed away by a flood and reconstructed at its present location.

The single span rests on beautiful, cut sandstone abutments without mortar. The exterior has freshly painted red plank siding with batten and a gray tin roof. The interior has a multiple kingpost truss without the kingpost center panel and new lengthwise floor planking.

Preserved in a small park, the bridge is open but does not serve normal traffic because it has been bypassed. The area surrounding the bridge site is well-maintained and offers easy visual access.

DIRECTIONS: Just south of SR 24 near I-79 at the northern edge of Bridgeport. (Donovan, 1980; West Virginia Department of Culture and History; West Virginia Department of Highways)

Odaville/Sandyville/New Era Bridge

The Odaville Bridge spans the Left Fork of Sandy Creek with 102 feet.

Built in 1892, the single span structure has added structural steel under the bridge and is supported by two steel piers close to the cut stone abutments. The bridge is covered with a shake roof and faded red plank siding that is in disrepair. The interior has a Long truss and an added segmented single Burr arch and new, crosswise 2" X 4" on edge, floor planking.

Structurally the bridge is sound and is open. Due to the added steel and missing planking on the sides, the bridge is not very pretty.

DIRECTIONS: From Odaville, south on SR 21, one mile, left on Route 21/15. (Donovan, 1980; West Virginia Department of Highways)

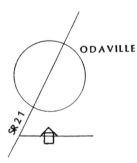

Staats Mill Bridge

Originally located three miles east of its present site over Tug Fork of Mill Creek, the bridge was named after a nearby mill owned by Enoch Staats. Staats Mill Bridge was built in 1887 by H.T. Hartley for $904. The stone abutments cost $820, for a total cost of $1724 for the structure.

In 1983, Staats Mill Bridge was moved to Cedar Lake Park and restored. The 97 foot bridge was placed over a pond and rests on cut stone abutments. The cost of the restoration was $104,000.

Today the bridge presents an impressive site over the pond exhibiting a camber throughout its 97 foot length. The interior has a Long truss and new crosswise floor planking.

Open only to foot traffic, the bridge is well-maintained at Cedar Lake Park.

DIRECTIONS: From Ripley, south on SR 25, one and one-half mile, left into Cedar Lake Park. (Donovan, 1980; West Virginia Department of Culture and History; West Virginia Department of Highways)

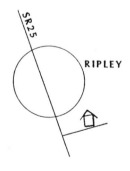

Marion County
48-25-02

Barrackville Bridge

Barrackville Bridge spans Buffalo Creek with 135 feet.

The single span structure was built in 1852 by Lemuel and Eli Chenoweth, brothers. The stone work was done by John and Robert McConnell.

Bailes Ice had a gristmill and sawmill near the bridge site and was responsible for saving the bridge during the retreat of a confederate band of soldiers. Because the Ice Family agreed to provide food and let the soldiers rest on their land, the army agreed not to burn the bridge. Consequently, Barrackville Bridge is the second oldest covered bridge in West Virginia.

For the first 20 years after construction, the bridge did not have siding. R.L. Cunningham was awarded the siding contract in 1872. In 1934, C.A. Short, an employee for the state of West Virginia, repaired the approaches, strengthened the bridge, and built the existing external sidewalk. In 1951, steel was placed under the bridge for additional support.

Today, the Barrackville Bridge is covered with dark red lap siding, a tarpaper roof, and rests on cut stone abutments without mortar. The interior has a multiple kingpost truss encased with a double Burr arch. The truss members are painted red and the side that has the walkway is open and the outside of the walkway is sided and roofed. The floor has crosswise planking and two runners that have pieces missing. The bridge was bypassed in February of 1987 by a temporary bridge. It is unknown when and if Barrackville Bridge will be reopened.

DIRECTIONS: In Barrackville, northernmost part of town, on CR 250/32. (Donovan, 1980; West Virginia Department of Culture and History; West Virginia Department of Highways)

Monongalia County
48-31-03

Laurel Point/Dents Run Bridge

Laurel Point Bridge spans Dents Run two miles west of the village of Laurel Point. William and Joseph Mercer built the bridge for $250 in 1889. The stone work was done by W.A. Loar for $198.

The 40-foot structure has a kingpost truss. The floor is crosswise with two lengthwise runners. The bridge is supported by cut stone abutments without mortar. Structural steel has been added to the underside of the bridge for additional support. The bridge is covered with a tin roof and red lap siding. Still open for traffic, the bridge is not used because of an adjacent concrete bridge.

Access to the creek is easy.

DIRECTIONS: From Laurel Point, west one mile on US 19, right on SR 43 one-half mile, left on CR 43/4, one-fourth mile. (Donovan, 1980; West Virginia Department of Culture and History; West Virginia Department of Highways)

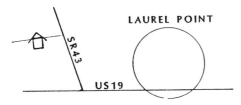

"Bridge Closed" signs often indicate the presence of a covered bridge. More than a few of the covered bridges are found closed. This could mean one of three things: 1) it is scheduled to be replaced, 2) it is in such poor condition that it is no longer safe and there are no funds to fix or replace it, or, 3) it is to be renovated.

Just east of Breezewood, Pennsylvania in Bedford County, this unique combination of signs appear. The "One Covered Bridge" sign indicates the direction to follow to find McDaniels Bridge (38-05-20). The "2 Covered Bridges" sign leads to Jackson's Mill Bridge (38-05-25) and Felton's Mill Bridge (38-05-03). These three bridges are clustered within two miles of each other.

Typically, all covered bridges are indentified with a weight limit. Twelve tons is considerable when compared to many covered bridges that limit the weight to three tons.

When bridging you will find that covered bridges are often clustered because a certain county or township has preserved their bridges.

This road is closed due to restoration. This is an interesting photo because it shows the restoration of Baumgardner's Mill Bridge (38-36-25) in Lancaster County, Pennsylvania in progress.

Originally, the covered bridge assumed its name after the road, the nearby mill, the stream it spanned, a close neighbor, or its builder. Now, once in a while the road has assumed the name of the bridge.

A three-ton weight limit for a bridge ahead is an excellent indication of an approaching covered bridge. I especially like the way I framed my car in this photo!

"Road Closed" signs help identify the location of a covered bridge. Sometimes the road is blocked off one-tenth to a mile or more from the bridge's site and a short walk is necessary. Sometimes by checking my map for access to the other side, I could get closer to the bridge by driving around the block.

Height limits are often posted for covered bridges. Some covered bridges have wooden headers nailed on the portals which limit use to cars only.

This unique sign indicates the existence of clustered, covered bridges.

Some covered bridges were built to accept excessively tall traffic, other bridges were built solely to accommodate a team of horses and a wagon.

I thought this sign was just a little redundant!

"Covered Bridge Ahead" signs just made things too easy. I always felt as if I was on a treasure hunt and then I was given an unfair advantage—it was verified, I was on the right trail!

Bibliography

CONNECTICUT

Allen, Richard Sanders. "Covered Bridges In Connecticut." *The Antiquarian.* 2 (November 1950): 11-19.

Allen, Richard Sanders. *Covered Bridges of the Northeast.* Brattleboro, Vermont: The Stephen Greene Press, 1957.

"Covered Bridge Links Town's Past, Present." *Waterbury Republican*, 18 March 1987.

Donovan, Richard T. *World Guide to Covered Bridges.* National Society for the Preservation of Covered Bridges, 1980.

INDIANA

Arnold, Eleanor. Rush County Heritage, Inc., Rushville, Indiana. Letter 30 January 1987.

Bailey, Dorothy. Brown County Historical Society, Nashville, Indiana. Letter 3 February 1987.

"Bean Blossom Bridge Closes After 105 Years of Service." *Brown County Gazette*, 31 March 1982.

Business and Professional Women of Osgood, Versailles, Milan and Holton. *History of Ripley County, Indiana.* Versailles, Indiana: Business and Professional Women of Osgood, Versailles, Milan and Holton, 1968.

"Council Votes to Fix the Bean Blossom Bridge." *Brown County Gazette,* 30 June 1982.

"Covered Bridge." *Noblitt Sparks Industries "Folks,"* June 1947.

"Covered Bridge is on the Original Route of the Cincinnati-to-St. Louis Pike..." *Outdoor Indiana* 40 (October 1975): 12.

Crawfordsville-Montgomery County Chamber of Commerce (a). "Crawfordsville and Montgomery County Visitors Guide." Crawfordsville, Indiana: Crawfordsville-Montgomery County Chamber of Commerce.

Crawfordsville-Montgomery County Chamber of Commerce (b). "Historical Montgomery County, Indiana." Crawfordsville, Indiana: Crawfordsville-Montgomery County Chamber of Commerce.

Donovan, Richard T. *World Guide to Covered Bridges.* The National Society for the Preservation of Covered Bridges, Inc. 1980.

Gobin, Jerry L. Surveyor Fayette County, Indiana. Letter 28 January 1987.

Gould, George E. *Indiana Covered Bridges Thru the Years.* Indianapolis: Indiana Covered Bridge Society, Inc., 1977.

Hardesty, Barbara. *Parke County Covered Bridges.*

Indiana Covered Bridge Society, Inc. *Indiana Covered Bridge Guide.* Indianapolis: Indiana Covered Bridge Society.

Indiana Department of Commerce, Tourism Development Division. *Parke County Covered Bridge Courier and Map.* Indianapolis: Indiana Department of Commerce, Tourism Development Division. 1986.

Indiana Department of Highways, Division of Planning. Bartholomew County, *Indiana General Highway and Transportation Map.* Indianapolis: Indiana Department of Highways, Division of Planning, 1982.

------. Brown County, *Indiana General Highway and Transportation Map.* Indianapolis: Indiana Department of Highways, Division of Planning, 1982.

------. Dearborn County, *Indiana General Highway and Transportation Map.* Indianapolis: Indiana Department of Highways, Division of Planning.

------. Decatur County, *Indiana General Highway and Transportation Map.* Indianapolis: Indiana Department of Highways.

------. Fayette County, *Indiana General Highway and Transportation Map.* Indianapolis: Indiana Department of Highways.

------. Fountain County, *Indiana General Highway and Transportation Map.* Indianapolis: Indiana Department of Highways.

------. Franklin County, *Indiana General Highway and Transportation Map.* Indianapolis: Indiana Department of Highways.

------. Jackson County, *Indiana General Highway and Transportation Map.* Indianapolis: Indiana Department of Highways.

------. Jennings County, *Indiana General Highway and Transportation Map.* Indianapolis: Indiana Department of Highways.

------. Lawrence County, *Indiana General Highway and Transportation Map.* Indianapolis: Indiana Department of Highways.

------. Montgomery County, *Indiana General Highway and Transportation Map.* Indianapolis: Indiana Department of Highways.

------. Parke County, *Indiana General Highway and Transportation Map. Indianapolis: Indiana Department of Highways.*

------. *Putnam County, Indiana General Highway and Transportation Map.* Indianapolis: Indiana Department of Highways.

------. Ripley County, *Indiana General Highway and Transportation Map.* Indianapolis: Indiana Department of Highways.

------. Rush County, *Indiana General Highway and Transportation Map.* Indianapolis: Indiana Department of Highways.

------. Vermillion County, *Indiana General Highway and Transportation Map.* Indianapolis: Indiana Department of Highways.

Merrell, Dorthy. Bedford Public Library, Bedford, Indiana. Letter 4 March 1987.

"Once Again Open for Automotive Traffic." *Brown County Democrate,* 1 June 1983.

Penturf, David E. Putman County Surveyor, Greencastle, Indiana. Letter 28 January 1987.

Puetz, D. J. *Indiana County Maps.* Lyndon Station, Wisconsin: C. J. Puetz.

Roeger, Charles O. "General Information: Covered Bridges in Jackson County." The Jackson County Historical Society, Inc.

Weber, Wayne M. *The Covered Bridges of Parke County, Indiana.* Indianapolis: Wayne M. Weber and Indiana Covered Bridge Society, Inc., 1980.

Watterson, Vivian. Lawrence County Historical Society, Bedford, Indiana. Letter 4 March 1987.

KENTUCKY

Donovan, Richard T. *World Guide to Covered Bridges.* The National Society for the Preservation of Covered Bridges, Inc. 1980.

"Kentucky's Covered Bridges." *Kentucky Images Magazine,* Special Edition No. 4, 1984, pp. 3-30.

Kentucky Historical Society. "Kentucky's Covered Bridges." Frankfort: Kentucky Historical Society.

Kentucky Transportation Cabinet. *General Highway Map, Bourbon County.* Frankfort: Kentucky Transportation Cabinet, 1986.

------. *General Highway Map, Bracken County.* Frankfort: Kentucky Transportation Cabinet, 1986.

------. *General Highway Map, Fleming County.* Frankfort: Kentucky Transportation Cabinet, 1986.

------. *General Highway Map, Franklin County.* Frankfort: Kentucky Transportation Cabinet, 1986.

------. *General Highway Map, Greenup County.* Frankfort: Kentucky Transportation Cabinet, 1986.

------. *General Highway Map, Lewis County.* Frankfort: Kentucky Transportation Cabinet, 1986.

------. *General Highway Map, Mason County.* Frankfort: Kentucky Transportation Cabinet, 1986.

------. *General Highway Map, Robertson County.* Frankfort: Kentucky Transportation Cabinet, 1986.

------. *General Highway Map, Washington County.* Frankfort: Kentucky Transportation Cabinet, 1986.

MAINE

State of Maine, Department of Transportation, Bureau of Planning. *General Highway Map, Oxford County.* State of Maine.

Donovan, Richard T. *World Guide to Covered Bridges.* National Society for the Preservation of Covered Bridges, 1980.

Burbank, Steve. "Legend of Maine's Covered Bridges." Bangor Historical Society.

Ewing, Abigail. Bangor Historical Society. Letter 2 March 1987.

MARYLAND

Allen, Richard Sanders. *Covered Bridges of the Middle Atlantic States.* Brattleboro, Vermont: The Stephen Greene Press, 1959.

United States Department of the Interior, National Register of Historic Places. "Dedication Ceremonies for the Reopening of the Jericho Covered Bridge." United States Department of the Interior, 1978.

Donovan, Richard T. *World Guide to Covered Bridges.* The National Society for the Preservation of Covered Bridges, Inc. 1980.

Frederick County Parks and Recreation. ''Roddy Road Covered Bridge.'' Frederick County Parks and Recreation.

Maryland Department of Transportation. *General Highway Map, Baltimore County.* Maryland Department of Transportation.

------. *General Highway Map, Cecil County.* Maryland Department of Transportation.

------. *General Highway Map, Frederick County.* Maryland Department of Transportation.

Maryland Historical Society. ''Gilpin's Falls Covered Bridge.'' Maryland Historical Society.

MASSACHUSETTS

Allen, Richard Sanders. *Covered Bridges of the Northeast.* Brattleboro, Vermont: The Stephen Greene Press, 1957.

Commonwealth of Massachusetts, Massachusetts Department of Public Works, Bureau of Transportation Planning and Development. *General Highway Map.* Regional Series, Region A. Commonwealth of Massachusetts.

------. *General Highway Map.* Regional Series, Region B. Commonwealth of Massachusetts.

Donovan, Richard T. *World Guide to Covered Bridges.* The National Society for the Preservation of Covered Bridges, Inc., 1980.

''One Hundred Turn Out In Sheffield for Bridge Rededication. '' *The Berkshire Eagle,* 5 October 1981, p. 19.

''Saving Sheffield's Kissing Bridge.'' *The Berkshire Eagle,* 17 August 1979.

''Town Cost Delays Work on Riverbank.'' *The Berkshire Eagle,* 1 August 1985.

''Work on Covered Bridge Should Start This Summer.'' *The Berkshire Eagle,* 31 May 1986, p. 21.

MICHIGAN

Donovan, Richard T. *World Guide to Covered Bridges.* The National Society for the Preservation of Covered Bridges, Inc., 1980.

Michigan Historical Commission. ''Fallasburg Covered Bridge.'' Michigan Historical Commission.

------. ''Langley Covered Bridge.'' Michigan Historical Commission.

------. ''White's Covered Bridge.'' Michigan Historical Commission.

Michigan State Transportation Commission. *General Highway Map, Ionia County.* Michigan State Transportation Commission, 1971.

------. *General Highway Map, Kent County.* Michigan State Transportation Commission, 1971.

------. *General Highway Map, St. Joseph County.* Michigan State Transportation Commission, 1971.

------. *General Highway Map, Wayne County.* Michigan State Transportation Commission, 1971.

NEW HAMPSHIRE

Allen, Richard Sanders. *Covered Bridges of the Northeast.* Brattleboro, Vermont: The Stephen Green Press, 1957.

American Society of Civil Engineers. *American Wooden Bridges.* New York: American Society of Civil Engineers 1976.

Donovan, Richard T. *World Guide to Covered Bridges.* The National Society for the Preservation of Covered Bridges, Inc. 1980.

New Hampshire Department of Public Works and Highways. Planning and Economics Division. *General Highway Map, Carroll County.* New Hampshire Department of Public Works and Highways.

------. *General Highway Map, Cheshire County.* New Hampshire Department of Public Works and Highways.

------. *General Highway Map, Grafton County.* New Hampshire Department of Public Works and Highways.

------. *General Highway Map, Merrimack County.* New Hampshire Department of Public Works and Highways.

------. *General Highway Map, Sullivan County.* New Hampshire Department of Public Works and Highways.

New Hampshire Department of Resources and Economic Development. ''New Hampshire Covered Bridges.'' Concord, New Hampshire: New Hampshire Department of Resources and Economic Development.

NEW YORK

Allen, Richard Sanders, "Covered Bridges Existing in New York State in 1947-49." Cooperstown, New York: New York State Historical Association.

Donovan, Richard T. *The World Guide to Covered Bridges.* The National Society for the Preservation of Covered bridges, 1980.

New York State Department of Transportation. Albany, Rensselaer and Schenectady Counties Map. New York State Department of Transportation, 1983.

------. *Delaware County Map.* New York State Department of Transportation, 1983.

------. Otsego and Schoharie Counties Map. New York State Department of Transportation, 1983.

------. *Sullivan County Map.* New York State Department of Transportation, 1983.

------. *Washington County Map.* New York State Department of Transportation, 1983.

OHIO

Architecture: Columbus. "Bergstresser Covered Bridge, Columbus, Ohio." Columbus, #322.

"Armstrong Bridge All That Remains of Clio, Once a Busy Place in County." *The Daily Jeffersonian*, 3 August 1963, p. 6.

Ashtabula County Engineer's Office. "Benetka Road Covered Bridge." Jefferson, Ohio: Ashtabula County Engineer's Office.

------. "Creek Road Covered Bridge." Jefferson, Ohio: Ashtabula County Engineer's Office.

------. *Dedication of the Ashtabula County State Road Covered Bridge State Road in Monroe Township.* Jefferson, Ohio: Ashtabula County Engineer's Office.

------. "Doyle Road Covered Bridge." Jefferson, Ohio: Ashtabula County Engineer's Office.

------. "Graham Road Covered Bridge." Jefferson, Ohio: Ashtabula County Engineer's Office.

------. "Harpersfield Covered Bridge." Jefferson, Ohio: Ashtabula County Engineer's Office.

------. "Mechanicsville Covered Bridge." Jefferson, Ohio: Ashtabula County Engineer's Office.

------. "Middle Road Covered Bridge." Jefferson, Ohio: Ashtabula County Engineer's Office.

------. "Olin's Bridge (Dewey Road)." Jefferson, Ohio: Ashtabula County Engineer's Office.

------. "Riverdale Covered Bridge." Jefferson, Ohio: Ashtabula County Engineer's Office.

------. "Root Road Covered Bridge." Jefferson, Ohio: Ashtabula County Engineer's Office.

------. "South Denmark Road." Jefferson, Ohio: Ashtabula County Engineer's Office.

------. "Wisewell Road Covered Bridge." Jefferson, Ohio: Ashtabula County Engineer's Office.

Associate Membership of the Indian Lake Chamber of Commerce. (Bickman). "In Commemoration of the Centennial Birthday of the Bickman Covered Bridge." Associate Membership of the Indian Lake Chamber of Commerce.

Associate Membership of the Indian Lake Chamber of Commerce. (McColly). "Covered Bridge History, Bridges." Associate Membership of the Indian Lake Chamber of Commerce.

"B & O Reservoir Bridge." *The Daily Jeffersonian,* 8 August 1963, p. 11.

Bliss, Alice, and Hakala, Paul E. eds. *Ashtabula County Historical Society Quarterly Bulletin.* 15 (March 1968): 1-9.

"A Bridge Without a Country." *Athens Messenger.* 29 March 1984.

Carrillon Historical Park. "The Old Mill and the Covered Bridge." Dayton: Carrillon Historical Park.

"Closed to Traffic." *The Sidney Daily News.* 9 August, 1985.

"A Cool Place on a Hot Summer Afternoon." *News Register.* 20 July 1977.

"Covered Bridge Due at Belmont." *Times Leader.* 23 April 1974.

Covered Bridge Festival Committee. *Annual Ashtabula County Covered Bridge Festival.* Jefferson, Ohio: Covered Bridge Festival Committee.

"Covered Bridges." *The Circleville Herald.* 17 February 1983.

"Covered Bridges are Charming Links to the Past." *Video View Union County Advertizer*. 11 July 1983.

"Covered Bridges, Part of the Past." *Vinton Courier*. 16 March 1983.

Cuyayoga Valley, National Recreation Area. *Everitt Road Covered Bridge*. Brecksville, Ohio: Cuyahoga Valley National Recreation Area.

Donovan, Richard T., ed. *World Guide to Covered Bridges*. Boston: The National Society for the Preservation of Covered Bridges, Inc., 1980.

Ellsworth, Catherine and Bottorf, Naomi, eds. *Ashtabula County Historical Society*. 12 (October 1984).

Fairfield County Visitors and Convention Bureau. *Relax. Discover the Covered Bridges of Fairfield County*. Lancaster, Ohio: Fairfield County Visitors and Convention Bureau.

"Finishing Touches." *The Daily Jeffersonian*. 1 April 1967, p. 2.

"Five Covered Bridges in Vinton County." *Vinton Courier*. 2 April 1975.

Goslin, Charles R. *Crossroads and Fence Corners, Historical Lore of Fairfield County*. Lancaster.

Greenberg, Ronald M. and Marusin, Sarah A., eds. *The National Register of Historic Places*. Washington D.C.: United States Department of the Interior National Park Service. 1976.

The Guernsey County Chapter 5 Ohio Genealogical Society, Guernsey County. *A Collection of Historical Sketches and Family Histories*. Cambridge, Ohio: The Guernsey County Chapter 5 Ohio Gelealogical Society.

"Historical Society Presents." *Vinton Courier*. 3 July 1985.

"Indian Camp Bridge." *The Daily Jeffersonian*. 25 July 1963.

"Indian Camp Span Improved; Likely To Be Last Covered Bridge in County." *The Daily Jeffersonian,* 12 November 1964, p. 12.

Ketcham, Bryan E. *Covered Bridges on the Byways of Ohio*. Oxford: Oxford Printing Company, 1969.

"Letter to the Editor." (Eakin Mill Bridge). *Vinton Courier*. 4 April 1984.

Lisbon Area Chamber of Commerce. *Historical Recreation Points Near Lisbon, Ohio*. Lisbon, Ohio: Lisbon Area Chamber of Commerce.

"More Research Shows Ponn Bridge was Burned in 1874 and Restored." *Vinton Courier*, 18 April 1963.

National Park Service, U.S. Department of the Interior. *Cuyahoga Valley, National Recreation Area Ohio*. Washington D.C.: National Park Service, U.S. Department of the Interior, 1985.

Noble County Chamber of Commerce. "Look to Noble County for the Quality Life." Caldwell, Ohio: Noble County Chamber of Commerce.

Ohio Department of Transportation. *Adams County Map*. Columbus: Ohio Department of Transportation.

------. *Ashtabula County Map*. Columbus: Ohio Department of Transportation.

------. *Athens County Map*. Columbus: Ohio Department of Transportation.

------. *Belmont County Map*. Columbus: Ohio Department of Transportation.

------. *Brown County Map*. Columbus: Ohio Department of Transportation.

------. *Butler County Map*. Columbus: Ohio Department of Transportation.

------. *Clermont County Map*. Columbus: Ohio Department of Transportation.

------. *Clinton County Map*. Columbus: Ohio Department of Transportation.

------. *Columbiana County Map*. Columbus: Ohio Department of Transportation.

------. *Coshocton County Map*. Columbus: Ohio Department of Transportation.

------. *Delaware County Map*. Columbus: Ohio Department of Transportation.

------. *Fairfield County Map*. Columbus: Ohio Department of Transportation.

------. *Franklin County Map*. Columbus: Ohio Department of Transportation.

------. *Greene County Map*. Columbus: Ohio Department of Transportation.

------. *Guernsey County Map*. Columbus: Ohio Department of Transportation.

------. *Hamilton County Map*. Columbus: Ohio Department of Transportation.

------. *Harrison County Map*. Columbus: Ohio Department of Transportation.

------. *Jackson County Map*. Columbus: Ohio Department of Transportation.

------. *Lawrence County Map*. Columbus: Ohio Department of Transportation.

------. *Licking County Map*. Columbus: Ohio Department of Transportation.

------. *Logan County Map*. Columbus: Ohio Department of Transportation.

------. *Miami County Map*. Columbus: Ohio Department of Transportation.

------. *Monroe County Map*. Columbus: Ohio Department of Transportation.

------. *Montgomery County Map*. Columbus: Ohio Department of Transportation.

------. *Morgan County Map*. Columbus: Ohio Department of Transportation.

------. *Muskingum County Map*. Columbus: Ohio Department of Transportation.

------. *Noble County Map*. Columbus: Ohio Department of Transportation.

------. *Perry County Map*. Columbus: Ohio Department of Transportation.

------. *Pickaway County Map*. Columbus: Ohio Department of Transportation.

------. *Preble County Map*. Columbus: Ohio Department of Transportation.

------. *Ross County Map*. Columbus: Ohio Department of Transportation.

------. *Sandusky County Map*. Columbus: Ohio Department of Transportation.

------. *Scioto County Map*. Columbus: Ohio Department of Transportation.

------. *Shelby County Map*. Columbus: Ohio Department of Transportation.

------. *Summit County Map*. Columbus: Ohio Department of Transportation.

------. *Trumbull County Map*. Columbus: Ohio Department of Transportation.

------. *Union County Map*. Columbus: Ohio Department of Transportation.

------. *Vinton County Map*. Columbus: Ohio Department of Transportation.

------. *Washington County Map*. Columbus: Ohio Department of Transportation.

------. *Wyandot County Map*. Columbus: Ohio Department of Transportation.

"Pickerington to Underwrite Cost of Moving Covered Bridge." *Lancaster Eagle-Gazette,* 16 July 1986.

"Plan to Save Covered Bridge." *The Daily Jeffersonian,* 9 March 1965, p. 14.

"Public Invited to Covered Bridge Meeting to Explore Moving of Armstrong Bridge." *The Daily Jeffersonian,* 19 March 1965.

"Reassembly Slated in Ohio." *News Register,* 26 August 1973.

"Residents May Restore Former Covered Bridge." *Newark Advocate,* 26 August 1986.

Riley, Gladys. Otway, Ohio. Letter, 12 July 1986.

"Rubber Neck Tour Stop." *Times Leader,* 6 October 1975.

"Save Our Bridge." *Vinton Courier*, 8 October 1970.

Schlotterbeck, Seth S. *Covered Bridges of Preble County, Ohio.* Eaton, Ohio: The Preble County Historical Society, 1976.

Ahannon, Marilyn and Simmons, David A. *The Bridges of Carrillon Park.* Dayton: Carrillon Historical Park.

Smolen, John (Ashtabula County Engineer). "Covered Bridge Rehabilitation in Ashtabula County." Jefferson, Ohio: Ashtabula County's Engineering Office.

Southern Ohio Covered Bridge Association, Inc. *Ohio Covered Bridge Guide.* Columbus: Southern Ohio Covered Bridge Association.

Southern Ohio Covered Bridge Association, Inc. (Fairfield County Map). *Highway Map of Fairfield County.* Columbus: Southern Ohio Covered Bridge Association, Inc.

"Township Residents Lament Loss of Covered Bridge." *Newark Advocate,* 23 August 1986.

"Unique Hump-Backed Covered Bridge at Geer's Mill In Good Condition, Vinton Engineer Says." *Vinton Courier,* 2 August 1962.

"Vinton County Has Bridge, But Lake Will Come Later." *Columbus Dispatch,* 23 July 1972.

"Vinton's Humpback Bridge Goes Down in History." Athens Messenger, 6 May 1973.

PENNSYLVANIA

Caruther, E. Gipe. *Seeing Lancaster County's Covered Briges.* E. Gipe Caruthers 1974.

Donovan, Richard T. *World Guide to Covered Bridges.* The National Society for the Preservation of Covered Bridges, Inc., 1980.

Pennsylvania County Maps and Recreational Guide. London Station, Wisconsin: Puetz.

Pennsylvania Department of Transportation. *Bedford County Map.* Middletown, Pennsylvania: Pennsylvania Department of Transportation, 1980.

------. *Bucks County Map.* Middletown, Pennsylvania: Pennsylvania Department of Transportation, 1980.

------. *Chester County Map.* Middletown, Pennsylvania: Pennsylvania Department of Transportation, 1980.

------. *Columbia County Map.* Middletown, Pennsylvania: Pennsylvania Department of Transportation, 1980.

------. *Juniata County Map.* Middletown, Pennsylvania: Pennsylvania Department of Transportation, 1980.

------. *Lancaster County Map.* Middletown, Pennsylvania: Pennsylvania Department of Transportation, 1980.

------. *Lawrence County Map.* Middletown, Pennsylvania: Pennsylvania Department of Transportation, 1980.

------. *Montour County Map.* Middletown, Pennsylvania: Pennsylvania Department of Transportation, 1980.

------. *Northumberland County Map.* Middletown, Pennsylvania: Pennsylvania Department of Transportation, 1980.

------. *Perry County Map.* Middletown, Pennsylvania: Pennsylvania Department of Transportation, 1980.

------. *Somerset County Map.* Middletown, Pennsylvania: Pennsylvania Department of Transportation, 1980.

------. *Washington County Map.* Middletown, Pennsylvania: Pennsylvania Department of Transportation, 1980.

Washington-Greene County Covered Bridge Map. Washington, Pennsylvania: Washington-Greene County Tourist Promotion Agency.

Zacker, Susan M. *The Covered Bridges of Pennsylvania, A Guide.* Harrisburg; Historical and Museum Commission, 1986.

VERMONT

Allen, Richard Sanders. "The Covered Bridge." *Vermont Life.* Spring 1969.

Donovan, Richard T. *World Guide to Covered Bridges.* The National Society for the Preservation of Covered Bridges, Inc. 1980.

Lovell, Frances S. "Some Covered Bridges." *Vermont Life.* Summer, 1951.

Morse, Victor. *Windham County's Famous Covered Bridges.* Brattleboro, Vermont: The Book Cellar, 1960.

Northern Cartographic. *The Vermont Road Atlas.* Burlington, Vermont: Northern Cartographic, Inc. 1985.

Royce, Edmund Homer. "Covered Bridges of Vermont." *Vermont Life,* Spring, 1947.

Vermont Agency of Transportation. *General Highway Map, Addison County.* Vermont Agency of Transportation.

------. *General Highway Map, Bennington County.* Vermont Agency of Transportation.

------. *General Highway Map, Chittenden County.* Vermont Agency of Transportation.

------. *General Highway Map, Franklin County.* Vermont Agency of Transportation.

------. *General Highway Map, Lamoille County.* Vermont Agency of Transportation.

------. *General Highway Map, Orange County.* Vermont Agency of Transportation.

------. *General Highway Map, Washington County.* Vermont Agency of Transportation.

------. *General Highway Map, Windham County.* Vermont Agency of Transportation.

VIRGINIA

Allen, Richard Sanders. *Covered Bridges of the Middle Atlantic States.* Brattleboro, Vermont: The Stephen Greene Press, 1959.

Arritt, Gay. *Historical Sketches of the Alleghany Highlands.* Alleghany Historical Society, 1982.

"Covered Bridge Attracts Visitors, Vandals." *Union Star,* 11 October 1983.

"Covered Bridge Still In Use." *The Bull Mountain Bugle,* 19 May 1976, p. 30.

"Covered Bridge Still Stands." *Danville Register,* 1976.

Department of Highways Public Information Office. "Covered Bridges in Virginia." Department of Highways Public Information Office, 1963.

Donovan, Richard T. *World Guide to Covered Bridges.* National Society for the Preservation of Covered Bridges. 1980.

"Few Covered Bridges Still Remain As Reminders of Virginia's Past. *Richmond Times,* 22 May 1955.

"Historical Landmarks Serve Patrick County." *The Interprise,* 21 January 1963, p. 1

Jackson River Vocational Center. *Yesterday, Today and Tomorrow.* Jackson River Vocational Center, 1976.

"Last In Country." *Daily News Record,* 31 December 1968.

Presbrey, Joseph L. "Covered Bridges - A Link to the Past." *Virginia Record.* May 1980 pp. 30-31.

Virginia Department of Highways and Transportation (s). "Covered Bridges In Virginia." Virginia Department of Highways and Transportation, 1985.

Virginia Department of Highways and Transportation (b). *General Highway Map, Allegheny County.* Virginia Department of Highways, 1985.

------. *General Highway Map, Giles County.* Virginia Department of Highways, 1985.

------. *General Highway Map, Rockingham County.* Virginia Department of Highways, 1985.

------. *General Highway Map, Shenandoah County.* Virginia Department of Highways, 1985.

WEST VIRGINIA

Allen, Richard Sanders. *Covered Bridges of the Middle Atlantic States.* Brattleboro, Vermont: The Stephen Greene Press, 1959.

Auvil, Myrtle. *Covered Bridges of West Virginia Past and Present.* Parsons, West Virginia: McClain Printing Company, 1977.

Donovan, Richard T. *World Guide to Covered Bridges.* The National Society for the Preservation of Covered Bridges, Inc. 1980.

McCallum, Barbara Beury. "Covered Bridges Span Over a Century." *Wonderful West Virginia,* July 1983, pp 2-11.

West Virginia Department of Culture and History. *Barrackville Covered Bridge.* West Virginia Department of Culture and History.

------. *Mud River Covered Bridge.* West Virginia Department of Culture and History.

------. *Simpson Creek Covered Bridge.* West Virginia Department of Culture and History.

------. *Staats Mill Covered Bridge.* West Virginia Department of Culture and History.

West Virginia Department of Highways Planning Division. *General Highway Map West Virginia, Barbour County.* West Virginia Department of Highways Planning Division.

------. *General Highway Map, Cabell County.* West Virginia Department of Highways Planning Division.

------. *General Highway Map, Doddridge County.* West Virginia Department of Highways.

------. *General Highway Map, Harrison County.* West Virginia Department of Highways.

------. *General Highway Map, Jackson County.* West Virginia Department of Highways.

------. *General Highway Map, Marion County.* West Virginia Department of Highways.

------. *General Highway Map, Monongalia County.* West Virginia Department of Highways.